FOOD SHOPPERS' GUIDE TO HOLLAND

A Comprehensive Review of the Finest Food Products in the Dutch Marketplace

First Edition 1996
Second Edition 1998
Third edition 2000

ISBN 90 5166 777 9

Art Work by Sook Hee Lee - Los Angeles, California and
Lee Dong Jin - Seoul, Korea

Cover Design by Rob Bergervoet, The Netherlands
Cover Photo by Cees van Leeuwen, The Netherlands

Published by:
Eburon Publishers
PO Box 2867
2601 CW Delft
00 31 15 2131484
Netherlands

FOOD SHOPPERS' GUIDE TO HOLLAND

A Comprehensive Review of the Finest Food Products in the Dutch Marketplace

By Ada Henne Koene

Ada Henne Koene is the granddaughter of German immigrants who reached the United States in the late 1800's by way of the Ukraine. They brought with them a knowledge and love of good European food and passed it on to their children and grandchildren. There was little these hearty people couldn't do in terms of food preparation including charcuterie, baking and wine and cheese making. It was no accident that Ada began travelling at an early age and she hasn't stopped since. While living in Hawaii she learned to appreciate the different Asian foods that were cooked in Hawaii's melting pot. She later joined an American engineering firm working on projects in Asia for the International Bank for Reconstruction and Development (IBRD), or the World Bank; the Asian Development Bank (ADB); and the United States Agency for International Development (USAID). She lived in Thailand, Korea, Indonesia and the Philippines for 18 years and travelled extensively in most of the Far East and Southeast Asian countries. When she wasn't working and travelling, she was honing her Asian cooking skills with her household staff who were all excellent cooks. In Korea, Ada met and married her Dutch husband, Arie Koene. Arie's work kept them abroad and together they have lived and travelled in South America, North Africa, South Africa, Western and parts of Eastern Europe, and some countries in the Caribbean and Indian Oceans and the South Pacific. In the meantime, Ada has called Holland home where she is a freelance travel writer and writes cooking columns for various women's magazines. The Koenes also own a Seattle-based 30-foot motor home with which they have toured all but a few of the continental American states including Alaska.

PREFACE

This booklet started out as my contribution to *At Home in Holland*, a book published by the American Women's Club of The Hague. It appeared in a condensed form as the Chapter "*FOOD*" in the 1983 edition. Since then, the contents evolved into a greatly expanded version which has been presented as a part of the "*Bloom Where you are Planted*" program for new members sponsored by the Amsterdam Chapter of the Federation of American Women's Clubs overseas. Because of its demand and volume, the material now deserves its own cover. My hope is that this handy pocketbook-sized edition is small enough to fit into your handbag, but complete enough to help you shop and prepare your meals in the best of American, Dutch and some international culinary traditions.

Many scenic fishing villages like Urk and Scheveningen dot the coastal landscape and fishermen and their families with historical connections to the seas, like this lady from Spakenburg, continue in the seafood business.

ACKNOWLEDGEMENTS

It would be impossible to compile a book such as this without the help of many. I owe a million thanks to my husband, Arie, who introduced me to the Dutch marketplace. He not only identified the Dutch equivalents of familiar products but pointed out those which were new to me, and coaxed me into trying them. Arie also gave me technical computer support for preparing the texts and proofread the manuscript.

When Arie's memory regarding the preparation of traditional Dutch foods failed him, we turned to his sister, Syn van Kerkhoff, whose didn't. From Syn, I also learned some "folksy" traditions like the true meaning of an often repeated Dutch phrase, "*en een beetje nootmuskaat*", meaning a small grating of nutmeg. This lovely spice enhances the flavor of many locally-cooked vegetables. Nutmeg, along with mace, cloves and pepper, are the aromatic and flavorful spice quartet grown in Dutch Indonesia which caused the former colony to be known as the "Spice Islands".

My neighbor, Truus Brandsma, who is at home in the Dutch, French and German kitchens, spent hours pouring over my manuscript and her knowledge of these cuisines was invaluable. Then when Ellie Kolthof, the wife of a colleague of ours, heard of this project she also lent a hand. Living abroad with her husband and family for many years, she believed a compilation such as this would also be helpful to Dutch housewives living in countries where English is the second language. This booklet could thus be used in the reverse.

Chef Peter van der Louw, formerly owner of De Boeier Restaurant in Huizen, reviewed the chapter on meats and added his professional comments. Like Ellie, Peter was one of the first to place an order for the book. Hans and Henk Groeneveld of Groeneveld Slagerij, who are considered by many as the finest butchers and sausage makers in Holland, looked at the meat chapter from a butcher's perspective and gave their final stamp of approval. Meanwhile, Mr. and Mrs. W. van Moolenbroek and their successor Fred de Lange, **De Kaasspecialist** in the Hamershof shopping center in Leusden, reviewed the cheese chapter; it is Mr. Moolenbroek that you see in the drawing of the cheese shop.

As they were being interrogated, my neighborhood butcher, baker, greengrocer, fish specialist and chicken man also made invaluable contributions to this booklet without even knowing it. To them I owe a very special thanks for their enduring patience and good humor.

I am grateful to my friends and compatriots: freelance photographer and Master Chef Brynn Bruijn who played the devil's advocate in terms of accuracy; and to editor and television script writer Linda Durieux and my former colleague and fellow Asian traveller Vonda Teal Gittins for reading the manuscript as copy-editors. Thanks also to Mary Fencl for her contribution to the Children's Foods chapter and to Susan van Onzenoort-Tam and Mona Willems-Laypa who worked behind the scenes on the Chinese and Indonesian food chapter. Finally, thanks also to my publisher, Eburon, and Freek van der Steen for their technical support in preparing this book.

CONTENTS

I	**INTRODUCTION**		2
II	**BEFORE YOU SHOP**		5
III	**FOOD MARKETS**		9
IV	**FOOD AND FOOD PRODUCTS**		13
	1	Basic Baking and Cooking Ingredients	13
	2	Herbs and Spices	27
	3	Dairy Products (Cheese, Eggs, Milk and Milk Products)	40
	4	Delicatessen and Gourmet Items	48
	5	Breads and Pastries	50
	6	Fish and Shellfish	54
	7	Poultry, Game Birds and Game	67
	8	Fruits and Vegetables	71
	9	Meats (Beef, Veal, Pork, Lamb and Sausages and Cold Cuts)	100
	10	Frozen, Canned and Dried Foods	124
	11	Children's Foods	127
	12	Health and Vegetarian Foods	130
	13	Beverages	132
	14	Traditional Dutch Foods	134
	15	Asian and other International Food Products	139
		Popular Indonesian Rijsttafel Dishes	139
		Popular Chinese Dim Sum Dishes	142
		Essential Indonesian and other Asian ingredients	143
		Exotic Asian Vegetables	150
V	**APPENDICES**		
	A	Housewares and Kitchen Supplies	171
	B	Cleaning Supplies	177
	C	Weights and Measures	181
	D	Oven Temperatures	184
	E	Vocabulary	185
		Basic Baking and Cooking Ingredients	185
		Herbs and Spices	189
		Dairy Products	191
		Delicatessen and Gourmet Foods	193
		Breads and Pastries	194
		Fish and Shellfish	195
		Poultry, Game Birds and Game	197
		Fruits and Vegetables	199
		Meats	204
		Children's Foods	208
		Beverages	209
		Indonesian Rijsttafel Terms	210
		Exotic Asian Vegetables	212
		Cleaning Supplies	213
	F	International Food Shops	215
VI	**INDEX**		221
		English	221
		Dutch	230

I - INTRODUCTION

Newly arrived residents of Holland are often dazzled by the large variety of food shops and food products. There are several supermarket chains, the stores of which range from diminutive to relatively large versions of food emporiums in other countries. Yet they supply everything needed for a well-stocked pantry. Most also have butcher counters, greengrocers, fresh bakeries and cheese counters and are conveniently located in every neighborhood and village center just a short bicycle ride from home. What they don't carry, the ubiquitous host of other small highly-specialized, family-owned "mom and pop" shops do.

There are family-run butcher shops whose showcases bulge with familiar fresh meats plus savory meat products such as fresh and smoked local hams, sausages and patés, the types and flavors of which are seldom available outside Western Europe. Their neighbors may also include greengrocers, cheese specialists, bakers, *poeliers* or poultry specialists and fish mongers. The greengrocers' bins and boxes will be chock-a-block full of the freshest of the fresh Dutch produce. These are supplemented by common and exotic fruits and vegetables from all over the world: grapes from Greece; avocados from South Africa; apples from my own Washington State; oranges from Florida, Spain and Israel; pears from Japan; mangosteen from Thailand; tomatoes from Egypt; and pomelos from Israel. The shelves of the cheese specialist's shop will sag from the weight of the large, golden wheels of Dutch cheese that are stacked to the ceiling; the display cases brim with cheeses galore from Denmark, France, Italy, Greece, Great Britain and Switzerland. The cheese specialists know their merchandize and can tell you the ages of the Dutch cheese and can recommend other cheeses in terms of flavors. The bakers' wholesome, mouthwatering breads and pastries are the envy of bakers from other countries. They arrive at work hours before their customers awaken and their breads are still piping hot when the first customers arrive. Besides the bakeries, there are also shops which specialize in pastries and confections. The *poelier* or poultry specialists have a large variety of chickens and chicken parts, turkeys, ducks and exotic game and game birds. Although the fishing fleets are a mere shadow of what they once were, you can't beat the variety and freshness of the fish sold by the fish mongers. The Dutch love their fish and they won't settle for anything less. Salmon is flown in from Norway every day and should you wish you can even order live lobsters. As if these weren't enough, the open or wet markets held daily in larger cities and weekly in smaller villages are other sources of fresh food stuffs.

Due to Holland's long association with Indonesia, and with Indonesian and Chinese cuisines, ingredients to prepare these foods are available in small *toko* (Chinese/Indonesian shops) located in almost every Dutch city and village. There are also larger Chinese supermarkets in major cities. In addition, if you search long enough you will find ingredients to prepare Mexican; Middle Eastern or Mediterranean; North and South American; other European; and Far East, South East and South Asian cuisines.

It is impossible not to eat well in Holland. Yet, cooking here can sometimes be daunting, even for the most experienced cooks. One of the culprits is the local beef. As cooks soon discover, perhaps too late, that the local beef is not marbled and is simply not suitable for long grilling or hours of oven dry-roasting that is popular in many English-speaking countries. To make my point, a Dutch waiter once aptly replied when asked to return a steak to the frying pan, "Madame, if we cook it any longer you won't be able to eat it."

Even preparing some vegetables can be a bit perplexing. Those who have never cooked Belgian endives or *witlof* and white asparagus cannot be expected to know that the bitter core at the base of the endive needs to be removed and the stringy outer skin of white asparagus needs to be peeled. Many other food products sold here may look similar to those sold in other countries but the similarities can be deceptive.

This book identifies some of the problem areas and takes much of the mystery out of food shopping and cooking in Holland. The first chapter discusses some of the things you need to know before entering the markets. The second identifies the types of food shops or markets where you can do your shopping. The following chapters describe in detail basic and international baking and cooking ingredients; herbs and spices; dairy products; delicatessen and gourmet foods; breads and pastries; shellfish and fish; poultry and game; fruits and vegetables; local meat cuts and how to cook them; frozen, canned and dried foods; children's foods; health foods; beverages; traditional Dutch foods and international foods.

In the Appendices you will find some lists of housewares and supplies, cleaning supplies, weights and measures and oven temperatures. An English/Dutch vocabulary list and a list of International food shops appear at the end of the Appendices.

While this book was written with the North American cook in mind, cooks from other countries who are versed in English will almost certainly find it helpful. Hopefully, the experiences of our readers in the Dutch market and kitchens will be happy ones and can be counted as a part of their overseas adventures. My own repertoire of international recipes has expanded considerably since coming to Holland and includes many excellent Dutch recipes. They have not only been a delight to my family and friends back home, but with the Dutch emphasis on vegetables in their meals, I believe my family is much healthier for it. As they say in Holland, *eet smakelijk*.

A good, innovative butcher like this one in Amersfoort prepares the meats for barbecues, fondues and snacks and sells prepared salads and sauces as accompaniments.

II - BEFORE YOU SHOP

Learning the language

While it is estimated that 75 percent of the Dutch speak English, you cannot expect the shopkeepers and clerks to know all of the English names for their merchandise. It would therefore be helpful if you were to enter the market-place with shopping lists in English and Dutch and a reasonable skill in the art of Dutch pronunciation. Don't worry if your pronunciation is not perfect. The person waiting on you will most probably be happy to help you improve on it. The test for mastering this art is when you can pronounce Scheveningen like a Dutchman. Recognizing that you are a foreigner, you might be surprised if the clerk answers you in English and then, at the end of the transaction, orders you to "have a nice day". The Dutch like to practice English as much as you like to practice your Dutch. You'll get praise for trying; and even if you falter, to most natives your Dutch will sound very cute. Here are some helpful phrases to get you started:

Q. *Wie is aan de beurt?* Who is next?
A. *Dat ben ik.* I am.

Q. *Kan ik u helpen?* May I help you?
A. *Ik wil ...... hebben, alstublieft.* I would like..... please. Or: *Ik word al geholpen.* I've been helped.

Q. *Kunt u mij helpen?* Can you help me?
A. *Een ogenblikje, alstublieft.* A moment please.

Q. *Hoeveel kost het?* How much does it cost?

Q. *Heeft u ......?* Do you have ......?

Q. *Waar kan ik een..... vinden?* Where can I find......?

Q. *Iets anders?* or *Nog iets?* Anything else?
A. Nee *dank u, dat is alles.* No thank you, that is all.

Q. *Ietsje meer of ietsje minder?* A little more or a little less?
A. *Ietsje meer.* A little more.

Q. *Heeft u een tas?* Do you have a bag?

Shopping hours - *Openings tijden*

Supermarkets are permitted to stay open daily, except Sunday, from 8 a.m. until 10 p.m. However, that doesn't mean that they all do, so check your local stores. Supermarkets are also permitted to open on 12 Sundays a year.

A few food stores are open late in the evening and on Sundays in the larger in cities, tourist areas, railway stations, hospitals, and border areas. Check the Yellow Pages - *Gouden Gids* of your telephone book under *avondverkoop* or *avondwinkels* to see if there are any evening stores open in your area.

Most specialty food shops are normally open from 8 a.m. to 6 p.m., Monday through Friday and 8 a.m. to 5 p.m. on Saturday. There is also a small but ample supermarket, the Food Village, in the shopping arcade in Schiphol Airport that is open from 7 a.m. to 10 p.m.

Shops close for holidays, but do not normally observe three-day holiday weekends. For instance, if a holiday should fall on Friday, the shops re-open Saturday.

Most cities observe one late evening shopping night per week known as ***koop avond***. This is usually Thursday or Friday night but also varies from city to city. The stores close for dinner and then re-open for about two hours.

This conflict in opening and closing times and days of shops among villages, towns and cities can be most frustrating. The most efficient way to solve the problem is to make a note of the opening and closing hours of the stores where you shop.

Don't be the first in the supermarket when it opens. Aisles are often blocked with boxes as clerks hurry to restock the shelves. However, don't go too late, for the shelves may quickly empty. Bread is baked daily; by late afternoon, there is very little selection.

Open, or wet, markets are held daily in larger cities and once or twice a week in the smaller towns and villages. Market days never change.

Shopping Procedures

Most specialty shops and supermarket counters work on the number system. Pull a numbered ticket from a conveniently located dispenser and wait for your number to be called or ticked off on a counter conspicuously located on the wall behind the clerks. Stay alert. If you miss your turn, you have to start all over again. You'll draw stares if you are caught napping. If there is no numbering system, customers are helped in the order that they entered the shop. Keep a sharp eye on the person or persons entering before and after you.

It is a custom to bring your own **shopping bags**. They can be in any form: large plastic bags, handwoven baskets and bags which are, or can be, attached to wheeled carts such as those used for carry-on airline baggage. Portable plastic crates which fold open are also handy when shopping in bulk. Shopping bags can be purchased at housewares stores such as Blokker. Most supermarkets have a plastic bag vending machine as you enter the store or have bags hanging on racks as you approach to check out. They normally cost a *kwartje* (25 guilder cents) per bag. There is, however, no extra cost for the cardboard boxes which some supermarkets have stacked near the checkout stands if you arrive early. The specialty shops will give you a plastic bag for your purchases upon request.

Deposits on bottles

Many glass and soft-drink plastic bottles have *statiegeld* printed on the labels which means you automatically pay a refundable deposit. Return the bottles to the stores where you bought them, as not all stores carry the same brands. Some liquor stores also bottle their own wines and have deposits on the "house wine" bottles.

Recycling glassware

The Dutch faithfully participate in the recycling process and deposit their non-refundable glassware in the round slot of the *glasbak* containers conspicuously located near every shopping center. There are usually three containers; one each for white, green and brown bottles.

Measurements

The Dutch use the metric system for weight, volume, bulk and temperature; but, they also have a curious way of expressing weights when ordering meats, cheese and vegetables. These weights are detailed below. Just to confuse the issue, they generally order sliced cold cuts in 100-gram (een ons) or 150-gram (*anderhalf ons*) stacks. Larger items may be ordered as 1½ pounds - *anderhalf pond* or 1½ kilos - *anderhalve kilo* (this is one of the little nuances that you will pick up as you gain more experience in shopping in this country). Other weights and measures are given in a later chapter.

Metric	Dutch Equivalent	American*
100 grams	*een ons*	3 ounces
150 grams	*anderhalf ons*	5 ounces
250 grams	*half pond*	8 ounces
500 grams	*een pond*	16 ounces
750 grams	*anderhalf pond*	24 ounces
1,000 grams	*een kilo*	32 ounces
1,500 grams	*anderhalve kilo*	40 ounces

*Approximate

Payment

Most customers pay with cash; however, shops also accept payment by "PIN-card" which deducts the amounts automatically from your bank account, or by *eurocheques*, the certified checks issued by your bank. A similar arrangement is available through the Postbank.

You can also obtain electronic payment cards at your bank or Post Office. Unlike the "PIN card" system where you have to pay for charges under *f* 30 in some stores, there is no charge for using these cards. With the chipknip, cash is loaded onto a computer chip on your Europas and it works much like a telephone card. Simply wipe them through a scanner and your milk is paid for; there is no fuss with change. Banks call their card "Chipknip" while the rival system at the Postbank is called "Chipper". Where you have not been able to use them interchangeably, actions are being taken to merge the systems. The good news is that cash will still be accepted.

While supermarkets offer a good selection of fresh and processed cheese, serious cheese lovers and connoisseurs shop at their local cheese specialist - *kaasspecialist*.

III - FOOD MARKETS

Food shopping usually begins at the neighborhood supermarkets. There you can browse around at your leisure while getting acquainted with the local products and buy your basics to stock your pantry. If you feel shy or awkward about the language, contact with store clerks can be kept to a minimum. The check-out system at the supermarket is relatively simple and not all that different from systems in other countries. However, there will be a time when you can overcome your fears and be lured by the sights and smells of the specialty shops or stalls in the open markets. After a while, you will find that shopping in Holland is, in fact, not so alien.

With patience and fortitude, you can find almost everything you need, or desire, to create a well-stocked kitchen, even if it means checking in at several supermarkets and specialty shops in the neighborhood. Tastes are changing in Holland and people are yearning for a wider range of dishes featuring ingredients from all over the world. Thus, while you may not find an item in supermarkets or shops on one day, there is a good chance that they will stock it on the next. Persevere.

Food markets in Holland generally fall into three categories: **supermarkets**, **specialty shops** and **open or wet markets**.

Supermarkets

The "super" in supermarkets is a bit of an exaggeration for few are built on a grand scale. Albert Heijn is Holland's largest food chain. They rate their stores from 1 thru 5 with the small #1 stores stocking only the basics. The #5 stores carry the full line of products. The sizes are displayed at the store entrances. Spar, Super, Boni, Profimarkt, C-1000, Edah and Komart are other reliable supermarket choices. Most carry a full range of items: meats; bakery goods; cheese and other milk products; fresh, canned and frozen fruits and vegetables; cereals; pastas; soft drinks; wines; teas and coffees; baby foods; cleaning supplies; cigarettes, cigars and pipe tobaccos; pet foods; candies; sauces; cake and bread mixes; and spices. Some carry in-house brands which may be marginally cheaper. Watch for specials or items marked *reclame*. Albert Heijn has membership "Bonus" cards where sale items are automatically deducted from the purchase price.

Supermarkets have shopping carts handy as you enter. Because of the number of carts that disappeared, many are now using the system where rows of carts are coupled with chains, locking one cart to the other directly behind it. You need a one-guilder coin to unlock the cart. The guilder is refunded once the cart is recoupled. You can always "buy" a cart from someone leaving the store.

Some of the supermarkets have clerks to help you with the meats, vegetables, fruits, cheese, cold cuts and delicatessen items, while some will weigh your fruits and vegetables at the check out counter. Others sell the meats and cheese pre-wrapped and expect the customer to select, bag, weigh and label the fruits and vegetables. They identify the produce by pictures on the scales. Drop the produce in the plastic bags provided for you, the like items in one bag. Put it on the scale. Press the corresponding picture button, then press the button marked *bon*, and a price tag with an adhesive backing appears from the side. Stick it onto the plastic bag. If there is no picture for the item you are buying, look at the bin from which you plucked it. See if the item is marked *per stuk* - per piece. Cucumbers, for instance, are sold by the piece. Alternatively, the produce may already have a price on it.

There are two common types of checkout stands. One is where you load your goods onto a conveyor belt and as each item is tallied by hand or by computerized sensors, or a combination of the two, it is pushed into a bagging ramp. The ramp usually has a movable divider which means it can accommodate two shoppers. Alternatively, the checkout clerk places your goods into a shopping cart which can be wheeled away for bagging at a counter set aside for that purpose. Your cart in turn replaces the one you wheeled away.

There are no supermarket baggers and only on rare occasions will any of the staff help. Thus, you will have to bag your purchases yourself. If there are people waiting behind you, you will sense the pressure to get moving and out of the way. Getting your purchases to your car is also your responsibility, although some supermarkets make home deliveries of large purchases.

After totalling up your purchases, the clerk will ask: "*Spaart u zegels?*" Having asked this hundreds of times a day, the question is usually unintelligible. Many supermarkets offer **savings stamps - *zegels***, the price of which is added onto your receipt by some supermarkets and are free in others. The return is relatively small. For instance, a 47 guilder book of stamps can be traded in for say 50 guilders. You have to be quick to say no or *nay* and hope for the best. Unless you are into licking glue, you probably won't want to participate. However, some brands have special promotional stamps which are redeemable for goods, or the store may be offering stamps toward free towels or crystal.

Specialty Shops

For a more generous selection, you cannot beat the specialty shops and there are many of them:

The Butcher Shop (*Slagerij*)
The Poultry and Game Specialist (*Poelier*)
The Fish and Seafood Shop (*Vishandel*)
The Bakery (*Bakkerij*)
The Pastry and Confectionary Shop (*Banketbakkerij*)
The Greengrocer (*Groenteman* or *Groenteboer*)
The Cheese Shop (*Kaashandel*)
The Delicatessen or Gourmet Shop (*Delicatessenwinkel*) or Food Departments in Major Department Stores
The Chinese/Indonesian Shop (*Toko*)
The Dairy Shop (*Melkwinkel* or *Zuivelhandel*)
The Beverage or Liquor Shop (*Slijterij*)
The Health Food Store (*Reformhuis*)

At times, your stops will also have to include a visit to the drugstore - *drogisterij*, pharmacy - *apotheek*, department store - *warenhuis* and housewares shop - *huishoudartikelen* for particular items not normally stocked elsewhere.

Open Markets

Open Markets, also called wet markets, are a Dutch institution and have been held in this country for as long as the recorded history of the Netherlands. There is a lot of local color here and you can get some good buys. In larger cities, the open markets are held daily, except Sundays. Smaller cities and villages hold them once or twice a week. However, there are some ethnic markets that are open on special occasions, or on weekends like the *Oosterse Markt* in Beverwijk near Amersterdam. The *Oosterse Markt* people cater to Middle Eastern or Mediterranean cuisines. Check with the local tourist office (VVV) for opening and closing times.

Open Markets are also central to any minicipal anniversary or theme celebrations. They usually have a hodge-podge of stalls featuring flowers, clothing, bric-a-brac, sewing supplies, accessories, fish, chicken, cheese, fruits, vegetables, prepared meats, breads and pastries, international foodstuffs and pet foods. There are also the ubiquitous stalls selling traditional Dutch treats like *Goudse stroopwafels, poffertjes* or *oliebollen.* You'll read more about these delectables in the Traditional Dutch Food chapter.

Farms

Another shopping possibility is buying cheese, poultry, eggs, fruits and vegetables directly from the farmers who grow or make them. Their products are generally cheaper than the shops and the visit gives you an excellent chance to get a close peek at what could well be some of the oldest, most singular farms in Europe. Some are absolutely ancient.

Look for the ***kaasboerderij*** **- cheese farm** signs and taste Holland's most delicious cheeses. Get there early and catch the farmer as he demonstrates the craft of cheese making. The *kaasboerderij* in Maarsbergen has been so successful that one of their barns has been turned into a cheese museum, a coffee shop and a restaurant where (upon advance request) they serve a most attractive Dutch *koffietafel* (a set lunch of soup and cold cuts centered around the afternoon coffee) to bus-loads of tourists.

Drive through the fruit-growing region of the Betuwe and you'll not only see some fetching thatched-roofed farms but the ingenious way the farmers ward off the birds with tin cans tied on strings.

In Beverwijk, between Amsterdam and Alkmaar, there is a very active weekend Eastern Market - *Oosterse Markt* which specializes in food stuffs for Middle Eastern cuisines.

IV - FOOD AND FOOD PRODUCTS

IV.1 BASIC BAKING AND COOKING INGREDIENTS

Today's Dutch cooking is not all that different from other Western kitchens and almost everything that you need in terms of basic baking and cooking ingredients is available in Holland. However, in terms of texture and composition, there are sometimes differences between local products and products manufactured in other countries. This chapter identifies the local products and their idiosyncrasies and recommends substitutions when helpful.

Stocking your pantry obviously should begin with the local supermarkets. Each supermarket chain has its own brand and product favorites; thus, you may need to visit more than one. They have baking sections where you can find leavening agents, gelatins, cake decorations, cake and tart glazes, aromas and essences, and many interesting cake and tart mixes. They also carry the basic types of wheat and non-wheat flours, vinegars, cooking oils, solid cooking fats (refrigerated), syrups, honey, baking chocolate, tomato pastes and sauces, bread crumbs, some noodles and pastas and dairy products.

Then, if you still haven't found everything you need, try the health food stores and delicatessens or gourmet shops which cater to kitchens of English-speaking countries. However, be aware that if you are depending upon imported ingredients, you must keep an extra supply on hand.

Almond paste - ***amandelspijs*** Made from finely-ground almonds mixed with confectioner's (icing) sugar and glucose syrup, almond paste is widely used in Holland as a filling for baked goods, especially holiday breads and pastries. It is sold in supermarkets, bakeries and cheese and delicatessen or gourmet shops in small rectangular bars. It is also the basic ingredient in **marzipan - *marsepein*** which is turned into sweetmeats with colorful animal, vegetable and fruit shapes. Marzipan is also rolled into sheets and used for covering cakes and for cake decorations.

Baking powder - ***bakpoeder*** Baking powder is a chemical raising or leavening agent used in baked goods. Baking powders are made from acids, sodium bicarbonate and flour or cornstarch. There are two major kinds: the **double-acting powder** and the **single-acting tartrate** and **phosphate baking powders**. Double-acting baking powder is the most commonly used in North America and it is clearly marked on the container. The basic difference between single- and double-acting powders is that the leavening agents of the double-acting powder work twice, once when mixed with liquid and again when exposed to heat while the single-acting baking powder begins to work when the liquid is added. Thus, when using the double-acting powder the batter can be mixed and the baking delayed until needed; but, the batter with the single-acting powder must be baked immediately in a pre-heated oven. Assume that, unless otherwise indicated, your local powders are double-acting. The amounts are the same.

To make double-acting baking powder mix ½ teaspoon cream of tartar with ¼ teaspoon baking soda and ¼ teaspoon cornstarch.

Baking soda - *maagzout or natrium bicarbonaat* Baking soda is bicarbonate of soda which is used in baked goods as a leavening agent. It causes dough or batter to rise immediately by releasing gas bubbles when mixed with acids such as buttermilk, yoghurt or vinegar. Its Dutch name translates as stomach salt, and is therefore available at the *drogist* - drugstore or the *apotheek* - pharmacist. Many Chinese or Asian shops and shops which cater to North American and British expatriates carry imported baking soda. Chinese cooks may use it to tenderize meats.

Bread crumbs - *paneermeel* There are basically two types of bread crumbs: crumbs made from fresh (soft) bread, and crumbs made from dry bread. Fresh bread crumbs can easily be made from chunks of fresh bread, with or without crusts, which are whirled in a food processor or blender. The Japanese ***panko*** sold in Asian stores are dried bread crumbs made from fresh bread. Like the fresh bread crumbs, they add a lovely texture to breaded meats and fish. They are also suitable for meat loaf. The locally-made **bread crumbs - *paneermeel*** are made from finely ground, dry Dutch rusks. They are perfectly suited for breaded meats such as **Wienerschnitzel**.

Cake and tart glazes and garnishes There are several glazes presently available in most supermarkets for cakes and pies. A **chocolate glaze - *chocoladeglazuur*** can be used for dipping and coating, spooned over the top of a cake and let drip down the sides of the cake, while **fruit glaze - *vruchtenglazuur*** (***taartgelei*** or ***tortengusz***) is spooned over the top of fruit tarts to add gloss. The fruit glazes come in two colors: clear - *helder* and red - *rood*. There are also several cake, pie and ice cream toppings to choose from such as: nougatine (coarsely-chopped sugar-coated peanuts, candy sprinkles, jimmies - *hagelslag,* chocolate flakes - *vlokken,* and pink and blue candy coated anise seeds - *muisjes.*

Candied fruit Candied fruits including whole fruit or fruit pieces are those that have been put through a process of dipping in sugar syrups. As the process progresses, the syrup replaces the water in the fruit. Almost any fruit (and some flowers) can be candied: cherries, plums, apricots, pears, figs, pineapple and citron peel; but **candied cherries - *glacé or bigarreau*, mixed fruits - *pudding vruchten*, citron peel - *sukade*** are most commonly found here. They are used in fruit cakes, breads and cookies and as garnishes on other pastries. The cherries are preserved in colored sugar solutions and are available in a mixture of red, green and gold. Candied fruits can be purchased in the baking section of supermarkets and some specialty gourmet shops.

Cereal grains Look for cereal grains and grain products such as **amaranth, barley - *gerst*, hulled barley - *gort*, pearl barley - *parelgort*, quick-cooking barley - *vluggort*; buckwheat - *boekweit*, buckwheat groats or kasha** - ***boekweitgrutten*, bulgur (bulghur), corn - *mais*, cous cous, kamut, millet - *gierst*, oats - *haver*, oatmeal**

- ***havermout*** or ***havervlokken***, **quinoa** (Incan rice), **rice** - ***rijst***, **rye** - ***rogge***, **spelt,** and **wheat** - ***tarwe*** in several places: supermarkets, health food stores, Asian shops or supermarkets and/or Middle Eastern shops. They also sell **wheat germ** - ***tarwekiemen***, **wheat bran** - ***tarwezemelen***, **cream of wheat** - ***tarwe griesmeel,*** and **oat bran** - ***haverzemelen***. Buckwheat, rye and wheat are all ground into **flour** - ***bloem*** or **meel** and the corn into **cornmeal** - ***maizmeel*** (for baking) or **coarsely ground cornmeal** - ***maisgriesmeel*** (for mush or polenta). The oatmeal is the old fashioned rolled oats. **Rice** grown in Surinam and American is good all- around **long grain rice** - ***langkorrelrijst*** which is light and dry when cooked. It is sold as: **unpolished rice** - ***zilvervliesrijst*** or ***bruin rijst***; **white or polished rice** - ***witte*** or ***geslepen rijst***; **converted or parboiled rice** - ***parboiled rijst***; **instant or quick white rice** - ***snelrijst*** or ***snelkookrijst***; and **broken rice** - ***gebroken rijst***. The Italian **Arborio** is a short grain variety that is moist and sticky when cooked. It is sold in some supermarkets and shops or market stalls which sell Italian or Mediterranean foods. **Wild rice** - ***wilde rijst*** (which is a grass seed and not rice) and **brown rice** are usually available in health food stores. See also Asian rice in Chapter IV-15.

Chocolate - chocolade There are several types of chocolate that are used in cooking. **Unsweetened chocolate**, often called **baking** or **bitter**, is unadulterated chocolate which contains around 50 percent cocoa butter. Sometimes lecithin, vanilla and sugar may be added to make the chocolate more palatable resulting in what is called ***puur chocolade*** or **pure chocolate.** This is made with various degrees of sweetness: regular, semi-sweet and extra bitter and it is available in bars and can be eaten as candy. A third type of chocolate, **milk chocolate** - ***melk chocolade***, is created when dry milk is added to sweetened chocolate. It is basically a sweet or eating chocolate which is used for candy bars and is rarely used in cooking except, perhaps, in the case of chocolate chip cookies, because it doesn't melt well. Baking and pure chocolate can be used interchangeably in some recipes but milk chocolate cannot. **White chocolate** consists mostly of cocoa butter and has no chocolate liquor (chocolate paste) in it. As a rule, it should not be substituted for baking chocolate in recipes. **Couverture** is a chef's chocolate and is usually used for glazing. It is sold in the baking sections of supermarkets as chocoladeglazuur. For baking chocolate, you can substitute three tablespoons cocoa mixed with 1 tablespoon melted butter in some recipes although there might be a little difference in texture. This equals one square or one ounce unsweetened chocolate. Baking chocolate is sold in some delicatessens and gourmet shops while pure and milk chocolate bars are found in the supermarkets. Callebaut, which is arguably Europe's finest maker of chocolate, produces a type of flattened chip which is available in 2½ kilo containers from a friendly baker or from wholesalers such as Ven Groothandelcentrum B.V. The chips are available in brown and white chocolate. The chips are good for making chocolate mousse, milk and sauce.

Chocolate chips Some delicatessens or gourmet shops carry the American (and some German) chocolate chips which are used to make the All-American Chocolate Chip Cookie but they are expensive. There are three types: semi-sweet, milk and white chocolate. However, as a last resort, remember that the original Toll House (chocolate chip) cookies were made with broken **pure chocolate – *puur chocolade*** bars.

Cocoa powder - *cacaopoeder* Dutch cocoa has long been highly prized for its lucious dark-brown color and mellow taste and many recipes in international cookbooks still specifying using it. The special appearance and flavor is achieved by treating the paste or chocolate liquor in an alkaline solution to help neutralize its acidity during the manufacturing process. Cocoa is sold in two forms: plain or mixed with milk powder and sweeteners to make instant drinks.

Coconut - *kokosnoot* The coconut is largest of all nuts, and in South and Southeast Asia the meat is eaten either when the coconut is quite young or when ripe while in the West the meat is eaten ripe. The fresh **young coconuts** - ***jong kokosvlees*** or *kelapa muda* (Indon.) have green outer layers and the flesh is like an opaque jelly that can easily be scooped out with a spoon and eaten from the shell. However, the outer layer of the ripe coconut is peeled away to expose a brown hairy shell. When the shell is cracked open it reveals a firm, white flesh which is chipped from the shell and grated. One coconut yields 3 to 4 cups of grated coconut. In the West the grated meat is primarily used for cakes, pies, puddings and cookies while in Asia milk is often extracted by pouring hot water over the grated coconut and then kneading it, see International Foods Chapter. Use it within four days or you can safely freeze it for up to six months. Fresh young and ripe meat is also available from the deep-freeze in many Asian stores. When selecting a ripe coconut, choose one that is heavy and makes the sound of liquid when shaken. The coconut eyes should be firm and dry. The thin liquid or juice can be drunk like a beverage, but one can get very sick if the juice isn't ready for drinking. However, this juice should not be confused with the coconut milk or coconut cream described above. The **desiccated** or **grated coconut - *gemalen kokosvlees*** sold here is dry and unsweetened. It can be used for making coconut milk and baked goods such as **Macaroons**, but for better results North American sweetened baking coconut sold at some import shops.

Cream of Tartar Cream of tartar is the fine, white, powdery acid salt which is a by-product of the crystalline sediment found in wine barrels. It is the acid salt of tartaric acid and is often confused with the tartaric acid - *wijnsteenzuur* or *gezuiverde wijnsteen* sold at pharmacies here. Cream of tartar adds volume and acts as a stabilizer for beaten egg whites when added half way through the whipping process. It also helps to create a less grainy consistency of candies and frostings. It is the acid ingredient in baking powder which is activated when moisture is added to the batter. Look for cream of tartar at delicatessen or gourmet shops which cater to cooks from English-speaking countries for it is not commonly used in the Dutch kitchens.

Crumb crusts While the original Graham crackers or Graham cracker crumbs are imported by some delicatessens or gourmet shops, there are reasonable locally-made substitutes such as Verkade's *volkoren San Francisco* or *Tarvita* biscuits. For crumb crusts, they can be crushed with a rolling pin or ground in a food processor. Fourteen biscuits usually make enough for one crust. A locally-made **crumb crust mix - *kruimelbodem*** is also sold in the supermarkets. It is made of wheat flour, salt and rice flour, and only needs to be mixed with melted butter. Albert Heijn's *Windsor Biskwie* biscuits can make a presentable **vanilla crumb crust**. Perhaps it can be improved a little if vanilla sugar is added.

Extracts and essences - *aroma* There are several types of extracts and essences - *aromas* sold in Holland, the most common being **almond - *amandel*, lemon - *citroen*, cherry water - *kirsch*, maraschino - *marasquin*, mocha - *mokka*, rum - *rhum***, and **vanilla - *vanille***. Most are packaged by Dr. Oetker and Baukje. According to the Baukje instructions, you should use two aroma bottle caps (about 1½ teaspoons total) for every 500 g/cc batter. For some, this may seem a little strong. The most popular extract is that which is made from the vanilla bean. It is available as *aroma* in supermarkets or McCormick's brand pure vanilla extract in import shops catering to North Americans. The vanilla essence can also be extracted from the whole **vanilla bean - *vanille stokje*** by soaking it in water then by boiling the water to reduce it, intensifying the flavor. Alternatively, you can use the French technique for sauces and custards which is to split the pod and scrape the seeds directly into the liquid. The seeds can be left in or removed by straining through a sieve after cooking. This method gives you the ultimate vanilla flavor. The seeds from one inch of bean equals one teaspoon pure vanilla extract. Another option to consider is the wonderfully fragrant **vanilla sugar - *vanille suiker***. It is made by burying two beans in a pound of sugar for about a week. One packet of commercially sold vanilla sugar equals about one teaspoon pure vanilla extract. Distilled essences such as **rose-, orange flower-** and **geranium-water** are available at some Asian shops and shops which cater to Middle Eastern or Mediterranean cuisines.

Fat, solid There are three basic types of solid cooking fats available in Holland. They include the **animal fats - dierlijke vetten** such as **butter - *boter*, lard - *reuzel*, beef suet - *rundvet*** or ***rund niervet***; two **deep frying fats - *frituurvet and Ossewit*** which are made from a mixture of vegetable oils and animals fats respectively and have very high smoke points; and **margarine - *margarine*** which is made with **vegetable oil - *plantaardig olie***. Butter is available salted - *gezouten* and unsalted - *ongezouten*. Chefs use the unsalted butter for it gives them control over the amount of salt added to any dish. Also available on the market are special types of **butter** and **margarine** for frying. They contain less water (they are 97-98% fat) than normal butter and margarine (which are 80% fat) and have a higher smoke point. They are called several things but are most commonly identified with the term **bak en braad** or **bak- en braadproducten**. Braderie braadboter is made of real butter. At the time of this writing, there is no Dutch equivalent of the (hydrogenated) **vegetable shortening** which is widely used in North American baking although some delicatessen or gourmet food shops which cater to North Americans may carry imported shortening. You can use butter or a special **baking margarine** - ***bakgraag*** which is sold under the brand name Bona. Some have used frituurvet or Ossewit with good results although they harden quickly (they are 100% fat) and are not as easy to work with as shortening, butter or margarine. For short crust pastry, try a combination of frituurvet and butter or margarine. Many of these fats are also now available in pourable form - ***vloeibaar***. The replacement for butter, margarine and shortening is the same in terms of cup measures but shortening is a little lighter since butter and margarine contain water. The manufacturers of Crisco shortening state that 1 cup Crisco + 6 teaspoons water equal 1 cup butter or margarine. Fats impart different flavors. Whereas the flavor of Mexican and Chinese food benefit from lard, the flavor of butter is essential to French and Italian cooking. While the French clarify butter to remove the milk solids that burn at high temperatures, the Italians might use ⅓ part vegetable oil. The smoke point of oil is higher than butter and adding the oil raises the smoke point, but you still get the desired butter flavor.

Flour, wheat While there are thousands of varieties of wheat, they can be placed into two broad categories: hard wheat, which is grown in the colder climates of the great northern plains of the United States and southern Canada; and soft wheat, which is grown in the more temperate climates of western Europe and the more southern United States. The most important characteristic of these two that concern the cook is the protein content for when water is added, proteins cling together with the water to form gluten sheets. These sheets trap and hold the gases and air that enable yeast bread to rise. Hard wheat contains more gluten-forming protein and thus is usually mixed during the milling process with soft to achieve the exact balance of proteins needed for various types of baking. Yeast bread, pasta and pizza require about 13 to 14 grams of protein per cup, while delicate cakes and pastries need only 8 grams. For cookies high protein flour holds them together better while low protein flour makes for tender cookies. For other types of baking, the miller blends the hard and soft wheat to create **all-purpose flour**. According to Shirley O. Corriher in her book ***Cookwise***, the amount of protein in these all-purpose blends vary from country to country, and in the case of the United States, from region to region. For instance, northern brand American bleached all-purpose flour has 11 to 12 grams of protein per cup while the bleached southern brand White Lily all-purpose has 9; the national brand Gold Medal has 11. In Holland, the Albert Heijn and Koopman brands of all-purpose flour contain 11 grams per 100 grams of flour (or 13 grams based on 125 grams of all-purpose flour per cup), Friso brand has 12. These proteins absorb water differently. Ms Corriher writes that: "The same amount flour and water that makes a firm dough with a high-protein flour makes soup with a low protein flour." In her book *La Varenne Practique*, Anne Willan, the founder of the famous cooking school writes: "Each type of flour has so many individual properties that substitutions are seldom successful, particularly in baking." While this might be true for the professional baker, for the home cook perfectly acceptable quick breads and cookies can be made with local commercial baking ingredients regardless of the regional origin of your recipes. Check your cakes and quick breads for doneness before removing from the oven and make one test cookie before baking the rest. Ms. Willan goes on to say that gluten development can be slowed by adding less flour to the dough: "A scant cup/110 grams of hard wheat flour has the same gluten strength as one full cup/125 grams pastry flour." To make cake flour, one cup stirred all-purpose flour less 2 tablespoons should have the same gluten content as 1 cup cake flour. Traditionally, the Dutch housewives have relied on their neighborhood bakery for their baked goods. Thus, there has been little choice in the local supermarkets. The best flour is in the hands of the professionals. Basically you have a choice of white **tarwe bloem** and ***patent bloem*** (*patent bloem* meaning an all purpose flour), ***volkoren*** **- whole wheat flour** (which contains the wheat germ and/or bran) and ***tarwemeel*** **- brown wheat flour**. **Self-rising (U.K. Self-raising) -** ***zelfrijzend bloem*** is an all-purpose flour to which baking powder and salt has been added. Soubrey manufacturers a **pastry flour -** ***bloem voor patisserie*** especially designed for fine pastries, waffles and pancakes and a **white bread flour -** ***witbrood bloem***. Both are sold in some gourmet shops and food wholesalers. **Instant flour -** ***vlug bloem*** is granular flour which is made to dissolve quickly in cold liquids then is added to hot mixtures such as gravies and sauces as a thickener. ***Cakemeel*** is a cake mix to which flavoring and coloring has been added. There is no commercial **unbleached flour** on sale here but Julia Childs, the guru of American cooking says that: "....when a recipe calls for all-purpose flour, you can use either bleached or unbleached all-purpose flour." Unbleached, however, is a little higher in protein.

Flour, non-wheat Several are available here; some are used for baking, others as thickening agents. **Rye - rogge** is milled from the grain of a cereal grass. It contains less gluten than whole wheat or all-purpose flour thus won't rise very high unless mixed with other high protein flour. **Buckwheat -** ***boekweit*** is milled from the seed of an herb rather than a cereal grain. It makes very dense and heavy bread and thus is usually mixed with other flour. **Arrowroot -** ***pijlwortel*****, cornstarch -** ***maizena*****, potato flour -** ***aarappelzetmeel*****, rice flour -** ***rijstbloem*** and **tapioca -** ***tepung tapioca*** (Indon.) are used mainly as thickening agents. They are sometimes preferred to wheat flour in particular applications such as in fruit pies and tarts. Wheat flour creates a cloudy liquid and the high acid in fruit sometimes neutralizes its thickening power while cornstarch and tapioca flour both thicken fruit juices into a bright runny gel with the fruit's true colors. However, tapioca doesn't work well in open-faced pies. Thus, for fruit pies and tarts use 3 tablespoons cornstarch or a mixture of cornstarch and tapioca for 6 cups of fruit. **Arrowroot** and **potato flour** produce lighter sauces than those made with wheat flour. However, they need to be added at the end of cooking because they lose their effect if cooked more than 2 or 3 minutes. They also should not be heated over 175°F. **Cornstarch** is a powdery "cornflour" most commonly used in binding sweet sauces and savory Chinese dishes. It can be cooked longer without losing its thickening properties. **Rice flour** is used in Asian cooking in some desserts, sauces and sweet and sour dishes. These four flours should be mixed with water to make a paste before adding to liquid. Look for them in Health Food and Asian Shops. Corn starch is also available in supermarkets.

Gelatin - *gelatine* Made from extracts of animal bones, skin and cartilage or from algae, gelatin is a thickening agent which is used in molded salads and desserts. It is basically sold in leaf or powdered form. **Leaf gelatin - *gelatine blaadje*** comes in rectangular leaves. Each leaf weighs 2 grams; it takes 6 leaves to equal one 11-gram package powdered gelatin. **Powdered gelatin - *poeder gelatine*** is packaged in 11-gram (1¼ tablespoon) packets. U.S. packets weigh ¼ ounce (1 tablespoon). One packet sets 2 cups (about ½ liter) of liquid. Soak both gelatins in cold water before dissolving in warm liquids.

Honey - *honing* A large selection of honey is sold in supermarkets and health food shops. The flavor varies according to the flower from which the honey is derived.

Marshmallows Originally made from the roots of the marshmallow plant, marshmallows today are made from light corn syrup, gelatin, gum Arabic and a coloring agent. Large American marshmallows are available in some supermarkets and the American style fluffy, whipped marshmallow is sold by Albert Heijn. The local pastel-colored marshmallows are called *spekkies* or *spekken* and can be used as well.

Noodles and pasta Supermarkets, cheese and gourmet shops, food stalls at open markets and shops that cater to Italian and other Mediterranean cuisines carry large selections of dried and sometimes fresh pastas. Supermarkets also carry Asian noodles; however, for the best selection of Asian soup and frying noodles, try the Chinese, Indonesian and Japanese shops - see also Chapter IV - 15.

Nuts - *noten* The term "nut" commonly refers to dried fruits or seeds that have hard or brittle outer shells. Those routinely used in the kitchen include **almonds - *amandelen***, **Brazil nuts - *paranoten***, **cashew nuts - *cashew noten***, **chestnuts - *kastanjes***, **coconuts - *kokosnoten***, **hazelnuts - *hazelnoten***, **macadamia nuts - *macadamia noten***, **pecan nuts - *pecan noten***, **peanuts - *pindas***, **pine nuts (also called piñon, pignoli and pignolia nuts) - *pijnboomnoten***, **pistachio nuts - pistachenoten** and **walnuts - *walnoten***. All are readily available in delicatessens and cheese shops and some are sold in supermarkets and Asian stores. Nuts can be used simply as snacks. They are roasted, toasted, smoked, candied or flavored with various seasonings. Nuts used in cooking are generally raw, blanched, dry-roasted or oil-roasted, salted or unsalted. Toasting or roasting the nuts enhances their flavor and this can easily be done at home. These nuts add flavor and texture to cereals, breads, desserts, soups, sauces, bread stuffings and stews and make attractive garnishes. The **almond** is probably the most versatile. It is a flat, oval nut and a brown skin hides a tasty ivory flesh. It is used as an ingredient or as a garnish. They can be used with fish, poultry, rice, sauces, vegetables, breads, cakes, cookies, and candy (see **almond paste**). They are sold blanched, roasted or smoked and whole, halved, or in slivers. To remove the dark brown skin, blanch them for two or three minutes until the nut pops out of the skin when squeezed between the thumb and forefinger. **Walnuts** and **pecans** are closely related to each other and thus are often used interchangeably. Their ivory flesh is encased in a thin brown skin. Toasted walnuts add a delicious flavor to green salads, fruit salads, breads, cakes, pies and cookies. They are much loved in the sweets of the Middle East. The pecan has a rich and almost buttery flavor. It is native to the United States and is grown mostly in the South and Southwest where it is paired with molasses to make the famous pecan pie. It is also used in ice cream, cakes, pies and cookies. When shelled, the pecan turns rancid quickly. **Hazelnuts** (or filberts) have a pale golden flesh encased in a brown skin. They also have a buttery flavor and they are prized by cooks and bakers. They are used for breads and cookies, poultry stuffing, pâtés and salads. Hazelnuts add flavor and texture to sautéed pork, chicken and vegetables. They are used chopped, ground or whole. To remove their skin, heat them in the oven for about 10 minutes until the skin begins to flake. Then wrap the warm nuts in a dish towel and rub them together until the skin is removed. The edible **chestnut** is common in many parts of Europe and Asia. A blight had more or less wiped them out in North America. They are eaten boiled, roasted, candied or puréed. In the winter they can be purchased in their shells or peeled and vacuum-packed. Unsweetened, peeled, whole or puréed chestnuts are available in tins and they are mostly sold under the French name *marron*. Sweetened chestnuts are sold as *marrons glacés*. Chestnuts are often eaten as a vegetable and are mixed with Brussels sprouts and red cabbage. Chestnut purée is used in desserts. They should not be confused with the Asian water chestnuts which are not nuts at all. **Peanuts** are actually legumes. They are also called groundnuts because the plant bends down after flowering and buries its pods in the earth. They are used in savory sauces such as the Southeast Asian saté and are added to Chinese stir-fry dishes. Chopped peanuts are added to breads, cookies and candies and are used as toppings on ice cream. Peanuts are also used in salads and slaws. In Africa they are used in stews and soups. **Pine nuts** come from the cones of certain pine trees. They are much appreciated in Korea, the Middle East and the Mediterranean and are essential to the Italian *pesto* sauce. They are often added to salads and stews and can be sprinkled over custard-filled tarts and pastries. They are sold blanched but toasting improves their flavor. **Pistachio nuts** are used in pâtés and terrines and are valued for their flavor in ice creams. They are available shelled and unshelled. Unshelled nuts will be partially open when they are ripe. **Macadamia** nuts are native to Australia but they are cultivated in Hawaii where they are used in pies, cakes, ice creams and macadamia nut candy. Because their shells are extremely hard, they are always sold shelled. **Coconuts** - see Coconuts above and in the Asian Food chapter. **Brazil nuts** are native to South America and although they are usually eaten as a snack, they can be used much the same as macadamia nuts. **Cashew nuts** are mostly used as snack foods here or are used in sweet and savory Asian dishes.

Oil, cooking Basic cooking oils - *olie* like **corn oil - *maisolie*, olive oil - *olijfolie*, vegetable oil - *slaolie***, and **sunflower oil - *zonnebloemolie*** and ***frituur olie* – deep-frying oil** which is made from a combination of vegetable oils and has a high smoking point are sold in most supermarkets while **peanut oil - *arachideolie*, sesame oil - *sesamolie*, safflower oil - *saffloerolie*** and **soya oil - *sojaolie*** can be bought at health food stores, supermarkets and Asian shops. Sunflower and safflower oils are favorites because they are high in polyunsaturated fats. **Peanut oil** is preferred by Chinese cooks because of its high smoke point. Buying **olive oil**, on the other hand, is more complex. The very best is the first pressed oil which is done at low temperatures using the best quality fruit. This is called "cold pressing" and appears on some labels in Holland as "1st cold pressing". It may be unrefined or clarified. In Europe the unrefined oil is graded according to acidity with "extra virgin" oil being less than 1% acid which is ideal. In the United States, all first pressed unrefined olive oil may be classified as "virgin". The oil pressed from ripe fruits will be golden, when pressed from partially ripe fruits, it will have a greenish tinge and will taste stronger. Some chefs prefer the Italian olive oil produced around Lucca and the French olive oil produced around Nice in Provence. Others prefer the oils of Greece, Portugal and Spain.

Oil, other There are several other oils which are available in local delicatessens or gourmet shops and deserve attention (they are often known by their French names): **walnut oil - *huile de noix*** with its aromatic, nutty flavor is used in dressings and seasonings; **grape-seed oil - *huile de pepin de raisin*** which is particularly good for marinating meats; **almond oil - *huile d'amande*** which is used to flavor salads and cold dishes and **hazelnut oil - *huile de noisette*** with its very special toasted hazelnut taste is used to flavor cold dishes such as salads and mayonnaise and is sprinkled over certain vegetables like artichokes, asparagus and green beans. **Sesame oil - *sesamolie***, which is made from toasted seeds, is used to flavor Asian foods and is found in Asian shops. Don't confuse it with the sesame oil made from untoasted seeds that is sold in some health food stores. The flavor of all of these oils is either destroyed or altered by heat.

Pastry dough Easy-to-use **puff pastry - *bladerdeeg*, dough for savory pies - *deeg voor hartige taart*, pizza dough - *pizzadeeg*** and **filo (phyllo) - *fillo bladerdeeg*** pastry dough are sold in most supermarkets in the frozen food section. **Puff pastry** is made with layers of butter and dough and is very flaky when baked. It can be used to make **Croissants, Palmiers, Napoleons, Danish Pastries** and tops for **Pot Pies**. It is mostly sold in sheets and 5-inch (12½-centimeter) squares. ***Deeg voor hartige taart*** is mostly used as the bottom crust of savory pies such as **Quiche Lorraine** and is also sold in 5-inch (12½ centimeter) squares. **Filo dough** consists of sheets of pastry which are rolled and stretched very thin, even thinner than the **strudel dough** which it resembles. It is used in Greek and Middle Eastern cookery. It is a prime ingredient in **Baklava** and **Spanakopita**. **Filo** and the Turkish ***yufka*** sold in Middle Eastern shops can be used in recipes calling for the Moroccan ***warka*** and Tunisian ***malsouqua***, although *yufka* is thicker than filo and *warka* and *malsouqua* are prepared by pouring a thin batter over a heated inverted pan.

Peanut butter - *pindakaas* Locally-made peanut butter is either smooth (**natural - naturel**) or **chunky - *met stukjes noot***. However, Albert Heijn also makes it with **sesame seeds - *sesam*** and **chilies - *pikante*.** Be sure to try the local peanut butter for it is made from all natural ground peanuts and has fewer additives than other peanut butters. American brands are also sold in some supermarkets and import shops.

Pectin - *pectine* Already present in many fruits and vegetables, pectin is used as a jelling agent for some jams, jellies and preserves. More sugar is required when using pectin. To keep the sugar content down, combine fruits with a high pectin content like apples, red currants, gooseberries, plums, and cranberries with low pectin fruits such as apricots, blueberries, cherries, strawberries, blackberries, grapes, and pineapples. If you still wish to use commercial pectin, there are several types sold here. Van Gils makes a **gelling sugar - *geleisuiker*** which is a sugar with pectin already added. They also make a gelling powder. Both are sold in supermarkets. Marmello and Opecta are two brands of gelling powders. For one kilo of fruit use 1 kilo *geleisuiker*, 25 grams van Gils powder, 15 grams Marmello powder or 30 grams Opecta powder. Marmello and Opecta are sold in health food stores.

Salt - *Zout* A fine-grained **table salt** is sold in all supermarkets and health food stores as are **sea salt - zeezout**, **mineral salt - Jozozout, iodized salt - Jozo met jodium, reduced sodium salt - Jozo Vitaal, salt substitute - dieet zout**, and seasoned salts such as **season all - kruidenzout, garlic - knoflook**, **onion - uien** and **celery - selderie**.

Stock, broth, and bouillon Most delicatessen or gourmet food shops and some supermarkets carry tinned or bottled concentrated white, brown, veal, poultry, vegetable, fish and lobster stocks. These are used as a base for many sauces or are diluted with water to enrich many soups. In addition, supermarkets sell several types of solid beef, chicken, vegetable, fish and herb bouillon cubes which can be mixed with water to make instant stocks. The following stocks sold here are known by their Dutch or French names or both while the bouillon cubes are expressed in Dutch. **White stock - *blanke fond or fond blanc*** is made from chicken carcasses (*gevogeltefond* or *fond de volaille*) or veal meat (*kalfsfond* or *fond de veau*) which have been simmered with veal bones and knuckles, carrots, onions, leeks, celery and a bouquet garni of aromatic herbs. **Brown stock - *bruine fond or fond brun*** is made from beef and veal meat and bones and aromatic vegetables which have been browned in fat to give the stock a richer color and fuller flavor. Brown stock can also be made using only veal in which case it is known as brown veal stock (*bruine fond de veau* or *fond brun de veau*). **Vegetable stock - *groentefond*** is made from any number of browned vegetables such as carrots, parsnips, potatoes, celery, mushrooms, leeks, garlic, onions, peas, beans and aromatic herbs. **Fish stock - *visfond or fond de poisson*** (or more correctly *fumet*) is made by simmering fish trimmings and bones, onions, shallots, mushrooms and aromatic herbs. **Lobster stock - *kreeften-fond* or *fonds d'homards*** is made by simmering lobster with aromatic vegetables and herbs. **Game stock - *wild fond* or *fond de gibier*** is made with meat and trimmings of venison, pheasant, rabbit and other game and carrots and onions and a bouquet garni of parsley, thyme and bay leaf plus sage, juniper berries and cloves. **Bouillon** - ***bouillon*** cubes come in several flavors: **beef - *rundvlees*, chicken - *kip*, herb - *kruiden*, vegetable - *groente*** and **fish - *vis*.**

Sugar - suiker Supermarkets carry a full range of **cane - *riet*** and **beet - *biet*** sugars. There is a **crystal** or **coarse sugar (British granulated) - *kristalsuiker*** (used for coffee or syrup), **super fine** or **castor sugar (American granulated) - *zeer fijne tafelsuiker*** (used for cooking and baking), **powdered** or **confectioner's - *poedersuiker*** (used for icings), **sugar cubes - *suikerklontjes*** and **candy sugar - *kandij suiker*** (a large crystal sugar used for coffee, baking and preserving). Powdered sugar is crushed granulated sugar. Locally, it is made from sugar beet. It is a little coarser than American and British powdered sugar but for all practical purposes it gets nearly the same results. In addition, the Dutch have three types of **soft cane sugar - *basterdsuiker*.** The **white - *witte*** has a little molasses clinging to it and is used to sweeten yoghurt and cereals. It dissolves much more quickly than the crystal or super fine sugar. The **light brown - *lichtbruine*** and **dark brown - *donkerbruine basterd*** sugars are like the brown sugars sold everywhere. The darker the sugar, the more molasses there is clinging to it. Health food stores and counters at supermarkets sell a rather coarse **raw cane sugar - *ruwe rietsuiker*** not processed with chemicals. This sugar and the dark brown sugar can be used instead of raw **Demarara sugar** which is favored by the British. For a special raw sugar, try the Indonesian ***gula Jawa*** which is made from palm sap. It comes in solid, cookie-sized slices and is sold at Asian stores. White sugar is made up almost entirely of **sucrose** which in turn is composed of glucose and fructose. Both inhibit crystallization. **Glucose** (also called dextrose, corn or grape sugar) is less sweet than sugar and is much like corn syrup which contains a high glucose content. It is available in health food stores in a thick colorless syrup or as a **powdered grape sugar - *druivensuiker*.** **Fructose**, or fruit sugar, is the sweetest sugar and is sold in the health food stores and health food sections of supermarkets in a very fine crystal. Since it is sweeter than normal crystal sugar it is often used on cereals and in coffee. It can also be used in cakes and pastries but loses some of its sweetness in cooking.

Syrup - *stroop/siroop* There are several types of commercial syrups such as molasses, golden syrup, corn syrup and maple syrup that are available on the Dutch market. They are used in baking, as dessert toppings, as toppings for pancakes and waffles and for making candies and cake icings. **Molasses - *melasse*** is a by-product of the sugar refining process of sugar cane and sugar beet. The first boiling of the cane or beet sap produces a light molasses which is the sweetest and most refined and is mainly used to make pancake and waffle toppings. The second boiling results in a darker, less sweet molasses which is popularly used to flavor ginger bread, molasses cookies and Boston baked beans. The third boiling produces a very thick, dark harsh-flavored residue known as **black-strap molasses** or **black treacle** which is consumed by health food enthusiasts and is used as fodder for the cattle that are fattened on feedlots in the United States. Premium table molasses can be made by blending cane or beet syrup with the first boiling of molasses. A dark molasses can be bought in health food stores and sections of supermarkets. **Golden Syrup**, which is usually identified by its brand name *Lyle's*, is available in many supermarkets here. It is made from simmering sugar cane sap. It is a light treacle with a lovely gold color and has the consistency of honey. It can be substituted for light corn syrup in cooking and baking and is used as pancake and dessert toppings. **Corn syrup** is a thick, sweet liquid derived from corn starch. It inhibits crystallization and is thus a popular ingredient in candies, jams and jellies. Corn syrup is available in two forms: light and dark, the dark being a mixture of light corn syrup and molasses. Some of the delicatessens or gourmet shops which cater to North Americans carry both light and dark corn syrups. What the Dutch traditionally use as a pancake syrup is actually a mixture of the lighter molasses and other syrups. It comes in two forms; **heavy - *huishoudstroop*** (a mixture of sugar and glucose syrup) and **heavy but more liquid - *schenk stroop*. *Siroop*** is a term which applies to the light and liquid berry syrups used to flavor drinks. **Maple syrup** is made from the sap of the sugar maple tree. Its unique flavor makes it the favorite American topping for pancakes and waffles. It can be used to glaze hams, sweeten spice cakes and apple pies and flavor ice creams, puddings and frostings. Some health food and import stores now carry pure New England **maple syrup - *ahornstroop*** and maple-flavored syrup which is a combination of a less costly syrup (such as corn syrup) and a small amount of real maple flavoring.

Tomato paste, purée and sauce - *tomaten purée* The term **tomato paste** generally applies to tomatoes that have been cooked for several hours, strained and reduced to a thick paste-like consistency. **Tomato purée** is cooked for a shorter period, strained and reduced to a thick liquid. **Tomato sauce** is a slightly thinner purée that is flavored with various seasonings. In Holland, the term ***tomaten puree* - tomato purée** generally applies to the thick **tomato paste**. Look for ***tomaten puree*, *gecondenseerde* - condensed** or ***dubbel geconcentreerd* - doubly concentrated**. For an unseasoned **tomato sauce**, try the ***gezeefde tomaten* - strained tomatoes** that are on the same supermarket shelves as Italian pasta sauces. Heinz has a new Spanish-type ***Tomato Frito***, which a tomato sauce with water, sunflower oil, sugar, and garlic and onion extracts. The American style **tomato sauce** is sold at import stores.

Vinegar - *azijn* Vinegar is made from the activity of an airborne bacteria on naturally fermented alcohol such as wine, malt and apple cider. The most common vinegars sold in Holland are **natural vinegar - *natuurazijn*, white wine - *witte wijn*, red wine - *rode wijn*, apple cider vinegar - *appelazijn*** or ***ciderazijn*** and **pickling vinegar - *inmaakazijn***. (Don't confuse them with *schoonmaakazijn* which is a cleaning vinegar used to remove nasty calcium deposits.) Supermarkets and delicatessens or gourmet food shops also offer a variety of herb-flavored vinegars such as an **herbal bouquet** - ***kruidenazijn*** and **tarragon** - ***dragonazijn***; fruit-flavored vinegars such as **raspberry** - ***frambozen***; **balsamic vinegar** and **rice** - ***rijstazijn*** (see also Chapter IV.15). **Apple cider** and **rice vinegars** are milder and not so acidic as many other vinegars. The most common usages for these vinegars are as follows: **Balsamic vinegar** is an Italian vinegar which is aged in wooden barrels for several years and is sold in various stages of ageing. We are talking decades here. A very old bottle is treated like an aged bottle of fine wine. A few drops can be used along with olive oil and vinegar on green salads. A few drops drizzled over strawberries enhances the flavor of even hothouse strawberries. It can be used in stews and meat dishes and on pastas. Add at the last minute for it loses its flavor when heated. **Cider vinegar**, made from the juice of apples, can be used for fruit and cabbage salads, for fish and shellfish court bouillon and for pickling. **Herb vinegar** is made with white wine flavored with various herbs like tarragon, basil and herb mixtures and are mostly used as salad dressings. ***Natuurazijn*** is a simple white all-purpose vinegar made from all natural products. It can loosely be compared to distilled white vinegar made from a grain-alcohol mixture. **Raspberry vinegar** is made from macerated raspberries in white wine vinegar. Its fruity aroma compliments chicken, duck and liver and is used in salads that have some fruit in them. **White wine vinegar** is made from white grapes and is used when a clear liquid is preferred. Use with fish, meat and game marinades; vegetable salads; and sauces such as **Hollandaise** and **Béarnaise**. Use this vinegar to make home-made aromatic vinegars. **Red wine vinegar** is obviously made from red grapes. It is preferred for use on green salads and red meat dishes. Made from rice, **rice vinegar** comes from China and Japan and has a subtle, sweet flavor. It can be used in dipping sauces, in sweet and sour dishes, salad dressing and pickles. Buy it in Asian stores.

Whipped Cream Stabilizer – ***slagroom versteviger*** When added to cream as you are whipping it, this stabilizer gives the cream body so it will hold its shape. The cream can then be used for a light frosting for cakes, pies and other desserts. It will keep, covered, for up to 48 hours.

Yeast - ***gist*** The most common types of yeast are fresh, active dry, rapid rise and instant. Formerly most supermarkets carried only the active dry yeast but instant yeast called *gist levure* (Dr. Oetker brand) or *instant gist* (Baukje brand) is now available on supermarket shelves. Developed by the French in 1960's, the "instant" means that you can add it to the dry ingredients without soaking it, although soaking does not do any harm. Instant yeast has a greater tolerance to temperatures than the other types of yeast. It contains "live" yeast cells so for recipes calling for active dry yeast, Julia Child, the guru of American cooking, says to use 25% less instant yeast although instructions on the packages of both active dry and instant state that one 7 gram packet dry yeast equals 25 grams fresh. For plain breads, reckon on 13 grams instant to 500 grams flour. For bread machines, use 6 grams instant for 500 grams flour.

IV.2 HERBS AND SPICES

In 1595 a group of nine north Netherlands merchants funded an expedition to the Banda Islands (in today's Indonesia) in search of spices. The party consisted of four ships manned by 249 men. After two years, three ships and 89 crew members returned with a modest cargo. While the trip was a failure in human terms, the profits were enough to cover the expenses. More expeditions followed. The second expedition of 22 ships realized 100 percent profit in spite of the loss of 8 ships. Profits eventually soared to 400 percent before the demand by Dutch traders and traders from other countries caused the growers to raise their prices. Sometimes the people of Banda sold the same spices twice. Finally in 1602, in a decisive move meant to gain a monopoly and stabilize prices, a large group of Amsterdam merchants formed the *Vereenigde Oost Indische Compagnie* (United Netherlands Chartered East India Company) or the VOC. They succeeded in monopolizing the Dutch spice trade and international navigation east of the Cape of Good Hope and West of the Straights of Magellan. Governed by seventeen directors known in history as the *Heeren XVII*, the VOC would eventually usher the country into one of the most profitable and illustrious chapters of Dutch history. The period would become known as the "Golden Years". The spices that caused this great stir were simply cloves, mace, nutmeg and peppers from Indonesia (the Spice Islands) and cinnamon from Ceylon.

To this day these spices are still an important part of the Dutch cuisine. Every housewife still has a handy nutmeg grater with a separate compartment for storing the whole nut and before many vegetables are brought to the table, there is a ritualistic scraping of the nutmeg nut - *en beetje nootmuskaat* over the top.

Other spices central to Indonesian cuisine would reach Holland much later. Today practically every dried herb and spice used in international cooking is available in Holland. Only dried or freshly ground exotic herbs, spices and blends peculiar to specific regional cuisines might be absent. If you don't find what you are looking for in the supermarkets, try the local Chinese and/or Indonesian specialty shops or the stalls at the open markets such as the Albert Cuyp Market in Amsterdam and the very active weekend *Oosterse Markt* - Eastern Market in Beverwijk. See also Chapter IV - 15, Asian and Other International Food Products.

Herbs and spices come from several sources. Some are imported in bulk and packaged by the vendors while Spice Islands, McCormick, and Silvo are commercial brands which are sold in supermarkets and specialty shops. Some supermarkets package their own in-house brands. Conimex and Go Tan are two local firms specializing in Indonesian and Chinese herbs, spices and blends.

In addition to the dried herbs, some greengrocers, supermarkets and garden centers sell fresh potted herbs like basil, chervil, chives, coriander, parsley, tarragon and thyme, albeit not always at the same time. Some frozen herbs, and herbs like basil, dill, oregano, rosemary and thyme and Italian and Provençal herb mixtures packed in oil, are also available. When substituting dried for fresh herbs use this formula: ¼ teaspoon dried, finely powdered herbs is equivalent to ¾ to 1 teaspoon of dried, loosely crumbled herbs and 1½ to 2 teaspoons freshly snipped herbs.

Herbs and spices all have special characteristics of their own. Spices change their personalities when they are heated in oil, dry roasted or ground while some herbs lose their character very quickly and must be added at the last minute. Herbs and spices are generally compatible with other herbs and spices and thus are combined in numerous blends. Keep them in a cool dry place, away from your stove, and replace the old with new ones at decent intervals — when green herbs turn brown and before the seeds are in danger of becoming rancid with age.

Allspice - *piment, Jamaica peper* A berry from a tree which grows in the West Indies, allspice has the flavor of cinnamon, cloves, nutmeg and mace combined. It is generally used in cakes, jams, fruit pies, pickles, sausages and ketchup, and in Jamaica it is used in soups, curries and stews. It is sold as dried whole berries or ground.

Anise - *anijs* This sweet, licorice-flavored seed is related to cumin, caraway, fennel and dill. It should not be confused with star anise - *steranijs* which is much stronger. Anise is considered by many to be a digestive, but in Holland anise-flavored sugar cubes - *anijsblokjes* dissolved in hot milk are taken to relieve cold symptoms. In the West it is used in cakes and cookies. In India and the Middle East, it is used in soups, stews and breads. It is also used in several countries to make sweet liqueurs like **Pastis**, **Ouzo**, **Arrack** and **Anisette**. Anise is sold as dried whole seeds or ground.

Basil - *basilicum* A member of the mint family, basil is a pungent herb most widely used in Mediterranean and Thai and other South East Asian cooking. Most basils are green with the exception of the dark opal which is a lovely purple. Basil has an affinity for tomatoes and is used to flavor tomato-based pasta sauces, pizzas, soups and meat stews. Fresh basil is also used in green salads and vegetable dishes. It is the primary ingredient in the Italian **Pesto** which is a mixture of fresh basil crushed together with pine nuts (also known as *piñon* or *pignoli*), garlic, olive oil and grated Parmesan and sardo or pecorino cheeses. Pesto is served on pasta or potato gnocchi or stirred into **Minestrone Soup**. There is a striking difference between fresh and dried basil but they are used interchangeably in many recipes. Dried, crumbled basil is sold in supermarkets and fresh basil can be purchased from greengrocers but it is suggested that you order it in advance. See also Basil in Other Asian Ingredients.

Bay leaf - lauierblad This aromatic herb is native to the Mediterranean. There are two main varieties of bay leaf, Turkish and Californian. Garden centers often carry small laurel trees but the fresh leaves are sometimes bitter. Dried leaves are sold in supermarkets and Asian stores.

Capers - *kappertjes* The small green flower buds of a native Mediterranean (and parts of Asia) bush, capers add a pleasant, but pungent flavor to many sauces and condiments. They are a usually added to mayonnaise to make **Tartar Sauce** which accompanies **Fish**. Capers are either dried and salted or preserved in a vinegar brine. Here the brined buds are sold in small jars in supermarkets, Asian shops and gourmet shops.

Caraway seed - *karwijzaad* Caraway is a member of the same family as parsley. It has a pungent, anise-like flavor. Caraway is often confused with cumin, probably because the French often refer to it as *cumin des prés*. The seeds are used in bread doughs and are added to cheeses, cabbage, soups and sausages. They are also used to flavor **kümmel**, a German liqueur. The seeds are sold whole or ground.

Cardamom - *kardemom* The dried fruit of a plant in the ginger family, cardamom or cardamon has an aromatic cinnamon-like flavor and enhances sweet and savory dishes. It is widely used in Indian *garam masala* and curry mixtures. Scandinavians use it to flavor sweet breads and **Lucia Buns**, cakes and braised meats. Arabs flavor their coffee with it. It is sold as whole or ground seeds.

Cayenne pepper - *cayennepeper* The finely-ground hot and pungent powder made from a variety of small, dried, ripe chilies, cayenne pepper can be used in any dishes calling for hot peppers.

Celery leaf - *selderij, bladselderij* or *snijselderij* Before the 16th century, leaf or wild celery was considered to be a medicinal herb. It looks very much like flat-leaf parsley. Today it is used to give an aromatic celery flavor to many European and Mediterranean soups and sauces. In Holland, it is used together with celery root - *knolselderij* to flavor the traditional **Dutch Pea Soup - Erwtensoep**, Chinese celery - *kun choy* (C), *qin cai* (M) is similar to the Dutch *selderij*; however, its flavor is a little stronger. It is used in many Chinese stir-fry dishes together with meat, poultry and seafood but can also be used in soups and with fried rice. The other celery varieties are vegetables: **garden** or **stalk celery - *bleekselderij*** which is grown for its stalks and **celery root** or **celeriac - *knolselderij*** which is grown for the root. *Bleekselderij* and *knolselderij* are used as vegetables in soups and salads. See also Exotic Asian Vegetables Chapter.

Celery seed - *selderij zaad* These tiny, pungent seeds are the fruit of the lovage or maggi plant. They add a celery- or fennel-like flavor to soups, stocks, pickling spices, mixed vegetables, cole slaw and potato salads. The seeds are mostly sold dried but whole.

Chervil - *kervel* Chervil is a mild-flavored member of the parsley family. It has feathery green leaves that have an anise-like flavor. Its flavor is strongest when fresh and it is usually added at the last minute. It is an important ingredient in the French *fines herbes* herb mixture. It compliments some egg, tomato and fish dishes, and is added to green salads, cream sauces and herb butters. A creamed **chervil soup - *Kervelsoep*** is quite popular here. Chervil is sold fresh in many greengrocers and supermarkets.

Chili peppers - *Spaanse peper/lombok* Members of the capsicum family, chilies range from large, mild-flavored peppers to the tiny, fiery-hot birdseye chilies. *Capsaicin*, which give chilies their heat, is present in the seeds, veins and skin. The strength depends on the species and ripeness. Native to Central and South America and the West Indies, they were widely used in Mexican and South American cooking when Christopher Columbus discovered them. Their popularity quickly spread to the Mediterranean and African countries. Chilies were introduced to Asia in the 16th century and are extremely important to most Asian cuisines; Japan and parts of China are exceptions. Today there are over 200 types of chilies. Several Indonesian chilies or cabé are available here, mainly; the finger-length ***lombok* or Spanish peppers** and the four alarm **cabé rawit - bird's eye chilies** which are either green - *hijau* or red - *merah*. Some Asian stores carry the explosive fresh ***habañero*** chilies and many supermarkets and Asian stores carry canned or bottled ***jalapeño*** and **green chilies**. They also market ***Tabasco*** and other hot sauces and pastes. Shops which cater to Middle Eastern and Mediterranean expatriates carry chili varieties dictated by their cuisines. Dried, crushed and powdered chilies are also available.

Chili powder This is the powder made from dried chilies sold in Asian stores and is mostly used in Asian cuisines. Chili peppers differ from country to country. Thus, for example, it is wise to use Indian chili powder for Indian recipes and Korean chili powder for Korean recipes. Chili powder can be combined with olive oil to make a chili oil (½ cup chili powder, 2 cups olive oil and 2 crushed cloves of peeled garlic) which is used in **Peri Peri**, a hot Portuguese sauce used on chicken and fish. It can also be used in Asian recipes calling for chili oil. This is not to be confused with the **Chili Powder** blend which is used for Tex/Mex cooking - see **Spice Blends**.

Chives - *bieslook* A delicate herb tasting much like onion, chives are used to season vegetables, cream soups, sauces and fish and shellfish dishes. They are frequently used fresh together with sour cream and bacon bits as a topping on baked potatoes. Chives bruise easily and are thus usually snipped with a scissors rather than chopped. Supermarkets and greengrocers market chives in small herb pots throughout the year. See also Chinese chives in the Exotic Asian Vegetables chapter.

Cinnamon - *kaneel* The reddish-tan inner bark of a tropical evergreen tree, cinnamon has a woody aroma which enhances the tastes of sweet and savory dishes. In the West cinnamon is used in fruit compotes, mulled wines, apple and pear sauces and pastries. It is widely used in the Indian curry blend, *garam masala*, and Middle Eastern foods where it is used flavor lamb and rice dishes. It is available ground or as **cinnamon sticks or quills - *kaneel stokjes***.

Clove - *kruidnagel* Clove is the tiny, dried bud of the evergreen clove tree. It has a sweet, pungent aroma which goes well with both sweet and savory foods and is thus one the worlds most important spices. Cloves are used in the Indian spice blend ***garam masala*** and as a part of pickling spice mixture. They are used in cakes and cookies, fruit pies and compotes and stews. Whole cloves are often used to decorate **Baked Ham** and are an important ingredient in the American Thanksgiving favorite, **Pumpkin Pie**. Cloves are sold as whole dried buds or nails or ground.

Coriander/Chinese parsley/cilantro - *koriander* A very pungent herb, coriander is related to the parsley family but its flavor is completely different. It is grown for its leaves and for its dried ripe fruit or seeds. In some cuisines, only the leaves are used in steamed fish and shellfish dishes, soups, Mexican salsa, salads and stews. Thai cooks use the leaves, stalks and roots while Indonesians use mostly the seeds. Both leaves and seeds are known as *koriander* here, but in the Asian stores the seeds might be known by their Indonesian name *ketumbar* (Dutch - *ketoembar*). Don't confuse the leaves and seeds for the flavors are remarkably different. Coriander leaves are sold fresh at some greengrocers and Asian stores, mostly by special order, and the seeds are sold dried.

Coriander seed - *koriander zaad (ketumbar - Indon.)* Coriander seed or fruit is the spice of the coriander plant and its taste and character is quite different from the leaves. The seeds are added to curry powders and pickling spice mixtures, minced meat dishes, sausages and stews. They are also used in baking. They are usually sold whole or ground.

Cumin - *komijn* The tiny aromatic seeds of a member of the parsley family, cumin has a strong, heavy flavor and aroma. It is often confused with caraway seed. It is a native of the Nile Valley and is used in Middle Eastern countries to flavor minced meat and vegetable dishes. Latin Americans use it in sauces, soups and stews. It is an important ingredient in chili powder which is used in Mexican foods while Indian cooks use it in their curry spice blend, ***garam masala***. Cumin seeds are sold whole or ground.

Dill - *dille* Once considered a magic herb which was used as a guard against witchcraft, dill is now grown for the refreshing anise-like flavor of both its seeds and leaves. The soft, feathery leaves called dill weed are used to flavor dill pickles, salads, vegetables, meats, soups and sauces. Fresh dill loses its flavor quickly so must be added toward the end of the cooking process. Dill seed is the dried fruit of the herb. It is stronger than the leaf. Scandinavians use both leaves and seeds in breads and pickles and with seafood. Poles and Russians use dill weed to flavor soups and stews. Dill weed is sometimes sold fresh or packed in oil but is usually dried.

Fennel seed - *venkelzaad* The fennel plant has the aroma of anise. The fresh leaves are sometimes used in place of dill or as a garnish and the seeds are used in both sweet and savory dishes. Its bulbous base is used as a vegetable. Fennel seeds also flavor many liqueurs. They are sold whole or ground.

Fenugreek - *fenegriek* A medicinal herb thought to reduce fever when applied to the body, fenugreek is generally noted for its aromatic seeds which resemble celery or lovage - *lavas* in flavor. It is used in curry powders, teas and Middle Eastern and Indian spice blends. Uncooked fenugreek tastes bitter, thus it is usually roasted to produce a more mellow flavor. The dried seeds are sold whole and can be ground at home when required.

Galangal - laos/kencur *Galangal* is a rhizome (underground plant stem) of the ginger family. There are two types: **greater galangal** (*Alpinia galanga*) is known in Indonesia as *laos*; **lesser galangal** (*Languas officinarum or Alpinia officinarum*) as *kencur*. They are sold here under the Indonesian names. *Laos* is sold fresh and has the most delicate flavor. It is more extensively used in Southeast Asian cooking. *Kencur* is also known as "aromatic ginger" but ginger and galangal cannot be used interchangeably. Both *laos* and *kencur* are also cut into small pieces and dried (soak before using) and are sometimes powdered. However, it is best to buy laos fresh and then stick it in the freezer - see Ginger below.

Ginger - *gember* Fresh **ginger root - *gember wortel*** is actually not a root but a rhizome (the underground stem of the ginger plant). It has a spicy, pungent aroma which is indispensable to Asian cooking and can be purchased fresh or dried and powdered at greengrocers, supermarkets and Asian stores. When buying fresh ginger select firm roots which show no signs of shrivelling. The mild young (or spring) ginger requires very little peeling but as it ages its flavor increases and the skin becomes tougher. Then it must be peeled. Ginger root can be kept in the freezer either whole and unpeeled or it can be ground to a pulp and frozen in an ice cube tray. Some Asians keep fresh ginger in a moist pot of earth to prolong its freshness. Europeans and Americans generally use the powdered ginger in baked goods such as ginger bread and ginger snaps. Tender pieces of ginger - *stem gember* preserved in syrup and ginger syrup are also sold in most supermarkets. This ginger is eaten as a sweetmeat or in desserts like ice cream. In addition to flavoring foods, ginger has other uses. A hot tea made from fresh ginger and honey is used in Asia as a panacea for colds and sore throats and as a digestive aid. A slice of ginger dropped in used hot cooking oil will refresh it. See also stem ginger in the Exotic Asian Vegetables Chapter.

Horseradish - *mierikswortel* One of the five bitter herbs of the Jewish Passover festival, horseradish is a pungent, spicy root which is grown mainly for its white flesh. Fresh roots are sometimes sold by greengrocers. They are rarely cooked but are freshly grated and used as a condiment or as an ingredient in sauces. Grated horseradish bottled in vinegar - *geraspte mierikswortel* is available in supermarkets and gourmet shops. Bottled horseradish must be white, not yellow or grey. Fresh and bottled horseradish should be eaten quickly as it loses its pungency.

Juniper berry - *jeneverbes* The berries of a prickly evergreen shrub, juniper berries are best known for the flavor they give to Dutch Jenever or gin. The Dutch, Germans and Alsatians use them to flavor sauerkraut dishes; the French in general use them to flavor brines and pâtés; and Scandinavians use them to flavor marinades for beef, game and pork. They are also used in game stock. The berries are sold dried.

Kaffir lime - *jeruk purut* Kaffir lime is the fruit of the small kaffir lime tree. The bitter rind of the fruit and the leaves are used in Thai and Indonesian cooking. The aroma of the leaves is much like lemon verbena. Lemon grass, lemon or ordinary lime rind can be substituted but there will be a difference in flavor. Fresh and dried kaffir lime leaves are generally known here by their Indonesian name, *daun jeruk purut* or *daon djeruk* and are available at Asian stores.

Lemon Balm - *citroenmelisse* The leaves of the lemon balm are very much like mint in appearance and have a lovely lemon scent. They are used to flavor salads and meat and poultry dishes and are brewed to make an aromatic tea. Lemon balm is usually found here as a garden herb.

Lemon Grass - *sereh* or *citroengras*. Also known as citronella, lemon grass is an Asian grass which resembles a fibrous green onion. It contains citral, an essential oil in lemon peel, which gives it the taste and aroma of lemon. It is an important essence in Southeast Asian cooking and dominates the flavors of some of their curries. Lemon grass is sold fresh, frozen or ground in most Asian *toko* where it is known by its Indonesian name, *sereh*.

Lovage - *lavas* A tall Persian plant which is now grown in many parts of Europe, lovage looks, smells and tastes like celery. Its leaves, seeds and stalks are used to flavor salads, soups and stews. It is especially good in fowl and game dishes. Here it is also known as the *maggiplant* for its aroma is much like the soup extract, Maggi. In Holland, it is basically a garden herb.

Mace - *foelie* Mace is the lacy growth which surrounds the nutmeg seed and turns bright red when ready for harvesting. The tastes of nutmeg and mace are similar but that of mace is more refined. It is used to flavor both sweet and savory dishes such as cheese soufflés and cream desserts. It can also be used in shellfish stock and **Béchamel** or other cream sauces. A pinch of mace in any chocolate dish doubles the chocolate flavor. It is usually sold here in large "blades" which are removed from the food when done. It is also sometimes ground.

Marjoram - *marjolein* or ***marjoraan*** Marjoram is a cousin of oregano but has a more delicate flavor. However, the Mediterranean marjoram sold here is stronger than American marjoram. It is good in fish, meat, poultry, egg and vegetable dishes and in tomato sauces. Fresh marjoram is sold by greengrocers and garden centers but it is mostly sold dried.

Mint - *munt* There are over 30 species of mint, the most common in Holland are **peppermint - *pepermunt*** and **spearmint - *kruizemunt***. Mint is mostly used to flavor sweet sauces, liqueurs and cocktails such as mint julep. It also freshens coleslaw and fruit salads and goes well with peas, carrots, onions and cucumbers. Middle Easterners make aromatic mint teas. Some greengrocers carry fresh mint and Middle Eastern stores carry the dried crumbled mint leaves. Garden centers sell it as a perennial garden herb.

Mustard seed - *mosterdzaad* There are three main types of mustard seed: white/yellow, Oriental/brown and black. The powder actually has relatively little flavor until a liquid such as wine, vinegar, water or beer is added at which time it becomes **prepared mustard**. The American prepared white/yellow mustard, sometimes referred to as "ballpark" mustard for it is used on hot dogs sold in sports stadiums, is flavored with sugar, vinegar or turmeric (which gives it the bright yellow color). Brown mustard seeds, used in the French Dijon-style, German and Chinese mustards, are zestier. Chinese and German mustard can sometimes be quite hot. Black mustard is not so popular. Mustard is sold prepared in numerous mustard blends, as whole mustard seeds and as a powder in Asian and gourmet stores and supermarkets. Don't ask for Chinese mustard in Chinese and/or Indonesian shops here for they use the English Coleman's mustard.

Nutmeg - *nootmuskaat* Nutmeg is the kernel of the fruit of the nutmeg tree. It has a rich, spicy, sweet aroma which makes it a popular spice for baked goods. It is also used in milk or cream custards, Béchamel and other cream sauces, and on fruits and vegetables. It is a Dutch favorite where it is used as a topping on vegetables; local butchers use it to season rolled pork roasts. Freshly grated nutmeg has a superior taste. The whole nut can be purchased here along with a nutmeg grater to grate it. It is also sold as a powder.

Oregano - *oregano* A member of the mint family, oregano is a pungent herb related to both marjoram and thyme. It is an essential herb in southern Italian, Greek and Mexican cooking although the Mediterranean oregano is milder than the Mexican variety. Oregano goes extremely well with tomato-based dishes such as pizzas and pasta sauces and with soups, stews, fish, roast pork and chicken. It is sold fresh or dried and crumbled.

Paprika powder - *paprikapoeder* Paprika is a red pepper powder made from grinding certain sweet dried red pepper pods. Its sweet, lightly pungent or hot flavors are highly prized in Hungarian and other Balkan cuisines. Paprika powder is made from Californian, South American, Spanish and Hungarian peppers but the Hungarian powder is considered to be superior. Most supermarkets carry only the mild paprika. This spice is not to be confused with the term *paprika* which the Dutch use for red and green bell peppers.

Parsley - *peterselie* Parsley is one of the world's most widely used herbs. It has a fresh peppery taste. Of its many varieties, **Italian** or **flat-leaf parsley** and the **curly-leaf** are the most common. The flat-leaf is the more pungent of the two but the curly leaf parsley is more plentiful in Holland. Parsley is always included in the mixed blends of *fines herbes* and *bouquet garni* and is used in soups and stews, cream and tomato sauces, vegetables, salads and with poultry, game, pork, beef and fish. It is popularly used as a garnish. It is sold fresh or dried and crumbled.

Pepper and peppercorn - *peper en peperkorrel* The world's most popular spice, pepper is a small berry that grows in clusters on the pepper plant vine. The berry is used to produce **black** - ***zwarte*****, white** - ***witte*** and **green** - ***groene*** peppercorns. The most popular is black pepper for it is most flavorful. Black and white pepper are available whole, cracked and coarsely or finely ground. Green peppercorns, which are the under-ripe berry, are usually preserved in brine. Freshly ground whole peppercorns release more flavor than pre-ground pepper for pepper loses it flavor rather quickly. A mixture of freeze-dried black, white, green, pink peppercorns is also available locally.

Poppy seed - ***maanzaad*** The seeds of the opium poppy, poppy seeds have a slight but nutty aroma. Most of the whole seeds sold here are blue-grey. They are used in Western and Middle Eastern breads, cakes and pastries, in salad dressings and as toppings for noodle and rice dishes. In India, they are toasted and ground with other spices and used to flavor and thicken sauces. They are also used to make pastry fillings.

Rosemary - ***rozemarijn*** A pungent herb which grows wild in the Mediterranean, rosemary has dark, needle-shaped leaves which emit a pleasant lemon and pine aroma. It is especially good for flavoring vegetables, soups and salads and for grilled meats such as chicken, pork, lamb and veal. It is usually sold fresh or as whole or powdered, dried leaves or as a pot herb in garden centers.

Rue - ***wijnruit*** Rue is a perennial herb with bitter tasting leaves. It is used to flavor some eastern European meat stuffings and the Italian marc brandy, *grappa*. Here, it is mostly a garden herb sold in garden centers.

Saffron - ***saffraan*** Saffron is the hand-picked dried stigma of a species of crocus. Each flower has only three stigmata and it takes around 15,000 to make an ounce. It is the most expensive spice in the world. Red-orange in color, saffron is pungent and highly aromatic. It is used to flavor and tint soups, sauces, fish and rice dishes in Indian and Mediterranean cooking. In the U.K. it is an ingredient of saffron cakes. When buying saffron, the very best strands should have very little of the yellow stigma left on it. Saffron should be dark (Buddhist) red. Soak a few threads in your cold cooking liquid for several hours before using it. It will give an even flavor through your dish. A little goes a long way. Saffron is sometimes powdered but is mostly sold in short threads.

Sage - ***salie*** A native Mediterranean herb which is best known for its use in poultry stuffing; sage has a pungent, musk-like aroma that enhances the flavor of chicken, duck, pork, soups and stews. It is sometimes sold as a pot herb in garden centers or is dried and crumbled and sold in supermarkets and Asian stores.

Salam leaf - ***salamblad***, Indonesian ***daun salam***, is a tree leaf much used in Indonesian cooking. It is sometimes erroneously called "curry leaf". It gives a subtle flavor to South East Asian dishes. Bay leaf is often substituted; but, Indonesian cooks advise to do without if salam leaf is not available.

Savory - *bonekruid* Savory is an herb related to the mint family. There is a summer savory and a winter savory. Summer savory is more delicate and is better suited for cooking. Its aroma is like a cross between mint and thyme. It is especially used to flavor beans but is also good in meat loaf, sausages, poultry and soups.

Sesame seed - *sesamzaad* Sesame seeds come in shades of ivory, brown and black and their taste is mild, sweet and nutty. The darker the seed, the nuttier the flavor. They are used in a variety of ways. In the West, sesame seeds are used in salad dressings and to decorate breads, cakes and other confectionaries. The oil from the seeds is used in cooking. In Chinese, Korean and Japanese cooking the seeds are often toasted first to enhance their flavor. The toasted seeds are also pressed to create a flavorful brown **sesame oil** which is favored by Asian cooks as a seasoning and not for frying. Mediterranean and Middle Eastern cooks grind the seeds into a paste, tahini.

Star anise - *steranijs* Native to China and Vietnam, star anise is one of the few spices used in Chinese cooking. It gets it name from the spiked star shape. It has a taste similar to anise and fennel but has a stronger licorice-like aroma. It is a key ingredient to Chinese five spice powder and is used to flavor pork and poultry dishes. It is also used in Chinese and other oriental medicines to relieve symptoms of colic and rheumatism. Buy it whole or ground.

Szechwan or Sichuan pepper/Fagara A reddish-brown dried berry of the prickly ash tree, the Szechwan pepper has a mildly-hot taste and spicy-woody aroma. Although it resembles black peppercorns, it is not related. Whole berries are often heated before using to release their distinctive flavor. They are an essential ingredient to the Chinese five-spice powder.

Tamarind - *asam or assem (Indonesian)* Also known as *Indian date*, tamarind is the fruit from a tall Asian and African tree. The pods contain small seeds and a sweet/sour pulp which, when dried, becomes quite sour. Tamarind is used much like lemon juice is used in Western cuisines. Many recipes call for tamarind water which means simmering dried tamarind slices in water for several minutes. The slices are then discarded. Tamarind is also sold in blocks of partly-dried broken pods and pulp or as a concentrate in Asian stores.

Tarragon - *dragon* An herb with a mild licorice-like flavor, tarragon is widely used in classic French cooking. It flavors **Béarnaise sauce**. It is also a part of the *fines herbes* blend. The flavor is fairly assertive so should be used with caution. It is especially good with chicken, fish and shellfish, eggs, cauliflower and tomatoes. It is also used to make tarragon vinegar. It is sometimes sold fresh in an herb pot or dried and crumbled.

Thyme - *tijm* A member of the mint family, thyme has many relatives. The most popular thyme is the garden variety which has a minty-lemon aroma. It is widely used to add flavor to meat, poultry and fish dishes. It is an important herb in French cooking for it grows wild in Provence. It is an integral part of the *bouquet garni* blend. You can buy it fresh, dried and crumbled, or dried and powdered.

Turmeric - *koenjit or kunyit, kurkuma* Another member of the ginger family, turmeric has a bitter, pungent flavor and adds its yellow-orange hue to curry dishes. It is widely used in South and Southeast Asian cooking. In the West, it adds color to mustard blends. It is sometimes sold fresh, but it is usually available in powdered form.

Wasabi Made from the edible root of the "mountain hollyhock" grown only in Japan, *wasabi* has a fierce aroma and a fiercer taste. It is often known as Japanese horseradish but is in fact not related to the European horseradish plant. It accompanies many raw dishes such as **Sashimi** and **Sushi**. Its pale green flesh is finely grated and is available in tins of powder and tubes of paste. The powder is mixed with water until it has a mustard-like consistency.

HERB AND SPICE BLENDS

Bouquet garni is the French name given to a fresh bouquet of herbs tied together and includes fresh parsley, thyme and bay leaf. It is removed from the dish before serving. Dried, crushed blends of oregano, summer savory, marjoram, rosemary, basil, sage, thyme, dill weed and tarragon are also marketed by Spice Islands as *bouquet garni.*

Bumbu (Indonesian) or boemboe (Dutch) The Indonesian word *bumbu* designates a mixture of herbs and spices, often a paste or a sauce, used to flavor a cooked dish. This term is also applied to a spice mixture for dishes such as **Bahmie (or Bami) Goreng** (fried noodles) or **Nasi Goreng** (fried rice). In Holland *bumbu* may also be called *kruidenmix.* Sometimes the *bumbu* is sold with dried vegetables for these dishes. Meat and perhaps some fresh vegetables can be added to freshen the dish.

Chili powder - *chilipoeder* Chili powder is a blend of ground dried chilies, cumin, coriander, cloves, garlic and oregano. This powder is used to season various types of Chili in Tex/Mex or Mexican cooking. This should not be confused with dried, ground chili peppers.

Curry powder - *kerriepoeder* Curry powder is a mixture of dried chilies, cinnamon, cloves, coriander, fennel, fenugreek, garlic, turmeric and more. In Indian and other South and Southeast Asian cooking, different blends are used for each type of meat or vegetable. There it is usually ground into a paste and bought fresh daily.

Fines herbes is a blend of herbs used in French cooking consisting of equal parts of chervil, chives, parsley and tarragon.

Five-spice powder is a Chinese mixture of star anise, fennel, Szechuan pepper, cloves and cinnamon or cassia. It is used to flavor many dishes including steamed chicken and roast pork.

Garam masala is another popular Indian blend which varies from region to region. A basic blend might simply consist of cardamon, cinnamon, cloves and coriander but other blends are more extravagant with a dozen or more spices. The name literally means "hot spice". It adds a final flavor at the end of cooking and is sometimes sprinkled over the top of a dish just before serving. It is generally available at Asian stores.

Harissa This a Tunisian hot chili sauce which is mixed with cumin, coriander, caraway and garlic. It can be used to flavor Tunisian couscous and other soups and stews. It is often mixed with olive oil and served as a dipping sauce with French bread and olives.

Herbes de Provence As the name suggests, this is a dried herb blend used in Provençal foods of Southern France. A traditional blend includes basil, lavender, rosemary, summer savory and thyme.

Italian seasoning - *italiaanse keukenkruiden* A dried herb blend including basil, marjoram, oregano, red pepper, rosemary, sage and thyme which is used in pasta sauces.

***Kipkruiden* - Chicken spices** A tasty spice blend to be used on chicken which is baked, grilled or southern fried, *kipkruiden* is a Dutch poultry spice mixture of paprika, black pepper, nutmeg, coriander and curry powder, among others. It is not to be confused with the American herb poultry seasoning.

Pickling spices - *inmaakkruiden* A savory blend used to flavor pickled vegetables, this pickling spice mixture incorporates both herbs and spices such as allspice, bay leaf, cinnamon, cloves, mustard seed and red pepper, among others. It is good when used as a seasoning in corned beef and chicken rice or noodle soups.

Poultry seasoning is a North American blend of herbs used in bread stuffing and is sold in shops which sell imported American products. To make your own, mix ¾ teaspoon dried thyme, 1 teaspoon ground sage and ¾ teaspoon ground dried rosemary for six cups of stuffing.

Pumpkin pie spice is a North American blend of allspice, cinnamon, cloves, ginger, mace and nutmeg. It is used in baked pumpkin pies, a traditional dish in the Thanksgiving Day meal. You can also use steamed, strained and drained pumpkin flesh seasoned with the following mixture: ½ teaspoon each ground allspice and cinnamon and ¼ teaspoon each ground ginger and nutmeg for one pie.

Quatre épices is French for **four spices** and is a powdered mixture of white pepper, cloves, cinnamon and nutmeg although ginger sometimes replaces the cinnamon or pepper. It is mostly used for making paté. It should not be confused with the Tunisian blend which includes white pepper, paprika, cinnamon and powdered rose hearts - *coeurs de roses.*

Sambal is an Indonesian condiment or relish. It is available in several blends. The most basic is *sambal olek* or *oelek* which is made up of fresh red chilies, salt and vinegar; sugar is optional. *Sambal bajak* or *badjak* is made of fresh red chilies, onions, garlic, candlenuts, *trasi* - shrimp paste, galangal, kaffir lime leaves, brown sugar, salt and oil. See Chapter IV- 15.

Shwerma spices - *shoarmakruiden* is a powdered mixture of spices very popular in Holland in recent years. It is made from curry powder, caraway seed and paprika and is used to season fried or grilled strips of various meats stuffed in pita bread to make a Middle Eastern *schwerma - shoarma* sandwich.

IV.3 DAIRY PRODUCTS

Of all the wonderful food stuffs produced in Holland, the Dutch are probably most proud of their milk - *melk* and milk products - *zuivelproducten*. The ubiquitous purveyor of this life sustaining substance, the Holstein cow, grazes everywhere. So important is the milk cow that in Friesland the statue of Frisian stadhouder Count Willem Lodewijk bears the inscription *us Heit* - our father, while a nearby statue of a record-breaking milk cow bears the inscription of *us mem* - our mother. Advertised as *de witte motor* - the white motor, milk drives millions of Dutchmen to supermarkets, cheese shops and cheese farms - *kaasboerderijen* to buy this precious commodity. Gouda and Edam cheeses are so well known around the globe that wherever cheese is sold, Gouda and/or Edam cheese are always present. Holland exports half a million tons of cheese annually. It is in fact the world's largest exporter of dairy products.

This chapter details the dairy products generally found in Holland; dairy products, for the purpose of this booklet, include margarine and eggs.

CHEESE - *KAAS*

While the supermarkets offer a good selection of fresh and processed cheese, serious cheese lovers and connoisseurs shop at their local cheese specialist - *kaasspecialist*. He not only has the largest selection of cheese, but he ages his Dutch cheeses naturally to obtain the optimum taste and perfection and his Dutch cheeses never hit the shelves until they are at least two months old. And, since most Dutch cheeses are classified according to age, he keeps a watchful eye on the ageing process. The older it gets, the stronger the flavor. Thus, when buying Dutch cheese you will have the following selection:

***Jonge kaas* - young cheese** (4 weeks) Has a mild, creamy flavor. It can be used for cooking but the protein can separate from the fat, forming strings.

***Jong belegen* - young but slightly ripe** (two months) Its definitive taste is beginning to develop. Good for cooking but don't overheat.

***Belegen* - ripe** (4 months old) Richer in flavor, ripe cheese can be used in both cold and warm dishes.

***Extra belegen* – extra ripe** (7 months) At this stage the cheese has developed a cheddar-or jack-like flavor and is good for all uses.

***Oud* – old (10 months)** Now quite piquant, it is in the same league as Parmesan. It can stand more heat and almost becomes crisp on the surface as it browns in French onion soup and gratin dishes.

***Overjarige brokkel* - old crumbly cheese** (1 to 2 years) This cheese gets its name from the fact that as you slice it, it crumbles. The taste now is pretty sharp. It is not recommended for cooking. Salt crystals in the cheese are a part of the ripening process.

In addition to all of the local cheese, the cheese specialist probably has on hand a good variety of French fresh and soft, ripened cheese; English Cheddar and Stilton; Danish blue; Swiss Emmenthaler and Gruyere; and

Italian mozzarella, mascarpone and Parmesan. He probably also has goat and/or sheep cheeses which come from the Mediterranean and parts of France. If he doesn't have the particular cheese you need, he will be happy to order it for you. Many of the cheese shops have also evolved into delicatessens of a sort. They offer a wide selection of dips, spreads, sauces, herb butters, crackers, patés, nuts, dried fruits and imported wines.

Cheese is made up of 60 percent solids and 40 percent liquid. Different cheeses are labelled according to fat content which in effect means the percentage of fat content of the solids.

You can buy pieces of the large wheels by the Dutch weight (**ons**, **half pond** or **pond**) sliced - *plakken*, cut in a wedge - *punt stuk*, flat chunk - *plat stuk*, grated - *geraspte* or ground - *gemalen*. It should be stored in a cool place but cover it with plastic that is renewed every few days to keep it fresh. It should be served at room temperature. Grated cheese can be frozen.

They are classified as full fat - *volvet* 48+; medium fat - 40+; and low-fat - *mager* or 20+.

Some terms you will see on cheese packages describe their taste - *smaak* as: aromatic - *aromatisch*, fresh/sour - *friszuur*, mild - *mild*, nutty - *nootachtig*, piquant - *pikant* or tasty - *pittig*. Others describe their texture as: creamy - *romig*, soft - *smeuig*, or firm - *stevig*. Special diet cheese - *dieetkaas* has less fat - *minder vet* or less salt - *minder zout* than normal cheese. Processed or spreadable cheeses are called *smeltkaas* or *smeerbaar*.

Popular Dutch cheeses to try:

Seventy percent of the cheeses produced in Holland are Gouda or types of Gouda, 27% are Edam. Both are easily recognizable for Gouda comes in flat, yellow wheels weighing anywhere from 4 to 20 kilos while Edam is ball-shaped with either yellow natural, or red paraffin, rinds. Edam generally weighs 1.7 kilos, the exception being baby Edam. Both types have rich yellow interiors. In terms of taste, Gouda has a tangier flavor and a higher fat content, 48+; Edam is just 40+ fat and is much dryer and doesn't melt as well in sauces. There is also a delicious **smoked Gouda – *Goudse rookkaas*** that is good in snacks and salads.

***Boerenkaas* - farmer's cheese**

Cheese is made from pasteurized and unpasteurized (or raw) milk. Since pasteurizing kills the bacteria that imparts special flavors into cheeses and raw milk cheese aged under 60 days cannot be sold in some countries, many people who have never been to Holland can not have sampled the exquisite **farmer's cheese - *boerenkaas*** favored by local cheese lovers. It is the celebrated farmer's raw milk cheese which is usually a type of Gouda. All the *boerenkaas* must be identified by a label on the rinds. You can buy it plain or seasoned with cloves, nettles, garlic, celery or cumin/caraway. In the spring you will see some of it advertised as ***graskaas* - grass cheese** which means it is the first cheese made from the milk of cows after they have been released from winter barns and have grazed in spring meadows or ***Meikaas* - May cheese** which is similar to *graskaas*. It is fresh and mild.

For people with no-salt diets, some local cheese farmers will make salt-free cheese upon special request.

Other Dutch Cheeses:
Old Amsterdam - a very old Dutch cheese that because of its age, it is probably the most expensive.
Reijpenaer - a naturally-ripened, superior Gouda-type cheese but because of tight quality control, it is only sold in select shops.
Friese nagelkaas 40+ is made with cloves - *kruidnagelen* and cumin/ caraway seeds - *komijn* and is slightly aged.
Kernhem 60+ - a slightly creamy dessert cheese.
Landana 50+ - a soft, creamy oval-shaped cheese with a mildly-sharp taste.
Maasdammer kaas 45+, also known as **Leerdammer** or **Hollandse *gaten kaas*** resembles the pale-yellow Swiss cheese with large holes. It has a mild, sweet and nutty flavor and is good for fondue and grilled sandwiches.
Leidse kaas 20+, a type of Gouda that is seasoned with cumin seeds and is thus known as *komijnekaas*. The most well-known is the original farmer's cheese - **Boeren Leidse** which has the red crust and the City of Leiden Coat of Arms pressed in it.
Maaslander 48+ - has less salt than other Dutch cheeses.
Centenaar and **Milner** have less salt and less fat (30+).
Pardano 45+ - is a low salt cheese that is more like an Italian cheese. It can be used for pizzas and pastas.
Althena 48+ is made especially for people on low salt diets.
Trenta 48+ - a vegetarian cheese for it has no animal rennet.
Subenhara 50+ - a soft dessert cheese that may be flavored with garlic - *knoflook*, garden herbs - *tuinkruiden* or nettles - *brandnetel*.
Dutch Goat and Sheep cheeses - *Hollandse geiten kaas* and *Hollandse schaapen kaas*.

Other cheeses:
The list of cheeses sold in Holland goes on and on. The following are representative samples of some you may find in your local supermarket or cheese shop. They are listed according to texture:

Soft, fresh cheese - *verse kaas* There is some confusion over soft, fresh cheese because they are sometimes used interchangeably by cookbook writers. However, their textures vary from fairly liquid and smooth to fairly firm or firm but crumbly. ***Fromage blanc*** or ***fromage frais*** and ***kwark*** (or *quark*) are similar to a fairly liquid English **curd cheese** or **soft cheese** in terms of taste and cooking properties although their fat content and manufacture may vary. The Italian **ricotta** (see **Whey cheese**) is also a curd cheese, but the commercial ricotta is made from the whey which is a by-product of other cow and sheep milk cheeses. These curd cheeses can be used interchangeably in cheesecakes or can be sweetened and eaten on fruits for breakfast or for dessert. **Cream cheese** (Mon Chou) is firm, smooth cheese which is similar to the French *Petit suisse*. It has a very high fat content and can be used on crackers and bread and is excellent in baked cheesecake. It is not suitable for most other cooking applications for it separates. Don't confuse this firm cheese with the new Philadelphia cream cheese (*zachte frisse zuivelspread*) and the Mon Chou cream cheese (*zacht en luchtig*) spreads. **Mascarpone** is a sweetened, whipped cream cheese which can be used as a topping for scones in lieu of **clotted cream** (which is available only in shops which cater to people from English-speaking countries) and for filling for fruit tarts or crepes. **Cottage cheese - *hüttenkäse*** is a granular, tart cheese made from skim milk. The local cottage cheese is recombined with some cream (it is however advertised as being low fat - *magere*) and has some yoghurt bacteria added. It can be eaten in salads, on crackers or plain. Some soft, fresh cheeses like Mascarpone and Boursin are double cream (60% butterfat) and triple cream (75% butterfat) and some are salted (Demi-Sel) or salted and beaten with cream (Petit Swiss). Some are **natural - *naturel*** while others are seasoned **with herbs - *met kruiden*, with garlic - *met knoflook*** and **with pepper - *met peper***; or topped or mixed **with walnuts - *met walnoten*** or **with ginger - *met gember***. They are good cheese-board snack cheeses. Soft, fresh cheeses include **Mon Chou**, **Philadelphia** and **La Cuisine** (firm or soft, spreading cream cheeses); **Mascarpone** (a sweetened, whipped cream cheese); **Danone Hüttenkäse** (cottage cheese); **Danone**, **Mona**, **Milram**, **AH Biogarde** and **Jockey leger** (*kwark*); and **Boursin**, **St. Moret**, **Rederijkertje**, **Chanteneige**, **Bon Ami**, **Cantadou**, **Paturain**, **Vonk** and **Rambol** (snack cheeses).

Soft to semi-soft, ripened cheese These cheeses are sprayed with spores and develop a soft, white, bloomy rind. Those which are washed with brine develop an orange-hued rind. They are excellent dessert cheeses. Some like the **Limburger** cheese can be particularly evil-smelling but once you get past the strong odor the tastes can be quite pleasant. Limburger cheese has its fans. Soft, ripened cheeses include: **Belle des Champs**, **Boursault**, **Bressot**, **Brie**, **Brillat-Savarin**, **Camembert**, **Chaumes**, **Chèvre**, **Géremont**, **Limburger**, **Münster**, **Pont l'Eveque**, **Reblochon**, **Saint Albray**, **Saint Nectaire**, **Saint Paulin** and **Tommes**.

Semi-soft cheese These cheeses range from mild to strong. Because of their fine texture they can be included in a selection for cheese boards and served with crackers and wine. Since they melt well, they can be used as toppings on melted cheese sandwiches and casseroles. Some semi-soft cheeses sold in Holland are: **Bel Paese**, **Gouda** (young and young but slightly ripe), **Passendale** and **Port Salut**.

Semi-firm to firm cheese Most semi-firm to firm cheeses vary from mild to sharp. Since they melt well, they can be used for sandwiches and grated for use in cooking omelets, casseroles and quiches. However, the softer of these cheeses, if overheated, will separate and form strings. Thus, when adding them to the cheese sauces, heat until just melted. If using cheddar, make sure it is a dry cheddar. In this category are: **Appenzeller**, **Beaufort**, **Cantal**, **Cheddar**, **Edam**, **Emmenthaler**, **Gouda** (ripe and extra ripe), **Gruyère**, **Morbier** and **Raclette**. Kits for making ***Fondue au fromage* - cheese fondue** consisting of Emmenthaler and Gruyére cheese are sold in cheese shops and supermarkets.

Firm to hard cheese Parmesan, Pecorino Romano, Old Amsterdam and **Gouda** are firm cheeses which can be sliced when young but when they age and harden, they are grated. These hard, aged cheeses can stand more heat than softer cheeses, which is the reason why they are so widely recommended for cooking. Use them for flavorings for pastas, soups and casseroles. Parmigiano-Reggiano is Italy's premier Parmesan. Cheese shops and supermarkets sell pre-grated and freshly grated Parmesan and Gouda cheese.

Goat/Sheep cheese - *geitenkaas/schapenkaas* are becoming very popular. Some goat cheeses to look for are **Geiten Kernhem, Bastiaansen** and **Marlijn** geiten.The most famous sheep's cheese is the hard **Pecorino Romano**. Also look for the softer **Pérail de brébis** and **Brebiou**.

String, spun paste or spun curd cheese (pasta filata) Because of their texture, the mild string cheeses such as **Mozzarella** and **provolone** are usually used for baked pasta dishes, pizza toppings and casseroles. They can also be served as part of a first course salad. Some are also smoked.

Blue-veined cheese Because they are inoculated or sprayed with spores of molds (Gorgonzola being an exception), blue-veined cheeses are generally strong. They are most widely used in salads, salad dressings, or mixed with cream and butter for cracker spreads. Some, like the **Fourme d'Ambert, Cambozola, Magor and Châteaux d'Arville**, are milder than others and can be used as is directly on snack toasts. **Bluefort**, **Bleu d'Auvergne**, **Bresse Bleu**, **Danish Blue**, **Roquefort** and **Stilton** are blue-veined cheeses most commonly found in Holland. **Gorgonzola** is available in Italian shops and in some cheese shops upon request.

Whey cheese Instead of being made from milk, whey cheeses are made from the whey which is drained from other cheeses. **Ricotta** is probably the most well-known. It is white and moist and is used in Italian cooking in salads, cakes and tarts and in fillings for pancakes and pastas.

Processed and diet cheese Processed cheese is a natural cheese which is ground and combined with emulsifiers until it is smooth and is then pasteurized. It contains coloring agents and preservatives. Most processed cheese in Holland is made into spreads. **Diet cheese** such as **low-fat - *minder vet*** and **low-salt - *minder zout*** are sold in most cheese shops.

EGG(S) - *EI(EREN)*

Eggs are sold in cartons of 6 or 10 and are classed according to weight and quality (supermarket quality is Class A) but the classification is in transition. From now on they will be sold in four sizes: S (small) - *klein* weighing less than 53 grams, M (medium) - *middel groot* weighing 53 to 63 grams, L (large) - *groot* weighing 63 to 73 grams and XL (extra large) - *extra groot* weighing 73 grams and more. They cannot be sold when they are more than one month old. Check use by date - *tenminste houdbaar tot* for freshness.

You can choose between eggs laid by battery hens (***batterij eieren***); free ranging birds (***scharreleieren***); birds with less freedom than free ranging birds (***volièreerien***); birds raised on corn, wheat, oats and millet (***viergraneneieren***) and free ranging birds fed on corn (***maïsscharreleieren***). There are also **eko-eieren** in health food stores from free-roaming chickens fed on organically-grown grains. You might also see eggs laid by Arcuna or Columbian Blacktail chickens. If any of these many types of eggs appear unclean, don't wash them for you will remove the protective outer coating and they will not keep as long. See also Chapter IV-7 for other types of eggs.

MILK AND MILK PRODUCTS - *MELK EN MELKPRODUCTEN*

Generally, the place to buy your milk and milk products is the supermarket. However, some neighborhoods are still serviced by a milkman. Your neighbors will know if there is such a service in your area. Also consider buying directly from cheese farms and cheese shops which sell fresh **farmer's milk - *boerenmelk*** and **buttermilk - *karnemelk***.

Biogarde or garde This is a purely Dutch product similar to yoghurt but has some different cultures. It is not as sour as yoghurt, thus it is easier to digest. It is sold in plastic tubs near the yoghurt and is available in two types: ***roer*** and ***stand***. *Roer* is processed in large vats where it is stirred until the process is completed and is subsequently packed. *Stand* is packed in the final shelf packing with the cultures and is held at specific temperatures while the *garde* develops. *Roer* has a creamier texture. There is also a drink.

Butter - *boter, roomboter* Butter is sold in supermarkets and in cheese shops. It is packaged in blocks and tubular forms of 250 and 500 grams. Unless specified, butter is always **unsalted - *ongezouten***. Others are **lightly salted - *licht gezouten*** or **salted - *gezouten***. **Herbed butter - *kruiden boter*** is nice on French bread and on grilled meats.

Buttermilk - *karnemelk* Buttermilk is sold in half-liter cartons in supermarkets and liter bottles in some cheese shops and cheese farms. Commercially, it is not always the milk left over after the butter has been churned but is made by adding certain bacteria to low-fat or nonfat milk. It can be drunk like milk. It also adds a tangy flavor to the American favorite, **Southern Fried Chicken** (chicken dipped in buttermilk and then flour).

Coffee milk - *koffiemelk* Coffee milk is a sterilized **unsweetened condensed milk** or **evaporated milk** from which 60 percent of the water has been evaporated. It is the same as the condensed milk sold in North America. *Koffiemelk* is available in three forms: whole - *volle* (about 8% milk fat), half full - *halfvolle* (about 4% milkfat) and *mager* (about 1% milk fat). **Sweetened condensed milk - *gesuikerde gesteriliseerde gecondenseerde melk*** or **gecondenseerde volle melk met suiker** milk is thicker for it is a mixture of milk and sugar (about 45% is sugar). It is similar to, and can be substituted for, what Americans call Eagle Brand sweetened condensed milk. It is, however, becoming hard to find as fewer Dutch people use it. Some Chinese and/or Indonesian food shops carry it. *Koffiemelk* is commonly sold in supermarkets in cans, jars, wax paper cartons and individual serving cups. **Powdered coffee creamers** are also on the same shelves as coffee milk.

Cream - *room* Pasteurized fresh (single) whipping cream - *slagroom* is sold in supermarkets and cheese shops by the half-liter in waxed paper cartons, one-quarter liter and one-half liter in plastic containers, or refundable glass half-liter bottles. In addition to the fresh cream, you can buy **whipped cream – *geklopte slagroom*** in the milk section of Albert Heijn and whipped cream in spray cans at all supermarkets. There are several types of dry, **powdered non-dairy whipping cream** such as ***klop klop*** and ***slag slag*** or **whipped cream in spray cans**. Look for the powdered cream on the shelves near the coffee milk. There is no half and half. A **sterilized whipping cream - *lang houdbaar slagroom*** which doesn't have to be refrigerated, can be whipped. A teaspoon or two of lemon juice turns it into a lovely sour cream. **Clotted cream** is known here as Devonshire or Devon cream. It is created through a process of heating a rich, unpasteurized milk until the cream rises to the top. The cream is then scooped off and is used together with jam as a topping for scones. It is available in shops that cater to English-speaking residents. ***Kookroom*** is a sterilized cream with a setting agent added. It doesn't curdle when cooked and is 20% fat.

Crème *fraîche* is a matured, thick French cream which in France is unpasteurized. It has a slightly sour taste. It is delicious not only on fresh fruits and warm cobblers but in soups and sauces and savory dishes. *Crème fraîche* is sometimes substituted for sour cream in cooking for it boils without curdling but sour cream should not be substituted for *Crème fraîche*. Sour cream is much sharper in flavor and less silky in texture. *Crème fraîche* also contains more fat, as much as 60 percent, as opposed to 18% butterfat in sour cream. Both are sold in cheese shops in similar containers. Some manufacturers identify their product as sour cream on one side and *crème fraîche* on the other but it is really *crème fraîche*.

Ice cream - *ijs, roomijs, or schepijs* For many years, the ice cream selection here was fairly limited. Flavors were varied by toppings of fruity, chocolate and butterscotch syrups. However, the American ice cream giant Häagen Dazs and Ben and Jerry, now sell their products locally which broadens the selection of flavors considerably. In addition to this block ice cream, there are also some very interesting frozen ice cream desserts on the market and many stores are carrying frozen yoghurt. Supermarkets sell ice cream by the liter or half-liter blocks, in tubs and in bars. Soft ice cream and hard ice cream cones are sold at small ice cream parlors or by street vendors.

Margarine - *margarine* (80% fat) is sold in blocks of 250 grams or in plastic tubs. There is a **diet margarine - *dieet margarine*** which is low in sodium and cholesterol, and a **low fat margarine** - ***halvarine*** (40% fat). The diet and low fat margarines are not suitable for baking. However, there is a local margarine which is especially designed for frying and roasting and it is called *margarine voor bakken en braden* - see Chapter IV-1.

Milk - ***melk*** Considering that Holland is a dairy country, most Americans are always amazed that milk is not sold in gallon containers but only in half-liter, liter or 1½ liter cartons or refundable glass bottles. Milk is pasteurized and comes in varying degrees of fat content: **full fat milk** - ***volle melk*, half full** - ***half volle melk*** *(2%)* and **skim** - ***magere melk***. The expiration dates are usually three days after the "sell by" dates that appear on the carton or cover. You can buy milk with added calcium - *calcium* + and **sterilized milk** - ***lang houdbaar*** or ***gesteriliseerde melk***, in plastic jars and waxed paper cartons and **powdered milk** - ***melkpoeder*** in packages.

Sour cream Sour cream is a cream that has been treated to give it a sharp sour tang. It is used for dips, salad dressings and toppings for baked potatoes. Sour cream is added at the last minute to season some soups and stews for it separates when cooked. It comes in small containers and is sold in supermarkets and cheese shops. It is generally called '**sour cream**'; however, it is sometimes sold by its German name ***saure rahm***. Don't confuse it with creme fraiche, see Creme Fraiche above.

Toetje This is a pudding which sometimes looks like an ice cream sundae. The name literally means "a small dessert".

Vla A popular locally-prepared custard or pudding-like dessert, *vla* is sold in containers like the milk or yoghurt and it is found in the same section. It comes in a variety of flavors; chocolate and vanilla are the most common. Kids love it.

Yoghurt The Dutch yoghurt is a bit more sour and liquid than say the Bulgarian yoghurt, which is also popular here. It comes in half-liter and liter milk cartons, and is either **full milk fat** - ***volle*** or **low fat** - ***mager***. It is delicious *au naturel* but when served with berries and the **white moist sugar** - ***witte basterd suiker***, it is a lovely dessert. To thicken yoghurt in the traditional Dutch way, pour it into a cheese cloth bag and hang it over the sink letting the extra liquid drip until it reaches the desired consistency. It is called ***hang op*** meaning "hang up". There are all sorts of yoghurts from other EC countries, especially from France, which deserve trying. Many have fruit added.

Yoghurt drink - ***yoghurt drank*** A variety of fruity yoghurt-based drinks such as strawberry, peach and raspberry are now also very popular. Some come in liter waxed paper containers. Yoghurt drinks are also made from sterilized milk so they do not have to be refrigerated until opened. The Japanese ***Yakult*** which is a yoghurt type drink is now also being marketed here - See Chapter IV-15.

IV.4 DELICATESSEN AND GOURMET ITEMS

For people on the go, there are many possibilities for picking up delicious meals ready-to-eat at delicatessens or gourmet shops, *traiteurs*, butcher shops, cheese shops, fish shops and greengrocers. Most of the delicatessens or gourmet shops and *traiteurs* are located in major cities like The Hague, which is the seat of the Dutch government and home to the foreign embassies. Other good sources are large department stores like Bijenkorf, Vroom and Dreesman and Marks and Spencer which have deli sections, and some Chinese/Indonesian restaurants and shops - *toko* that have take-away food counters. Delifrance, a French *boulangerie* and *café* chain, also has a take-away window for plain croissants or croissants and baguettes stuffed with ham and cheese as well as delectable French sweets. You can go for months without cooking a single meal.

Some delicatessens or gourmet food shops specialize in tinned, frozen and dried gourmet foods from particular countries like the United States, Japan, China/Indonesia and/or the combined countries of Asia, and combined countries of the Middle East while others carry gourmet foods from all over the globe. *Traiteurs* sell prepared gourmet meals, some are ethnic, and may cater or come into your home to cook as well. Look for the gourmet shops under ***delicatessen*** and ***traiteurs*** in the ***Gouden Gids*** **- Yellow Pages** of the telephone book. Most gourmet shops carry cheese while cheese shops may carry gourmet items.

MAIN COURSES - *HOOFDGERECHTEN*

Many butcher shops sell ready-to-eat traditional Dutch winter foods. Included are the famous Dutch stamppot dishes: ***Hutspot*** **- Hodgepodge**, ***Zuurkool met worst*** **- sauerkraut with sausage** and ***Boerenkool met worst*** **- curly kale with sausage**. They also might offer the famous ***Erwtensoep*** **- Dutch pea soup** and ***Bruinebonensoep*** **- brown bean soup** and the basic Indonesian dishes of ***Nasi goreng*** - **fried rice**, ***Bahmi (or Bami) goreng*** **- fried noodles** and Indonesian ***Saté*** **- kabobs** in addition to various ***schotels*** **- casseroles**, **pasta**, **lasagna** and **pizza**. You only need to reheat them.

Fish shops often sell ready-to-eat **Spanish paella**, a dish of rice with a selection of any of the following: shrimp, lobster, clams, chicken, pork, or ham flavored with garlic, onions, peas, tomatoes. They also sell deep-fried fish, the famous rice dish from Louisiana - **Jambalaya** and the famous fish soup from Provence, France - **Bouillabaisse**.

The gourmet table top cooker has become very popular in recent years. Many butchers prepare special platters of meats for these cookers. In the warmer months they offer marinated meats ready for the summer barbecues.

NUTS - *NOTEN*

Cheese shops, delicatessens and special counters in supermarkets usually stock the largest and freshest assortment of nuts which may include **almonds** **- *amandelen***, **Brazil nuts** **- *paranoten***, **cashew nuts** **- *cashew***

noten*, chestnuts - *kastanjes*, coconuts - *kokosnoten*, hazel nuts - *hazelnoten*, macadamia nuts - *macadamia noten*, mixed nuts - *gemengde noten*, pecans - *pecan noten*, pine nuts - *pijnboomnoten*, pistachios - *pistachenoten and **walnuts - *walnoten***. Some shops roast the nuts on the premises. Nuts are sold by weight. Supermarkets also carry nuts in cans and plastic bags.

SALADS - *SALADES*

Many fish shops have a good selection of seafood-based salads usually made from **salmon - *zalm*** and **shrimp - *garnalen***. Butcher shops sell salads to accompany their meats and cold cuts; i.e., **celeriac root - *knolselderij*, cucumber - *komkommer*, ham and leek - *ham en prei*, egg - *eier*, potato - *aardappel*** and **hussar's salad (potato and meat) - *huzaren salade***. Cheese and gourmet shops also sell some of the above. Salads can be eaten as accompaniments to meals; and others, such as the *knolselderij salade*, make delicious luncheon snacks when stuffed in ham rolls. Greengrocers sell **mixed vegetable or fruit salads - *rauwkost*** without the dressing. Most salads, except those specified as *rauwkost*, are heavily laced with mayonnaise.

SAUCES - *SAUZEN*

Almost all of the above-mentioned shops sell an assortment of savory sauces namely **curry - *kerrie*, dill - *dille*, fish or tartar - *vis or Remoulade*, garlic - *knoflook or aioli*, whiskey - *whiskey cocktail*** which can be used with meat fondues, barbecued meats, fish, seafood cocktails and salads.

SNACKS - *HAPJES*

Butcher shops and butcher counters in supermarkets sell **sausage rolls - *saucijzen broodjes*** (skinless sausages baked in puff pastry), **Dutch meatballs - *bitterballen*** and Dutch deep-fried **minced meat snacks - *frikadel* and *croquette***. Some butchers make elaborate savory quiches filled with minced meats and vegetables as well as the famous ***quiche Lorraine***. Also popular these days at butcher shops is the savory **Flemish liver paste - *Vlaamse likkepot***. Supermarkets and shops which specialize in dried snacks such as dried fruits, nuts and potato chips also have a large assortment of bridge snacks, which include tiny Japanese crackers.

SOUPS - *SOEPEN*

The Dutch are very fond of soups. Thus, in addition to the main course soups mentioned above, supermarkets and specialty shops sell canned gourmet soups and soup stocks. Fish shops also sell some fish-based soups and stocks while the greengrocers offer sliced or chopped fresh soup vegetables.

IV.5 BREADS AND PASTRIES

The shops which probably delight foreign residents most are the **bakeries,** or ***bakkerijen***, which turn out the most mouth-watering fresh breads and pastries and creamy bonbons. At Christmas time they have a full range of seasonal breads and cookies; then at Easter they outdo themselves with a stunning array of brilliant, foil-wrapped chocolate bunnies, bonbons, marzipan animals and fruits and cakes decorated for the season. Enjoy them while you are here. To find these bakeries, look for ***Brood en banket*** in the **Yellow Pages** or ***Gouden Gids*** of the telephone book for the bakery nearest you or for the ***Warme Bakker***, ***Brood en Banket***, or ***Banketbakkerij*** signs in your shopping area.

In addition to these wonderful bakeries, you might want to try the Middle Eastern breads such as *lavash* or *khubz Arabi* (*pita*) sold in Turkish shops and bakeries; *fococcia*, *ciabatta* and *panzarotti* sold in shops which cater to Italians; the French *croissants*, *baguettes*, *petit pains*, *brioches* and *pistolets* sold in many bakeries and delicatessens; and the English breads like *scones*, *crumpets* and *muffins* which are sold in shops which cater to those from English-speaking countries. The shops from the U.K. and some supermarkets might also carry the Indian breads, *naan* and *poppadam*.

The ***warme bakker*** or ***brood en banket*** specializes in baked breads, rolls and cookies, but also carries some types of pastries and bonbons; while the ***banketbakkerij*** specializes in pastries such as cakes, tarts, Danish rolls and cream puffs and confections such as chocolate bonbons and marzipan. Some have a limited variety of breads. Most supermarkets also have in-house bakeries and they also stock some factory-made breads which are sometimes referred to as breads from the *kouwe bakker - cold baker.*

The term *warme bakker* means that the breads are baked fresh daily. Thus, if you arrive when the shops just open, there is a good chance that the breads and pastries will be direct from the baker's ovens. Arrive there too late and you may find that your favorite bread is sold out. There are no preservatives in these Dutch treats so they must be eaten quickly. Freeze what you can't eat in the course of the day. However, breads from the *kouwe bakker* or factory breads, have a longer shelf life. Bonbons should also be eaten rather quickly or stored in the refrigerator since many are made from fresh cream. Eating all the goodies from these shops on the day of purchase is generally not a problem.

Bread can be purchased by whole - *heel* or half - *half* loaf, sliced - *gesneden* or unsliced. Some bakeries charge a token amount for the slicing; with others, it is gratis. The baker's assistant will generally ask if you want your bread sliced. The rich cakes and tarts or pies are sold whole or by the piece and cookies by the weight.

Since the Dutch traditionally only eat one hot meal a day, breads and cold cuts are central to the two cold meals, which explains the large variety of baked breads and rolls from which to choose.

BREAD - *BROOD*

There are at least 200 types of bread baked in Holland, albeit not by the same baker. There are two basic types, those which are made with water (like French bread which needs to be eaten as soon as possible) and milk bread which lasts longer and has a crunchy taste.

Whole wheat and whole grain breads such as **brown - *bruin*, whole wheat - *volkoren*** and **four- or five-grain - *vier of vijf granen*** are the most popular breads in Holland. They are often sold out in the course of the morning or early afternoon. They are baked in regular bread loaf tins except for the brown **sandwich bread - *casino brood***, which is square, and when sliced is perfect for the toaster.

White bread - *witte brood* comes in all shapes and forms. In addition to the ordinary **white bread - *wittebrood*** which is in the shape of a rectangular loaf, there is the **tiger bread - *tijgerbrood*** with a spotted crust; **cut bread - *knipbrood*** which has been cut across the top before baking; **white round loaf - *lampionnebrood***; **milk bread - *melkbrood*** which is made with powdered milk; and, white **sandwich bread - *casino brood***. **French bread - *Frans stokbrood*** made in Holland is absolutely scrumptious. There is a difference between this and its relative, the Dutch-style **French bread - *Hollands stokbrood***. Don't confuse them for French bread has a crunchier crust.

Raisin bread and currant bread - *rozijnenbrood en krentenbrood* are traditional Dutch breads which are eaten plain or toasted and generously spread with butter.

Rye bread - *roggebrood* is not generally baked fresh by local bakers. On sale here is the dark, heavy, coarse and slightly sour Scandinavian-style ***roggebrood*** and the German-style ***pumpernickel***. However, the lighter German-style rye breads are baked in some Dutch bakeries. Some delicatessens have the mini-loaves of dark rye for use as appetizers and snacks.

Rolls - *broodjes* There are several types of basic breakfast and sandwich rolls and these are slowly being supplemented by other types like the French ***brioches*** or dinner rolls. The varieties surely will increase. **Currant buns - *krentebollen*** are hamburger-sized rolls that are studded with currants. **Hard rolls - *harde broodjes*** have crisp crusts and are best when used for sandwiches or as accompaniments to a meal. **Soft rolls - *broodjes*** are 'little breads' that can be used for regular sandwiches. They are either round - *bolletjes* or oval - *puntjes* and they are either made of white or whole wheat flour. The round, white, soft rolls resemble hamburger buns. The term *broodje(s)* can also mean the sandwiches which are made with the *broodje(s)* or buns.

Rusk or **Dutch rusk** - ***beschuit*** is a dry slice of bread which is made from a special kind of white or whole-wheat dough. The bread is baked in a round loaf mold then is sliced and baked again until it turns crispy and golden brown. It is a breakfast bread which, in Holland, is eaten topped with butter and cheese or cold cuts. The French rusk - ***biscotte***, originally a diet food, is also eaten here for breakfast and some other meals. Dutch rusks are lighter. Rusks can be soaked in milk and used in stuffing, or powdered to make bread crumbs.

CAKES, COOKIES AND PASTRIES - *GEBAK*

The coffee or tea break is an important part of the Dutch day. In fact, the country stops working around 10:30 in the morning and again at 3:30 in the afternoon for a coffee or tea break. Thus, there is an ample selection of accompanying cakes, pastries and cookies, especially cookies.

Cake - ***cake*** Cakes which are baked in Holland are rich (often loaded with whipped cream), heavy and elegant but the variety of flavors is limited. Those covered with *marzipan* frosting are exquisite. They can be purchased whole, by squares or by slices. ***Boter cake*** is a type of butter cake which resembles **pound cake**. It can be used as a coffee cake or in some desserts like **Baked Alaska**. However, there is another type of **butter cake** - ***boterkoek*** which is an unleavened shortbread. It is used as a coffee cake.

Cookies - ***koekjes***, freshly baked, are types of sweet **sugar cookies** - ***zoete koekjes*** or **butter cookies** - ***roomboter koekjes***. **Salt cookies** - ***zoutjes*** are also made by the bakers and are meant to be eaten like any salty snacks. A greater variety of cookies from the *kouwe bakker*, including the famous American chocolate chip cookie, can be bought in the supermarkets.

Cream puffs and Danish pastries - ***soezen en koffie broodjes*** Although limited in terms of variety, these pastries are delicious. They are filled with whipped cream, custard or custard and fruit. Smaller cream puffs are known by the diminutive name - *soesjes*.

Pies or tarts The local **tarts** are similar to pies so we can say that they are related. There are, however, differences in the type of crusts and the shape of pans in which they are baked. The Dutch make tarts with a sweet tart pastry - *pâté sucrée* or sweet bread dough placed in shallow tins. Some are filled with a somewhat thin layer of fresh fruits or fresh fruits and custard and then topped with a jelly glaze. However, some fruit tarts are fully baked and have lattice pastry toppings. Ready-to-eat tart bottoms are also available at the supermarkets along with **tart** or **pie filling** - ***vlaaivulling***. **Vlaai** is a popular tart originating in the southern province of Limburg. It is made with fruit or rice-custard fillings. Shops selling only these delectable pastries are now opening up north of the rivers that divide the country. **Savory pies**, like **quiche Lorraine** and meat pies, are also offered from time to time in bakeries.

Puff pastry shells - ***pasteitjes*** These small puff pastry shells are made for the French dish, ***vol au vent***. They are filled at home with creamed chicken or veal stews (*ragout*). You can by them individually from the baker or in packages from the supermarket.

DUTCH SPECIALTIES:

Holiday breads like ***Kerststol*** **- Christmas bread**, ***Kerst tulband*** **- Christmas turban** and ***Kerstkransje*** **- Christmas wreath** appear just before St. Nicolaas arrives on 5 December and disappear after the New Year. Some reappear at Easter. ***Oliebollen***, literally meaning oil balls, are New Year's Eve treats and bakers only carry them at that time of the year. However, they are also sold at yearly regional markets and children's fairs. Some sweets like ***appelbol*** **- apple ball**, ***appelflap*** **- apple turnover** and ***appelbeignet*** **- apple fritter** are fall and winter pastries while ***appelgebak*** **- apple cake**, ***boterkoek*** **- butter cake or short bread** and ***gevulde boterkoek*** **- *filled shortbread***, ***speculaas*** **- spice cookie** and ***gevulde speculaas*** **- filled spice cookie** and ***ontbijtkoek*** **- spiced breakfast cake** are available all year. These and other Dutch sweets typical to Holland are described in detail Chapter IV-14.

IV.6 FISH AND SHELLFISH

While not the great seafaring nation it once was, Holland still retains its reputation for being purveyors of fine seafood. Many scenic fishing villages like Urk and Scheveningen dot the coastal landscape and fishermen and their families with historic connections to the seas continue in the seafood business. In addition to the fish caught by local fisherman, fish from other European Union member states and different countries of the world pass through the Dutch market. The quality and quantity available here is excellent. Your best selection of fresh fish and shellfish is from the well-stocked fish and seafood shops which may also offer creative varieties of seafood salads and cocktail snacks and sauces (like **Tartar sauce**) to accompany fish dishes. Naturally, shops in larger cities have the best selection. For shops specializing in seafood products, look for ***Vishandel*** in the ***Gouden Gids***, or **Yellow Pages**, of the telephone book. Weekly markets also have vendors where you can purchase fish.

On Fridays, mobile fish vendors park their vans around shopping centers or conspicuous intersections all over the country. They sell cooked and fresh fish. While the selection may be limited, for very little money you can buy ***gebakken kibbeling*** **- deep-fried cod pieces** and ***gebakken lekkerbekjes*** **- deep-fried haddock**. A literal translation of *lekkerbekjes* is *lekker* = delicious, and *bekjes* = mouths. Just heat them up in a shallow, greased frying pan when you get home. Other Dutch specialties sold here are the raw, salted ***nieuwe haring*** **- new herring** which are sold with an optional topping of chopped raw onions, ***gerookte paling*** **- smoked eel,** ***mosselen*** **- mussels,** ***gerookte makreel*** **- smoked mackerel** and ***gebakken kuit*** **- deep-fried roe**.

When buying whole fish, you might be asked if you want the fish head and skin removed - *kop en vel eraf*. Give a prompt yes - *ja* or no - *nay* lest you end up having to clean it yourself. The fish can also be scaled - *geschrapt* (to scale - *schrappen*). Upon request, the fish specialist will give you a fish head - *kop* and bones - *graten* for making stock or you can buy the stock in tins or in powdered bouillon cubes.

The fish is normally fresh but if you smell it, it isn't. Beware of cheap fish or cod with a flesh that has a slightly yellow tinge. They don't come out of the sea that way. Frozen fish with white spots suggests freezer burns meaning it has been in the freezer too long.

The availability of fish and shellfish varieties depends largely on the seasonal catches. Mussels and oysters, for instance, are traditionally eaten only during the months which have an "R" in them although you may find them in some of the other cooler months. You can rely on finding haddock, cod, flounder, sole, herring, eel, prawns and shrimp throughout the year. The fish names given are the most commonly used names but they are sometimes confusing. For instance, certain types of rockfish are called red snappers when they are not even true snappers.

The fish on the following pages are grouped into three categories: Lean Sea Fish, Rich-fleshed Fish and Fresh-water Fish. Shellfish (crustaceans, mollusks and cephalopods) are lumped together.

Vis, Schaal- en Schelpdieren
In Nederland verkrijgbaar
Schelvis
Leng
Heek
Kabeljauw
Wijting
Zwarte koolvis
Schar
Tong
Griet
Heilbot
Tarbot
Schol
Tongschar
Paling
Geep
Haring
Sprot
Makreel
Rode poon
Mul
Sardien
Spiering
Goudbrasem (dorade)
Rog
Tilapia
Diklipharder
Zalm
Zeewolf
Zeeduivel
Roodbaars
Regenboogforel
Snoekbaars
Bonito
Mossel
Kreeft
Krab
Kokkel
Oester
Noorse kreeft
Noordzeegarnaal
Pijlinktvis
Inktvis (zeekat)
Illustraties: Berna van Rest

SCHELVIS
Gadus aeglefinus
(Melanogrammus aeglefinus)

Eng.: *Haddock;* **F.**: *Eglefin;* **D.**: *Schellfisch;* **Sp.**: *Eglefino;* **I.**: *Asinello.*

LENG
Molva molva

Eng.: *Ling;* **F.**: *Linque;* **D.**: *Leng;* **Sp.**: *Maruca;* **I.**: *Molva.*

HEEK
Merluccius merluccius

Eng.: *Hake;* **F.**: *Merlu;* **D.**: *Seehecht;* **Sp.**: *Merluza;* **I.**: *Nasello.*

KABELJAUW
Gadus morhua

Eng.: *Cod;* **F.**: *Morue,Cabillaud;* **D.**:*Kabeljau, Dorsch;* **Sp.**: *Bacalao;* **I.**: *Merluzzo, Baccalà.*

WIJTING
Merlangius merlangus

Eng.: *Whiting;* **F.**: *Merlan;* **D.**: *Wittling;* **Sp.**: *Merlan;* **I.**: *Merlano.*

ZWARTE KOOLVIS
Pollachius virens

Eng.: *Saithe, Pollock;* **F.**: *Lieu Noir;* **D.**: *Seelachs, Kohler;* **Sp.**: *Carbonero, Colin;* **I.**: *Merluzzo nero.*

SCHAR
Limanda limanda

Eng.: *Dab;* **F.**: *Limande;* **D.**: *Kliesche;* **Sp.**: *Limanda nordica;* **I.**: *Limanda.*

TONG
Solea solea

Eng.: *Common sole;* **F.**: *Sole commune;* **D.**: *Seezunge;* **Sp.**: *Lenguado común;* **I.**: *Sogliola.*

GRIET
Scophthalmus rhombus

Eng.: *Brill;* **F.**: *Barbue;* **D.**: *Glattbutt;* **Sp.**: *Rémol;* **I.**: *Rombo lèscia.*

HEILBOT
Hippoglossus hippoglossus

Eng.: *Halibut;* **F.**: *Flétan;* **D.**: *Heilbot;* **Sp.**: *Fletan, Halibut;* **I.**: *Halibut.*

TARBOT
Scophthalmus maximus

Eng.: *Turbot;* **F.**: *Turbot;* **D.**: *Steinbutt;* **Sp.**: *Rodaballo;* **I.**: *Rombo chiodato.*

SCHOL
Pleuronectes platessa

Eng.: *Plaice;* **F.**: *Plie, Carrelet;* **D.**: *Scholle;* **Sp.**: *Solla;* **I.**: *Passera.*

TONGSCHAR
Microstomus kitt

Eng.: *Lemon sole;* **F.**: *Limande-sole;* **D.**: *Echte Rotzunge, Limande;* **Sp.**: *Mendo limon;* **I.**: *Sogliola limanda.*

PALING
Anguilla anguilla

Eng.: *Eel;* **F.**: *Anguille;* **D.**: *Aal;* **Sp.**: *Anguila;* **I.**: *Anguilla.*

GEEP
Belone belone

Eng.: *Garfish;* **F.**: *Orphie;* **D.**: *Hornhecht;* **Sp.**: *Aguja;* **I.**: *Aguglia.*

RODE POON
Trigla lucerna

Eng.: *Tub gurnard;* **F.**: *Grondin perlon;* **D.**: *Roter Knurrhahn;* **Sp.**: *Lucerna;* **I.**: *Capone gallinella.*

MUL
Mullus surmuletus

Eng.: *Striped red mullet;* **F.**: *Rouget de Roche;* **D.**: *Streifenbarbe;* **Sp.**: *Salmoneta de roca;* **I.**: *Triglia di scoglio.*

TILAPIA
Tilapia spp.

GOUDBRASEM (DORADE)
Sparus aurata

Eng.: *Gilthead seabream;* **F.**: *Dorade;* **D.**: *Goldbrassen;* **Sp.**: *Dorade;* **I.**: *Orata.*

ROG
Raja montagui

Eng.: *Spotted ray;* **F.**: *Raie douce;* **D.**: *Fleckroche;* **Sp.**: *Raya pintada;* **I.**: *Razza maculata.*

DIKLIPHARDER
Chelon labrosus

Eng.: *Thicklip grey mullet;* **F.**: *Mulet lippu;* **D.**: *Dicklippige Meeräsche;* **Sp.**: *Lisa;* **I.**: *Cafalo bosega.*

ZEEWOLF
Anarhichas lupus

Eng.: *Wolffish;* **F.**: *Loupe de Mer;* **D.**: *Seewolf, Katfisch;* **Sp.**: *Perro del Norte, Lobo;* **I.**: *Bavosa lupa.*

ZEEDUIVEL
Lophius piscatorius

Eng.: *Anglerfish;* **F.**: *Baudroie, Lotte;* **D.**: *Seeteufel;* **Sp.**: *Rape;* **I.**: *Budego.*

ROODBAARS
Sebastes marinus

Eng.: *Redfish;* **F.**: *Grand sébaste;* **D.**: *Rotbarsch;* **Sp.**: *Gallineta nórdica;* **I.**: *Scorfano di norvegia.*

BONITO
Sarda sarda

Eng.: *Atlantic bonito;* **F.**: *Bonite à dos rayé;* **D.**: *Bonito;* **Sp.**: *Bonito atlantico;* **I.**: *Palamita.*

SNOEKBAARS
Stizostedion lucioperca

Eng.: *Pike-perch, Zander;* **F.**: *Sandre;* **D.**: *Zander;* **Sp.**: *Lucioperca;* **I.**: *Sandra.*

HARING
Clupea harengus

Eng.: *Herring;* **F.**: *Hareng;* **D.**: *Hering;* **Sp.**: *Arengue;* **I.**: *Aringa.*

SPROT
Sprattus sprattus

Eng.: *Sprat;* **F.**: *Sprat;* **D.**: *Sprott;* **Sp.**: *Espadin;* **I.**: *Papalina.*

MAKREEL
Scomber scombrus

Eng.: *Mackerel;* **F.**: *Maquereau commun;* **D.**: *Makrele;* **Sp.**: *Caballe del Atlántico;* **I.**: *Maccarello.*

SARDIEN
Sardina pilchardus

Eng.: *Pilchard, Sardine;* **F.**: *Sardine;* **D.**: *Sardine;* **Sp.**: *Sardinas;* **I.**: *Sardina.*

SPIERING
Osmerus eperlanus

Eng.: *Smelt;* **F.**: *Eperlan;* **D.**: *Stint;* **Sp.**: *Eperlan;* **I.**: *Sperlano, eperlano.*

ZALM
Salmo salar

Eng.: *Salmon;* **F.**: *Saumon;* **D.**: *Lachs;* **Sp.**: *Salmón;* **I.**: *Salmo.*

REGENBOOGFOREL
Oncorhynchus mykiss
(Salmo gairdneri)

Eng.: *Rainbow trout;* **F.**: *Truite arc-en-ciel;* **D.**: *Regenbogenforelle;* **Sp.**: *Trucha arcoiris;* **I.**: *Trotta iridea.*

KRAB
Cancer pagurus

Eng.: *Edible crab;* **F.**: *Tourteau;* **D.**: *Taschenkrebs;* **Sp.**: *Buey, Masera;* **I.**: *Granciporro.*

MOSSEL
Mytilus edulis

Eng.: *Blue mussel;* **F.**: *Moule commune;* **D.**: *Miesmuschel;* **Sp.**: *Mejillon;* **I.**: *Mitilo, Cozza.*

KOKKEL
Cerastoderma edule

Eng.: *Common edible cockle;* **F.**: *Coque commune;* **D.**: *Herzmuschel;* **Sp.**: *Berberecho;* **I.**: *Cuore edule.*

OESTER
Ostrea edulis

Eng.: *European flat oyster;* **F.**: *Huître plate européenne;* **D.**: *Auster;* **Sp.**: *Ostra;* **I.**: *Ostrica.*

KREEFT
Homarus gammarus

Eng.: *European lobster;* **F.**: *Homard européen;* **D.**: *Europäischer Hummer;* **Sp.**: *Bogavante;* **I.**: *Astice.*

NOORSE KREEFT
Nephrops novegicus

Eng.: *Norway lobster,* **F.**: *Langoustine;* **D.**: *Kaisergranat;* **Sp.**: *Cigala;* **I.**: *Scampi.*

NOORDZEEGARNAAL
Crangon crangon

Eng.: *Common shrimp;* **F.**: *Crevette grise;* **D.**: *Nordseegarnele;* **Sp.**: *Quisquilla;* **I.**: *Gambero dello sabbia.*

PIJLINKTVIS
Loligo vulgaris

Eng.: *European squid, Calamary;* **F.**: *Encornet, Calmar;* **D.**: *Gewohner Kalmar;* **Sp.**: *Calamar;* **I.**: *Calamaro.*

INKTVIS (ZEEKAT)
Sepia officinalis

Eng.: *Cuttlefish;* **F.**: *Seiche commune;* **D.**: *Sepia;* **Sp.**: *Jibia, Choco;* **I.**: *Seppia.*

Stichting Nederlands Visbureau. Postbus 72, 2280 AB Rijswijk. Telefoon 070 - 336 96 00

The fish in each group may be of different families; but their most important characteristics, such as taste and flesh tone, are similar enough to use them interchangeably in most recipes.

Some popular French fish cooking terms you'll encounter in the following descriptions are: ***à la meunière*** meaning "like the fisherman's wife" (dip in milk then in seasoned flour and pan-fry in butter, garnish with lemon slices and chopped fresh parsley); ***en papillote*** (moisten with white wine or lemon juice and bake in parchment paper until the paper browns and puffs and the fish is done) and ***au gratin*** (top with bread crumbs and dollops of butter or top with cheese then brown in a hot oven or under the oven broiler).

LEAN SEA FISH

The common characteristics of lean sea fish are that they have white, lean, firm and mild-flavored flesh. The percentage of fat is one to about five percent and most of the fat is in the liver, which is discarded. This means that the flesh tends to be dry and thus should be poached, steamed or pan-fried; but it can be baked, grilled or broiled as long as it is basted frequently. However, because of their texture, some are more suitable to specific dishes than others.

Angler, lotte, monkfish or goosefish - *zeeduivel* Angler is an extremely ugly fish but has a fine, sweet flavor which has been compared to lobster. Only its tail is good for eating. It is usually sold filleted and can be pan-fried, sautéed, or roasted and, because of its firm texture, it is commonly used in soups and the French fish stew, **Bouillabaisse**.

Brill - *griet* A flatfish found in European waters, brill is similar to, but is cheaper than, turbot. It can be prepared in many ways: grilled, broiled, fried, baked or poached, and served with cold sauces. It is often braised with white wine, champagne or cider and is garnished with shrimps, prawns and mussels. Brill is relatively small, 12 to 30 inches (30 to 75 centimeters), and weighs around 2 to 4 pounds (±1 to 2 kilos) so can be cooked whole.

Cod - *kabeljauw* Cod is called "the beef of the sea". It can grow to an enormous size, sometimes up to six feet long. It is abundant in the North Atlantic. Its flaky, delicate white flesh can be broiled, grilled, pan-fried, baked *au gratin*, or poached or braised in the oven in a court bouillon. It is especially good for **Fish and Chips**, **Cod Fish Cakes** and **Cod Chowder**. Large cod are generally cut into fillets - *gefileerd*. Hake, haddock, pollack and whiting are close relatives and can be easily substituted. However, the cooking time can vary. **Salted, dried cod** (and **pollack** and **hake**) are called ***stokvis***.

Dab - *schar or limande* Dabs are small flatfish of several varieties and a member of the flounder family. The true or European dab has a delicate, moist flesh. They can be purchased whole or filleted and can be prepared in the same manner as brill, plaice or flounder.

Flounder - *bot* A large flatfish, flounder is often mistakenly called "sole" like in "filet of sole" in the United States. Flounder has a fine texture and mild flavor and can be cooked in the same manner as the other flatfish: brill, sand dab, halibut, etc. Flounder is sold whole or in fillets.

Haddock - *schelvis* is a small, mild fish 2 to 6 pounds (±1 to 3 kilos) which is related to the cod family. It is the fish of choice in the local deep-fried delicacy, **lekkerbekje**. It can also be sautéed, grilled or pan-fried, but is particularly good when stuffed and poached or baked. It is available whole or in fillets.

Hake - *heek* A smaller relative of the cod, hake can weigh anywhere from 1 to 9 pounds (½ to 4 kilos). Its white, delicate flesh has little flavor but it is very popular, probably because it has few bones. Hake benefits from being baked either *au gratin* with a topping of Mornay sauce or baked and basted with butter and lemon and served cold with accompanying sauces such as mayonnaise and dill. It shouldn't be cooked too long. Purchase it whole or in fillets or steaks.

Halibut - *heilbot* Halibut is a member of the flatfish family which includes brill, flounder, sand dab, sole, plaice and turbot. Halibut can grow up to 440 pounds (200 kilos) although most halibut caught weigh around 55 to 110 pounds (25 to 50 kilos). Its pure-white, mild-flavored, firm flesh is cut into fillets or steaks and like cod, it is especially suited for **Fish and Chips**. However, it can also be grilled, broiled, baked or poached.

Ling - *leng* A member of the cod family, *leng* can grow to an enormous size. That which is found in the North Sea can reach up to 5 feet (1½ meters) in length. It is usually sold in fillets and can be prepared in the same manner as cod. The lingcod fished on the American West Coast is really a greenling rather than a cod but it also can be used in the same manner as cod. Because of its firm, sweet flesh, it makes a very nice **Lingcod Chowder**.

Mullet - mul There are several species of mullet which are found in coastal waters. The **grey mullets** are the largest striped mullets and they grow to about 2 feet (60 cm) long. The **thick-lipped mullet - *diklipharder*** is a type of grey mullet with very thick lips. The French call it *mulet lippu*. It has a lean, white slightly-soft flesh. It can be cooked in bouillon, baked or grilled. It must first be scaled. The **red mullets** are called *rouget-barbet* in France and are related to the *goatfish* in the United States for they have two barbels under their chins. The best is bright pink with gold streaks and the flesh is white and tasty. They are very popular in the Mediterranean where they are often not gutted but are grilled whole with the skin left on. The flesh deteriorates very quickly so must be consumed in a very short period (see also **Sea robin**).

Plaice - *schol* Fairly popular in Holland, plaice is a flatfish which is abundant in the North Sea and the Atlantic. Although it can grow to 12 pounds (5½ kilos), it is usually around 2 to 3 pounds (1 to 1½ kilos). It has a delicate flavor and texture and can be prepared in the same manner as sole or brill. It is particularly good in the recipe **Plaice à la florentine** (plaice poached on a bed of spinach topped with Mornay sauce).

Pollack - *pollak* Either of two large North Atlantic fish, pollack is yellow or black. Both have lean, white, firm flesh but the yellow pollack has a finer texture. **Black pollack - *zwarte koolvis*** (or the French *lieu noir*) is more commonly available here. Pollack can be substituted for cod in all recipes. It can be sold whole, filleted or cut into steaks but is more commonly available dried as *stokvis* or smoked and packed in oil in tins. It is a cheap substitute for smoked salmon. Pollack is often used to make imitation crab.

Ray or skate - *rog* This kite-shaped fish has a firm, pinkish-white, sweet flesh which comes from the winglike fins. It may be called a ray - *rog* or ray wing - *rogvleugel*. It should be washed several times or soaked in milk to get rid of its ammonia-like smell. It can be poached, baked, sautéed or steamed.

Redfish - *roodbaars* Also known as Norwegian haddock, redfish is related to the scorpion fish or goatfish. Its firm, white flesh tastes rather like crab. It can be baked, broiled or fried. See also **Sea robin** below.

Red snapper - *rode zeebaars* Red snapper has a juicy, firm flesh and an exceptional flavor. It ranges from 2 to 10 pounds (1 to 4 ½ kilos) It is the fish of choice for **Chinese Steamed Fish** or for deep-fried **Sweet and Sour Fish**. It can also be baked, broiled or grilled, or stewed in chowders. Smaller snapper are sold whole but the larger snapper may be sold in steaks and fillets.

Sea bass - *zeebaars* is a term loosely applied to many unrelated saltwater and freshwater fish; many are not necessarily members of the bass family. Their flesh is lean to moderately fat. They can be purchased whole or in fillets or steaks. They are suitable for almost any method of cooking.

Sea bream/gilthead - *goudbrasem (dorade)* The name bream is applied to many fresh or salt-water fish. In this group would be the American **porgy**, the French ***daurade*** and the Japanese **sea bream**. The flesh is firm and has a delicate, mild flavor. It is suitable for any type of cooking but it is particularly good for grilling. It is especially popular in the Mediterranean region.

Sea robin/gurnard - *rode poon*, red mullet/goatfish - *mul/rode mullet or rouget* and redfish/red drum - *roodbaars* are members of the same family and they are often confused with each other. Their flesh is lean, white and firm but their taste and texture varies. They can, however, be cooked in a similar manner; i.e., they can be pan-fried, poached, grilled, baked *en papillote* or used in soups and fish stews like **Bouillabaisse**. Their meat is rather perishable so must be eaten rather quickly. (See also **Mullet**).

Sole - *tong or zeetong* A member of the flatfish family and related to sand dab, flounder, brill, plaice, turbot and halibut, sole has a lean, delicately-flavored, fine-textured flesh. While many flat fish like the **lemon sole - *tongschar*** (which is actually a member of the flounder family) are called "sole", true sole is found only in European waters. There are several types of true sole but the most well known is **Dover sole**, which averages about 12 inches (30 cm) in length. It is the most prized fish of this family and its exquisite taste is best when simply fried *à la meunière*. Sole can also be sautéed, poached, steamed, baked or poached. It is usually sold gutted and skinned and filleted.

Turbot - *tarbot* A highly-prized fish in Europe, turbot is rated right up there with Dover sole, which is reflected in its price. It is found in the Atlantic and Mediterranean. It has a mild, firm, flaky, white flesh and is sold whole or in chunks. It can be poached in milk to retain its whiteness, braised, grilled or broiled. Don't cook it too long or the turbot loses its flavor.

Whiting - *wijting* Whiting grows from 10 to 16 inches (25 to 35 cm) in length and is related to the cod. It is essential to certain regional fish soups in France but it can be grilled, steamed, dipped in breadcrumbs and pan-fried, poached in wine, or stuffed with herbs and onions and baked. It is sold either whole or in fillets.

Wolf fish - *zeewolf* Wolf fish is a fairly large salt water fish with large teeth. It has a very firm, white, coarse flesh and a distinct flavor. The French call it **loup de mer** or wolf of the sea. It can be poached, baked, stewed or grilled. However, the wolf fish should not be confused with the handsome *loup* which is a type of bass or sea perch caught principally in the Mediterranean. This *loup* has a fine, firm flesh and delicate flavor. It is relatively rare and expensive.

RICH-FLESHED FISH

Rich-fleshed fish range anywhere from 5% to 35% fat. The meat tends to be darker, richer and stronger in flavor than the lean sea fish. The fat is distributed throughout the flesh; and, with a few noted exceptions, it is suitable for dry-heat cooking such as grilling, broiling and baking. Some of these fish live in salt water, and then swim to fresh water rivers and streams to spawn.

Anchovy - *ansjovis* Anchovy is a small silvery fish which comes from the Mediterranean, the Black Sea and Atlantic and Pacific coastlines. They are usually filleted, salt cured and canned in oil and are commonly used as a garnish for pizzas and salads or in traditional seasonings such as anchovy butter and anchovy sauce.

Eel - *paling/zeepaling* is considered a delicacy in Holland. Its flesh is rich, sometimes pungent, sweet and firm. It is a rather long snakelike fish, of which there are two varieties, freshwater eel - *paling* and saltwater eel -

zeepaling. In some parts of the country eel is called *aal*. Because it is oily, the flesh deteriorates rather quickly. Fresh eel is usually sold alive and then killed and skinned while you wait. It is sometimes cooked and preserved in its own gelatine or smoked, and served as hors d'oeuvre. Fresh eel is often used in Mediterranean fish soups and stews. The Dutch are very fond of ***Gestoofde paling*** (eel stewed in wine) and ***Gebakken paling*** (breaded fried eel).

Garfish - *geep* A very long fish with a pointed snout, garfish is much appreciated by the Dutch, Danes and the Belgians. The bones are green before cooking and mauve when cooked and the fish has a very strong smell, a combination of which can be off-putting. It can be prepared in the same way as eel, or fried.

Herring - *haring* is the name given to a huge family of saltwater fish of which there are many varieties. So important were Holland's great herring fleets that the first catch of the season is still offered to the sovereign. It is called ***nieuwe haring,*** *nieuwe* meaning "of the new season". When fresh, it can be baked, sauteed or grilled. In Holland, it is usually sold fresh, but it is also salted, pickled or smoked. ***Maatjes haring*** are herring caught after they have been feeding then salted and cleaned. They are fat and plump and are considered to be the tastiest. There are many types of cured herring: **rolmops - *gemarineerde haring*** are herring fillets marinated in spiced vinegar and wrapped around onions or gherkins; **kippered herring** are flattened, salted and lightly smoked over an open fire; and **smoked herring - *bokking*** are strung on a spit and smoked.

Mackerel - *makreel* is a rather fatty fish (6 to 8%) caught in the North Atlantic, the North Sea and the Mediterranean. It is sold fresh (whole or in fillets), smoked or salted. Fresh mackerel can be grilled or poached and served with mustard or tomato sauces. It can also be used in soups.

Salmon - *zalm* is one of the world's favorite fish with its firm flesh and distinctive flavor. It is a migratory fish which swims from the ocean to spawn in the rivers and streams. The **Chinook or king salmon** with its off-white to bright pink flesh is considered by many to be superior. Other high fat salmon are the **coho** or **silver salmon** with pink to orange flesh and the sockeye or red salmon with its deep red flesh. The **pink** or **humpback salmon** with a more delicate flavor is usually canned. The fresh salmon sold in Holland generally come from salmon farms in Norwegian fjords or from the North Sea around Scotland, Denmark and Norway but some American salmon is imported. Uses for salmon are endless. It can be marinated and grilled, pan-fried in butter, steamed Chinese style, baked *en papillote* with white wine and leeks, or braised whole with or without stuffing. It is good hot or cold accompanied by a variety of sauces. Fresh salmon is sold whole or cut into steaks or fillets. It is also sold smoked.

Salmon trout - *zalm forel* is a type of trout which feeds on shellfish until its flesh turns pink. In recent years, it has become very popular in Holland. Buy it from a reliable fish monger for improper treatment can severely alter its mild, but distinctively salmon taste. Salmon trout can be used in any recipe calling for salmon. It is generally sold whole.

Sardine - *sardine* is a term applied to many small saltwater fish such as the young pilchard which is related to the herring family. The small sardine is usually smoked or salted; but in Holland, it is often sold preserved in oil or in tomato sauce and canned. Much of the flavor depends on the type of oil used in canning; that packed in first quality olive oil is considered to be the best. Some sardines are packed whole while others are boned and sold as fillets. They are mostly served as hors d'oeuvres.

Smelt - *spiering* is a small saltwater fish which spawns in fresh water. Its fine, mild, delicate flesh is oily. The classic cooking method is *à la meunière*. It can also be marinated and grilled or baked *au gratin*. It is quite perishable so it is usually frozen.

Sprat - *sprot* Sprat is often compared with herring and sardine. It is most often sold smoked, preserved or marinated, but fresh sprat is available in some parts of the country. Fresh sprat is pan-fried and the flesh is eaten off the sides leaving the head and tail intact. Sprats are very popular in Scandinavian countries (in Norway they are called anchovies) and are used in open-faced sandwiches and salads.

Tuna - *tonijn* is a name given to any of several large sea fish which are similar in appearance. The most common varieties of tuna are the albacore, yellowfin, bluefin, blackfin and skipjack or bonito. Albacore or big eye is very popular because of its mild-flavored white flesh. The Japanese are very fond of tuna. They eat it raw as **Sashimi** and use the dry bonito as the base for their ubiquitous soup stock - **Daishi**. The Mediterranean countries are also fond of tuna and seem to have countless ways of using both fresh and tinned. Tuna is available here either fresh in steaks or tinned tuna. In tins it comes in three grades: solid or fancy, chunky, and flaked or grated. It is packed in water, oil, or with vegetables in a piquant sauce.

Whitebait - *witvis* is a young herring or smelt. It is usually fried and eaten whole.

FRESHWATER FISH

Carp - *karper* A freshwater (or sweetwater) fish, carp is found in quiet rivers and on fish farms. It is best to soak the carp in a bowl of vinegar and water to remove its muddy taste before cooking. Carp can be roasted, grilled, cooked in court bouillon or stewed. It is suitable for cooking Chinese-style **Sweet and Sour Fish**.

Catfish, European - *meerval* Easily distinguished by its huge barbed head, European catfish (called *poisson chat* by the French) are freshwater fish caught mostly in the Danube, some Swiss lakes and the River Doubs in France. The meat is firm, white and rather fatty. It can be pan-fried, baked, grilled, broiled, poached or steamed and can be used in soups and stews.

Perch - *baars* and its relative the **pike perch - *snoek, snoekbaars*** are considered by many to be the tastiest of all freshwater fish. Their firm flesh is mild with a delicate flavor and has a low fat content. Small ones can be sautéed. Medium ones can be fried *à la meunière*; and the larger ones baked, broiled, steamed or poached and used in soups and stews. Don't confuse these fresh-water perch with some saltwater fish such as white perch, ocean perch and sea bass which are erroneously nicknamed perch. They are not the same.

Trout - *forel* A name given to a large species of fish related to salmon and whitefish, trout are mostly sweetwater fish. Some do grow in salt water. Rainbow trout - *regenboogforel* is a species imported from the United States and bred in a big way in Europe. You can buy it fresh or smoked, whole or in fillets. Its flesh is firm-textured and the fat content ranges from medium to high. Any salmon recipes can be used for trout.

FISH EGGS

Roe - *kuit* and ***hom*** can either be female fish eggs - *kuit* (hard roe) or the reproductive gland or milt of the male fish - *hom* (soft roe). The choicest roe comes from various fish like cod, haddock, salmon, trout and sturgeon. Roe can be sautéed and poached and roe from certain fish like whiting, cod or salmon can be grilled. It can be purchased fresh, frozen, canned or deep fried - ***gebakken kuit***. Salmon, trout and lumpfish roe or eggs are substituted for **caviar (sturgeon)** when salted.

SHELLFISH

There are three major types of shellfish: crustaceans (crabs, crayfish, lobsters, prawns and shrimp); mollusks (clams, mussels, oysters and scallops); and cephalopods (squid, octopus and cuttlefish) which have no shells.

Abalone - *zeeoor* Abalone is a mollusk of which only the foot that clings to the rocks is edible. It is widely used in Chinese and Japanese cooking and should be bought canned, dried or salted from the Chinese/Indonesian stores or Chinese supermarkets.

Clam Mussels and cockles have always been the more popular bivalve mollusk in Europe while clams are preferred in North America where Clam Chowder is an American classic. You can, however, find fresh clams from time to time in the larger seafood shops like Simonis in Scheveningen. They will most likely be the soft-shell clams that are found from the White Sea down to France. The test for freshness in clams is similar to the mussels, but for soft-shell clams touch the protruding neck, if it moves it is alive. You can also buy the tiny Italian canned clams at some food shops, look for ***vongole*** on the small jars.

Cockle - *kokkel* This tiny ribbed bivalve mollusk is harvested from the sandy areas of the Waddenzee. They are removed from their shells and frozen and exported or are sold fresh in fish shops. They are, however, not as popular here as mussels. They should be left in cold water for 12 hours to get rid of the grit, thoroughly washed, then cooked like mussels.

Crab - *krab* is one of a large group of crustaceans with five sets of legs. The **King** and **Snow Crabs** from the North Pacific, the **Dungeness Crab** of the American West Coast and **Rock Crab** from Florida waters are the most famous. However, most crab sold in Holland comes from France, England and Scandinavia. It is usually sold cooked, cooked and frozen, or canned. Cooked cold crab can be used in salads like the famous San Francisco **Crab Louis** or in **Crab Cocktail**. A crab-flavored fish cake (surimi) made from fish products is sold in fish shops here and makes a reasonable substitute for crab in cold dishes.

Cuttlefish - *inktvis*, octopus - *octopus* and squid - *pijlinkvis* are all closely related and can be substituted for each other. Squid, however, is the most widely available of the three. The Japanese eat their squid and octopus like ***Sashimi*** while in the Mediterranean area the cuttlefish, squid and octopus are poached, deep-fried, sautéed, stewed or barbecued. All have ink sacs which contain a dark liquid which is also used in some Mediterranean cooking. These cephalopods can be quite tough and chewy but the cuttlefish in particular must be beaten quite vigorously to soften it before cooking. Then the meat should either be quickly cooked over high heat or long, slowly cooked over low heat. Cooked squid or calamari and octopus slices are available in some local fish shops while fresh cuttlefish can be purchased whole or cleaned. Asian stores often sell dried cuttlefish and squid.

Lobster - *kreeft* A saltwater crustacean, lobster is related to crab. There are two major types: the **Northern lobster** which is fished off the Atlantic coasts of the United States and Canada, and the closely related **European lobster** that lives along Europe's Atlantic coast, the Mediterranean and South Africa. These lobsters have five pairs of legs, the first legs form into large claws. Lobster can be purchased cooked or alive; although, it generally has to be ordered ahead of time from your local fish shop. The average lobster weighs around 1 pound (450 grams). Lobster can be grilled, baked, stir-fried or sautéed in butter. Two dishes for which it is famous are **Lobster Newburg** and **Lobster Thermidor**. The **spiny lobster** which is also known as **rock lobster**, **crawfish** or **langouste** has five pairs of matching legs with no claws and is often confused with the true lobster. It is caught in the warmer waters of Florida, Southern California, Australia and the Gulf of Mexico. It is also known as **crayfish**, which is again confused with the diminutive **freshwater crayfish - *ecrevisse*** which look like mini-lobsters. Spiny lobster can be prepared in much the same manner as the true lobster. **Crayfish or crawfish - *rivierkreeft* or *ecrevisse*** is widely used in Louisiana and French cooking. It grows in fresh water and is available here in a cooked and frozen state. It can be used in a variety of ways: au gratin, in soufflés or in pies. It can also be cooked in stock and served whole.

Mussel - *mossel* This delicious mollusk is farmed in Dutch waters and is very popular in Holland. Still, you must buy them from a reliable source. To make sure they are alive and fresh, check the bag to see if they are tightly closed or snap shut when the shells are tapped. Keep them refrigerated and use them within one or two days. They have traditionally only been available during the colder months, those with an "R" in them; but those months can be stretched. Three or four hours before cooking, rinse the mussels and place them in cold water. Some cooks add one or two tablespoons flour. The mussels feed on the flour and release the old salt water and sand trapped inside. Just before cooking, toss out any mussels that have broken shells or those that float to the top of the water, then pull out the dark thread (beard) from the back of the shells. After cooking, throw out any that have not opened. Mussels are cooked very simply: sautéed in butter, steamed in white wine and vegetables, cooked in a cream sauce, stewed in soups, or cooked in the Spanish rice dish ***paella***. It takes 35-40 mussels in shells to make 2 pounds (1 kilo). Allow 36 per person when served as a main course and 18 as starters. The Dutch use the hinged shell of the first large mussel as a tweezers to pull out and eat the rest of the other mussels.

Oyster - *oester* Like mussels, oysters have traditionally only been available during the colder months from September to April. However, sometimes these months are stretched. Oysters are cultivated in Holland, so they are sold fresh. The shells must be closed tightly when you buy them. They are sold by the dozen. Reckon on six to eight per person. Oysters are usually eaten alive and raw, but can be cooked and eaten hot or cold.

Prawns - *kreeft garnalen*, shrimp - *garnalen* and **scampi** are often confused with each other. The term **prawn** is applied to describe a type of marine crustacean which looks like a tiny Maine lobster about 6 to 10 inches (15 to 25 centimeters) long with pincers or claws. It is widely available in western Europe. The French langoustine, Dublin Bay prawns, Italian scampi and Florida and Caribbean lobsterettes are all part of this category. The term prawn is also applied to the freshwater prawn (it travels from salt water to spawn in fresh water like salmon) which looks like a cross between a lobster and a shrimp. Its body is narrower and it has longer legs than shrimp. To further confuse the issue, the term prawn is also used to describe "jumbo" shrimp or gambas which weigh in at 10 or less to the pound (½ kilo). **Shrimps** grow in salt water and vary in size from 10 or less to a pound (½ kilo) to the tiny **Dutch shrimps - *Hollandse garnaal*** or ***Noordzee garnaal*** which weigh in at 100 to a pound. These brownish-pink sweet shrimp are considered a delicacy in Holland as are the somewhat larger pinkish-red Norwegian shrimps. Both are used in shrimp cocktails, hors d'oeuvre and salads. Shrimps and prawns can be stir-fried, sautéed, steamed, poached and grilled. Most shrimps and prawns on the market are cooked and peeled, but fresh shrimp and prawns in their shells are also available. Frozen shrimps and prawns are always available in the Chinese supermarkets or other Asian shops.

Scallop - *St. Jacobsschelp* This mollusk has two beautiful shells that are used as serving containers for dishes such as ***Coquilles St. Jacques***. The entire scallop including the roe is edible; but, in the United States, only the sweet white muscle that holds the two hinged shells together is eaten. To clean, sever the muscle from the top shell with an oyster or clam knife. Discard the top shell. Loosen the muscle from the bottom shell and tip into a bowl of water. Cut out the white muscle and red coral then cut off the small crescent shaped muscle from the white meat and discard the muscle. The red coral should be cooked gently for it has a tendency to explode when heated too fast. Scallops can be baked with buttered bread crumbs; sautéed with butter, herbs and wine; floured and deep fried; added to soups; eaten raw in ***Sushi***; or skewered and grilled. The meat toughens when overcooked. When fresh, the shells should be tightly closed. In Holland, scallops are sold fresh or the contents are cleaned and sold (without shells but with the red coral) from the deep freeze. Allow 3 to 4 shells per person.

Sea cucumber - *zeekomkommer* Also known as a sea slug, sea cucumber gets its name from the fact that it looks like a cucumber. It is usually sold dried in Chinese/Indonesian food shops and is widely used in East Asian cooking.

IV.7 POULTRY, GAME BIRDS AND GAME

While most supermarkets and butcher shops and some stalls at open markets carry whole chickens, chicken parts and eggs, there are some shops which specialize in all kinds of poultry, game birds, game and eggs. The signs outside these shops either read "**Chicken Specialist**" or "***Poelier - Wild en Gevogelte***". In the **Yellow Pages**, or ***Gouden Gids***, of the telephone book, they are listed under ***Poeliers***. The *poelier* might also have whole chicken grilled on a spit - *gebraden kip*, grilled chicken pieces on sticks, saté and fried chicken wings (t.v. sticks) ready for heating and eating with accompanying sauces.

Game and game birds are extremely popular in Europe during the late autumn and winter months. In the more populated areas, they are sold fresh but in the rural areas they are mostly sold frozen. Don't expect that a full selection will always be in stock. Order ahead of time if you have your heart set on serving something special. Game birds have very little fat and should be barded or larded before roasting, and basted frequently. Barding means to cover the joints with thin slices of pork or bacon fat - *bardeer vet* to keep them from drying out. Old game birds should be cooked with moist heat (braised) or cooked in stews. Only the game and game birds commonly found in Holland are listed below.

EGGS

Chicken eggs - ***kippen eieren*** are sold in supermarkets, by the chicken specialist, at stalls at open markets and sometimes by the cheese specialist. For a description of chicken eggs, see Chapter IV.3, Dairy Products. In addition to chicken eggs, **quail eggs - *kwarteleieren*, lapwing eggs - kievits eieren** and **duck eggs - *eende eieren*** are sometimes sold by the game specialist. Quail eggs can be hard cooked, soft cooked or poached, while duck eggs should be cooked 12 minutes or longer. Lapwing eggs are available from mid-March until the first or second week of April, after that it is forbidden to collect them. Lapwing eggs should be cooked from five to seven minutes and can be served with rye bread or white toast. In Holland, once the lapwing egg is cooked, it is peeled then placed in the left palm, and the right hand is clapped over it to distribute the yolk. The egg white is velvety and transparent.

POULTRY AND GAME BIRDS

Chicken - *kip* or *kuiken* The chicken specialist stocks the common chicken and chicken parts, including giblets. They also usually carry the more flavorful **corn-fed chicken - *mais kip***. You can recognize them by their jaundiced skins. Some are imported from France and Belgium where they are called *poule jaune*. The prized French **Bresse chicken - Bresse poularde** is expensive but delicious. It is fed on corn, buckwheat, milk and buttermilk and is considered to be the queen of all chickens. Other types of chicken sold in Holland are **spring chicken - *piepkuiken*, broiler chicken - *jong haantje*, roasting/stewing chicken - *poularde*, roasting chicken/pullet - *braadkip* or *braadkuiken*** and **soup chicken - *soepkip***. The soup chicken makes a tasty soup; but since they are old laying hens, they must be simmered for several hours to get all of the flavor out of them. Free ranging ***scharrelkip*** are always good. Cut-up chicken parts are and are usually sold by the piece or weight: **breast with bone - *kippenborst*, breast deboned - *kipfilet*, drumsticks - *kippenpootjes*, drumstick and thigh - *kippenbout*, wings - *vleugels*, wing drumsticks - *t.v. sticks*** and **liver, heart and gizzard - *lever, hart and maag***. Dutch butchers leave small back portions attached to the thighs which is a nuisance if you like a clean cut thigh for your Southern Fried Chicken. Cut the offending portions off and use them for chicken stock. **Rolled roast - *rollade*, chicken cordon bleu - *kip cordon bleu*** and **breaded chicken cutlet - *kipschnitzel*** are offered in almost every shop that sells chicken. Chicken spices - *kipkruiden* are automatically added when rolling the roasts but they can be special-ordered without the spices if you like. You have the following choices: *kiprollade met vel* - a deboned whole chicken with skin; *kipdij rollade* - a rolled roast made of deboned chicken thighs; and *kipfilet rollade* - a rolled roast made of deboned chicken breasts. You can also buy ready to eat **grilled roasts - *gegrillde rollade(n)***. Chicken cordon bleu is made of chicken breast stuffed with cheese and ham slices and breaded. Fry them about three to five minutes on each side until done.

Duck - *eend* **Tame duck - *tamme eend*** and **wild duck - *wilde eend*** are generally eaten in Holland around the winter holidays. However, **Peking duck** which is especially fattened for use in Chinese cooking is available all year round at the Chinese supermarkets and/or Chinese/Indonesian stores known as *toko*. Tame or domesticated ducks from Rouen and Nantes in France are considered to be the best. **Wild ducks - *wilde eenden*** are trapped in Holland from the end of July until the end of January. Thus, there is no buckshot damage. Young wild ducks can be roasted on a spit or in the oven but older ducks should be braised. Recipes for tame ducks are also suitable for wild ducks.

Goose - *gans* In spite of the fact that turkey is gaining in popularity in Holland, the holiday goose is still cooked in many homes. It is mostly domesticated goose but wild goose is also available at times. Goose can be roasted in the same manner as turkey. Goslings, when available, are more tender than the larger older birds which, because of their toughness, should be braised. A tart fruit sauce offsets its fatty taste.

Grouse - *korhoen* is no longer sold in Holland.

Guinea fowl - *parelhoen* sold in Europe is a lovely black domesticated bird with pearly white spots. It descended from the wild African Guinea fowl. It has a dark flesh and a slightly gamey flavor and can range from ¾ to 4 pounds (340 grams to 1.8 kilos). The youngest birds are the most succulent and can be prepared in the same way as young chicken. The older birds weighing over 2¼ pounds can also be prepared in the same manner as chicken but should be barded with fat or bacon and basted or cooked in a casserole to keep the flesh moist.

Partridge - *patrijs* is still hunted in some European countries like France and Britain but they are relatively rare in Belgium and Holland. A partridge weighs around 12 to 14 ounces (360 to 420 grams). Partridges must be eaten fairly soon after they are killed. The young bird has a white, slightly gamey flavor and can be wrapped in vine leaves and stuffed with juniper berries or grapes and roasted. It can also be broiled and braised.

Pheasant - *fazant* is hunted in Holland and Belgium from 15 October until the end of January and some birds are grown on farms. A full-grown male pheasant can weigh from 2½ to 5 pounds (±1 to 2¼ kilos) and the female averages 3 pounds (1½ kilos). Connoisseurs prefer the female to the cock because it is juicier and more tender. Very young cocks and hens can be roasted but older pheasants need to be barded and braised.

Pigeon - *duif* and wild pigeon - *houtduif* are available in Holland. Young tame pigeons are especially tender and can be grilled (broiled) or roasted. Young pigeon only needs to be lightly barded while full barding is a must for older birds. Older ones can also be cooked in casseroles or in a rich, well-seasoned stew. Wild pigeon or wood pigeon is more flavorful and can be prepared in the same manner as the domestic pigeon.

Quail - *kwartel* found in Europe is a small migratory bird quite different from the quail found in North America. They are protected birds in Holland so cannot be hunted. However, a breed from the Far East is raised on farms in Belgium and France and is available here in autumn and winter months. They are rather small so allow two per person. Young quail can be roasted, broiled (on a skewer) or fried. Older birds should be cooked with moist heat or braised. Wild quail should be barded with bacon before roasting.

Turkey - *kalkoen* Whole turkeys appear in shops around Christmas, while deboned turkey breasts, turkey thighs and rolled roasts made from thighs - *rollade(n)*, are sold throughout the year. Thanksgiving turkeys can be bought fresh from the chicken specialist, chicken man or *poelier*, as well as from some butchers. Farms that raise turkeys sometimes also sell them directly. The Dutch turkeys are not fed growth enhancements other than their normal food and are full of flavor. The size normally eaten in Holland is around 8 pounds (3½ kilos). Ask for a 22-pound/10 kilo turkey and see the look of amazement. You can order a large turkey a month or two ahead of time. There is always one walking around which survived the holidays the previous year. You can ask for the giblets but that doesn't mean you will get them. Try making gravy from chicken necks, hearts and gizzards.

GAME

Boar, wild - *wild zwijn* is the ancestor of the domestic pig. It was once abundant in Europe but is now becoming rare. It is hunted in parts of Holland, Belgium and France. Young boar has delicate flesh but as it ages, the taste becomes more pronounced. The best boar meat is that which is one to two years old. Boar is sold in roasts or cutlets; however, only the meat from the young boar, six months or less, is truly suitable for dry roasting.

Roasts from older boars should be braised and the cutlets pan-fried. Any older boar should be marinated in a red wine; the length of marinating time should increase with the age. Younger boar should be marinated two to three hours, the older animals for five to eight hours. The older boar needs to undergo long and slow cooking.

Deer - *ree and hert* is still hunted in Holland and is available at the *poelier* and some butcher shops. The smaller deer is known as **ree** while the larger deer is called **hert**. It is butchered into fore and hind legs, back, chops, fillets and stew meat. The cuts correspond to cuts of beef or pork. The haunch or hindquarter cut includes the leg and loin. It is roasted after being hung and marinated. Deer is much leaner than beef and its meat is less tender. It should be cooked using the moist heat method (braised) or barded and larded and roasted in dry heat. Steaks from younger deer can be pan-fried.

Frog's legs - *kikkerbilletjes*. While frog's legs would normally be listed under fish, they are included in this section for they are sold by the *poelier*. They are also available through farms which specialize in raising frogs for the markets. The only parts of the frog which are edible are the legs. Their delicate flesh must be cooked very briefly and they are delicious when sautéed in butter or olive oil with garlic and herbs.

Rabbit and **hare** **Tame rabbit - *tamme konijn***, **wild rabbit - *wild duinkonijn*** and **hare - *haas*** are all available on the Dutch market. Some are actually hunted in Holland while others are imported. There are several main differences between rabbits and hares: rabbits are smaller, have shorter ears and rear legs and rabbit meat is white to pink, while hare meat is light to dark red. A medium-sized hare is usually cut into two front legs, - *hazenvoorbout(en)*, two back legs - *hazenachterbout(en)*, filet - *hazenrugfilet* and two halves of the saddle. The most popular cut is the **saddle of hare - *hazerug*** which is the unseparated loin from rib to leg of both sides. The saddle can also be cut into steaks and chops. Rabbits are sold whole or legs - *konijnenbout(en)* only.

Venison - *wildbraad*, though generally thought of as pertaining to deer, can apply to meat from other game animals.

IV.8 FRUITS AND VEGETABLES

Dutch farmers provide this country with a stunning variety of fruits and vegetables. There is a large concentration of apple, pear and cherry orchards in the Betuwe Region while vegetable gardens and greenhouses dot the countryside. Vegetables play a leading role in the Dutch diet. In fact, if you ask any Dutch cook what they are having for dinner, they will invariably mention the vegetable first and not the meat. Many are used in a variety of *stamppot* dishes where vegetables are cooked with potatoes and mashed together (see Chapter IV.14). Meat portions in these dishes are small, usually 3½ ounces or less per person.

Ordinary fresh fruits and vegetables can be purchased at supermarkets, greengrocers and at stalls in open markets. The greengrocer is known as ***de groenteboer*** or ***groentewinkel*** and is listed under ***Groenten en fruit*** in the ***Gouden Gids***, or **Yellow Pages**, of the telephone book. However, for the best selection of exotic fruits and vegetables try those who specialize in certain regional foods such as the Asian shops or vendors at the Eastern Market in Beverwijk.

At the supermarkets, you are expected select and weigh your own produce or they will weigh it for you at the check-out counter; however, at the greengrocers there are usually people to wait on you—don't touch the merchandise. New designer varieties of fruits and vegetables (like green cauliflower) are developed from time to time. They sometimes appear and disappear very quickly. Fruits and vegetables new to the Dutch market retain the names by which they are known in their native countries; i.e. broccoli is simply known as broccoli.

Many greengrocers, including those in supermarkets, offer prepared *rauwkost* or uncooked cut fruits and vegetables ready for mixed salads, soups, stews and casseroles. The best selection is offered during the late fall and winter months when the hearty winter stews like *Hachee* or *stamppot* dishes appear on the Dutch tables. Tell the greengrocer the number of people you are cooking for and he can tell you how much to buy.

Fruits and vegetables are sold by the piece or by the Dutch weight; i.e. *ons* (100 grams), *pond* (500 grams), *1½ pond or anderhalf pond* (750 grams), *kilo* (1,000 grams) or *1½ kilo* (*anderhalf kilo*). Some greengrocers will sell halves of larger vegetables like cabbage or cauliflower.

FRUITS - *VRUCHTEN*

Apple - *appel* The fruit of the apple tree is the most widely cultivated in the world. When stored properly, it is available year round. Out-of-hand eating apples are best from September through November and as dessert fruits from October through April. In Holland, there are two classifications: apples best suited for eating raw, or ***handappelen***, and apples also suited for cooking, or ***stoofappelen***. Apples most commonly available in Holland are: **Cox's Orange Pippin**, a juicy, aromatic, very popular, out-of-hand eating apple; **Alkmene**, a firm baking and out-of-hand eating apple which resembles Cox's Orange Pippin; **Elstar**, a slightly tart, firm, juicy, baking and out-of-hand apple; **Golden Delicious**, a slightly sour, all-purpose apple which is a good out-of-hand eating apple and is especially suited for fruit salads and pies; **Goudreinet**, a fresh, slightly sour, out-of-hand eating apple which is also good for making apple sauce and apple juice; **Granny Smith**, a firm, juicy all-purpose apple with a sweet, tart flesh which is a good for eating out-of-hand and for cooking and baking; and **Jona gold (Jonathan)**, a juicy and aromatic out-of-hand eating apple and all-purpose cooking apple. **Pink Lady (Cripp's Pink), Fuji** and **Early Red One** are relatively new to the Dutch marketplace and all are sweet, juicy, out-of-hand eating apples. The Pink Lady is green with a pretty pink blush while the others have skins of various shades of green, red and gold.

Apricot - *abrikoos* This fruit has a fragrant, sweet, highly-perishable flesh like its cousin the peach. It is in season during June and July. Fresh apricots can be eaten out-of-hand or used in fruit salads and compotes, cakes and pastries and preserves. **Dried apricots** can be rehydrated and used in fruit breads and cakes and together with fresh cranberries make a lovely relish for the Thanksgiving dinner. Apricots are also available canned.

Banana - *banaan* A tropical fruit, the banana is generally imported from Central and South America. There are many varieties of banana; Indonesia alone has around 40 types. Bananas can basically be divided into two categories: the **common fruit or dessert banana** and the **cooking banana** or **plantain - *bakbanaan***. The **yellow dessert banana** is the most popular in the West but from time to time the short, chubby **red** or **apple banana** and **finger banana** also appear on the market; both are much sweeter than the common yellow banana. The **plantain** is frequently used in West Indian, South American, South and Southeast Asia and African cuisines. Cooking brings out their flavor; they cannot be eaten raw. The Asian stores often carry Asian varieties of cooking bananas. However, if you cannot find them, slightly unripe bananas can also be used for hot banana-based dessert dishes like **Bananas Foster**, which consists of bananas lightly sautéed in butter and flavored with rum, brown sugar and banana liqueur accompanied by a scoop of ice cream. Bananas are picked green and must ripen at room temperature before eating out-of-hand.

Berries - *bessen* The berries sold in Holland can be divided into two categories: soft such as **raspberries - *frambozen***, **blackberries - *bramen*** and **strawberries - aardbeien** and firm such as **blueberries - *blauwe bessen*, gooseberries - *kruisbessen*, cranberries - *veenbessen*** and **currants - *krenten*** (see currants below). Most berries appear in the shops at the beginning of summer while strawberries are now available throughout the year. Health food enthusiasts love these berries for they are rich in vitamins and minerals. The soft berries are best when eaten fresh. Cooked, they and the firm berries are turned into jams and jellies, syrups for beverages, liqueurs, tarts and pies. The **strawberry** is by far the most popular of all berries. In the words of William Butler, a 16th-century author: "Doubtless God could have made a better berry, but doubtless God never did." The sweet, **wild strawberries - *bosaardbeien*** or ***fraises des bois***, are considered to be the "queen of strawberries". Strawberries are widely used as a filling in the French puff pastry or are baked together with rhubarb in pies in the United States but they are never better than when eaten fresh with sugar and yoghurt, a small amount balsamic vinger, or whipped or clotted cream. The **raspberry** is an excellent dessert fruit and is often made into dessert sauces. They can also be eaten much like strawberries. The taste of the lovely **blackberry** with its black or deep purple sacs is often enhanced with cooking and is used crushed but whole in cooked jams. The **blueberry**, with it smooth bluish-black skin and silvery frost coating, is bland when raw but improves in flavor when cooked in muffins, cobblers, pancakes and pancake syrups. The **gooseberry** is a large green to amber-green tart berry which flourishes in Northern Europe. It is a prime ingredient in the famous dessert known as **Fool** and is used as a condiment with smoked meats and strong tasting fish. The **Cape gooseberry**, also called *physalis*, is also sometimes found here. Because it is such a pretty fruit, it is often used for decoration on French gateau or cakes. **Cranberries** are cultivated berries mostly imported from North America although you will sometimes find them Dutch-grown. They are sold fresh in 12-ounce plastic bags in the late fall and winter months or as canned cranberry sauce (whole or jellied) throughout the year. Raw cranberries are not eaten out-of-hand but can be chopped fine and mixed with other fruits in salads and relishes or cooked in sauces and chutney or baked in pies and quick breads. Fresh cranberries will keep, tightly wrapped, in the refrigerator for up to four weeks and in the freezer up to one year. Place them in an airtight plastic bag and pop them in the freezer. When thawed, discard any berries that are discolored or shrivelled. The tiny **lingonberry, cowberry** or **bilberry** so popular in Germany and Scandinavia is its wild relative.

Carambola - ***carambola*** The carambola is often called the star fruit, for when cut crosswise the slices are star-shaped. Its flesh should be soft, juicy and fragrant. Its waxy, golden-yellow skin is tender but the ridges are rather tough and should be trimmed. Choose a fruit with a bright even color with shiny skin. They can be eaten out-of-hand or used in salads or as a garnish. Indian cooks use them to make pickles and chutney or cook them in stews.

Cherimoya, custard apple or sour sop - ***cherimoya*** **or** ***annona*** A large tropical fruit with dull green skin, cherimoya has creamy-colored, custard-like flesh and large, black seeds. Its flavor has been compared to a combination of pineapple, mango and strawberry or banana, pineapple and pear. It is best when served chilled. Cut the fruit in half, remove the seeds and scoop out the flesh with a spoon. Eat it plain or purée it to make ice cream. Pick a fruit that does not have skin blemishes. It is ripe when the flesh gives a little when squeezed.

Cherry - ***kers*** It is unfortunate that this delicious fruit is so perishable and the season so short. Cherry season in Holland is May, June and July. There are two kinds of cherries: sweet and sour. Sweet cherries are good for eating out-of-hand or added to fruit salads, compotes, pies and tarts and ice cream. Sour cherries are used to make commercial syrups, brandies, liqueurs, wines, jams and jellies. ***Glacé*** or ***bigarreau*** are **candied cherries** which are used in cakes and puddings and for decoration. A specially-treated

maraschino is available for use as a garnish for desserts and for cocktails. Cherries preserved in syrup are available in glass jars. They can be drained and used in cherry pies. However, there is also a type of canned cherry which has a thickened sauce that is used in **Limburg tarts - *vlaaien***. It is called *vlaaivulling*.

Currant - *krent* The term currant is used to describe two distinctly different fruits. One is a tiny, dried grape produced mainly in Greece. It is called the Zante grape and resembles a raisin. Currants are also grown in Australia, California and South Africa but production is limited. This type of currant is traditionally used in baked goods such as breads - *krentebrood* and rolls - *krentebollen*. The other currant is a tiny berry related to the gooseberry. The berries can be **black - *zwarte bessen***, **red - *rode bessen*** and **white - *witte bessen*** and they are not dried. This berry is also called *aalbes* here. **Black currants** are made into ***cassis*** (a delicious liqueur) and into syrups, juices, and jams and jellies. **Red currants** are acid-tasting while the **white currants** are sweeter. They are eaten with sweetened yoghurt or in salads, sauces, and jams and jellies. The famous French preserve **Bar le Duc** is made from red and white currants. Currant season is from end-June through August.

Dried fruit Holland imports many varieties of **dried fruits** from California and the Mediterranean region. They include apple - *appel*, apricot - *abrikoos*, currant - *krent*, date - *dadel*, prune - *gedroogde pruim*, raisin - *rozijn*, sultana and fig - *vijg* plus a mixture apricots, apples, pears and peaches called *tutti frutti*.

Fig - *vijg* Originally from Asia Minor, the fig is the fruit of the ficus tree which grows in warm climates. There are hundreds of varieties but all have a soft, moist, intensely sweet flesh with thousands of tiny edible seeds. The skin of the cultivated fig is purplish-black to nearly white. They have soft, fragile skins and they are highly perishable; thus they are a bit of a luxury when they are available on the local market. Figs can be eaten out-of-hand or sliced and covered with cream. Fresh figs are in season from September through November. Dried figs can be purchased from supermarkets and specialty food stores.

Grape and grape leaves - *druif* and *druiven bladeren* Grapes are considered to come from one ancient species with many varieties. Some are raised to produce wine while others are cultivated as dessert or table grapes or are dried to produce raisins, currants and sultanas. Grapes are usually described as either white or green with a yellow hue or black with a deep dark color (also known as red). Italy and France are Europe's largest suppliers of sun-ripened dessert grapes while those from Holland and Belgium are usually grown in hot houses. Thus there is usually a wide variety available on the Dutch market. Table grapes can be used for fruit and chicken salads and are a classic garnish for **Filet of Sole** and **Chicken à la Veronique**. They also make wonderful preserves and jellies. Grapes are on the market year-round and will keep refrigerated for up to a week. **Grape**

leaves are wrapped around certain snacks like the Greek **Dolmas**. They are available in jars packed in brine in specialty foods or gourmet shops like those that carry Greek and Middle Eastern foods. Bottled or canned grape leaves should be washed before using.

Grapefruit - *grapefruit*, pomelo - *pompelmoes*, ugli - *ugli* and ***tangelo*** A tropical citrus fruit, **grapefruit** comes in two colors: white, with a yellowish-white flesh and pink, with pale pink to ruby red flesh. The darker the color, the sweeter the fruit. The delicious **ruby red grapefruit** developed in Texas but also grown in Florida is very popular here and is marketed as **double red grapefruit - *dubbel rode grapefruit***. Grapefruit is a good breakfast fruit and is also a welcome addition to fruit and green salads. Chilled **grapefruit juice** is a delicious breakfast drink and it can also be added to punches and cocktails. **Pomelo**, **Shaddock** or **pamplemousse** was first discovered by the Dutch in Indonesia and Malaysia, and they called it *pompelmoes*, or pumpkin citron. It is the ancestor of the grapefruit and its flesh can be from yellow to pink, sweet to tart but it is a bit dry. The peel is very thick. In the Indonesian *toko* it would be sold as *jeruk Bali*. **Ugli** is another fruit that appears from time to time. Its name probably means ugly, which it is. It is thought to be a grapefruit/tangerine hybrid. Its flesh is sweeter than grapefruit and sharper than tangerine. It can be eaten like grapefruit. The tangelo is a cross between the pomelo and tangerine. There are many hybrids but the one you will see in Holland is the sweetly-tart Minneola.

Kiwi - *kiwi fruit* or **Chinese gooseberry - *Chinese kruisbes*** is an exotic fruit named after New Zealand's kiwi bird. It looks like a fuzzy brown goose egg. Its brilliant green flesh dotted with tiny black seeds is the secret to its success. Kiwi fruit can be eaten out-of-hand or sliced in fresh fruit salads or as an attractive garnish on fruit tarts. It grows in many parts of the Northern and Southern Hemispheres so it is available all year. Kiwi fruit should be firm but must give a little when pressed and should have no soft spots.

Kumquat - *kumquat* The tiny kumquat is about the size of a quail egg but looks like an orange. It is eaten out of hand skin, pips and all. The skin is actually sweeter than the flesh. Rub them around the palms of your hands to increase their aroma. Kumquats are also used in preserves, relishes and liquers.

Lemon - *citroen* is too tart to eat on its own like most other citrus fruits but is probably used more than any other. It is the principal flavor in a number of desserts; it adds zest to many meat dishes and fruits and enhances the flavor of fish. Fresh lemon juice, when mixed with water and sugar, makes a refreshing summer drink, lemonade. Lemon juice rubbed on various cut fruits inhibits discoloring. The oil of its peel (yellow part only) is the essence of many cakes and it is pertinent to the success of **Crepes Suzettes**. Lemons are available year around. Bottled lemon juice is sold in supermarkets although it hardly resembles fresh lemon juice.

Litchi, lichi or lichee - *lychee* This tropical fruit with a rough-textured, reddish hull is much cherished in China. Its flesh is white and sweet. Shell and seed it and eat plain out-of-hand. Canned lichees are available in most supermarkets and Asian stores but it is worth trying to find them fresh. Dried lichees are sold in Asian stores and are eaten like candy.

Lime - *limoen* Limes, like lemons, are too tart to eat on their own and thus are added to sweet and savory dishes. Their flavor is, however, distinctly different from lemon and are thus not interchangeable. The most common is the Persian lime which has a green skin and juicy, pale-green pulp. However, it has many cousins. Most Americans know the Florida Key Lime which has more of a yellowish flesh than green and is the main flavor of the **Key Lime Pie**. In Mexico, limes are used in place of lemon in dips and seafood and fruit salads. But they are probably most famous for the flavor they impart on mixed drinks such as **Margaritas**. In Asia, the lime of choice is the diminutive orange-fleshed Asian lime (*jeruk nipis* in Indonesia, *manao* in Thailand) which are sweeter than their Western counterparts so adjust recipes accordingly. Key limes would be the best substitute. If anyone has them, it will be the Asian stores. Bottled lime juice is also available.

Mango - *mango or manga* A fragrant tropical fruit, the mango has a juicy, deep-orange flesh which clings to a large central seed. The flesh should be smooth as custard; avoid the mango that has a fibrous flesh. Mangoes have different shapes (oblong, kidney and round) and different colors. The orange and red-skinned mango is a favorite. Mangoes can be eaten out-of-hand; they should be cut in half and the flesh scooped out with a spoon. They can also be sliced in a mixed fruit salad. In Thailand, the ripe mango reaches its ultimate flavor when sliced and eaten with sticky rice sweetened with coconut milk and topped with coconut cream, **Khao niew mamuang**. In many tropical Asian countries, green or unripe mangoes are eaten out-of-hand dipped in seasoned salt or sugar. They are also used in fruit salads or in mango chutney. Mangoes imported into Holland come mostly from North Africa and South America. They are usually not ripe but they can be ripened in a paper bag at room temperature until the flesh gives a little when squeezed.

Mangosteen - *mangosteen* is an exquisite tropical Asian fruit with an exotic perfume-like flavor. It has a thick, dark reddish-brown skin when ripe and is shaped like a tangerine. A knife cut around its circumference (piercing only the skin) reveals a delicate pearly-white fruit in five to eight fat, juicy segments. Its flesh discolors rather quickly so it must be eaten as soon as it is peeled or sprinkled with lemon juice to stop the action. Fresh mangosteen is sometimes available but it is also sold canned in light syrup at Asian stores.

Melon - *meloen* There are two broad classes of this succulent fruit which has been eaten by man since ancient times; the **Watermelon** and the dessert or **Muskmelon**. Because of the many varieties and their easy cross-pollination, they are difficult to categorize. Probably the most popular of them all is the **watermelon - *watermeloen*** which has a dark green skin and crisp, juicy, red flesh. It is cherished all over the world. The **cantaloupe - *cantaloup***, which is a muskmelon with netted skin, seems to be another favorite. It has a cream-colored netting over yellowish green background and moist, orange flesh. It is not as sweet as many melons and is commonly served with a slice of Ardennen, Parma or Westfalian ham draped over it. However, to eat a true cantaloupe, you have to eat it in Europe for according to food historians, the first recorded melon imported into the United States was the "Netted Gem" variety of muskmelon and not the cantaloupe which came from France. In comparison, the **net melon - *netmeloen***, with a cream-colored netting over yellowish-orange skin and orange flesh, has little aroma. Other common local melons are the **Ogen melon - *Ogen meloen*** which has a green-skin with orange or yellow stripes and yellow/green sweet flesh; the succulent sweet **honeydew - *honingmeloen* or *Spaanse meloen*** which has a creamy yellow to green skin and pale green or light orange flesh and is eaten much like the cantaloupe; the **Galia melon - *galiameloen*** which is related to the *Ogen* melon and has a green to brownish netted skin when ripe and light green flesh; and the **sugar melon - *suikermeloen*** which has a light green almost white skin and a pale-green, juicy, sweet, aromatic flesh.

Nectarine - *nectarine* A smooth-skinned relative of the peach, the nectarine's rich flesh is sweet and succulent. When ripe, its skin should be a deep golden yellow with red blushes. Slightly ripe nectarines can be ripened at room temperature. Eat them out-of-hand or use them in fruit salads and cooked desserts.

Olive - *olijf* The fruit of the olive tree, olives are too bitter to be eaten fresh. Thus they are either pressed for oil or are cured in salt or brine. They are then eaten like vegetables in casseroles, pizzas, salads or as snacks. The dozens of varieties of olives come in many sizes, colors and flavors. Under-ripe olives are always green but older olives can be green or black. The most popular olives here are the **Spanish olives** which are soaked in lye and then fermented in brine for several months, the Greek ***kalamata*** olives and the French ***Niçoise***. Olives are sold with pits or pitted and some are stuffed with pimento, almonds or anchovies. Supermarkets carry some canned olives but specialty food stores and stalls at open markets have better selections.

Orange - *sinaasappel* and **mandarin - *mandarijn*** The orange is the world's most popular fruit after the apple. It can be divided into three basic types, sweet, loose-skinned and bitter. The most popular sweet orange is the **common orange** such as the **Valencia** which is valued for the quantity and quality of its juice; in Holland they are called **juice oranges - *pers sinaasappelen***. The juicy, seedless **navel orange**, which owes it name to the navel-like appearance of its blossom end, is an excellent eating orange and it slices easily for fruit salads and garnishes. The **blood orange - *bloedsinaasappel*** is valued for its pink or red flesh and its berry-like flavor. Sweet oranges are better when eaten fresh and not cooked for their vitamin C content dissipates quickly after being cut. **Mandarin oranges** are thin, loose-skinned oranges of which there are many varieties. They vary in size, color and flavor and can be sweet as honey or tart; the **clementine** is the sweetest. **Tangerine** is the name used for deeply colored mandarins. Oranges are imported from all over the world throughout the year. Mandarin segments are also available in tins and are popular in fruit salads and for decorations on cakes.

Papaya - *papaja* is a large tropical fruit with a creamy, aromatic orange to orange-red flesh. Its central cavity is filled with black seeds which are scraped out and discarded. It is a popular breakfast fruit. It is simply cut into quarters and sprinkled with lime juice. It can also be used in fruit salads, compotes and fruit tarts. Papaya contains papain which is used as a commercial meat tenderizer. The papain inhibits jelling so raw papaya cannot be used in gelatine-based desserts and salads. Cooked papaya presents no problem. Its leaves, when cooked with meats, will tenderize them. Canned papaya is also sold locally.

Passion fruit - *passievrucht* is a tropical fruit which is commonly known by its Spanish name *granadilla* (meaning little pomegranate). The "passion" comes from the shape of its flowers which are said to resemble certain instruments of Christ's crucifixion. There are many varieties but a common type has an unattractive dimpled, dark-purple skin and soft, golden, fragrant flesh surrounding small black seeds. It can be eaten out-of-hand, cut in half and sprinkled with sugar or strained and made into juices, ice cream, dessert sauces and jellies.

Peach - *perzik* There are hundreds of varieties of peaches. They all have two things in common: the stone of the **freestone peach** falls out rather easily while the flesh clings to the stone in the **clingstone peach**. The peach skin is fuzzy so the fruit needs to be peeled; when quickly blanched in hot water it can be peeled quite easily. It is a fragrant fruit which is eaten fresh, out-of-hand or covered with sugar and cream. Peaches are also used in jams, compotes, soufflés, sorbets and fruit salads or simply canned in sugar syrup or water. A peach is ripe when its flesh gives to slight pressure.

Pear - *peer* There are around 5,000 varieties of pear, but only a few are of commercial importance in Holland. Pears can be classified as **hand pears - *handperen*** or **stewing pears - *stoofperen***. **Hand pears** are mostly eaten as a breakfast food or dessert. As a dessert, they can be prepared in numerous ways. They are baked in fruit tarts, charlottes, mousses, and compotes and are delicious when poached in light sugar and eaten with blue cheese or when poached in raspberry or wine syrups. Pears can also be cooked with chicken and game. They should be picked firm and ripened at room temperature. They are considered ripe when they become soft around the stem. The hand pears most commonly found in Dutch greengrocers are the juicy and slightly sweet **Clapp's Favorite**; the juicy, sweet **Conference**; the sweet, succulent, highly aromatic, firm, fruity-flavored **Doyenne du Comice**; the juicy, sweet **Triomphe de Vienne** and the juicy, aromatic **Bonne Louise**. There are at least two types of stewing pears which appear from year to year; the soft, sweet ***Gieser Wildeman*** and the slightly sour ***Saint Remy***. Their lovely flavor is often not apparent until cooked. Ask your greengrocer about the cooking time. Supermarkets carry **pear nectar** and canned pears. Most pears appear on the market in August and finish by January or February. However, the Conference pear is available through May. You also sometimes see the Asian pear (also known as Chinese, Japanese, Korean, or apple pear) in Holland. They are many varieties that range in color from huge, golden yellow to tiny, yellow green. These pears are very crunchy when you bite into them and are slightly sweet and very juicy.

Persimmon - *kaki* or *Sharon fruit* In late autumn, persimmon trees with their bright orange fruits color the rural landscapes of Korea and Japan. There are two basic types: the *Hachiya* which is elongated and the *Fuyu* which looks more like an orange tomato. Both have orange flesh. A fully-ripe Hachiya is soft and sweet. When firm or under-ripe, it will pucker the mouth. The *Fuyu* may be eaten when it is still firm. Persimmons should have a smooth glossy skin without blemishes. They can be eaten out-of-hand or used in baked goods such as puddings. The Koreans preserve persimmons by hanging them in the sun to dry. In the winter they make a delicious and warming honeyed spiced tea.

Pineapple - *ananas* If any dish is labelled "Hawaiian", you can count on its being flavored or garnished with pineapple. In fact, the Hawaiians didn't see pineapple until the late 1800's when it was imported for local agricultural production. It gets its English name from the pine cone which it resembles. In Holland, it is called *ananas* after the Paraguayan word *nana* which means "excellent fruit". In Chinese cooking, pineapple is roasted with pork and duck or used in **Sweet and Sour Pork**. In the Caribbean, it is baked in brown sugar and rum. Thais stuff scooped out pineapple halves with fried rice and the pineapple flesh and bake it in the oven. Vietnamese flavor soups with it and Indians and Indonesians serve it with curry. Fresh pineapple should be slightly soft and have a strong, sweet aroma. It does not ripen after it is picked. Avoid those which have too much green on the skin. Fresh or frozen pineapple cannot be used for gelatine dishes because its natural enzymes neutralize the gelling. Canned pineapple poses no problems.

Plum - *pruim* and prune - *gedroogde pruim* There are hundreds of varieties of plum; they vary in size, flavor and color. They are smooth-skinned and have soft, moist flesh and large center pits. They can be eaten out-of-hand or used to make delicious tarts, crisps and cobblers or chutneys, jellies and preserves. In China, plums are stewed with apricots, sugar and vinegar to make a plum sauce to accompany roast duck. They are also distilled to make brandies and wines. When buying, avoid those which have breaks in the skin, have soft spots or are discolored. The **prune** is a variety of dried plum. It can be eaten out-of-hand or stewed.

Pomegranate - *granaatappel* The pomegranate is about the size of a large orange. Inside are hundreds of small seeds surrounded by a translucent brilliant-red pulp. The seeds are separated by a bitter white membrane. They can be eaten as a fruit or pressed to extract the tart but sweet juices which are very good with game.

Prickly pear - *cactus or woestijn vijg* The fruit of the prickly pear cactus, it is named for its pear-like shape. It is also known as **cactus pear, Indian fig** or **barbary fig**. The flesh is sweet and moist and it contains small hard edible seeds. It is extremely popular in Mexico, Central and South America, southern Africa and Mediterranean countries. Peel or eat raw with lemon or lime or use it in a dessert sauce.

Rambutan - *ramboetan* A member of the litchee family, rambutan is a tropical Asian fruit that has a tough, red shell with soft, hooked spikes which makes it look like a hairy sea urchin. A cut or tear around the shell reveals a lovely white fruit similar to the lichee. It is eaten out-of-hand. Buy only those that are bright red and the spikes are firm not dried.

VEGETABLES - *GROENTEN*

Artichoke - *artisjok* A member of the thistle family, the artichoke has a green, globular bud surrounded by tough scaly leaves. An artichoke is usually cooked whole, in salt water, allowing one to a diner. Before cooking, the stem is cut off and the sharp leaf points are clipped and rubbed with lemon juice to keep them from discoloring. After cooking each leaf is broken off and dipped in melted butter or mayonnaise and drawn through the teeth to remove any tasty flesh clinging to the part nearest to the core. Finally, when the leaves are all gone, the fuzzy interior is exposed and scraped away and discarded and the tender bottom is then eaten. Raw artichokes are also trimmed of the leaves forming a fiber-free cup which can be cooked, then stuffed to accompany meat dishes. Select fresh artichokes with rich green leaves with no browning. In Holland, they are also sold canned in brine or marinated in olive oil in jars. They are picked when very young and the hearts and buds are tender enough to be eaten whole. They are best when dressed in a vinaigrette and served in an artichoke, artichoke and tomato or mixed green salad.

Asparagus - *asperge* is a member of the lily family. Its shoots range in size from pencil thin to nearly an inch thick. There are basically four kinds: white, green, purple and wild. The **white asparagus** is the height of elegance in Holland, Belgium and Germany where it is prized for its delicate, nutty taste. During the asparagus season, many restaurants in these countries boast of serving up to 200 dishes featuring this lovely white stalk. It is colorless because it is grown underground and is harvested when the tip barely breaks ground. It has a relatively short season; from the beginning of May until 21 June. At this time you can buy it directly from the farmers. The fields are easy to spot because the asparagus grows in long, raised furrows. Most of it is grown in Limburg and Brabant. The stalks have a stringy outer peel which should be removed with a potato peeler before cooking. They should be cooked for 10 minutes or until just tender. In Holland, white asparagus is traditionally served with thinly sliced ham, hard-boiled eggs, new potatoes and melted butter. Allow one pound per person. **Green asparagus** is a relative newcomer here and has yet to be widely known; although in some countries, green asparagus is considered to be a luxury vegetable. Most of the green asparagus sold in Holland comes from Spain. **Purple asparagus**, which is full of flavor, is grown in parts of Italy and in the Loire, Charentes and Aquitaine regions of France. It should be peeled up to the tip. When boiled the tips turn green and the taste is much like broccoli. Purple asparagus is only available here on occasions. A tiny, pencil thin asparagus grown in Thailand has recently made its appearance on the Dutch market although as of this writing it is quite expensive. While asparagus is generally boiled or steamed, it can also be stir-fried or sautéed. When buying asparagus, choose only those that have brittle spears and the tips are tightly closed. The base of the stalks should be moist, not dry. They can be kept refrigerated tightly wrapped in a wet cloth in a plastic bag for three to four days. They are grown in sandy soil so must be thoroughly washed.

Avocado - *avocado* While the avocado grows on trees and is considered a fruit, it is eaten like a vegetable. The two most widely marketed avocados are the **Haas**, which has a rough dark-green to purplish-black skin and the **Fuerta**, which has a thin, smooth, dark-green skin. Both have a smooth, pale-yellow flesh with a buttery flavor. They are picked before they are ripe; to ripen, place them in a paper bag or newspaper with a banana or apple, and keep in a dark spot at room temperature for two or three days. The Haas avocado is ripe when the flesh gives a little when squeezed. In South Africa (which exports avocados) the Fuerta avocado is ripe when the large avocado seed rattles when shaken. The cut flesh darkens quickly so should be added at the last minute or rubbed with lemon, lime or other citrus juices. Avocado is the basis for the Mexican *guacamole dip*, and it is often stuffed with shrimps in mayonnaise or used in cold soups.

Beans - *bonen* Members of the legume family, beans are part of the most important food group. Some are cultivated primarily for their edible pods (snap, string or French or green beans) and others for their seeds (Asian soya, American haricots, European broad or fava beans and Peruvian Lima beans). There are hundreds of varieties and they vary in color and shape and in flavor. Holland doesn't have the bean culture of some of the countries like the United States where producers compete to see how many types of beans they can mix to make a viable commercial soup or stew before the consumers say "enough". However, there are plenty of bean varieties sold in Holland to satisfy everyone.

Beans cultivated for their edible pod (Green beans) The most common **green beans** in Holland are **string or snap beans** which are known as ***sperziebonen*** (also known as *sla-* or *princessenbonen*) and ***snijbonen***. ***Snijbonen*** (meaning cut beans) are long, flat green runner beans that are about ¾-inch wide. They are sold whole or cut diagonally in very thin strips. In American cooking they are called Frenched or French green beans. Less common is the **scarlet runner - *pronkboon*** which is like the *snijboon* but unless picked when very young can be large, rough and stringy.

The Dutch usually overcook their green beans in boiling water; the Italians add them to soups or sauté them with ham; the Chinese stir-fry them with minced pork or oyster sauce; and Indonesians and other Southeast and South Asians braise them in coconut milk and spices. Green beans are mostly eaten fresh but are also frozen or canned. The pale **yellow snap or wax bean - *boterboon*** is usually canned. The **dwarf French green beans** or **haricots vert** are like small snap beans and should be cooked very briefly until the beans turn bright green and then "scared" under cold running water to stop the cooking process. Roll them in a tea towel and refrigerate, and reheat when they are to be used. On the other hand, **Chinese long bean, yard-long bean or asparagus bean - *kouseband*** grows to about 3-feet long. It looks like a green bean but is related to the black-eyed pea. It is mostly sold in Asian stores and it must be young and flexible. It really needs to be cut into 2-inch lengths and stir-fried.

Beans cultivated for their seeds (Asian soya, American haricots, European broad or fava beans and Peruvian Lima beans The **adzuki bean** is a small, sweet-flavored red bean used in Asian cooking to make sweet bean paste for confections. Adzuki beans are mostly sold in Asian shops. **Black or turtle beans - *zwarte bonen*** are small with jet-black skin and a cream-colored flesh. They are popular in the Caribbean, Mexico, Central and South America and the southern United States where they are used to make soups, stews and salads. They are available in Holland, either tinned or dried, in shops which cater to these cuisines and some Asian stores. The small, cream-colored **black-eyed pea - *zwarte ogenboon*** or **cow pea** with a central black eye and earthy flavor is popular in Africa and the southern United States where it is often cooked with ham in soups, stews and salads. They are sold in some supermarkets, Asian and Middle Eastern stores, shops that cater to North Americans and at stalls in open markets. ***Tuinbonen*** are the most common **broad or fava beans** which are cultivated for their seeds. They look like **lima beans - *lima bonen*** but taste quite different. They are shelled and the tough outer skin of the bean may be removed. They are available fresh, frozen or canned. **Brown bean - *bruine boon*** and **white bean - *witte boon*** are American haricots which are very popular here. They are mostly used in soups but are very good in **Boston Baked Beans**. They are available dried or canned. **Kidney beans - *kidney or nier bonen*** are the seed of a common shell bean. It is easily identified by its kidney shape and color. There is also an Italian white kidney bean which is called *cannellini* but it is not widely distributed here. Supermarkets sell tinned red kidney beans, sometimes in chili sauce, and the Asian stores carry them tinned or dried. They are always associated with the Tex/Mex dishes of **Chili con Carne** and **Refried Beans** but are appealing in other soups, stews and in salads. Also popular in Tex/Mex cooking is the **pinto bean - *kieviet boon*** which is a pretty, mottled reddish-brown and pink bean. Alas, they lose their mottled appearance once they are cooked. They can be used interchangeably with kidney beans in American Southwestern and Mexican cooking in soups, stews and chili with beans or meat. The **Lima bean - *lima boon*** is a Peruvian bean (also called butter bean) which is relatively large, light green and kidney shaped. They can be used in soups and stews but are also nice served hot and dressed with butter or in salads with a vinaigrette dressing. Americans use them in the native dish, **Succotash**. They are sold in tins or dried in some Asian stores and those which cater to North Americans. **Mung beans - *katjang idjo* (Indonesian)** are green, yellow or black in color and are most commonly used to grow bean sprouts. They are also ground into flour and turned into Chinese noodles or Korean mung bean pancakes. They are mostly sold in Asian shops and health food stores. The Asian **soy bean - *soya boon*** has a dark green pod covered with a grey soft fuzz. They are rather bland when cooked but they have a firm texture. Dried soy beans can be substituted for lima, fava or other dried beans in soups, stews, casseroles, etc. Dried soy beans can also be sprouted and used in salads, stir-fried dishes, or used as vegetables. Soy beans and soy bean by-products are sold in Asian and health food shops.

Bean and seed sprouts are the crisp, tender sprouts of various germinated beans and seeds. There are several varieties of sprouts and mixes on the Dutch market, namely **mung bean**, **alfalfa**, **radish seed, shiso green and red** (from the perilla or beefsteak plant), red beet sprouts – *rode biet kiemen* and an interesting **bean sprout mix**. The **mung bean sprouts - *taugé*** are the most common and are widely used in Asian cooking. When fresh, the sprouts with buds attached should be crisp and white with no brown areas. Any brown ends of root should be pinched off. Canned mung bean sprouts are also available but do not compare with the fresh. **Alfalfa sprouts - *alfalfa groente*** and **shiso green - *groen*** and **red - *purper*** are sold in their soil in small plastic tubs. They are cut off at the base and are mostly used in sandwiches and green salads. The red beet sprouts are an interesting new addition. A local **bean sprout mix - *kiemmix*** consisting of mung beans, chick peas and white beans can be stir-fried in butter or used in salads and sandwiches. **Radish seed sprouts - *radijssla*** have a definite radish flavor and they can be used like alfalfa sprouts. Sprouts are sold in supermarkets, greengrocers and health food stores. Refrigerate for no more than two days.

Beet - *biet* The beet commonly available in supermarkets and grocery stores in Holland is the **red beet or garden beet - *rode biet***, a root vegetable with a beautiful garnet flesh and edible green leaves. They sell fresh or cooked - *gare* beets here. Fresh beets should be gently cooked in their skins to prevent color and nutrient loss and then peeled and used in salads or served hot with a sweet and sour sauce. They are the principle ingredient of the famous Russian beet soup, ***Borscht***. When fresh they will keep, refrigerated, three to four weeks; when cooked, one or two days. Young beet leaves can be added to borscht or eaten raw in salad. Older leaves must be cooked and are served cold with lemon and oil or hot with butter and oil.

Broccoli - *broccoli* When George Bush was President, he announced to the world that his mother always made him eat broccoli and now that he was President of the United States he didn't have to eat it. In response, American broccoli growers sent truckloads of this wonderful vegetable to the White House. Studies quickly proved that it is one of nature's most nutritious gifts. A member of the cabbage family, there are several varieties. That which is commonly sold locally has a thick green stalk with flowering green or purplish-green heads. Don't buy them if the seeds have started to yellow. The flowerets are cut away from the stalks and are usually used separately; but, the stalks can also be peeled, chopped and cooked with the flowerets. Broccoli can be steamed (to retain its rich color) and served with cheese or Hollandaise sauce, sautéed in butter and garlic, baked with a bread crumb topping (*au gratin*) or used in broccoli soup.

Brussels sprouts - *spruitjes* This diminutive member of the cabbage family, consists of numerous mini-heads that grow around one thick, long stalk. Locals say they are best when picked after the first frost. They should be small with bright green outer leaves. Any outer discolored leaves should be discarded. They can be kept, refrigerated, for no longer than three days. Cooked sprouts, Belgian-style, are often embellished with glazed chestnuts or sliced almonds. A small ***x*** cut across the base ensures even cooking and less separation. Whatever you do, don't overcook them. Brussels sprouts are sold fresh or frozen.

Cabbage - *kool* The cabbage or brassica family is one of the oldest vegetables cultivated by man. This large family includes green, red and white cabbage; Chinese cabbage; and kale. The common **white or Dutch cabbage - *witte kool*** has a large, round, tightly-packed head. It is generally combined with savoy cabbage to make sauerkraut. The **pointed-head green cabbage - *spitskool*,** on the other hand, is loosely packed like the round-headed green cabbage favored in North America. It is a spring cabbage that can be baked, stewed or stir-fried by itself or with other vegetables, used in stews and soups or it can be shredded and eaten raw in coleslaw. Individual leaves can be also be blanched and filled with any of variety of meat and/or rice stuffings, then rolled and braised. **Green cabbage - *groene kool*** and **Savoy cabbage - *Savooie kool*** can be used in much the same manner as *spitskool*. They have pretty green, ribbed crinkly leaves that lighten the closer you get to the heart. They are often confused with each other. They are so beautiful that porcelain serving bowls have been made in their image. **Sauerkraut - *zuurkool*** is shredded cabbage aged in vats in a salt brine. It is sold here in plastic bags packed in wine or with spices. Some greengrocers sell it fresh from the vat. It can be rinsed before cooking to wash away the brine. **Curly kale - boerenkool** is a very popular winter vegetable in Holland. ***Stamppot boerenkool met worst*** (chopped curly kale cooked with browned onion, bacon, smoked sausage and potatoes) is one of Holland's national dishes. It is best after the first frost. **Red cabbage** - ***rode kool*** ranges from red to very dark purple. It can be pickled or eaten raw in salads. It is also braised, steamed or sautéed. Sometimes it is stewed with vinegar, apples and sugar to give it a sweet and sour taste. Lemon juice or vinegar added to the cooking water will help preserve its color. **Chinese cabbage - *Chinese kool*,** also known as **napa cabbage, Chinese leaves or Peking cabbage (*pe-tsai*)** is a long plump or thin cabbage with tightly packed green crinkly leaves running up and down wide white stalks. It is widely used in Chinese soups or braised with mixed vegetables. Chinese cabbage is sometimes confused with its relative ***bok choy, bok choi*** or ***paksoi***, also known as **Chinese white cabbage** or white mustard cabbage. Bok choy has a long, milky white stem and large crinkly green leaves like Swiss chard. It has a light fresh taste and can be stir-fried then flavored with soy sauce, salt, garlic and chicken stock. A miniature variation is very nice braised. See also Exotic Asian Vegetables in Chapter IV. 15.

Carrot - *worteltje or peen* The carrot is a root vegetable with lacy, bright-green leaves. There are several types on the market. There are the ***bospeen*** which are sold in bunches with their leaves attached, the ***waspeen*** which are *bospeen* that have the leaves removed and are washed and scrubbed, and the large **winter carrots - *winterpeen*** which are used for stews and soups. The larger winter carrots are bospeen which have been left in the ground longer. They become less sweet as they age. There is also small marble-sized carrots, ***mini worteltjes*** or ***parisienne*** that are used in soups but are associated with ***Poularde à la bonne femme*** (a French chicken, pearl onion, mushroom, potato and bacon or salt pork stew which calls for the vegetables to be cut to the size of olives).

Cauliflower - *bloemkool* is a member of the cabbage family and is composed of small white flowerets which grow on stalks in compact rounded heads. Cauliflower can be cooked or steamed whole and served in one piece or the flowerets can be cut and cooked separately. It is then dressed with cheese sauce, Hollandaise sauce, vinaigrette, or simply with melted butter. A teaspoon of lemon and ¼ cup of milk added to the cooking water will help to preserve its whiteness. Blanched cauliflower flowerets are served as part of a ***crudités*** assortment with a dipping sauce, or stir-fried in butter with garlic. They can also be used in cauliflower or vegetable soups.

Celery - *selderij* There are three types of celery on the market: **stalk celery - *bleekselderij*** with long, crisp, green-leaved ribs around a tender heart; the **leafy soup green - *selderij***; and **celery root** or **celeriac - *knolselderij***. The **stalk celery** sold here is undergoing a transformation. It was formerly the golden variety where the plant was covered and not exposed to sunlight to keep it from turning green, thus the term *bleek* or pale. Now it is mostly sold green. Celery ribs can be eaten raw, stuffed with cream cheese and served as hors d'oeuvre, or used in salads. They can be used to flavor soups, stews and stuffings. The **leafy soup green** which is more an herb than a vegetable and the **celery root** or **celeriac** are essential flavorings in **Dutch Pea Soup**. Poached, grated celeriac can also be dressed with mayonnaise to make a delicious salad.

Chicory, **Belgian** or **French endive - *witlof*, escarole - *andijvie*, curly endive - *krul andijvie*** and **radicchio - *roodlof*** are often confused with each other. They are members of the *chicory* family of which there are two kinds: one which is grown for its root (**chicory**) and the other which is grown for its leaves (**Belgian** or **French endive**, **escarole**, **curly endive** and **radicchio**). Raw **chicory root** is rarely sold commercially, but is dried and powdered and used as a substitute for coffee or as an additive. The **Belgian** or **French endive - *witlof*** or ***Brusselslof*** (called **chicory** in the U.K.) is the blanched shoot of the chicory root. The root is dug up and stored in a dark room until the shoot is about six inches in length. It is shiny and firm and has light green unblemished stalks with white ribs. **Witlof met ham en kaas saus** is a popular Dutch dish of steamed or boiled Belgian endives wrapped in ham and baked in a creamy cheese sauce. Before cooking, about 1/4 to 1/2 inch of the core is removed with the tip of a sharp knife or the cooked *witlof* will be very bitter. Lemon juice added to the cooking water helps prevent discoloration. Whole raw leaves can be used in salads or as finger food with dollops of cream cheese on the base. **Escarole or flat chicory - *andijvie*** (also known as Batavian endive in Britain) is a sturdy salad green with broad, wavy, jagged-edged, crispy, pale-green leaves. It is similar to the curly endive but has a milder, slightly bitter taste. It can be chopped and added raw to a dish of mashed potatoes mixed with strips of browned bacon to make ***Spekkie sla***, a Gelderland dish. Wilted escarole can also be added to vegetable soups. **Curly endive or *frisée* - *krul andijvie*** is often called *chicory* in the United States and **endive** in England. There are several winter and summer varieties. Basically, it has a white or yellow heart with thin, frizzy, spiked, yellow leaves in the center which darken to green near the outside. The leaves are slightly bitter. It can be used as a salad green in a mixed green salad or alone with a vinaigrette made with mustard, oil and garlic. It can also be braised. **Radicchio - *radicchio* or *roodlof*** is a red-leafed Italian chicory. The Vaneto variety sold here has a small round burgundy head with white ribs. The narrow, pointed, elongated leaves of the **radicchio de Treviso - *Trevisla***, on the other hand, grow from a thick stock. They are somewhat bitter but make an attractive garnish or addition to salads.

Corn - *mais* Corn is one of the New World's gifts to mankind. It is important as a whole grain. Without it we would not have corn oil, corn flour, cornmeal, cornstarch, corn bread and corn whisky. Yet it is not wildly popular in Europe and thus good corn is hard to find. There are two basic types: **field corn and sweet corn - *zoete mais* or corn on the cob - *maiskolven***. Most corn grown here is **field corn** for animal feed. The Israeli sweet corn is very good when it is available but it is expensive. Often it is not very fresh. To test for freshness, a milky substance should ooze out of the kernels when pricked. The silk should be moist and golden brown; the husks fresh and green. There is also some good frozen sweet corn on the cob and cut corn that is either frozen or canned. Watch out for the locally-canned "crispy" corn for it is an acquired taste. **Baby corn - *babymais*** can be purchased in cans or jars in some supermarkets and in Asian stores. **Popcorn** becomes light and puffy when heated in oil. It is generally imported from the United States and is sold in the health food section of supermarkets and in health food shops.

Corn salad, field lettuce, lamb's lettuce or mâche - *veldsla*. There is some confusion regarding this small leafy green. Some greengrocers call lamb's lettuce *veldsla* although it technically should be called *ezeloren* (donkey's ears) or *grof veldsla*. It grows in clusters and its sweet, nutty-tasting, tongue-shaped leaves can be eaten raw in salads or steamed and eaten like spinach. There is another *veldsla* with small leaves and long stems which is also known as *Amsterdamse vet* and *broeivet.* What the Dutch call ***lamsoren*** **(lamb's ears)** is the **sea aster** - ***zeeaster*** which grows in the wetlands.

Cress - ***kers*** is any of a number of members of the mustard family. The best known is **watercress** - ***waterkers*** which grows wild in freshwater streams. It has small, crispy, green leaves which have a distinct peppery flavor. It is used mainly as a salad or sandwich green. Unfortunately, it is not widely distributed in Holland. Some health food stores carry it. **Garden cress** - ***tuinkers*** **or** ***sterrekers*** is a smaller purple or green relative which is sold in Holland in small plastic containers like the alfalfa sprouts. It can be clipped at the base of the bloom and used in salads and sandwiches or as a garnish.

Cucumber - ***komkommer*** The cucumber is a gourd related to pumpkin, zucchini and other squashes. Those grown here are of two varieties: **eating or slicing** and **pickling**. The **eating or slicing cucumber** sold in Holland is the long, thin-skinned English cucumber which is generally used in salads or sandwiches. It can also be sautéed in butter or baked (*au gratin*) and makes a wonderful cold cucumber soup. If firm with no soft spots when purchased, it will last, refrigerated, for one week. The **pickling** varieties such as **gherkin** - ***augurk*** and ***cornichon*** (small French pickle) are available in jars. They are either sour or sweet/sour. Large sour gherkins called *zure bommen* are sold out of large jars by the piece. **Dill pickles** are available at specialty food stores that cater to expatriates.

Eggplant - ***aubergine*** The eggplant belongs to the night shade family. Thus, while it is eaten as a vegetable, it is actually a fruit. It varies in size and shape from the small Thai pea-sized eggplants to those the size and shape of eggs and to the larger fruits the size of a melon. In color they can vary from white, green and yellow to deep purple. In Holland, the large, globular purple eggplant is most common. When young, the dark skin can be eaten. As it ages, the skin toughens and the flesh becomes bitter. Older eggplants can be salted and rinsed after 20 minutes to eliminate the acrid taste. They should be cut just before cooking because the flesh discolors. Sliced eggplant can be baked in casseroles or dipped in egg and flour and fried in butter. Halved eggplants can be baked with tomato sauce, garlic, oil and herbs. They give depth to the Mediterranean vegetable stew ***Ratatouille*** and add character to minced lamb in the Greek ***Moussaka***. In the Middle East, grilled eggplants are mashed and mixed with sesame seed paste - *tahini*, lemon, garlic and oil to make the flavorful dip, ***Baba Ghannouj***. Tahini can be purchased at health food stores and Mid-Eastern markets. The Asian varieties which are elongated or egg-shaped are smaller and sweeter than the European. The Thai pea-sized eggplants are added whole to curries and raw to chili sauces. The others can be cooked, baked, grilled or braised. Some Indonesians eat the egg-sized eggplants raw. They are generally available in Asian stores that carry other vegetables.

Fennel - ***venkelknol*** There are two basic types of fennel: the **Florence fennel** or ***finocchio*** and the **common fennel**. **Florence fennel** is valued for its leaves, bulb, flower, seeds and celery-like stems; the **common fennel** for its stems and greenery. Fennel has an anise-like flavor but is sweeter and more delicate than anise; and when cooked, the taste is subdued. The bulbs of the Florence fennel can be cut into slices or wedges and braised in olive oil, baked in butter with bread crumbs (au gratin), sautéed with other vegetables or added to soups and stews. Young fennel bulbs and stems are used raw in salads or dipped in a vinaigrette. Common fennel seeds are used in pickling spices or to flavor liqueurs.

Garlic - *knoflook* A member of the lily family, garlic is related to onion, leek, green or spring onion and shallot. It has a bulb with several cloves - *teentjes* surrounded by a parchment-like skin. When selecting garlic, choose bulbs which are firm and free from the gray, powdery mold which sometimes collects between the cloves. Much of the garlic used in Holland is grown in France and Spain. There are three main varieties which are all grown in France: a garlic which has a white or greyish skin, a pink garlic with a mauve-colored skin and a garlic with reddish-brown skin. The white-skinned French garlic is considered to be less pungent than the others and the white skinned Spanish garlic is even milder. You often don't have a choice of garlic in the greengrocers for most only carry one type at a time. The most common white-skinned garlic grown in the United States is more pungent than its Spanish and French white-skinned cousins. Thus, you may have to compensate when using American recipes. Pressed, chopped or crushed garlic is stronger than whole garlic cloves or sliced garlic. For a mild garlic flavor, lightly brown the whole cloves in butter and/or oil or roast them in the oven. Remove them from the pan just before adding the other ingredients. Fully roasted, whole, unpeeled garlic cloves are wonderful when spread over French bread. Garlic can be purchased fresh by the bulb, or minced into a **paste - *knoflook pasta*** and preserved in a jar. **Garlic salt - *knoflookzout*** and **garlic powder - *knoflook poeder*** are also available.

Kohlrabi or **cabbage turnip - *koolrabi*** is a member of the cabbage family but its flavor is more like a mild turnip. It is not a root vegetable but has a bulbous stem with a light green peel and grows above ground. It is commonly steamed and dressed with butter or a white sauce. It can be used in place of turnip in soups and stews or can be eaten raw.

Leek - *prei* is native to the Mediterranean area and it has been prized by European gourmets for centuries. Nero loved leeks not only for their flavor but because he thought they would improve his singing voice. Unfortunately, leeks are still relatively hard to find in North American markets. They look like giant spring or green onions but their taste is much more subtle. They are generally used in soups and casseroles. The younger, thinner leeks can also be grilled, baked (*au gratin*) or steamed and served warm or cold with a heated olive oil, lemon juice and mustard vinaigrette sauce. Generally, only the white root and a couple of inches of light green leaves are used. Sand tends to gather between the leaves so they must be washed thoroughly. Try slicing the root lengthwise to the core or center leaves; then fold the leaves back and rinse them one by one but keep the round leek intact.

Lentil - *linze* is a tiny flat pulse or legume which is very high in protein. It is always dried. Commonly sold here is the brown **German lentil** which is normally used in lentil soups, stews and salads. Some stores might carry the small slate-green **French lentils or *lentilles de Puy***. They can be used interchangeably with German lentils. The yellowish-red **Egyptian lentils**, best suited for soups and purées such as the spicy **Indian *dals***, are sold in Middle Eastern or Asian stores.

Lettuce - *sla* There are hundreds of varieties of lettuce but the main types that find their ways to Dutch markets are **butterhead, cabbage** or **round lettuce** which includes Bibb, Boston or limestone; **crisphead** such as **iceberg**; **loose-leaf** such as **red leaf, oak leaf, red** and **green lollo rosso** and long-leaf such as **Cos** or **romaine.** The local **butterhead lettuce - *kropsla*** has soft, delicate, loose, green outer leaves and yellow leaves near the heart. It is the most widely used salad lettuce here. It is also considered to be **cooking lettuce - *stoof sla*** meaning that it can be steamed or cut into strips and mixed with hot mashed potatoes flavored with fried bacon strips or can be added at the last minute to add color to some soups. **Iceberg - *ijsbergsla*** is a crisphead lettuce with tightly packed, succulent, crisp leaves. It is mostly used in salads and sandwiches, but the Chinese parboil it and flavor it with oil and oyster sauce. **Red leaf - *rode*** or ***Bataafse rood*, oak leaf - *eikenbladsla*** and **lollo red and green - *lollo rosso*** and ***biondo*** are looseleaf lettuces which grow on stems and have no central heart. They make a lovely addition to mixed green salads. **Cos - *cos sla*** or **romaine lettuce - *sla romaine*** forms an elongated head and has crisp, dark-green leaves. It is generally associated with Caesar Salad. Unfortunately, cos lettuce is not so common here and may need to be special-ordered.

Mushroom - *paddestoel* A member of the fungus family, mushroom varieties number in the thousands. There are basically three types: **common cultivated mushroom**, **cultivated mushroom** (which used to grow only in the wild) and **wild mushroom**. **Common cultivated mushroom varieties** on the market in Holland are the ***champignon***, **chestnut - *kastanje*** and **crimini** and **portobello** (an adult version of the crimini). The very large common mushrooms might also be known here as ***reuzenchampignons***. Common mushrooms are good in pizzas, stews, sauces, stir-fries, soups and stuffings. The portobello is dramatic when brushed with oil and grilled. **Cultivated mushrooms** include **oyster - *oesterzwammen*** and **shiitake**. The pale grey **oyster mushroom** should not be sliced but gently torn from the lip to the base with the grain of the gills. It, like shiitake, porcini and chanterelle mushrooms are best when simply sautéed in butter with minced garlic and shallots and served on toast or pasta. The **shiitake** or **golden oak mushroom** grows wild in Korea and Japan. It has a delicious, slightly smokey flavor and can be grilled or baked or used in soups or stews. Shiitakes are either sold fresh at the greengrocer or dried in the Asian stores. They are sometimes referred to as Chinese black mushrooms. **Wild mushrooms** include **truffles - *truffels*, morels - *morieltjes*, porcini (*bolete or cèpes*) - *eekhoorntjesbrood***,

chanterelles - ***cantharellen*****, hedge hog (sweet tooth, wood urchin, pigs trotter)** - ***pied du mouton*****, lion´s mane (monkey´s head,** ***yamabuchi-take*****)** - ***pom pom blanc***, and **trumpets of death or horn of plenty** - ***trompette de la morts*** **or** ***hoorn van overvloed.*** **Truffles** are among the most highly prized and expensive foods in the world. They grow underground and truffle hunting is carried out in the age old tradition where pigs and dogs sniff them out. The superior French black and Italian white truffles are best when shaved or grated raw and dressed with a walnut oil dressing then scattered over salads, cheese fondue or pasta. The **morel** is related to the truffle. It is conical in shape. Gourmets love it for its earthy, nutty flavor. After the truffle and morel, the **porcini** are the most highly prized. They can range from one ounce to one pound. They have a meaty texture and earthy flavor and can also be used in soups and stews. The **chantarelle** or **girole** is respected for its delicate, perfumed taste. Chanterelles can be rather tough so should not be cooked too long. They and the dark **horn of plenty** can be baked, stir-fried and broiled and used in soups and stews. Sometimes called winter chantarelle, the **pied du mouton** actually looks like a chantarelle and can be used in much the same manner. The **lion´s mane** is a pretty puffy mushroom which deserves its French name, *pom pom blanc*. Mushrooms lovers are attracted to its lobster-like flavor when cooked. Slice across the cascading teeth for a lacy appearance. Like the other wild mushrooms, simple preparations are the best. All fresh mushrooms should be plump and firm and not dry, moldy or discolored. Dried mushrooms can be reconstituted by soaking in warm water for 20 minutes. Most of the wild mushrooms are available dried. Since they are expensive, they usually have to be special ordered. One pound fresh common mushrooms equals about six cups sliced and two cups cooked.

Okra - ***okra*** is native to Africa. It was widely used in Africa and the Middle East and in the plantation cooking which is still popular in the American South. It has a green pod and a tapered oblong shape. Okra can be fried in cornmeal or used in stews and soups. It is not widely available in Holland. Check in shops and markets that cater to Middle Eastern, Indian and Caribbean cuisines.

Onion(s) - ui(en) The onion is related to the lily and comes from an extensive family which includes chive, garlic, shallot, leek and scallion, spring or green onion. They are all used worldwide to flavor salads, soups, stews, sauces, vegetables, meats, savory tarts and salad dressings. **Dry onions** are mature onions which are covered with a dry papery skin. They can come in various shapes, colors and forms. However, when it comes to onions, the local markets are not very creative. Generally what you will find are the bronze-skinned globular or elongated yellow onions and the common white simply known as ***ui***, the Italian or Spanish **red** or **purple onion** - ***rode ui*** and the tiny white **pearl** or **silver onion** - ***zilveruitje***. Some greengrocers are now selling **sweet onions** - ***zoete uien***. The pearl onion is only available for a very short period but they are usually pickled. Pearl onions can be peeled and frozen and used in stews. Dried or freeze-dried **onion**

flakes - ***uien vlokken*** and **onion powder** - ***uien poeder*** are also available in the supermarkets. See also chive, leek, scallion, shallot.

Parsnip - ***pastinaak* or *witte peen*** is a pale-ivory member of the carrot family. Some are long like carrots while others are round and chubby. When cooked, parsnip tastes like a cross between a carrot and a sweet potato. Parsnips can be peeled, sliced and cooked like carrots; or they can be used in soups and stews. They are difficult to find in Holland but can be special ordered.

Peas - ***erwten*** There are many varieties of peas, all are members of the legume family. Most peas are picked from their pods; but the **Chinese snow peas** - ***peultjes*** and **sugar snap peas** (called sugar snaps here) are cooked and eaten pod and all. The most popular Dutch pea is the small ***doperwt* or *petits pois*** that remain sweet after they are picked. They are mostly sold frozen or canned. However, the **English** or **common garden peas** - ***tuinerwtjes*** (which are like the peas favored in North America) are now available in the frozen food section of the supermarket. These peas can be simply cooked in butter or with a cream sauce, cooked with bacon, pearl onions or carrots or cooked in a fresh pea soup and flavored with mint. They are a classic accompaniment to lamb, veal and poultry. There might be some confusion on the origin of **snow peas** – ***hoh laan dau* (C), *he lan dau* (M)** for the Cantonese name translates as "Holland bean" (say it fast *hoh lan dau*, *dau* meaning bean).They, however, have been cultivated in China since the 7th century AD. There are basically two types in the Chinese shops: robust and dainty; the dainty being the most tender. You might not always have a choice. The dainty peas can be eaten raw or cooked. They are also stir-fried with meat, poultry and/or seafood or simply sautéed in a little butter. They and the sugar snap peas should only be cooked briefly and can also be used raw in salads. The larger field peas like the **green pea** - ***groene erwt*** and **yellow pea** - ***gele erwt*** are usually dried and **split** - ***spliterwten***. ***Kapucijners*** are a type of **marrowfat pea** originally from Turkey which are now a part of the Dutch cuisine. They are available fresh and dried. When fresh, they are green and can be cooked as ordinary garden peas. They get their name from their color for, when dried, they resemble the light, cocoa-colored robes of the capuchin monks. They look like chick peas or garbanzo beans when dried. The ***kapucijnertafel*** is a popular way of eating *kapucijners*. It resembles the famous Indonesian *rijsttafel* in presentation except the *kapucijners* are used in place of rice. They are accompanied by several side dishes; i.e., fried bacon, meat balls, Vienna sausages, pickled onions, piccalilli and pickled cucumbers. **Chick peas** or **garbanzos** - ***kikkererwten*** are widely available in supermarkets, health food shops, greengrocers and shops which cater to expatriates and Mediterranean or Middle Eastern cuisines.

Pepper, sweet - ***paprika*** Sweet peppers are members of the capsicum family and they grow in abundance here, albeit in greenhouses. They are grown on cotton as part of the feeding system and the lights in the greenhouses are kept on at night so that they have to grow 24 hours a day.

Peppers are classified as sweet or hot. **Sweet peppers** can be **green - *groen*, red - *rood*** and **yellow - *geel***. Lately there have been some orange and even purple bell peppers on the market. They are commonly called **bell peppers** because of their bell-like shape. Don't confuse them with the name also used for the ground spice of capsicum peppers - *paprika*. Green peppers are less sweet than red peppers; red peppers are simply green peppers which have ripened and reddened with age. Bell peppers are used all around the world. Asian cooks use them with other vegetables in stir-fries. In Japan they are dipped in tempura batter and deep-fried; and in Korea, they are stuffed with minced or ground beef, dipped in egg and fried. Mediterranean cooks roast and peel them and serve them in stews and salads. **Pimiento** or **pimento - *zoete rode paprika*** is a large heart-shaped, bright orange, sweet pepper. Its flesh is thicker than that of the bell pepper. It shouldn't be confused with the pimento tree from which allspice comes. Peeled, bottled pimento is sold in supermarkets and specialty shops in Holland. However, red peppers are sometimes canned under the pimento name. You can tell the difference by the color. The rather longish sweet peppers favored in Middle European and Middle Eastern or Mediterranean cuisines are available at the Middle Eastern shops and market stalls and some greengrocers.

Peppers, hot - *Spaanse peper/lombok* Also members of the capsicum family, these hotter varieties are used mainly in flavoring although some are mild enough to be eaten as a vegetable. They are mostly sold as fresh green, fresh red and dried. The most common fresh **chili peppers** sold here are the slim, relatively mild peppers about 3 to 4 inches (7.5 to 10 centimeters) long and the tiny, fiery Asian chilies known here as *cabé* and *cabé rawit* (*cabé rawit* being smaller and hotter). If you can't stand the heat, the seeds and membranes can be removed to make the chili less hot. Fresh peppers should have smooth, full skins without cracks and should be firm and shiny. Dried chili peppers should be orange red all over. The capsaicin in chilies irritates the skin, and burns to the tongue or eyes can be severe. In Korea, cooks rub moistened salt over the hands to remove the capsaicin from cracks and crevices. Rubber gloves are, of course, more effective. More easy to use are the canned **green chilies** for Mexican foods and the ***pepperoncini***, ***Tabasco*** and ***jalapeño*** which are available in many specialty foods or gourmet shops.

Potato - *aardappel* One of Europe's major food crops, there are now hundreds of varieties of potatoes. When selecting them remember that the Dutch effectively steam their potatoes by placing them whole in a half-inch of water. They are covered, brought to a boil and then cooked over a reduced heat for about 20 minutes. They are drained, returned to a very low heat and the saucepan is shaken until the potatoes are dry and flaky on the outside. The potatoes used for this type of cooking are known as *afkokers* or *droogkokers*. Those that are not *afkokers* are identified as *kookt niet af*. Potatoes that are best suited for **baking** are described as *aardappelen om te poffen*. Potatoes for **mashing** are called *aarappelen om to pureeren*. Like everything else, potatoes have their bad years. As a rule it is a good idea to ask your greengrocer for advice on the best potatoes for each application. Potatoes are also seasonal and after the year's crop of Dutch potatoes are used up, potatoes from Cyprus and Malta are imported until the new crops are in. Potatoes that are designated as ***kookt niet af*** include the following: **Alpha** is a powdery potato but does not cook off and is good for boiling, frying and mashing or puréeing. **Bildstar** is a good potato for scalloped potatoes and hash browns. **Eersteling**, which is similar to the Bintje, is neither too mealy nor too powdery and it can be steamed or used for cottage fried potatoes, French fries or potato salad. **Gloria** is a firm potato which is good for pan-frying and French fries. **Kleibintje** and **superbintje** are members of the **Bintje** family. The *klei* or clay means that the potatoes are grown in clayey soil. Bintjes are good for French fries (*frites*) especially the larger ***zelf bak*** Bintjes which are sometimes sold at stalls in open markets. **Resonant** is powdery but does not become flaky when cooked. It can be boiled or fried and is especially good for mashed or puréed potatoes. **Super arkula** is similar to the *bintje* and is best when cooked, pan-fried or deep-fried. Probably the most popular ***afkoker*** is the **Eigenheimer**. It is a mealy, but tasty, potato and is excellent for mashed or puréed potatoes. For better results, add warm milk to the potatoes before mashing. **Dore** is a delicious but mealy potato that can be boiled, pan-fried or mashed. **Irene** is a reddish-skinned potato which crumbles rather quickly when boiled. Steam it gently or boil it for mashed potatoes. **Nicola** is a good all-purpose potato. Greengrocers and supermarkets also sell **peeled or scrubbed new potatoes** - ***nieuwe aardappelen*** or ***krieltjes***, among others. They are either kept in sinks with running water to keep them from discoloring or are vacuum packed. The vacuum packed potatoes have a shelf life of several days.

Pumpkin - ***pompoen*** **see Squash.**

Purslane - ***postelein*** is a leafy plant with a slightly spicy flavor. It can be cooked like spinach or used as a salad green with a vinaigrette dressing. The leaves are also used as a garnish.

Radish - ***radijs*** Most people are familiar with the small, round or elongated, red-skinned (with or without white tip) **radish** - ***radijs*** which is usually used for garnishes, sandwiches and salads. In Holland, there are two additional kinds of radish. The large **white winter radish** or ***rettich*** resembles the winter carrot but is bigger. In taste it can be compared with the large Asian radish. This radish can be sliced and eaten raw; but in Korea, it is grated and mixed with grated carrot, soy sauce, sugar, red pepper powder, green onions, garlic, vinegar and sesame seeds to make a lovely summer salad or used to make one of many types of Korean preserved vegetables or ***Kimchee***. It can be cooked like a turnip or pickled like the Japanese ***daikon***. The **black-skinned radish** - ***ramenas***, when peeled, reveals a white flesh. It tastes like the small radish but is stronger in flavor. It can be used in sandwiches and in salads.

Rhubarb - ***rabarber*** is a hardy perennial vegetable which is treated like a fruit. Its long celery-like stalks are edible but its roots and leaves are toxic. The flesh of the stalk is very sour. It was the English who first started using it in sweetened compotes and sauces and the Americans who started mixing it with strawberries or pineapple in pies. Look for rhubarb that has crisp unblemished stalks.

Rutabaga, **Swede** or **Swedish turnip** - ***koolraap*** is a member of the cabbage family and is thought to be a cross between wild cabbage and wild turnip. Its flesh is golden and slightly sweet. Its skin is yellow with purple at the stem end. It can be peeled, boiled and served with butter or a white sauce or used in any way suited for turnips but takes longer to cook. It is especially good in soups and stews.

Samphire - ***zeekraal*** There are two types of samphire: one grows along the coasts of Great Britain and Northern Europe and is known as **rock samphire** and the other is **salicornia** (also called Marsh samphire or glasswort) which grows in the United States. Samphire has spiked green leaves or stems and looks like a small cactus without the needles. It is eaten like a vegetable and has a crisp aromatic taste that goes well with seafood. It is sold fresh or pickled in seafood shops and fresh at greengrocers.

Salsify or oyster plant - ***schorseneer*** is a root vegetable of which there are two varieties: the white-skinned **true salsify** and the black-skinned **scorzonera**. The latter is easier to peel and is most commonly found in Holland. It gets its name from the Catalan word *escorso*, or viper, for it was formerly used to treat snake bites. They can be peeled and boiled and served with butter or baked with bread crumbs or cheese topping (*au gratin*) or baked in savory pies. In Italy, they are dressed in lemon juice and olive oil.

Scallion, spring onion and green onion These are all members of the onion family and are frequently confused with each other. The scallion is a distinct variety with a straight base while spring or green onions are actually immature onions and show the beginnings of the onion bulb. The scallion is milder and sweeter but since you rarely get scallions here, the green or spring onion - *sla-*, *lente-* or *bos-uitjes* or even leeks can be substituted. Scallions are native to Asia and about the only place you might find them in Holland are in the Chinese stores, ask for *tsung*, *cheong* (C) or cong (M). They are indispensable to the cooking of many Asian countries. Both the white and green parts are used to flavor many meat, poultry, sea food dishes or are used as garnishes on soups.

Shallot - ***sjalot*** The pungent **shallot** - ***sjalot*** is a member of the onion family but is quite different from the onion. It is actually formed more like garlic in that it has two or more cloves. Shallots are highly prized in French cooking and are essential to certain butter sauces. French recipes will tell you not to brown the shallots, but the Indonesians fry them until crisp and sprinkle them over fried rice, fried noodles and chicken soup. When a recipe calls for the small **Indonesian red onion** - ***bawang merah***, you can use the European shallot although they are not quite the same.

Sorrel - ***zuring*** is a member of the buckwheat family of which there are several varieties. The **garden** or **belleville sorrel**, also called *sour dock* or *sour grass*, is more commonly found in Northern Europe. It has the strongest flavor. Sorrel is considered both an herb and a vegetable and is cooked like spinach. However, its lemon-like tang is especially pleasing in cream soups, sauces and fish stuffings. A few leaves can also be used to freshen up green salads. If the leaves are shiny and firm when purchased, they will keep refrigerated for several days. Cooked, canned sorrel is sometimes sold in specialty foods or gourmet shops.

Spinach - *spinazie*, with its crisp dark green leaves, has a slightly bitter taste. There are basically two kinds sold here: **wild spinach** and **leaf spinach**. The wild spinach has large, thick, dark-green leaves and is stronger in taste than the leaf spinach. Use only the leaf, trim off the stem. Leaf spinach is lighter green and has thinner leaves than the wild spinach and it has a very delicate taste. Yet, it is the vegetable that kids love to hate. Even Popeye with all of his persuasive powers can't convince them that they should like it. However, it can be disguised in a number of ways in which case it is delicious. Spinach can be used raw as a salad green or it can be cooked like a vegetable. It changes its character when cooked. It can be served with a white or cheese sauce or baked in a spinach soufflé. It makes a delicious soup and a savory spinach pie. It is a classic accompaniment with chicken and veal, as well as eggs. Its name is often connected with Florence, Italy; thus dishes with spinach in them are often called à la Florentine. Spinach is often gritty so should be washed several times to remove the sand. Shake off most of the water clinging to the leaves then drop it in a saucepan and let it cook in its own juices. Turn often as the spinach "melts down". Do not overcook as it turns gray and sour very quickly. Spinach is also sold frozen. The leaves are either whole or chopped. According to the noted English cook book writer Jane Grigson, one kilo (2 pounds) fresh spinach equals ½ kilo (1 pound) when cooked (it serves 4). One kilo (2 pounds frozen leaf spinach equals 1½ kilos (3 pounds) fresh equals ¾ kilo (1½ pound) when cooked. Fresh spinach, of course, is superior to frozen. See also **Amaranth**, **Water spinach** and **Slippery vegetable** in the Exotic Asian Vegetables Chapter IV.15.

Squash - *pompoen* Squashes are members of the gourd family which are native to the Americas. They can be divided into two categories: summer squash such as **zucchini and patty pan** and winter squash such as **pumpkin**, **butternut** and **turban squash**. **Summer squashes** are picked before they ripen and have soft, edible skins and soft seeds. Of these **zucchini - *courgette*** is the most prolific. The entire vegetable can be eaten. In Italy and France, even the zucchini flowers are stuffed and deep-fried in batter. Zucchini has a smooth skin that can be anywhere from light to dark green and its watery flesh is off-white to pale green. It can be eaten raw but its delicate flavor usually needs to be enhanced by cooking with other stronger vegetables or smothered with sauces. It can be deep-fried and served with fish, mutton or veal or simply dipped in egg then seasoned flour or crushed cracker crumbs and pan-fried. **Patty pan** is a cymling summer squash which appears on the Dutch market in late summer. It is known here by several names: *pattison, bonnet de prètre, artichaut de Jerusalem, squash* *melon* or *Jerusalem artichoke*. It is, however, definitely not an artichoke. It can be stuffed with an herbed bread or corn dressing and baked in its skin. One grower has claimed that they now produce 80 types of **winter squashes** in Holland, however, most of these are used for decoration. Eating them is not a Dutch tradition and many a Dutch greengrocer will tell you that they all taste the same. To further complicate matters, they are not yet familiar with all of their names. Here are some varieties to look for: **winter luxury pie pumpkin** or the ***gele centenaar*** with a yellow netted rind, which are widely used by North Americans especially during the Thanksgiving holidays, and the French-grown bright orange ***rouge vif détamps*** or **cinderella pumpkins** make wonderful pumpkin pies and soups. Also good for pies and soups is the rather rough looking **hubbard squash** that comes in various shades of blue, green and gold. For baking, cooks like to use the **acorn squash** because of its rich flavor and the pretty pattern that forms when you cut it across into ½-inch slices. It has a dark green skin and orange flesh. The creamy yellow **spaghetti squash** is different again for when cooked it separates into yellow-orange strands. It has a fragrant honey or lemon flavor and is good with garlic butter or pesto and served on pasta. The **butternut squash** is pretty versatile for it can be baked, steamed or boiled. The rind ranges from tan to yellow and its flesh is orange and sweet. If you cannot find the squash you are looking for at the greengrocers, check the shops that cater to folks from the Caribbean and Africa.

Swiss chard - *snijbiet* This is an old fashioned vegetable in Holland. It is a member of the beet family. It is cultivated for its leaves and stalks but they should be eaten very young when they are eaten whole. The leaves taste like strong spinach and they can be cooked like any other hearty green. The outer stalks have a string running lengthwise like celery which must be removed.

Sweet potato - zoete *aardappel* is sold at greengrocers and Asian stores as ***bataat***, ***yam*** or ***oebi***. It is actually not a potato but a member of the morning glory family. To further confuse the issue, in America the darker-skinned sweet potato is often called "yam", although true yams and sweet potatoes are not related. They can, however, be similar in size and shape to each other but yams can grow to enormous sizes. There are two varieties of sweet potato sold here: one has a thin, pale-yellow skin and the other has a thicker copper-colored or purplish skin. The flesh of the pale sweet potato is light yellow; and when cooked it becomes dry and chalky. Its flesh is not sweet. The flesh of the darker-skinned variety is sweet and moist and its flesh turns a vibrant orange when cooked. The sweet potato can be puréed, candied or glazed and baked, or baked as a sweet potato pie. Sugar or honey and sweet spices are added to emphasize the natural sweetness. Fresh sweet potatoes are available in the autumn month but may have to be special ordered. Be specific in regards to type. Canned sweet potatoes are sold in stores which import American foods and are labelled "yams". Yams, because they are preferred in the West Indies, Latin America, Africa and parts of Asia, are sold in shops which cater to the cuisines of these countries.

Pattypan

Winter luxury

Rouge vif d'etamps

Hubbard squash

Acorn squash

Spaghetti squash

Butternut

Tomato - *tomaat* The tomato is a New World plant native to the Andes. Although it is a fruit, it is eaten like a vegetable. It is a member of the deadly nightshade family and for years was considered poisonous. Many people are allergic to it. The tomato didn't become popular until the 1900's. In the south of France it is affectionately called the "love apple" or "golden apple", in Italy it is called *pomodoro*. Today, tomatoes are used worldwide in appetizers, salads, soups, sauces and stews. The Dutch are large producers and exporters of greenhouse tomatoes which are known more for their perfect color and shape than for their taste. The common **slicing tomato** or **globe tomato** is good both raw and cooked but the **beefsteak tomato - *vleestomaat*** is considered to be more tasty. It is larger than most tomatoes and is especially good sliced raw and served with a vinaigrette with chopped garlic and onions. The **vine tomatoes - *trostomaten*** are presently in fashion. They are vine-ripened and are sold by the bunch like grapes. They have more flavor than those that are picked green and ripened on the window sill. The **plum tomato - *pomodori***, also known as Italian plum, Roma or sauce tomato, has thick meat and few seeds thus making it the tomato of choice for sauces. **Cherry tomatoes - *kriel-, kers-cocktail or cherry tomaten*** are mainly used as stuffed appetizers or for garnish and salads. **Sun-dried tomatoes - *gedroogde tomaten*** are also widely available in supermarkets, some cheese shops and gourmet shops. They are usually preserved in olive oil and are valued for their intense flavor. They can be used in a variety of ways, but especially in soups and sauces. **Canned tomatoes** are available peeled - *gepelde* and whole, cut into chunks - *blokjes*, condensed into tomato purée or paste, sieved in Italian *pomodori* sauce, or strained to make tomato juice. Good tomatoes should give a little when pressed but should not be overly soft. They should be richly colored and fragrant. Under-ripe tomatoes ripen quickly when left at room temperature. Cold temperatures during refrigeration decrease their flavor.

Turnip - *meiknolletjes* or ***meiknol*** The turnip is a crisp root vegetable, yellow or white in color, with a tinge of purple near the leaves. When young, it has a delicate sweet flavor; when it ages, the taste is more pronounced. It is a pot vegetable and can be used in soups or boiled or steamed and served with butter and parsley or a variety of cream sauces. The turnip should be firm and heavy with an unblemished smooth skin. They are not so popular so may have to be special ordered.

Turnip leaves - *raapstelen* Young slightly sweet tasting turnip leaves are a popular soul food. They must be picked before the turnip is fully developed and sautéed, steamed, fried or blanched or cooked alone or with other milder greens.

Watercress - see Cress

Zucchini - *courgette* see Squash.

IV.9 MEATS

Dutch farmers produce very fine **lamb**, **veal**, **pork** and **poultry**. However, for those raised on succulent, marbled steaks and roasts carved from grain-fed beef cattle, the **beef** in Holland can sometimes be disappointing. There is, nonetheless, much to be said in favor of Dutch beef. It is leaner and has a fuller flavor than its grain-fed cousins. Thus, a good butcher is invaluable. You'll find him behind butchers' counters in supermarkets and butcher shops. He is called a *slager* and his business is called *slagerij*. Butcher shops are listed under ***slagerijen*** in **the Yellow Pages**, or ***Gouden Gids***, of the telephone book. Visit him when there is a lull in the day and he is usually willing to discuss the various ways of cooking his meats. Notice the singular way he trims and presents his beef. Almost all fat and bones are removed. If you want them, you will pay extra. The cost differential between cuts is minimal. For instance, ground beef costs relatively very little less than the more expensive cuts. This can be in your favor if you know how the meat is cut.

A good, innovative butcher prepares the meats for barbecues, fondues and snacks and sells prepared salads and sauces as accompaniments. He might also prepare delicatessen meat dishes such as bacon, cheese and onion quiches, and savory meat pies. He most certainly offers standard items such as ***verse worst*** **- fresh sausage**, ***rookworst*** **- smoked sausage**, ***Wiener schnitzel*** **- breaded cutlets** (veal, chicken, pork or turkey), ***kip cordon bleu*** **- chicken cordon bleu**, ***tartaar or filet Américain*** **- steak or beef tartar**, ***saucijzen*** **- skinless sausages**, ***saucijzen broodjes*** **- skinless sausages baked in puff pastry**, and meat for ***shoarma broodjes*** **- Schwerma sandwiches** (a Middle Eastern sandwich of grilled, spiced, shredded meat served in pita or Arab bread pockets).

Prepackaged meats are only available in some supermarkets; thus, nearly every piece of meat will have to be plucked individually from the butcher's display case or cut to order by the butcher or his assistants. You will have to familiarize yourself with the names of cuts and the pronunciation.

Variety meats or offal (heart, liver, kidneys, etc.) retain some popularity here; however, they generally must be ordered ahead of time. If your butcher has them on hand, they are probably in the deep freeze.

Meat Cooking Terms and Methods

Bake, baked - ***bakken, gebakken*** See **roast**.

Bard, barded - barderen, gebardeerd To wrap bacon or fatback - *bardeerspek* around a roasting piece.

Boil, boiled/cook, cooked - ***koken, gekookt*** To prepare food for eating in a boiling liquid/to heat liquid until bubbles break the surface (212°F/100°C for water at sea level).

Braise, braised - ***smoren, gesmoord*** To cook by moist-heat method in a Dutch oven. Brown in oil on all sides for color and flavor and cook slowly with a small amount of liquid in a tightly covered pot on top of the stove or in the oven. The browned meat is often set on a bed of aromatic vegetables (celery, carrots, and onions) and herbs (thyme, bay leaf, parsley, cloves, allspice berries and garlic) with a flavorful liquid (red wine and/or beef broth). After cooking, the vegetables are puréed or strained to make a gravy.

Fry, fried - ***bakken, gebakken*** To **pan-fry** is to cook food in a small amount of hot fat over moderate to high heat in a frying pan. **Sautéeing** is a form of pan-frying but uses much higher heat and less fat. It sears the outside and seals in the juices. It is done very quickly.

Grill, grilled - ***grilleren, gegrilleerde*** To grill (or to broil) is to cook by radiant heat about 4 to 6 inches (10 to 15 centimeters) under a broiler element or over hot coals. To **pan-grill** is to cook in a frying pan over a moderately high heat using little or no fat.

Lard, larded - ***larderen, gelardeerde*** To lard is to insert long strips of larding fat - *lardeerspek*, or bacon, into a dry cut of lean meat usually with the help of a larding needle. It adds additional moisture to the roast.

Poach, poached - ***pocheren, pocheerd*** To cook food in liquid just under the boiling point. Chicken is usually poached in chicken stock, beef in beef stock and fish in court bouillon (a broth made by cooking various vegetables and herbs).

Roast, roasted - ***braden, gebraden*** or ***roosteren, geroosterd*** To cook by dry-cooking method; i.e., uncovered without water in an oven. Local beef and veal roasts should either be larded or barded and must be cooked very rare. Larding needles are available in kitchen ware shops. Roasting can be done at high temperatures for a short period, at low even temperatures for longer periods, or a combination of the two; i.e., starting the roast in a very high heat and then reducing the heat after 15 minutes. High temperature cooking produces a well-browned crust which seals in the meat juices.

Simmer, simmered - ***sudderen, zachtjes koken*** To cook food gently in liquid below or just at the boiling point. Bubbles should just barely break the surface.

Smoke, smoked - ***roken, gerookt*** To preserve fresh meat through prolonged exposure to smoke from a wood fire.

Steam, steamed - ***stomen, gestoomd*** To cook covered over a pot of boiling or simmering water. Steaming helps preserve the food's vitamins and minerals and its flavor, color, shape and texture.

Stew, stewed - ***stoven, gestoofd*** To cook with the food barely covered with liquid (water, wine, stock, or a combination) and simmered slowly in a tightly covered stewing pot for a long period of time. Stewing meat is generally cut into 1-inch (2.5 centimeter) cubes and browned before stewing.

Stir-fry, stir-fried To quickly fry small pieces of meat or vegetables over a very high heat (usually in a Chinese *wok*), while stirring the food briskly. The meat should be just cooked through and the vegetables should be wilted but crispy.

BEEF - RUNDVLEES

The cattle traditionally raised in Holland are dairy cattle. There are no enormous feedlots where beef cattle are fattened on grain in a controlled environment to produce moist and tender, self-basting, marbled meat (marbling being the creamy white fat running through the red flesh giving it a marble or granite effect). However, the Dutch beef has a very full flavor, it is not chemically treated and the growth of the cattle is not enhanced by hormones. The local meat is lean. Therefore, when you think of beef, think of dry-roasted roasts and pan-fried steaks cooked just briefly, or of braised and stewed meats cooked until they are very well done.

Local cuts are quite different from butcher shops in other countries. This can at times be problematic. Therefore, a detailed description of the cuts is given on the following pages, along with suggestions for cooking them. To supplement these cuts, many accommodating butchers will prepare alien cuts providing they receive detailed descriptions and/or photos.

The butcher shops listed in the Appendices of this book carry imported beef and are acquainted with the English and American cuts.

In the meantime, you can expand your culinary horizons for the local beef is compatible with French and, of course, Dutch cooking. If cooked properly, it can be delicious. Try Julia Child's *Mastering the Art of French Cooking, From Julia Child's Kitchen* or *The Way to Cook* for many of her recipes are well-suited for local beef.

Since no preservatives are added, the meat is sometimes discolored. This doesn't mean it has spoiled.

A Dutch side of beef is cut into three major wholesale cuts: ***Schouder* - shoulder**, ***Voorvoet* - foreshank** and ***Achtervoet* - rear shank**. They are cut and trimmed into roughly sixteen primal or wholesale cuts, depending upon your sources. The descriptions below offer some comparisons between these cuts and the eight or nine American wholesale cuts. Keep in mind that the nomenclatures of both the Dutch and American wholesale and retail cuts are not standard.

DUTCH WHOLESALE AND RETAIL BEEF CUTS WHERE THEY COME FROM

1. *Hals or Nek and Onderrib* corresponds with a portion of the **Chuck (1)**. It is a less tender part of the beef and is either cut into **lean slices - *magere runderlappen*, soup meat - *poelet*** or ground into **hamburger - *gehakt***.

2. *Dikke en Fijne Rib* are rib pieces which basically correspond with the American **Rib (2)** section. The tender cuts from here are a **rib piece - *ribstuk***, and **rib slices** or **steaks - *riblappen***. Whole **rib roast bone-in - *riblap met been*** is available upon request.

3. *Contrefilet (Dunne Lende)* is a large piece of first quality meat which roughly corresponds with parts of the **Short Loin (3)**, the closest to the rib, and **Sirloin (4)**, the closest to the rump. Two muscles run through it. When separated from the bone, they are called **top loin - *entrêcote*** and **fillet or tenderloin - *ossenhaas or haas***. **Steaks** cut from the ***entrêcote*** are called ***entrêcote*** or ***lendebiefstuk*** and are the local equivalent of the **New York Steak**. The ***ossehaas*** is a choice **roast**. When sliced it yields some of the prime cuts: ***tournedos* - medallions**, ***chateaubriand* - chauteaubriand** (the cut from the center of the tenderloin large enough for two), and ***biefstuk van de haas* - filet mignon**. The short loin can also be cut into **Porterhouse** and **T-bone** steaks. They are bone-in steaks sliced across the top loin and tenderloin muscles and thus include portions of both muscles. They are not truly Dutch cuts although some butchers do offer them. The top loin meat is generally rolled and tied to produce the **loin roast - *lenderollade***. **Rib eye steaks** have become popular here and are simply called ***rib* eye**. They are cut from between the short loin and chuck.

4. *Staartstuk, Dikke Lende or Zijlende* include parts of the **Sirloin (4)** and the **Round (5)**. The **roast beef - *lende rosbief*, steak - *biefstuk*** and **minute steak - *runderquicksteak*** cut from here is relatively tender.

5. *Bovenbil*, which also includes the wholesale pieces of ***Spierstuk*, *Platte bil met muis*, *Binnenbil*** and ***Ronde bil***, roughly corresponds to the **Rump** and **Round (5)**. Cuts from here include **rump steak - *biefstuk*, eye of the round - *kogelbiefstuk*, rolled roast - *rollade*, lean slices - *magere runderlappen*, minute steak - *runderquicksteak*** and a **frying piece - *baklap***.

6. *Klaprib* consists of part of the **Rib** piece **(2 & 3)** and part of the **Brisket** and **Short Plate (7 & 8)**. Local butchers cut it into **streaky slices - *doorregen runderlappen*** and **streaky rolled roasts - *doorregen rollade***. *Doorregen* describes the layers of fat that run through it like bacon or short ribs. To order **short ribs**, ask for ***doorregen borstlappen*** or ***klaprib met been***. If you don't succeed, try showing a photo.

Rundvlees

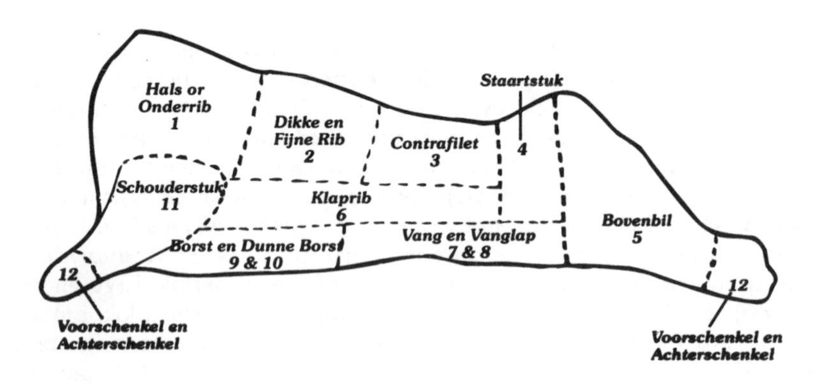

Beef

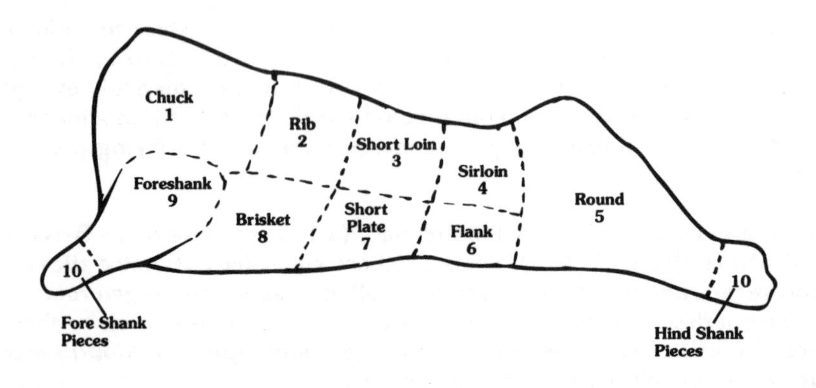

The bones add flavor to the meat when braising or stewing. ***Middenrif*** is the tender inside piece cut from under the **Short Loin** and **Flank** which is sliced into ***lap van de klaprib*** and ***vlees van middenrif***. These cuts are not very common.

7 and 8. ***Vang or Slip van de Lende and Vanglap*** are the pieces between the **Short Loin (3)** and **Sirloin (4)** and the **Flank (6)**. The meat is tasty but not exceptionally tender. Cuts include **streaky slices** - ***doorregen runderlappen***, cut up **stew meat** - ***hacheevlees***, **streaky rolled roast** - ***doorregen rollade*** and **roast beef** - ***rosbief***.

9 and 10. ***Borst (Puntborst) and Dunne Borst (Naborst)*** are basically the **Short Plate (7)** and **Brisket (8)**. Retail cuts include a type of **brisket** - ***borststuk*** or ***klapstuk***, **streaky slices** - ***doorregen runderlappen***, **breast slices** - ***borstlappen*** and **rolled roast** - ***doorregen rollade***.

11. ***Schouderstuk*** is the **Fore Shank (9)** and part of the **Chuck (1)**. It accounts for some of the toughest meat. The wholesale cuts: ***Baklap***, ***Sucadestuk***, ***Bloemstuk***, ***Schoudermuis*** and ***Driehoekstukje***, are cut into **roast beef** - ***rosbief***; a fairly large **roasting piece** - ***braadstuk***; various slices such as ***lendelappen***, ***sucadelappen***, ***braadlappen*** and ***magere runderlappen***; **minced beef** - ***tartaar*** and **soup meat** - ***poelet***.

12. ***Voorschenkel and Achterschenkel*** are the **Fore and Hind Shank (10)** pieces just above the leg. Cut from here are **shank cross cuts with bone** - ***schenkel met been*** and the gelatinous **marrow bone** - ***mergpijp***.

Variety meats or offal - ***orgaanvlees*** such as **brains** - ***hersen***, **heart** - ***hart***, **kidney** - ***nier***, **liver** - ***lever***, **sweetbreads** - ***zwezerik*** **and tongue** - ***tong*** are available upon request.

HOW TO COOK THEM

Poelet, Schenkel met been and Mergpijp - **cook in soups.** ***Poelet*** is **soup meat** cut from various parts of the beef. Together with the **shank cross cut with marrow bone** - ***schenkel met been*** and the **marrow bone** - ***mergpijp***, they make wonderful beef broths and stocks.

Ossestaart - **cook in soups, braise.** This is the flavorful bony **ox tail** which has rich gelatinous meat. It is often cooked in a clear soup with basil, thyme, marjoram and savory or with pot vegetables such as carrots, onions and celery. It can also be braised, coated with breadcrumbs, then broiled.

Hacheevlees - **stew.** Cut from the neck or flank - *nek* or *vang*, ***hacheevlees*** is cut into **stewing cubes**. It gets its name from **Hachee**, a delicious Dutch onion and beef stew.

Lappen or Runderlappen - **braise, stew, pan-fry, slice thinly for Sukiyaki.** These are cuts or slices that come from many parts of the beef.

They may be called ***stooflappen*** meaning they are braising or stewing cuts. Their quality and tenderness varies. ***Riblappen*** cut from the rib - *dikke rib* and the short loin - *fijne rib* are more tender than the ***lendelappen***, ***braadlappen***, and ***baklap***. They need a shorter cooking time than other stew meats and are sometimes tender enough to pan-fry. ***Doorregen runderlappen***, ***sucadelappen*** and ***magere runderlappen*** need to be braised for as long as two or three hours. ***Borstlappen*** cut from the *klaprib* are especially good for hearty soups like Ukrainian **Borscht**. Use the various ***lappen*** in the French **Boeuf Bourguignon**, Hungarian **Goulash** and other glorious stews. ***Runderquicksteak*** or ***malse bieflappen*** are similar to **minute steaks**. Pan-fry and serve with a gravy made from the pan juices. A large piece of ***magere riblappen*** is suitable for the thinly sliced **Sukiyaki meat**. Partially freeze the beef and slice thin like *rookvlees* or U.S. chipped beef (about ⅛ inch or 3 millimeters thick). A good butcher can or will do it for you with sufficient notice. Order ahead.

Klapstuk* - braise.** ***Klapstuk is a fairly fatty piece of meat cut from the breast - *borst*. It can be compared to a **brisket**. It is used for **Hutspot** (a Dutch carrot and onion stew). Braise at least 1½ hours before adding the vegetables.

Ossehaas* - pan-fry, roast, braise, stir-fry, grill as kebabs, deep-fry as fondue.** The ***ossehaas **- fillet or tenderloin** is the most tender and expensive cut of beef. It weighs about 3 to 4 pounds/1½ to 2 kilos. To pan-fry, brown on all sides, lay a loose piece of buttered aluminum foil over the meat only, then cook on top of the stove. It can also be brushed with oil and browned then roasted in a preheated 475°F/250°C oven for 15 minutes, then in reduced heat of 350°F/175°C for a further 15-20 minutes. The whole ***ossehaas*** can be used for **Beef Wellington** or in **Filet de boeuf en croûte** (beef baked in puff pastry). Tenderloin can also be used for **Beef Stroganoff** but should only be sautéed for seconds. It is safer to lay the meat on top of the onions and cook without letting the meat touch the pan. When using tenderloin for **Fondue, Kebabs**, or **Chinese stir-fry**, cook very briefly.

Biefstuk* - pan-fry, grill, broil.** ***Biefstuk gets its name from the English term for **beef steak**. The steaks are cut from various parts of the beef. The most expensive piece is the **fillet mignon** - ***biefstuk van de haas*** which is cut from the tenderloin - *ossehaas*. A standard local fillet weighs around 3½ ounces/100 grams but thicker fillets are available upon request. An ideal fillet should be around 1¼ inches/3 centimeters thick. ***Tournedos*** are **small steaks** also cut from the tenderloin and weigh around 3-3½ ounces/±80-100 grams. ***Chateaubriand*** is cut from the center of the tenderloin and is large enough for two. It is better known as a recipe than a cut of beef. The recipe calls for a grilled or broiled fillet which is served with the rich butter sauce - ***sauce Béarnaise***. Brush with oil then sear the outside quickly under a very hot grill, reduce the heat and cook for about 20 minutes, basting occasionally with butter. ***Kogelbiefstuk*** can be compared to the **eye of the round**. It is a tender cut from the rump and each steak usually weighs around 3½ ounces/100 grams. Cooking time for these steaks is less than 10 minutes for they should be cooked rare. To grill, brush with oil and place about 3 inches/7.5 centimeters from the preheated grill. Traditional **steaks** - ***biefstukken*** are cut from the *zijlende* and *spierstuk*.

Entrecôte **- pan-fry, grill, stir-fry, grill as kebabs, deep-fry as fondue.** The **top loin** - ***entrecôte*** is cut into **steaks** - ***entrecôte*** or ***lendebiefstuk***. They are juicy pieces of meat about ¾ inch/2 centimeters thick and weigh around 8 ounces/250 grams each. In Holland, one steak is meant to serve two. Pan-fry briefly and serve rare with **sauce Béarnaise** or **Hollandaise**, a rich sauce made of egg yolks, butter and lemon juice.

Rosbief **- roast, grill, stir-fry, grill as kebabs, deep-fry as fondue.** **Rosbief** - **roast beef** is cut from various parts of the beef: *dikke lende, platte bil, bovenbil, schoudermuis* or *spierstuk*. The most tender *rosbief* is cut from the *dikke lende* - rib. Ask for ***rosbief van de dikke lende***. It can be brushed with oil and grilled on a spit or roasted for about 15 minutes per pound. The butcher can bard it to add moisture when dry-roasting. Sear and roast 2-pound/1 kilo pieces, basting frequently, in a preheated 475°F/250°C oven for 30 to 40 minutes. *Rosbief* must be served rare. It is sliced thin after it has rested for at least 20 minutes, then it is eaten hot with sauces or cold in sandwiches. *Rosbief van de dikke lende* can be cut into cubes for fondue and **kebabs** or into thin strips for stir-frying. Cook very briefly.

Rollade **- braise, roast, stir-fry, grill as kebabs, deep-fry as fondue.** These seasoned and spiced **rolled roasts** - ***rolladen*** come from several parts of the animal. You can ask the butcher to roll them without the spices. ***Lenderollade***, the most tender of the rolled roasts, comes from the top loin - *contrefilet* or *dunne lende*. To braise, allow up to 2 to 2½ hours for browning and braising and resting for ½ hour before cutting. Braise until a sharp-pronged fork can be inserted with relative ease. It should still be a little chewy. To roast, start it at high heat for 10 to 12 minutes per pound then reduce the heat and roast for another 8 to 10 minutes per pound for rare beef. ***Lenderollade*** can be cut into 1-inch cubes for **Fondue** or **Kebabs** or in thin strips for **Chinese stir-fry dishes** and **Beef Stroganoff** (see ***Ossehaas***). They should be sautéed very briefly or they will become dry and chewy or not chewable. The rolled roasts made from the *bovenbil, klaprib, vang* and *borst* may need to be cooked longer.

Staartstuk **- braise, roast, grill.** This is a **rump roast** which weighs around 3 to 4 pounds/1½ to 2 kilos. It benefits from being marinated like **Sauerbraten** before braising. It can also be tied into a rolled roast.

Losgesneden ribben **- braise, grill.** These are individual **beef ribs** from the rib section. Braise until they are very tender or grill briefly.

Ribstuk **- pan-fry, dry-roast.** A fairly large piece cut from the *fijne* or *dikke rib*, *ribstuk* can be pan-fried or barded with a thin layer of fat and roasted.

Rundergehakt* - pan-fry, grill. Ground beef - *rundergehakt is sold regular or lean - *mager rundergehakt*. Be specific when ordering because the word *gehakt* may get you ***half om half* - half ground beef, half pork**.

***Tartaar or filet Américain* - beef or steak tartar - eat uncooked.** This is a minced, first-quality, lean beef which is garnished with onions, capers, anchovies, raw egg, Worcestershire sauce and hot pepper sauce. In fine restaurants steak tartar is made from tails of the tenderloin - *ossehaas*. The Dutch *Filet Americaine* is a variation of steak tartar with the addition of tomato sauce.

VEAL - KALFSVLEES

The best veal is the meat from milk-fed calves that are not more than three to four months old. Their flesh is creamy white with just a blush of pink. After 6 months, calves that are considered **baby beef** and the flesh ranges from pink to light red. Milk-fed veal is available in the spring and summer --at other times of the year older calves are sold as veal. It is a very lean and must be cooked more like poultry than beef. Braising, pot-roasting and gently simmering it over low heat is ideal.

French, Italian and Austrian cooks have a way with veal. Some of their most notable dishes are **Blanquette de Veau**, **Ossobuco**, **Veal Scaloppine**, **Veal Parmigiana**, **Veal Piccata**, **Wiener Schnitzel**, **Saltimbocca** and **Veal Cordon Bleu. Blinde vinken** or "veal birds" are Dutch specialties which are sold by most butchers. They consist of ground veal rolled in thin veal cutlets.

The wholesale veal cuts are similar to those of the full-grown steer but there are not as many. The local cuts described below are compared, as much as possible, with the American wholesale cuts.

DUTCH WHOLESALE AND RETAIL VEAL CUTS WHERE THEY COME FROM

1. *Hals* is the **Neck (1)**. The meat from here is cut into **slices - *lappen*** and **soup meat - *poelet***. It is also possible to buy a large piece for braising or poaching and meat with neck bones for making stocks. **2. *Bovenhals*** is a cut from just above the **Shoulder (2)**. Retail cuts from here are a **roasting piece - *braadstuk*** and **chops or cutlets - *koteletten***.

3 and 4. *Ribstuk* and ***Koteletten*** are roughly the same as **Rib (3)**. Most of the retail cuts are **cutlets - *koteletten***, with or without the bone, and **rolled roast - *rollade***.

5. *Dunne Lende* is the **Loin (4)** of the veal. Retail cuts from here are the **tenderloin - *kalfshaas***, **rolled roast - *rollade***, **cutlets - *koteletten*** and the **kidney piece - *kalfsnierstuk***.

Kalfsvlees

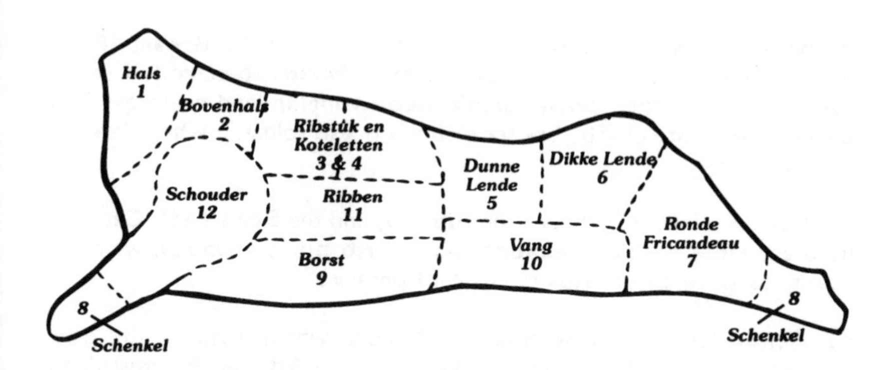

Veal

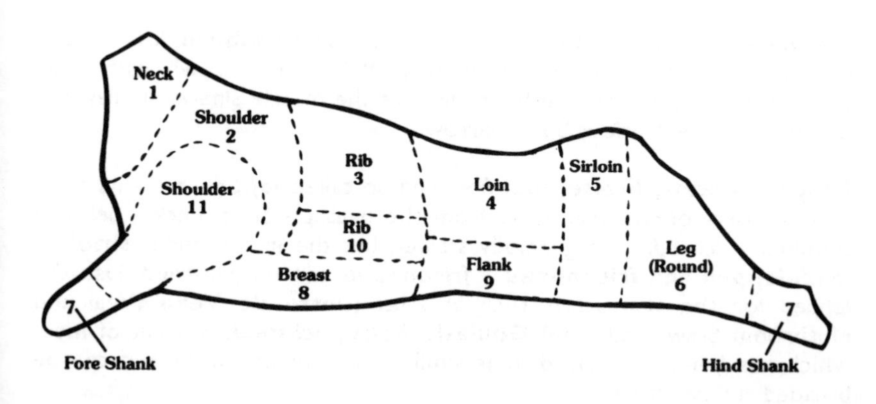

6. *Dikke lende* or **Sirloin (5)** is a prime section of the calf or veal. Cuts from here are **loin roast - *fricandeau*** and **loin slices - *lendelappen*.**

7. *Ronde Fricandeau*, *Platte fricandeau* and ***Spierstuk*** are wholesale cuts from the **Leg** or **Round (6)** of the veal. Their retail cuts are **fillet slices - *oesters*, veal cutlets - *schnitzels*, steak - *biefstuk*, roast - *fricandeau*, slices - *lappen*** and **minute steak - *kalfsquicksteak*.**

8. *Schenkel* is part of the **Front** or **Hind Shank (7)**. Cuts from here are **cross cut veal shanks - *ossobucco*** (hind shank), **soup meat - *poelet*** and **calves feet - *kalfspoten*.**

9 and 10. *Borst and Vang* correspond with part of the **Breast (8)** and **Flank (9)**. Retail cuts include **breast slices - *borstlappen*, rolled roast - *rollade*, soup meat - *poelet*, flank slice - *vanglap***, and **boneless flank cutlet - *vangkotelet*.** The **breast** or ***borst*** is also sold as a **whole breast - *hele kalfsborst*.**

11. *Ribben* is located between the **Rib (10)** and the **Breast (8)**. Cuts from here are **riblets - *ribkarbonade*** and the **rib piece - *ribben***, which are usually deboned. **Short ribs** can be cut from here.

12. *Schouder* is the **Shoulder (11)** piece which includes the other wholesale cuts like ***Voorschenkel*, *Muis*, *Driehoekstukje*, *Bloemstuk*** and ***Sucadestuk***. Retail cuts are **soup meat - *poelet*, roast - *fricandeau*, stewing slices - *stooflappen*** and **ground veal - *kalfsgehakt*.**

HOW TO COOK THEM

Kalfspoten* - stock.** The veal bones from the **calves feet - *kalfspoten are preferred for making soup stocks because they are high in natural gelatin. They are usually cooked with **soup meat - *poelet*.**

Poelet* - boil in soup, stew, braise. *Poelet is cubed meat from the neck - *nek*, leg - *achterschenkel* and flank - *vanglap*.

Ossobuco gets its name from the Italian veal dish, **Ossobuco**. It is a cross-cut, rear veal shank or knuckle, bone-in. It is braised slowly with wine, onion, tomato, garlic and herbs to dissolve the muscle sinews. Its flavor is enhanced by the delicious bone marrow.

Lappen* - stew, braise, pan-fry.** The so-called ***lappen are cuts from various parts of the veal. Cuts from the breast - *borst*, neck - *nek* and shoulder - *schouder* are generally stewed but the more tender **sirloin - *lendelappen*** and **fricandeau - *fricandeau*** can be pan-fried. Use the *lappen* for the veal stews such as **Blanquette de Veau** (Veal and Mushroom Stew) and **Veal Goulash**. ***Kalfsquicksteak*** is a cut of meat which has been tenderized. It is similar to a minute steak and can be breaded and pan-fried.

Schnitzel* - pan-fry.** The term ***schnitzel applies to any thin slice of beef, pork or veal but is most popularly associated with veal. ***Schnitzels***, which are also called scallops or cutlets, are cut from the various parts of the veal but the best are cut from the fricandeau. The standard weight is 3 to 4 ounces/±100 grams per *schnitzel.*

***Fricandeau* - roast, grill, braise, pan-fry.** A large piece of meat coming from the *platte fricandeau*, *ronde fricandeau*, *dikke lende*, *spierstuk* and *muis*. In English, the term '**fricandeau**' is used to describe "larded veal roasted and glazed in its own juices". It is basically a roasting piece; bard the *fricandeau* then baste frequently. To braise, lard it with strips of fat.

***Kalfsborst* - braise, poach.** This is the boned - *uitgebeende* **breast of veal** which is commonly filled with a ground meat and vegetable stuffing and is braised in the oven covered only with aluminum foil. It can also be poached or simmered.

Rollade* - braise, roast. Rolled roasts - *rolladen are cut from the loin - *dunne lende*, rib - *ribstuk* and the breast - *borst*. **The loin roast - *lenderollade*** is more tender than the others. *Rollade* can be opened and stuffed. Unless requested otherwise, the butcher will have already added his own spices. A roast shouldn't be cooked any longer than 25 to 30 minutes per pound. It should be rare in the center.

Kalfshaas - **pan-fry, grill**. The ***haas*** is the **filet** or **tenderloin** of veal which weighs around 1½ to 2 pounds/700 grams to 1 kilo. It is generally cut into the finest **medallions - *oesters*** and **small veal steaks - biefstukken**.

Kalfsbiefstuk and ***kalfsoesters*** **- pan-fry, grill. *Kalfsbiefstuk*** is a steak cut from the *ronde fricandeau* and *spierstuk*. The **biefstuk** from the *ronde fricandeau* weighs around 7½ ounces/200 grams. A smaller **veal steak - kalfsbiefstukje** weighs around 3½ ounces/100 grams. ***Kalfsoesters*** or ***médaillon de veau*** are small round slices trimmed from the *ronde* and *platte fricandeau*, *haas* and the *schouder*. They normally weigh around 1½-2½ ounces/±50-75 grams. These steaks and medallions should be cooked just briefly.

Koteletten - sauté, grill. These chops can be purchased with or without bone. Those with the bone are juicier and more tasty. They come from the *dunne lende*, *ribstuk*, *koteletten*, *ribben* and *bovenhals* and weigh around 7-8 ounces/±200-250 grams bone-in. Brush with oil and grill or sauté briefly. They cook in just minutes.

Ribkarbonaden* - grill. *Ribkarbonaden are small riblets which are cut from the *ribben*.

Braadstuk* - braise, roast. *Braadstuk is a large roasting piece cut from the shoulder - *bovenhals* and breast - *borst*. It can be cooked like *rollade*.

***Kalfsnierstuk* - roast, braise.** A special roast from the *dunne lende*, *kalfsnierstuk* contains the kidney and the kidney fat.

Kalfsgehakt* - pan-fry, grill.** A **lean ground veal**, ***kalfsgehakt can be mixed with beef suet. In Holland, it is used mostly in ***blinde vinken*** or **veal birds** which are ground veal rolls wrapped in veal cutlets. Ground veal is often mixed with ground beef and/or pork in meat loaf.

PORK - VARKENSVLEES

Raising pigs is a thriving business in Holland and some delicious pork is sold in supermarkets and butcher shops. It is cheaper than beef and in terms of quality, it is excellent. Cuts are very similar to American-style cuts. The pork raised in Holland is quite lean. In fact, some of the cuts compare favorably with chicken as lean white meat. There are fewer wholesale and retail cuts of pork than beef; however, the choice is less critical since all pork cuts are relatively tender.

Pork has traditionally been cooked until it is well-done because of worries about pork-related diseases. However, due to improvements in feeding techniques, this is no longer the case. Pork meat is considered "safe" with an internal temperature of 137°F/55°C. Many chefs recommend that a pork loin roast should be around 155° to 160°F/65° to 70°C in internal temperature. This is from 10 to 15°F less than the temperatures recommended on some commercial thermometers. The meat will be juicy, tender and slightly pink.

In addition to pork cuts, ground pork is turned into savory sausages and **sla vinken**, a Dutch specialty of lean minced pork wrapped in streaky bacon. Sla vinken can be pan-fried or barbecued.

Bacon and **ham** are sold at the butcher's counter in supermarkets and in butcher shops. They come in various types and forms. However, since the Dutch are not big meat eaters, they are mainly cut into thin slices to be eaten as cold cuts and in slabs or cubes for flavorings for soups and casseroles. Hams are rarely sold whole although most cooked hams are suitable for baking and frying. The Black Forest, Ardennes, Westfalian and Parma hams are salted and air-dried and are mainly used as cold cuts.

Dutch pork is cut into four major wholesale cuts: ***Schouder* - Shoulder Butt and Shoulder Blade**, ***Rib* - Loin**, ***Buik* - Side** and ***Achtervoet* - Leg** and then seven or eight wholesale pieces. The descriptions below compare them with the six American wholesale cuts.

DUTCH WHOLESALE AND RETAIL PORK CUTS WHERE THEY COME FROM

1. *Kop* is the **pig's head (1)** which is used in some countries to make **head cheese - *zure zult***. It is a wholesale cut.

2. *Schouder* is the **Shoulder Butt** and **Arm or Picnic Shoulder (2)** which includes the other wholesale cuts ***Schouderham***, ***Borstlap*** and

Varkensvlees

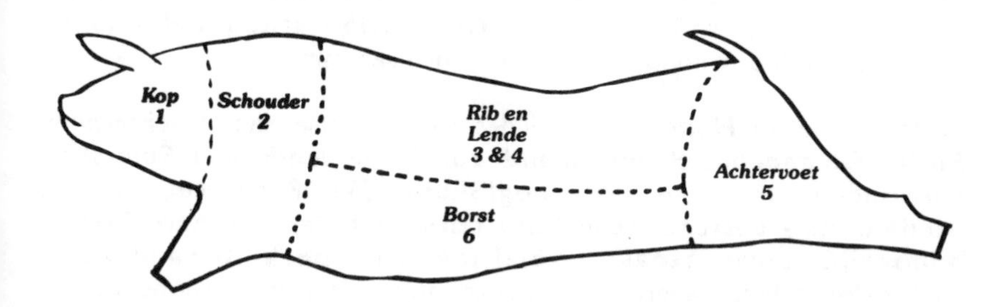

Pork

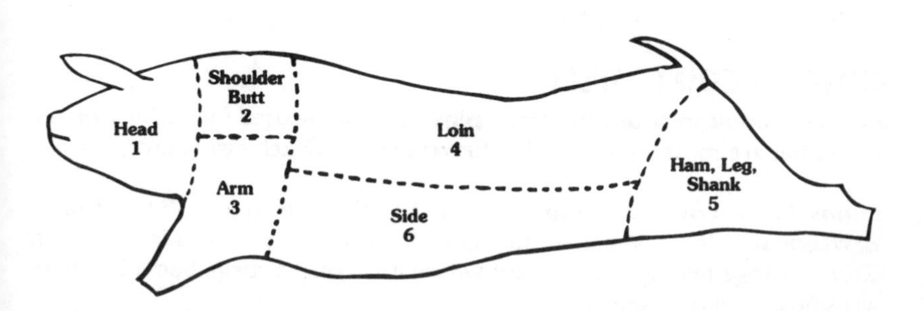

Schouderstuk. Local retail cuts are **rolled roast** - ***rollade***, **ham hock** - ***hamschijf*** and **lean pork slices** - ***magere varkenslappen***. The smoked and cooked ham from here is called ***schouderham***.

3. and 4. ***Rib*** and ***Lende*** correspond with the American **Loin (4)**. They include ***Haasje***, ***Haas*** or ***Lende***, ***Rib*** and ***Procureur***. Retail cuts from here are the prized cuts of pork: **fillet** or **tenderloin** - ***varkenshaas***; **fillet** - ***filet***, **boneless blade chop** or **blade steak** - ***schouderfilet***, **blade rolled roast** - ***schouderfilet rollade***, **blade chop** - ***schouderkarbonade***, **loin chop (with tenderloin)** - ***haaskarbonade***, **rib chop** - ***ribkarbonade***, **loin roast** - ***lenderollade*** and the **fat back** - ***rugspek*** or ***vet spek***. Several cuts from here are put through a curing process: the fat back has little or no lean streaks and is used as a **larding fat** - ***lardeerspek***, **salt pork** - ***zuurkool spek*** and a **smoked pork** - ***rookspek*** which resembles bacon. The local ***bacon*** is salted and lightly smoked and is made from the boneless rib chop --it tends to be quite salty. ***Casselerrib*** - **salted and smoked pork loin**, with or without bone, tastes much like ham.

5. ***Achtervoet*** or ***Ham***, which includes the wholesale cuts of ***Achterham***, ***Platte fricandeau***, ***Bovenfricandeau***, ***Dikke lende*** and ***Spierstuk***, corresponds with the **Ham/Leg/Shank (5)**. Retail cuts include **medallions** - ***oesters***, **fresh ham cuts** - ***hamlappen***, **ham hock** - ***hamschijf***, **pork steak** - ***biefstuk*** and **pork fricandeau** - ***varkensfricandeau***. Several **Leg** parts are also put through a curing process to make what is generally referred to as ham. ***Achterham*** is a **smoked, cooked ham**, while the salt-cured and air-dried German Black Forest and Westfalian, Belgian Ardennen, French Bayonne and Italian Parma hams are **uncooked ham** - ***rauwe ham***.

6. ***Borst*** is the **Side (6)** or lower portion of ribs and breastbone of a hog. **Spareribs** - ***krabbetjes***, **streaky fresh cuts** - ***doorregen verse lappen***, **fresh lean pork belly** - ***vers mager spek*** and **streaky rolled roast** - ***doorregen varkensrollade*** are taken from here. The **pork belly** - ***borst*** or ***buik spek*** is also called ***doorregen spek*** for it has streaks of meat running through it. It can be purchased in the following forms: **fresh slices** - ***doorregen lappen*** or ***speklapjes***, **pork cured in a salt brine** - ***pekelspek*** or ***zuurkoolspek***, **smoked and salted pork belly** - ***rookspek***, **salted and smoked breakfast bacon** - ***ontbijtspek*** and **smoked and cooked bacon** - ***katenspek***.

HOW TO COOK THEM

Pootjes* - cook in soup.** ***Pootjes - **pigs feet** can be used for various winter dishes but are most widely used in **Erwtensoep** (Dutch Pea Soup).

***Hamschijf* - cook in soup.** *Hamschijf* is the ham hock often used in **Erwtensoep**. It is sometimes sold grilled but not smoked and is cooked in Germany together with sauerkraut where it is called Eisbein. Some butchers will smoke it upon request.

Lappen* or *varkenslappen* - stew, braise, boil in soup, stir-fry or grill as kebabs.** The ***lappen are cut from the various wholesale sections of the hog. All can be used as stewing meats but have many other uses. The most tender *lappen*, ***hamlappen***, are cut from the *achtervoet* or *ham*. They are especially good in the stir-fried Asian dishes. ***Magere varkenslappen*** are lean pork slices cut from the shoulder with an outer rim of fat - *met een randje vet*. They are well-suited for marinated and grilled kebabs. ***Doorregen verse lappen*** are streaky belly cuts. They contain equal amounts of lean and fat. They are very popular here and are sometimes fried first to remove some of the fat. ***Varkenslappen*** are used in Chinese and Indonesian dishes like **Bahmie** (fried noodles) and **Nasi Goreng** (fried rice), **Saté** (small kebabs) and **Tjap tjoi** (chop suey). This is part of the Dutch influence as the majority of the Indonesians are Muslim and do not eat pork. *Varkenslappen* are also stewed in various Dutch winter *stamppot* dishes.

Varkensschnitzel* - pan-fry.** A thin slice of pork cut from portions of the leg, the ***schnitzels are usually breaded and pan-fried very briefly.

***Varkensfricandeau* - stew, braise or pot roast.** This is a lovely, thick piece of pork which is cut from the **Leg** or **Shoulder** - *fricandeau* cut from the leg is the tastiest. It should have a layer of fat - *een randje vet* on the outside. Smaller 1-pound (±500-gram) pieces can be braised on top of the stove. Larger ones should be done in the oven. Sear the meat in frying butter - *braadboter* or a combination of butter and oil then add a little water. Cover and cook, basting from time to time. It can be also be dry-roasted. Brush with frying butter and set in a preheated oven of 475°F/±250°C. After 15 minutes, reduce the heat to 325°F/165°C. Roast, basting frequently, for one hour.

Varkenshaas* - pan-fry. *Varkenshaas is the pork tenderloin which weighs about ½ pound (±250 grams). Simply brown it gently on all sides in frying butter - *braadboter*, or a combination of butter and oil for about five minutes. Reduce the heat, lay a piece of buttered foil over the meat only, and cook for an additional 20 minutes. Remove it to a plate and make a cream or mushroom sauce by deglazing the pan juices. Reckon on one-half or one tenderloin per person. It also benefits from a fine red wine marinade.

Varkensbiefstuk* and *varkensoester* - pan-fry**. Cut from the leg - *achterham* and the tenderloin - *haas*, each ***biefstuk weighs around 4 ounces (±125 grams) and each ***oester*** weighs around 2½ ounces (75 grams). They are considered to be the most prized pieces. Sear, cover with buttered foil, and cook over a low fire for 20 minutes. Good with a cream sauce and/or various spices.

Karbonaden* and *koteletten* - pan-fry**. These bone-in and boneless chops are cut from the loin and shoulder butt. They include **loin chops (with tenderloin) - *haas karbonaden*, rib chops - *ribkarbonaden and the **blade chops - *schouder karbonaden***. The loin and rib chops are leaner than the blade chop and are more expensive. All can be brushed with oil and pan-fried or grilled. Allow about four to five minutes on each side for a ¾-inch thick chop.

Krabbetjes* - broil, grill or stew. *Krabbetjes are spare ribs which are most frequently eaten with a rich tomato-based barbecue sauce. To cook on a charcoal or gas grill, roast until the meat is half done and the initial juices are cooked out. Baste with a barbecue sauce which then sticks to the meat. Total grilling time is roughly 30 minutes. Don't char them. They can also be woven on an oven spit and broiled under a low 325°F/±165°C heat, or simply baked in the oven. Spare ribs are also good cooked with sauerkraut. In Chinese cooking, they are used in soups or are spiced and steamed and served as a part of a Dim Sum meal (Chinese High Tea - *yam cha*).

Spek* and *bacon* - stew, pan-fry or serve as cold cuts.** Spek and bacon come from the back (*rugspek*) and belly (*buikspek*). The local fatback is available fresh - *vers*; salted - *gezouten*; salted and smoked - *gezouten* and *gerookt*; and salted and smoked with a portion of the loin - *bacon*. The local belly pork - *buikspek* or *doorregen spek* is sold fresh - *vers* as *doorregen* or *spek lappen*; salted - *pekelspek* or *zuurkoolspek*; or salted and smoked and sometimes cooked - *ontbijtspek* (breakfast bacon), *rookspek* (uncooked) and katenspek (cooked). The fresh *spek* is often used for **larding - *lardeerspek and **barding - *bardeerspek*.** The *pekelspek* or *zuurkoolspek*, *rookspek*, *ontbijt spek* and *katenspek* are used in soups and *stamppot* dishes such as ***Zuurkool met Worst*** (Sauerkraut and Sausage) and ***Boerenkool met Worst*** (Curly Kale with Sausage). ***Katenspek*** is probably the closest to, but leaner than, English- and American-style bacon. It can be fried or used in various soups and casseroles or eaten as cold cuts. **Canadian bacon** is back bacon which is the cured and smoked boneless loin. It is available in gourmet shops such as the food department of Marks and Spencer.

Ham and ***Casselerrib* - stew, pan-fry, cook in soups or serve as cold cuts. *Ham*** is cured and smoked meat from the arm shoulder - *schouder* and leg/shank - *achtervoet*. **Ham**, like bacon, is cut into thin slices and consumed as a cold cut or is cut into slabs or cubes for soup and casserole flavorings. Fully-cooked hams can be baked or reheated in the oven. ***Casselerrib*** - **salted and smoked loin** tastes very much like ham. It can be purchased as a smoked pork chop with or without the bone. It is sometimes very salty and can be soaked before frying. *Casselerrib* is also used for cold cuts but thick slices - *dikke plakjes* can be used in soups and casseroles, or fried.

***Rollade* - roast or braise. *Rolladen* - rolled roasts** are cut from various parts of the pork. ***Lenderollade* - rolled loin roast** is the most lean and tender. For pieces over 2 pounds (±1 kilo), place in a roasting pan and baste with frying butter. Put the pan into a preheated, very hot oven (475°F/250°C). After 15 minutes, reduce the heat to 325°F/165°C. Roast for 25-30 minutes per pound or until the meat thermometer reads 150° to 160°F/65°

to 70°C. It can also be braised in a Dutch oven on top of the stove with the lid slightly ajar. The ***schouderfiletrollade*** is the second most tender rolled roast followed by the ***doorregen varkensrollade*** which has more fat running through it. Prepare them all in the same manner. They are pre-spiced by the butcher but a plain roast is available upon request.

Schouderstuk **- roast or braise.** ***Schouderstuk*** is a wholesale cut weighing about 6 pounds (±3 kilos), bone-in. It can be purchased with or without the bone. The bone-in roast is a succulent piece for it has some fat running through it.

Varkensfilet is a fairly large, choice piece of meat that can be cut from the loin (with tenderloin) or the blade shoulder. It is boneless and weighs about 1¼ to 2 pounds/±600 grams to 1 kilo. Preheat the oven to 475°F/250°C, place the roast in the oven, reduce the heat to 325°F/165°C and roast for 20 to 30 minutes per pound. Baste it with pan juices.

LAMB - LAMSVLEES

In the springtime if you drive along the dikes and in the polders of Holland, you can't miss the lambs basking in the Lenten sun. Raising sheep for wool and meat is big business in Holland and lamb and mutton is featured in most supermarkets and butcher shops.

Lambs which are less than one year old are known for their mild and tender meat. They are slaughtered at various ages: milk-fed **baby lamb** or ***zuiglam*** when it is less than eight weeks old, **lamb** (which appears in the shops around Easter) when it is from two to five months old, and **regular lamb** when it is between ages six to 12 months. The Easter or spring lamb is considered to be ideal. The most famous Dutch lamb comes from the island of Texel. This lamb, fattened in pastures bordering the sea, is similar to the prized *pré-salé* (pre-salted) lamb from Brittany, France. Because of its salty taste, Texel lamb only needs to be seasoned with pepper to compliment its unusual flavor. When selecting lamb, let color be your guide. The flesh of baby lamb is light pink; it darkens to a pinkish-red in regular lambs and to red as it ages and becomes known as **mutton**. Mutton is stronger in flavor than lamb; but, the flavor can be neutralized with vinegar, wine and herbs.

Dutch lamb is cut into three major pieces and six lesser wholesale cuts. The descriptions below compare them with American wholesale cuts.

DUTCH WHOLESALE AND RETAIL LAMB CUTS WHERE THEY COME FROM

1. and 2. Hals and **Schouder** are the **Neck (1)** and **Shoulder (Blade Shoulder) (2)** wholesale pieces. The neck is sold whole or cut into **cutlets -** ***halskoteletten***. The whole neck is often deboned, filled with a stuffing, and poached. Although the **shoulder meat -** ***schouder*** is firmer than the rear **Leg**, it is quite tender and is rich in gelatin. It is generally deboned and tied into a **rolled roast - *schouderrollade***, or cut into **slices - *schouderlappen***. Scraps are cut into **soup meat - *poelet***.

3. *Rib* or ***Lamsrugribstuk*** compares with the **Rib (3)** and is divided into two pieces; the ***Voorribstuk*** (that nearest the **Shoulder**) and the ***Ribstuk*** (that nearest the **Loin**). The rib can be served as a whole **rack of lamb - *lamsrugribstuk***; it can be tied into a **crown roast - spinnekop**, or it can be cut into **chops and cutlets - *karbonaden* and *koteletten***. The deboned rack is rolled into a **rib roast - lamsrib rollade** or cut into **rib steaks - *schijf lamsrib rollade***.

4. *Rug* or ***zadel*** compares with the **Loin (4)** and **Sirloin (5)** and contains the **fillet** or ***haasje***. It is the **saddle of the lamb or double loin - *zadel*** which is the tender unseparated loin from both sides of the lamb. It can be cut into **single chops - *enkele ribkarbonaden*** from one side or **double chops - *dubbele ribkarbonaden*** from both sides. It can be roasted whole, bone-in, or deboned and tied into a **rolled roast - *lamsrollade van de rug***. This rolled roast can also be cut into **thick slices - *schijf lamsrugrollade***.

5. *Bout* is the **Leg of Lamb (5)** that can be purchased whole or divided into the *voorstuk* - center leg and the *achterstuk* - shank, with or without the bone - *met of zonder been*. Otherwise, it is cut into ***lappen* - slices**. It can also be deboned and tied into a **boneless rolled roast - *rollade***.

6. *Borst* and ***vang*** compare with the **Breast (6)**. The breast is fatty and tasty. It can be roasted whole, with or without bone, or cut into **slices - *borstlappen***. The **flank - *vang*** or ***klapstuk*** is deboned and tied into a **rolled roast - *rollade van het klapstuk*** or cubed for use as **stew meat - *ragoûtvlees***. Although not a standard local cut, the **riblets - *krabbetjes*** are available upon request.

HOW TO COOK IT

Lamb is mostly associated with countries of the Middle East or the Mediterranean, especially Greece, although it is very popular in a number of areas. They have wonderful recipes for roasted, broiled, grilled, pan-fried, braised and stewed lamb. Because of its mild flavor, its taste is enhanced by the addition of herbs, spices, aromatic vegetables and wine.

***Poelet* - cook in soup. *Poelet* - soup meat** consists of scraps cut from the neck, shoulder and breast. While lamb-based soup stocks are very popular in the Middle Eastern or Mediterranean countries, lamb in soup can be overpowering. Use it sparingly or mix with veal bones.

***Lamspootjes* - cook in soup.** The lambs feet are cuts from below the shoulder and leg. The meat and bone are used to make soup.

Lamsvlees

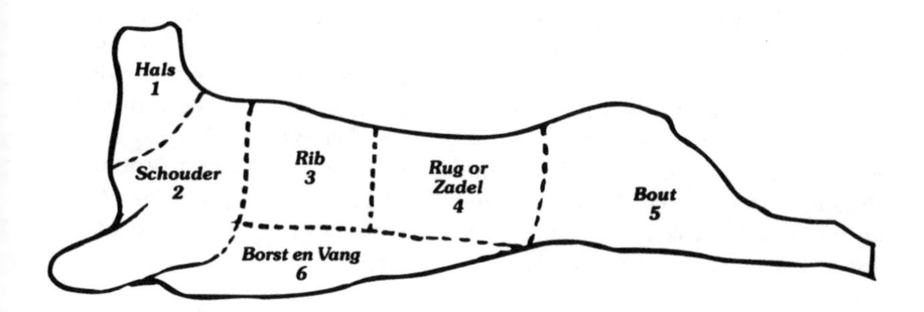

Lamb

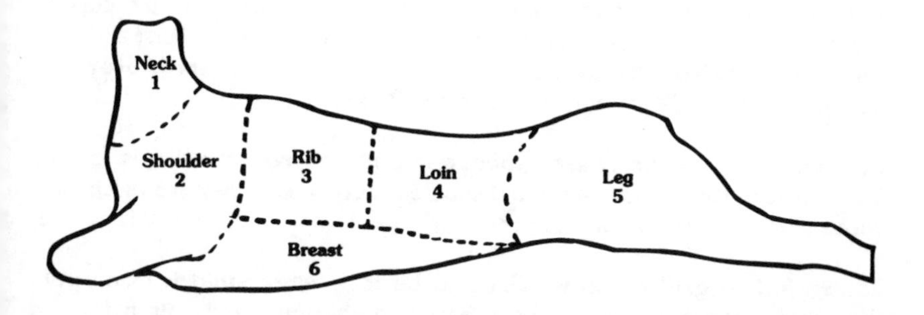

Schouder* - braise, stew, roast or grill as kebabs and saté.** The shoulder is the hardest working muscle of the lamb and it is mostly boned and tied into a **rolled roast - *schouder rollade. It is delicious when stuffed with pork sausage, poached with aromatic vegetables then braised in its own juices. It can also be cut into slices or pieces and stewed like the French dish, **Daube**. Use this piece of lamb for the Middle Eastern ***Schwerma or shoarma*** - grilled sandwiches.

***Lamsbout* - roast, grill or braise.** The ***lamsbout* - leg** is considered to be the loveliest part of the lamb for it is juicy and tasty. For a bone-in leg, have the butcher remove the hip bone and tail but leave the shank intact for it is easier to cut when the leg is not bent at the knee. The most popular way of cooking it is by inserting slivers of garlic cloves in the meatier parts and rubbing it with butter seasoned with thyme, salt and pepper. Start with a high 450°F/230°C oven and reduce the heat after 15 minutes to 350°F/ ±175°C. A medium rare roast takes about one hour. To grill bone-in, cut several deep slashes into the thick parts to allow for even cooking. A boneless leg is butterflied by making an incision down the length of the leg and removing the bone. To grill, brush it with olive oil first. The leg can also be cut into cubes and used for **Kebabs** (also known as **Shish kebabs** or **Shaslik**) and for Asian **Saté**. A bone-in 8-10 pound/3.9-4.8 kilo leg of lamb, hip bone and shank removed, serves eight or more. A 6½-pound (3 kilo) butterflied leg easily serves 10-12.

Rug or ***zadel*** and ***lamsribstuk* - roast.** These are the **saddle** and **rack of lamb** which (when left whole) make fine rib roasts that can be prepared much the same way as roast leg of lamb. The **whole rib piece - *ribstuk*** can be decoratively tied into a **crown roast - *spinnekop***. Start with very high heat 425°F/220°C, reduce heat to 325°F/170°C after 10 minutes. Total roasting time is 10 minutes per pound for rare and 15 minutes per pound for well-done.

Koteletten and ***karbonaden* - broil, grill, pan-fry or stew.** These cutlets and chops are cut from the rib - *rib*, back - *rug* or neck - *hals*. Of the three, the rib and back cutlets and chops are the most tender and juicy. They should have a rim of fat around them. Rub with herbs and brush with olive oil before grilling and serve with herbed sauces.

Lamslappen* - stew, pan-fry or grill as kebabs. *Lappen are cuts or slices of meat from the leg - *bout*, shoulder - *schouder*, breast - *borst* and neck - *nek*. The cuts from the lamb's neck, bone-in, are used for **Irish Stew** and deboned cuts for the creamy French stew, **Ragoût**.

Rollade* - braise or roast. *Rollade is a **rolled roast** which is formed from meat of the breast - *borst* and shoulder - *schouder*. They are often filled with savory stuffings before cooking.

Lamsgehakt* - grill or stew. Ground lamb - *lamsgehakt is made from the more fatty meats from the breast and shoulder. It is often formed around skewers and grilled as Middle Eastern **Kofta** or used like other ground meats in dishes such as **Moussaka** (a Greek lamb and eggplant stew). It is also popularly used to stuff various vegetables like zucchini and cabbage leaves.

SAUSAGES AND COLD CUTS - WORST EN VLEESWAREN

As in many European countries, the Dutch as a rule only have one hot meal a day. Thus, a large savory assortment of cold cuts is imperative. A basic breakfast consists of Dutch rusks - *beschuit*, breads or rolls, cheese and/or cold cuts, and sometimes a boiled egg. Lunch usually includes breads, rolls, cheese and cold cuts and occasionally a cup of soup (which does not count as a hot meal).

While some supermarkets keep a stock of pre-sliced and pre-packaged meats, on the whole cold cuts are freshly sliced as the customer waits. The sausages and cold cuts listed below are those which are widely available in the country. Other types may be found at ethnic stores or specialty shops.

Bacon There are various types of bacon that are mainly eaten raw as cold cuts in Holland although they can be used in soups and stews or pan-fried. They are mostly made from the belly and are thus streaked with fat. ***Ontbijt spek*** is a salted, smoked, cooked breakfast bacon which usually is rolled before cooking; ***katenspek*** is a type of smoked and cooked bacon which is probably the closest to, but leaner than, English- and American-style bacon; and ***bacon*** is a salted, lightly smoked, cooked bacon made from boneless rib chop.

Blood sausage, blood pudding or black pudding - *bakbloed-worst* A sausage basically made of pig's blood and suet, *bakbloedworst* can be grilled or sautéed in butter and served with mashed potatoes, potato salad or sauerkraut.

Bologna - *boterhamworst* Also spelled baloney in North America, Bologna is a term loosely applied to various lightly-smoked, pre-cooked sausages which may be lightly or highly spiced. They are fine or coarse in texture and made from pork, chicken, veal, beef or ham. The most widely used types of Bologna in Holland are fine ground *gekookte worst* and chunky *boterhamworst* which is made with cubes of fat much like the Italian *mortadella*. These sausages are usually eaten cold in sandwiches.

Casselerrib is a salted and smoked pork loin with or without bone which tastes much like ham. Check the salt content. It may have to be soaked before cooking. A cooked, boneless *casselerrib* can be sliced as cold cuts.

Cervelat - *cervelaat* A type of summer sausage which is cured, dried and smoked, cervelat resembles **salami**. It contains herbs and spices and other seasonings, namely garlic. Cervelat can be used as an appetizer and cold cut or diced and added to soups and salads.

Chipped beef - *rookvlees* is a thinly-sliced, lightly salted, smoked dried beef. This is not to be confused with ***paarderookvlees*** which is made of horse meat. The *paarderookvlees* is much darker than the regular beef *rookvlees. Rookvlees* can be used as a sandwich filling but can also be used to make **Creamed Chipped Beef on Toast or Biscuits** or in American G.I. terms, SOS.

Chorizo A spicy, hot Spanish sausage of coarsely-ground, smoked pork and highly seasoned with chilies, cumin, garlic and vinegar, *chorizo* is a relative newcomer in most Dutch shops and is a tasty addition to various soups, stews and casseroles.

Corned beef is imported from North and South America. It is similar to the corned beef one gets in cans, not at all the deli-type. It can be thinly sliced and served cold, sliced thickly and fried or chopped and fried with cabbage and/or potatoes which is called **Corned Beef Hash**. The local *pekelvlees* is probably the closest one can get to North American type corned beef.

Frankfurter knakworstjes are obviously the forerunner of the American hot dog in Holland. However, American hot dogs are becoming available at some stalls at open markets and prepared hot dogs are available at fast food stands and gas stations which promote "American hot dogs". Albert Heijn sometimes carries them in a ready-to-heat microwave packet, buns, napkin and all.

Ham Like bacon, ham is eaten cooked, or raw, as cold cuts. The local whole cooked hams, such as *achterham* and *schouderham* are also suitable for baking or frying. ***Achterham*** is cut from the leg/shank and is both smoked and cooked. ***Schouderham*** is cut from the arm shoulder and is salted, smoked, and cooked. The raw ham - ***rauwe ham*** includes the salt-cured and air-dried Black Forest, Westfalian, Ardennen and Parma hams which are eaten thinly sliced and uncooked. These hams are commonly eaten with fruits like cantaloupes and melons.

Head cheese - *zure zult* A sausage made from certain parts of the calf or pig, head cheese contains a gelatinous meat broth and is firm enough for slicing. In England it is known as *brawn* and in France as *fromage de cochon* or *pâte de tête.* It is available in some butcher shops and supermarkets.

Liver sausage - *leverworst* is available in several forms. There is a **Berliner leverworst**, a **Haagse leverworst**, a **Saksische leverworst**, and so on. All have different ingredients and have subtle differences. They are made of pork liver mixed with pork and other meat. Most are creamy smooth and **spreadable - *smeerleverworst*** but **hausmacher** is chunky and can sometimes be sliced. **Braunschweiger** is a spreadable, smoked liver sausage made from pork liver and soft pork fat mixed with eggs and milk. The delicious **Vlaamse likkepot** is a spread made from liver sausage, onions and a mixture of garden herbs.

Meat loaf - *gebraden gehakt* is readily available in most butcher shops. It is thinly sliced as a cold cut.

Pâtés and **terrines** are spreadable, seasoned, ground meat and liver pastes which can be used as snacks and appetizers or first courses. Some popular ones are mushroom, green pepper and garlic.

Roasted meats such as **beef - *rosbief*, pork - *gebraden fricandeau***, and **chicken - *gebraden kip*** are on sale in most butcher shops. They are thinly sliced and eaten as is. The pork and chicken are fully cooked but the roast beef is rather rare. If the rareness bothers you, it is excellent when lightly fried and used to make **French dip sandwiches** (hot slices of roast beef between two slices of French bread that are dipped in a cup of hot beef juice or *jus*). Use the powdered *jus* for the dipping sauce.

Salami is a term applied to a family of highly-seasoned, air-dried, sliceable sausages usually made of a mixture of pork and beef. They vary in size and shape and in curing processes. It is similar to *cervelat*. They can be used on pizzas and in soups and salads. **Pepperoni** is a type of salami which is not generally distributed in this country. The locally-made ***Rotterdammer*** is a reasonable substitute.

Sausage, fresh - *verse worst* Fresh sausages sold here are basically ***beierse braadworstje*** **- Bavarian bratwurst** made of pork and veal and fresh sausages which are the butchers' own specialties.

Sausage, smoked - *rookworst* is mostly available during the winter months. The most well-known local smoked sausage is ***Gelderse rookworst*** or smoked sausage from Gelderland. Butchers also have their own in-house specialties. They are either ***fijne rookworst*** (made from finely ground meat) or ***grove rookworst*** (coarsely ground meat) and are used for local *stamppot* dishes which include sauerkraut and curly kale and pea soup (see Dutch Traditional Foods). They are also good for **Jambalaya**. **Gelderse kookworst** is a large cooked sausage which, is sold by weight as a cold cut.

IV.10 FROZEN, CANNED AND DRIED FOODS

As most supermarkets in Holland are relatively compact neighborhood stores, shelf or freezer space is limited (as is shelf or freezer space in most homes) and products are displayed in moderation. Among the kinds of frozen foods sold are vegetables, T. V. or prepared dinners, fish, poultry, berries, juices (orange and grapefruit), snack foods and a very small variety of meats. These frozen foods are supplemented by several deep-freeze specialists who make home deliveries in large refrigerated trucks. Look under ***diepvriesprodukten*** in the ***Gouden Gids***, or **Yellow Pages**, of your telephone book or ask your neighbors whether such a service is in your area. Their catalogs are filled with a delicious assortment of ice creams and ice cream desserts, fruits, vegetables, Dutch traditional *stamppot* dishes, fish, meats and cold cuts, snacks, soups, pizzas, quiches, pastries and some T.V. dinners. They have a minimum amount for which they will make special deliveries, but if you happen to stop them when they are on your street the minimum is waived.

There is a more liberal selection on the canned food shelves of vegetables, fruits, catsup and other prepared seasonings, tomato pastes and sauces, prepared meats, seafood, stews, Asian foods and soups galore. Dried snack foods (sweet and salty), soups and pastas are well represented here.

Can sizes in Holland are expressed in content weight. For those using American recipes which call for can sizes, see the following chart:

Can sizes	Approx. Cups	Volume
5 oz	5/8	5 oz/150 gr
8 oz	1	8 oz/240 gr
No. 300	1¾	14 to 16 oz/420 to 480 gr
No. 303	2	16 to 17 oz/480 to 510 gr
No. 2	2½	20 oz/600 gr
No. 3	5¾	46 oz/3 kg

Breads and pastries

The supermarkets have a limited selection of frozen pastries; but what they do have is frozen pastry dough such as puff pastry - *bladerdeeg*, dough for savory tart - *deeg voor hartige taart* and filo - *fillo bladerdeeg* with which pastry crusts and Danish pastries are made. Unbaked croissants and pizza shells in tins are available and they only need to be baked. The frozen food specialists, on the other hand, have a nice selection of tarts, croissants and Danish pastries.

Fish

There is a good selection of frozen fish in the supermarkets. They are packaged in boxes and opaque plastic bags with pictures on them. Some frozen fish such as cod and sole are sold plain or as breaded filets and fish fingers. Canned fish and seafood like anchovies, crab, salmon, sardines, tuna and shrimp are also available. Check the contents of the cans carefully. Tuna fish, for instance, is sold water-packed, packed in oil or packed in a piquant sauce. Dried fish is only sold in seafood shops, Asian specialty stores and at fish and seafood stalls or wagons. The frozen food specialists might also carry fried or poached plaice and cod fillets, fish fingers, fried or smoked salmon, breaded shrimps and fish dinners.

Fruits and vegetables

The frozen fruits and vegetables are sold in plastic bags and paper cartons with pictures of the contents. You can usually find some berries and lots of corn, green beans, peas, spinach (whole leaf and chopped) and mixed vegetables for soups and stir-frying. Others, like curly kale, are more seasonal. There is also a generous selection of frozen potatoes which come in a variety of forms (French fries, croquettes and hash browns - *rosti*) produced by several manufacturers. Some need to be reheated by deep- or pan-frying, others can be baked in the oven.

There is a larger range of canned vegetables which, in addition to those mentioned above, include artichoke hearts, asparagus, beans, mushrooms, red bell peppers, red beets, tomatoes, hearts of palm and salsify. Canned fruits include apple sauce, berries, berry pie fillings, cherries, fruit cocktail, peaches, pears and pineapples (see also individual fruits and vegetables).

Packaged dried vegetables for stews and soups are sold in some supermarkets and greengrocers. They also carry dried pulses like split peas, brown and white beans and *kapucijners* - marrow fat peas. Occasionally, you can find lentils and kidney beans (see also individual vegetables).

Ice creams and frozen desserts

The choices of ice cream, ice cream desserts and ice cream bars are growing as new brands like Häagen Dazs are introduced from time to time. Supermarkets also have a good selection of ice cream toppings.

Meats

The selection of frozen meats in supermarkets is limited but the deep-freeze specialists will have various types of chicken pieces, hamburger patties, whole duck, sausages, schnitzels, etc. The poelier has a good selection of game and game birds in the late fall and winter. Canned meats include corned beef, spreads and pâtés, frankfurters and prepared hams. The frozen food specialists carry some lamb, pork and turkey ready for the frying pan or the oven and some ready to eat - *kant en klaar* sausages and hamburger patties.

Noodles and pastas

There is a wide choice of dried Asian noodles and Italian pastas in all supermarkets. However, for the best assortment for dried noodles and pastas visit the Asian specialty stores, gourmet shops, and stalls at open markets. Fresh pastas are also sold in Italian delicatessens that are proliferating in larger communities. Frozen pizzas are available in various assortments as are pastas like lasagna, spaghetti, macaroni with meat and cheese, and some Asian noodle dishes.

Ready to heat and eat meals - MRE's

Until recently there has been a rather paltry offering of prepared frozen or T.V. dinners but the selection is now growing. Some supermarkets now offer freshly-prepared dishes and sauces in neat vacuum-packed plastic containers. There is also an assortment of canned prepared foods including side dishes for Indonesian meals.

Sauces and salad dressings

Supermarkets carry a full range of dried and prepared sauces for beef fondue and vegetables plus salad dressings of various sorts. In addition to the European firms, Heinz and McCormick are here with some good barbecue and chili sauces plus their own salad dressings. Other prepared salad dressings are available at the import stores. Heinz catsup is here as is Worcestershire sauce. All supermarkets carry regular mayonnaise and a special mayonnaise that the Dutch and Belgians like to eat on their French fries - *fritessaus.*

Snacks

The list of ready to heat snacks is impressive. These snacks are also called *tussendoortjes* meaning in-betweens. Deep-freeze specialists carry the Indonesian *satés* and the Dutch *bitterballen* - breaded meatballs, *kroketten* and *frikandel* - croquettes, *kaassoesjes* - cheese puffs, *gehakt ballen* - regular meatballs and cheese soufflé - *kaassoufflé*. The list at the supermarket for frozen snacks is not so extensive; but they have canned Vienna and cocktail sausages, pickled gherkins and silver onions, and a mixed assortment of nuts. There are shelves of dried snacks: potato chips, soda crackers, rye and wheat breads, Melba toast, nuts and snack cups for hors d'oeuvres.

Soups

Supermarkets carry some frozen soups and an extensive collection of tinned soups and dried instant soups which are dissolved in a cup of hot water. They and the Asian stores also carry the dried Asian *ramen* and *saimin* soup packages. There is also a limited but adequate selection of Campbell's soups at some supermarkets.

IV.II CHILDREN'S FOODS

Everything is in place for raising healthy babies in Holland, and babies and children raised in Holland are among the healthiest in the world. Supermarkets, drugstores - *drogisten* and pharmacies - *apotheken* all carry baby food in jars, vitamins and infant formulas (plus non-food items such as diapers, baby wipes and pacifiers). For evening or weekend emergencies, at least one designated pharmacy stays open in each area on Saturdays, Sundays and evenings. The name of the appointed pharmacy is posted on all other pharmacy doors.

It is the custom in Holland to establish a relationship with a doctor, usually in your vicinity, who will in turn become your family's general practitioner - *huisarts*. He or she can recommend foods for your baby and will refer you to specialists when such services are required. In addition to this, as a foreign resident in Holland you are entitled to the services of a consultation bureau - *consultatie bureau* by joining the *Kruisvereniging*, a nationwide health organization. The *consultatie bureau* is the semi-equivalent of the wellness clinics for children in the United States, and among other things can give you nutritional guidance. However, until you have a *huisarts* or have access to the *consultatie bureau*, this is a quick overview of baby and children's foods available on the Dutch market.

FOOD FOR INFANTS - *ZUIGELINGEN*

Infant formulas for healthy babies - *volledige zuigelingen voeding*
There are three major producers of baby formulas: Nutricia, Friesland Nutrition or Friese Flag and Abbott B.V. All three have 24-hour hot lines: Nutricia, Tel: 0800-0 22 26 26; Friesland Nutrition Tel: 0800-022 74 34 and Abbott Tel: (020) 545 45 00. They should have someone on duty who can speak English. Their standard cow's milk formulas for healthy babies are: Nutrilon, Friso and Similac, respectively. They are sold in supermarkets, drugstores and pharmacies, primarily in powdered form, although Nutricia and Friso products are also available in liquid - *vloeibaar* form. Nutrilon Premium 1, Frisolac and Similac are for babies from 0-6 months - *vanaf de geboorte* and Nutrilon Plus 2, Frisomel and Similac 2 are for babies from 6 months - *vanaf 6 maanden*, and Nultrilon 3 for babies from 10 months – *vanaf 10 maanden.*

Infant formulas with special food requirements - *speciale voedingsbehoefte* are sold in some supermarkets, drugstores and pharmacies. Each manufacturer of infant formulas has a variety of products for babies with special needs. Nutricia products come in two types - Premium 1 for babies 0-6 months and Plus 2 for babies older than 6 months. For Friesland products, all those with 1 in the title are for babies 0-6 months, products with 2 in the title are for babies older than 6 months. However, you should consult your doctor before using them. Special formulas can be much more expensive, but the cost is usually covered by insurance. Small packages of these formulas can often be found at *apotheken* and larger supermarkets - it's best to try them before you buy a month's supply:

For premature or underdeveloped babies - *zuigelingenmelk voor prematuur en dymatuur geboren kinderen:* Nenatal and Nental BMF or Frisopré.
For hungry - *hongerige babies:* Nutrilon Forte.
For babies that spit up - *spugen:* Nutrilon A.R. and A.R. Plus 2
For babies that spit up, are constipated or have cramps - *bij spugen, obstipatie en krampjes:* Frisovorm.
For babies that have cramps, spit up and are tired – *helpt bij krampjes, spugen en moeisame ontblasting:* Nutricia Omnea 1 and 2
For babies with cramps - *krampjes:* Nutrilon Farilon.
For babies with cow's milk allergy - *koemelk allergy:* Nutrilon Pepti & Frisopep.
For babies with serious allergies from birth - *ernstige voedsel allergy:* Nutri-junior.
For mild lactose intolerance - *milde lactose-intolerantie:* Nutrilon Laag Lactose.
For babies with serious lactose intolerance - *ernstige lactose-intolerantie:* Nutrilon Soya and Frisosoy.

For making up formulas, you may wish to use bottled water as the Dutch water is hard in some places and leaves a residue in bottles even after boiling. Friesland Nutrition also has a disposable system with Frisopré, Frisolac, Frisomed glucose, Frisomed water and Frisomed O.R.S. in various sizes of disposable bottles. The disposable nipples - *spenen* are free and come with the bottles. Oral rehydration powders or O.R.S. solutions are available at the pharmacist and the drugstore. They are made with sucrose in place of glucose and often come in different flavors. Ask at the pharmacy if you can try one envelope of each flavor, rather than buying a box of one type and having it rejected by a sick, and possibly cranky, child.

FOOD FOR BABIES AND SMALL CHILDREN

Baby food in jars - *baby voeding or baby maaltijd* The most widely available jarred baby foods are sold under the name Olvarit by Nutricia.They offer a delicious array of pureed vegetables, fruits, vegetables mixed with meats and dairy products mixed with fruit - *zuivelhapjes met fruit.*There are pictures on the label to identify the ingredients. In addition, the labels specify the ages - *leeftijd* in terms of months - *maanden* for which the food is suitable; i.e. *baby vanaf 4 maanden, baby vanaf 8 maanden* and *peuter vanaf 15 maanden.* The ages of the *baby* - baby, and *peuter* - toddler vary according to manufacturer.

Beverages - *drank* There are many different types of juices and colas on the market. Baby juice is usually labeled *puur sap* - pure juice (with no additives or chemical preservatives) and is in the baby food section of the supermarkets. It is most often sold in concentrated, or syrup, form. There are many kinds of syrup that can be mixed with water or, for older children, carbonated mineral water. The rose hip syrup - *rozenbottel siroop* is exceptionally high in natural vitamin C. For special situations, Roosvicee has developed two fruit syrups, Stop and Laxo, which can be used by children with mild diarrhea and constipation, respectively. Other fruit mixtures are available, with or without added vitamins. Many fruit syrups - *limonades* are produced organically - *biologique*, meaning grown without pesticides. Look for the EKO mark. Due to the fact that most Dutch kitchens have very small freezers, juice is generally not available frozen. Kindercola is cola meant for older children, and has a lower caffeine content.

Cereal, breakfast - *ontbijt granen* There are several brands of baby cereals or pablums. Molenaar's Kindermeel is available in rice flour - *rijstebloem,* grain flakes - *graanvlokken* and seven grains - *7-granen.* Nutrix and Bambix *rijstebloem* comes in natural and various flavors. Rice flour is easier to digest than wheat flour - *tarwebloem. Bambix groei ontbijt, volkoren ontbijt met fruit* are other baby cereals while older children can enjoy cereals or porridge such *as Brinta, Nutricia nutrigraan volkoren pap* - porridge, muesli and *havermout* - oatmeal. Ages are indicated on the boxes. In addition, there is a limited selection by international brands like Kelloggs, Quaker and Nestle. Some gourmet shops featuring imported goods have a bigger variety.

Children's biscuits - *kindervoeding* Liga brand children's biscuits are available in the supermarket section for children's foods. These crackers are developed for different age ranges, i.e. Liga for children aged from 4 months - *Liga van 4 maanden*, etc. The useful phrases to know are: gluten free/no wheat protein - *gluten vrij*; no chicken eggs - *kippen-eiwit vrij;* milk free - *koemelk-vrij*, and rich in fiber - *rijk aan vezels.* Some cookies and crackers are available prepackaged, in twos and threes, and can be handy for taking along in the diaper bag.

Bread topping - *brood beleg* Children in the Netherlands generally eat sandwiches for breakfast and lunch. Kids and adults love the interesting selection of bread toppings. Hagel or *hagelslag*, *vlokken*, and *muisjes* are small chocolate or fruity candy bits, flakes and balls that are sprinkled over buttered bread, rusks or rolls. They come in various forms: *chocolade vlokken melk en puur* - milk and pure chocolate flakes, *chocolade hagel melk en puur* - milk and pure chocolate bits, *vruchten hagel* - fruit lumps, *anijs hagel* - anise flavored bits, *vlokfeest* - white and brown chocolate flakes, *rose en witte muisjes* - pink and white "mice" (candy-coated anise seeds), *gestampte muisjes* - coarsely ground "mice" and *toffee-feest* - mixed toffee flakes. Buttered rusks sprinkled with *muisjes* are usually served to guests to celebrate the arrival of newborns. In addition, there are several spreads and pastes such as peanut butter - *pindakaas*, hazelnut butter - *hazelnotenpasta*; and chocolate spread - *chocoladepasta* and various jams and jellies. Children's sandwiches sometimes contain meat. The favorites are *boterhamworst, smeerworst*, and *smeerpastei.* Small children often eat sandwiches of *smeerkaas* - a cheese food product.

Vitamins - *vitaminen* There are many brands of children's vitamins. Davitamon AD or D and Zymofluor combi-drops have been around for a long time. In the Netherlands, tap water is not fluorinated, thus babies and children are given fluoride drops along with vitamins or formula.

IV.12 HEALTH AND VEGETARIAN FOODS

The Dutch are very aware of the benefits of eating well and there is a limited health food counter in every supermarket. There are also health food stores - *reform winkels* or *reform huizen* in most cities. Look for them under ***reform-artikelen*** in the **Gouden Gids**, or **Yellow Pages**, of the telephone book. Theirs are natural products with no chemicals added and are made of organically-grown or *biologische* materials. There is an emphasis on vegetarian foods, vitamins and special low sugar, low salt, low cholesterol or gluten free diets. Some health food stores also carry baby foods, pet foods, cooking oils, coffee substitutes, herbal teas, grains and flours, pastas, juices, sugars, candies, bread spreads, jams and jellies, soya bean products, nuts and seeds, fresh and canned vegetables, syrups, cleaning and laundry supplies and cosmetics. They also carry fresh milk and milk products such as yoghurt, *garde*, *acidophilus melk*, margarine and ice cream and milk substitutes such as soya milk. *Unigel* and *Marmello* are pectin based gelling agents used to thicken jellies, jams and preserves. The food stuffs are listed in other chapters. The articles listed below are only representative samples.

Calorie counts on food packages are expressed in joules. One calorie (actually a kilo calorie or kcal) equals 4.2 kilo joules.

Vegetarian foods - *vegetarisch eten*

Many supermarkets and health food shops are also carrying some type of meat substitutes - *vleesvervangers* and prepared products.

Burgermix A mix of soya bean protein, grains, potato flakes and herbs, you can mix this product with water to create burgers or meatballs. Fry them in hot oil.

Cheese Trenta is a Dutch vegetarian cheese in that it uses no animal rennet.

Quorn Quorn belongs to the mushroom family. It is made by fermenting the myco-protein from the plant in a process similar to yoghurt or cheese. The result is a yoghurt-like mass from which the water is extracted. What is left is a dough-like product to which plant seasonings and egg white is added to thicken it. It comes minced, diced and marinated and can easily be used in stir-fry dishes and fried rice and fried noodles in place of meat.

Tahoe (tofu) - See Asian food chapter

Tempe - See Asian food chapter

Vegetarian cold cuts - *vegetarisch broodbeleg* With the help of vegetable oils, yeast powder, soya flour, and tivall, food makers prepare a variety of vegetarian dishes including those which look like cold cuts of various flavors, sausages and paté.

Tivall was created as a Kosher food in Israel. It is made from soy flour, wheat gluten and sunflower oil. It looks like meat or vegetables. It is used to make burgers, sausages and schnitzels.

General health food terms:

additives	*toevoegingen*
additives, artificial	*kunstmatige toevoegingen*
color	*kleurstoffen*
sweetener	*zoetstoffen*
flavoring	*smaakstoffen*
preservatives	*conserveermiddelen*
additives, without	*zonder toevoegingen*
bran (grain)	*zemelen*
chemicals	*chemische stoffen*
diet	*dieet*
easy on your stomach	*maagvriendelijk*
flakes	*vlokken*
fats	*vetten*
animal fat	*dierlijk vet*
butter fat	*botervet*
vegetable fat	*plantaardig vet*
germ (grain)	*kiemen*
gluten free	*glutenvrij*
healthy	*gezond*
lactose (non-dairy)	*lactose (melkvrij)*
mild	*milde*
nutrients	*voedingsstoffen*
nutritional value	*voedingswaarde*
protein	*eiwit*
carbohydrates	*koolhydraten*
fat	*vet*
energy	*energie*
sodium	*natrium*
percentage of	*procent van*
pure	*zuivere*
organic	*biologisch*
salt	*zout*
salt free	*zoutloos*
low salt	*natriumarm*
sea salt	*zeezout*
sugar	*suiker*
fruit sugar	*fructose*
grape sugar	*dextrose*
no sugar added	*geen suiker toegevoegd*
sweetened	*gezoet*
unsweetened	*ongezoet*
vegetarian	*vegetarisch*
vitamins	*vitaminen*

IV.13 BEVERAGES

One doesn't have to go thirsty in Holland. Almost every major beverage manufacturer is represented here. Supermarkets carry some soft drinks, mineral waters, mixes, juices, beers and wines, and beverage or liquor stores sell hard liquors, liqueurs, brandies, wines, coolers and mixes. Look under ***slijterijen*** in the ***Gouden Gids***, or **Yellow Pages**, of the telephone book. In addition to the well-known imported brands, there are some excellent local brews which are worth trying. Typical Dutch drinks are described in detail under the chapter on **Dutch Traditional Foods**.

Apple juice, apple cider and apple Brandy. The local **apple juice** - ***appelsap*** is a pasteurized juice made from Dutch apples. What many know as **apple cider** is the pure unprocessed apple juice. It is not sold retail as such but is allowed to ferment and become 'hard' cider or **apple wine**, which in Europe is called **apple cider** or ***cidre***. *Cidre* is either **still** or **sparkling** - ***mousserend***. ***Calvados*** or **applejack** is a potent **brandy** distilled from apple cider. Both cider and brandy are sold in beverage stores or *slijterijen*.

Beer Amstel, Grolsch and Heineken are probably the most famous of the Dutch beers. In addition, there are many other small breweries that turn out some superb beers to the delight of beer lovers and connoisseurs. Neighboring Belgium also enjoys a very fine reputation for its excellent beer.

Coffee - ***koffie*** The Dutch initiated the commercial exploitation of coffee when a shipment arrived in 1637. By 1660 they were trading coffee on a large scale. It is still arguably the world's finest. A good cup of Dutch coffee is dark and rich and full of flavor without being bitter. The secret of this wonderful combination is in the roasting. **Regular** and **caffeine-free** - ***caffeinevrij*** coffees are available as **whole beans** - ***bonen*** or in **coarse grind** - ***grof gemalen***, **regular grind** - ***normaal gemalen***, **fine or drip grind** - ***snelfilter-maling*** and as **instant coffee** - ***oploskoffie*** **or instant freeze-dried coffee** - ***vriesdroog koffie***. Unless specifically stated otherwise, ground coffee is always drip-grind. Coffee substitutes such as chicory are available at health food stores. Specialty shops also carry a good variety of coffee and coffee blends from around the world and Italian delicatessens located in the larger communities carry Italians blends.

Coffee milk - ***koffiemelk*** is sold either full - *volle* or half full - *half volle* and is known as **sterilized** and **condensed** or **evaporated milk** - ***gesteriliseerde geëvaporeerde koffie melk***. It is delicious and can also be used in dessert or savory pie recipes calling for evaporated milk. There is also a liquid non-dairy coffee cream (Menkomel) and some **powdered creamers** - ***koffiecreamers*** available here.

Juice - *sap* There is an ample selection of fruit and vegetable juices and fruit-flavored drinks. Orange, apple, pineapple and tomato juices are the most popular and they are sold in bottles or in paper cartons. Frozen orange and grapefruit juices are available in some supermarkets. Fruit drinks include guava, mango, papaya, passion fruit and strawberry/cherry mixed. Fruit flavored iced teas are a recent addition to the Dutch marketplace.

Liquor and liqueurs - *sterke dranken* There is a extensive array of **Scotch, bourbon, vodka, gin, rum, brandy** and **liqueurs** on Dutch shelves. Most are imported, but many excellent liqueurs and brandies are manufactured by local companies such as the Bols. You should try some of the traditional Dutch drinks like **Jenever**, ***Advocaat*** and ***Bisschop's Wijn***. They are described in the chapter **Traditional Dutch Foods**.

Soft Drinks - *fris dranken* Coke and Coke-Light, Pepsi and 7-Up have cornered the soft drink market although other types are also well represented. Many Dutch families make their own soft drinks by adding one of the many fruity syrups to a bubbling mineral water.

Tea - *thee* The first tea to arrive in Europe came to Holland in 1610 and like coffee, the Dutch started its commercial exploitation. It is still a very popular drink here. Twinings, Lipton and Pickwick teas, as well as herbal and fruit teas (such as Celestial Seasonings) are available at supermarkets, health food stores and Asian shops or *toko*. Several iced tea drinks have recently been introduced to the market. Some are carbonated.

Water - *water* Probably the least consumed beverage in Holland is tap water. Most people drink bottled water, partially because it is *chique* and partially because restaurants do not serve tap water. Spa is a big name brand. It comes carbonated - *koolzuurhoudend* (*Spa rood*), plain (*Spa blauw*) and with lemon and sugar added (*Spa groen*). The *blauw* (blue), red (*rood*) and green (*groen*) refer to the color of the labels. **Spring water** is known as *bronwater*.

Wine - *wijn* Wines from all over the world can be found here, especially those from France, Italy and Germany. Some American and South African wines are also available at selected beverage dealers. Albert Heijn, the largest supermarket chain in Holland, has established a good name for their wines; and if you know a little about the subject, this is a good place to shop. Prices vary but you can still get a good bottle for around f10. Many beverage or liquor stores bottle their own reliable house wines. Wine can be red - *rood*, white - *wit*, rosé - *rosé*, dry - *droog*, very dry - *brut*, sweet - *zoet*, light - *licht*, full-bodied - *vol* or sparkling - *mousserend*.

IV.14 TRADITIONAL DUTCH FOODS

While the local cuisine is rich in variety, due to the inclusion of many recipes which criss-cross international borders, there is a basic Dutch cuisine that is best described as "home cooking". It is "comfort food" which most Dutchmen crave when away from home for prolonged periods or after a summer of light meals.

The Dutch usually only eat one hot meal a day; it can be served for lunch or dinner, but it is generally served as the evening meal. The other two meals are sandwich meals consisting of Dutch rusks or *beschuit*, sliced breads, rolls and croissants topped with butter, jams or jellies, cheeses, sausages or cold cuts. Breakfast might be accompanied by a boiled egg. Lunch could be served with a cup of soup, croquettes or an *uitsmijter* - an opened-faced sandwich consisting of two slices of bread topped with ham slices and two quivering fried eggs. The hot soup does not necessarily make them "hot meals". A kind of lunch with several varieties of breads and toppings is commonly referred to as a *koffietafel*, meaning that it is a lunch which accompanies coffee, much the same as *Dim Sum* snacks accompany the Chinese High Tea - *yam cha*.

Vegetables are central to the hot meal. Any of the local dishes can contain a pound of vegetables cooked with 3 to 4 ounces (100 grams) of meat per person. The vegetables are often the integral part of one of the many *stamppot* dishes which are vegetables cooked with potatoes, often with meat. The meat is removed and sliced and the vegetables are mashed together. The local butcher sells ready to eat *stamppot* dishes beginning in the autumn months through spring. He also sells pre-cut vegetables so the local housewives can make their own. The hot meal may include shrimp cocktail, salted herring or a Hussar's salad for starters and is finished with a healthy serving of fruit. Coffee is served after the meal.

Most of the entertaining takes the form of coffee at eight, served with luxury sweets. The evening visit is extended when and if the host offers Scotch, wine or gin.

Since the days when Indonesia was a Dutch colony, the Dutch have been fond of the Indonesian rice table - *rijsttafel* which consists of numerous side dishes served with a central bowl of steamed white rice.

BEVERAGES

Advocaat Not so well known outside Holland, *Advocaat* is made with eggs and brandy and is actually eaten with a spoon and topped off with a dollop of whipped cream. It is not unlike egg nog in flavor and is delicious on pancakes and ice cream.

Bisschopswijn A Christmas drink of mulled red wine, bishop's wine is sweetened then spiced with stick cinnamon and cloves stuck in a whole lemon and served piping hot.

Boerenjongens and ***Boerenmeisjes*** are Dutch brandies aged with raisins and apricots, respectively.

Jenever Arguably Holland's national drink, *Jenever* is the "mother of all gins". Originally a stomach medicine with a little alcohol added to improve the taste and make it more palatable, the British loved it enough to smuggle barrels into their country before developing a gin of their own. *Jenever* is mostly drunk as an aperitif when it is called a *borrel.* It is kept in the freezer and consumed neat, ice cold, like vodka. You can buy it ***jong*** - young or ***oud*** - old, as is or with berries when it becomes ***bessenjenever.***

SNACK FOODS AND SANDWICHES

***Snoepjes* - candies** It would be an exaggeration to say that Dutch babies are born with *snoepjes* in their mouths but long before they are able to pronounce the word *snoepje,* Dutch mothers are popping these little sugary morsels between the lips of every little Hans or Mieke. You'll recognise these candies for they are sold from bins in supermarkets, drugstores and shops that specialize in candies (as opposed the more sophisticated shops which make bonbons). The most well-known *snoepjes* are the various licorice-flavored drops - *dropjes* which the Dutch enjoy throughout their lives. They are not to be confused with the licorice drops of say North America and come salty or sweet.

Bitterballen Breaded, deep-fried, minced meatballs, *bitterballen* resemble croquettes in texture and flavor and are eaten with the before-dinner aperitif or *borrel.* They are not, as their name suggests, bitter. They get their name from the *bittertje,* a kind of *jenever* sipped before dinner.

Kaassoesjes These delectable little cream puff pastries are filled with grated cheese mixed with butter.

Belegde broodjes *Broodjes* can mean sandwich buns or the sandwiches themselves. *Belegde* means that the *broodjes* are served with a filling, usually with ham or cheese.

Saucijzen broodjes are snacks made with skinless sausage meat rolled and baked in puff pastry. They are good for morning coffee for those who don't eat sweets.

Uitsmijters are very popular open-faced sandwiches consisting of two slices of bread topped with slices of ham, roast beef or cheese and always topped with two or three lightly-fried, quivering *spiegeleieren* (literally meaning mirror eggs) and lots of butter.

SOUP

Erwtensoep* - Pea Soup** Ask ten Dutch nationals to name Holland's national dish and nine will mention the hearty Dutch Pea Soup - ***Erwtensoep or ***Snert*** as it is commonly known. It has a special blend of ingredients: dried split peas, celery root, celery leaves, leeks, onion, fresh parsley, winter carrot and a selection of smoked ham or pig's knuckle, pork chops, smoked sausage and pork belly or smoked bacon. The flavors are enhanced by a sprig or two of fresh thyme. Greengrocers sell pre-cut

Erwtensoep vegetables during the autumn and winter season; but the time spent on peeling, cutting and chopping your own vegetables is well rewarded. Butcher shops also sell the soup ready-to-eat.

***Bruine-bonensoep* - Brown Bean Soup** This is another delicious Dutch favorite made of dried brown beans, bay leaf, dried chili pepper, cloves, smoked bacon, leek, celery, onions, potatoes and chopped fresh parsley.

***Groentensoep* - Vegetable Soup** This tasty soup is made of mixed green vegetables with a bouillon base. Tiny spiced meatballs are sometimes added. The fresh soup packet is available in supermarkets and greengrocers.

DAIRY PRODUCTS

***Vla* - custard or pudding** *Vla* is a custard or pudding of sorts which is sold in milk cartons and comes in a variety of flavors, usually vanilla, chocolate and strawberry. You can find it snuggled up to the milk and yoghurt in the dairy cooler - see *vla* and Dutch yoghurt in the **Dairy Products** chapter.

MEATS AND MAIN COURSE DISHES

***Blinde vinken* and *Sla vinken* - veal birds** These little "veal birds" made up of ground veal rolled in thin veal cutlets are best when fried, while *sla vinken* are made up of lean minced pork wrapped in streaky bacon which are good fried or barbecued.

***Asperges met ham en eieren* - asparagus with ham and eggs** This is an interesting combination of cooked white asparagus served with sliced boiled eggs, mixed ham slices and boiled potatoes topped with generous helpings of melted butter. This is a traditional spring treat.

***Boerenkool met worst* - Curly kale with smoked sausage** Dear to the Dutch stomach and heart is this curly kale *stamppot* dish which is made from smoked sausage, lardons of bacon or unprocessed bacon slices - *speklapjes* and browned onions cooked with sliced potatoes. The sausage is removed and the vegetables and bacon are mashed together to a consistency thick enough for a wooden spoon to stand up in it. The kale is sold frozen in supermarkets or can be purchased chopped and ready to cook at the greengrocers or ready to heat and eat at the butcher shop.

***Hachee* - Beef and onion stew** A simple to prepare savory beef and onion stew, *Hachee* is traditionally made with leftovers from a roast beef and its pan juices. The leftovers are by design and not by poor meal planning. A mixture of vinegar, bay leaves, cloves, Worcestershire sauce or meat extract give it a unique flavor. It is served with boiled potatoes.

***Hutspot* - hodgepodge** This is a historical *stamppot* dish. In October the people of Leiden eat it to remember the Spanish siege in 1573 and '74 and the subsequent lifting of the siege of the Dutch. It consists of browned brisket or *klapstuk* cooked with one part sliced onions, one part shredded carrots and two parts boiling potatoes. This is cooked in as little water as possible so that after the vegetables are soft and are puréed, a wooden spoon should stand straight up in them. The meat is removed before the vegetables are puréed.

Witlof met ham en kaassaus - **Belgian endives with ham and cheese** A simple but delicious dish, *Witlof met ham en kaas* is made from steamed endives wrapped with ham slices and baked in the oven with a rich cheese sauce. They are served with boiled potatoes.

Zuurkool met worst - **Sauerkraut with sausage** This is another great *stamppot* dish which consists of smoked sausage and smoked bacon cooked with boiled potatoes and sauerkraut. It is flavored with white wine and juniper berries. The meats are removed and the vegetables mashed together. The sausage is sliced and arranged on top.

BREADS AND PASTRIES

Appelbeignets - **apple fritters**, ***appelflappen*** - **apple turnovers**, ***appelgebak*** - **apple cake** (apples baked in sweet crust pastry) and ***appelbollen*** - **apple balls** (whole peeled cored apples filled with sugar and cinnamon and baked in a puff pastry shell) are popular apple pastries available here.

Botercake is a butter cake similar to a pound cake.

Boterkoek is a type of short bread. It is sometimes filled with almond paste - ***gevulde boterkoek***.

Flensjes Thin crepes which can be served with any number of delicious fruity and/or creamy fillings and sauces.

Goudse stroopwafels These thin Gouda waffles are more like wafers than waffles. Two are sandwiched together with a thick syrup in between. Many travellers take these home as gifts.

Kerstkransjes Christmas wreaths made of puff pastry and filled with almond paste.

Kerststol A delicious Christmas bread with raisins and almond filling, *Kerststol* is like the German ***stollen***.

Kerst Tulband/Paas Tulband Christmas or Easter turbans filled with currants, raisins or almond paste.

Oliebollen Literally translated as ‘oil balls’, *oliebollen* are similar to donuts in taste and are made with currants and raisins. They are specifically eaten on New Year’s Eve but are a hot item during the summer village fairs.

Ontbijtkoek A spiced heavy breakfast cake.

Pannenkoek This must be the forerunner of the American pancake but the Dutch scorn those who eat them for breakfast. They come in two sizes, big (over a foot in diameter) and bigger. The most common pancake is fried with bacon and covered with **stroop**, a very thick local syrup. They also cover them with fruits and some other delicious toppings. Restaurants specializing in pancakes are abundant here.

Poffertjes Delicious mini-pancakes served with dollops of butter and sprinkled with powdered sugar, *poffertjes* are served at some pancake houses and at *poffertjes* booths at local festivals.

Speculaas Generously spiced with cinnamon, cloves and nutmeg, these cookies may take several forms; i.e., St. Nicolaas during the Christmas season and Abraham for 50th birthday celebrations. They are known as *speculaas poppen*. Some speculaas pastries are also filled with almond paste - *gevulde speculaas*.

Taai Taai are small, soft doll-shaped cookies which are similar to *speculaas* dolls - *speculaas poppen* but have a different combination of seasonings.

Vlaai These tarts are better known as *Limburgse vlaai* - Limburg pies, the province where they originate. They are made from a sweet bread dough, filled with custard and fresh or dried fruits or cooked, spiced rice. Tea rooms serving nothing but different types of these tarts are now the trend.

IV.15 ASIAN AND OTHER INTERNATIONAL FOOD PRODUCTS

Holland is a former shipping and colonial power which had interests in Indonesia, South Africa and the Caribbean. Many people from these countries eventually came to live in Holland. They were later joined by guest workers from the Mediterranean countries and by international businessmen and women and their families, as Holland became the hub of their business interests in Europe. Thus, Holland is a truly international country; and it is relatively easy to find delicatessen or gourmet food shops and supermarkets which cater to most culinary needs. Look under ***delicatessen*** in the ***Gouden* Gids**, or **Yellow Pages**. In addition to these food shops, there are usually a few stalls at open markets which carry ethnic food stuffs for different palates. In Beverwijk, between Amsterdam and Alkmaar, there is a very active weekend Eastern Market - *Oosterse Markt* which specializes in food stuffs for Middle Eastern cuisines.

Mexican food has become very popular in recent years with supermarkets, gourmet shops and Asian stores carrying dried, frozen and/or canned corn tortillas; fresh flour tortillas; salsa; taco seasonings; taco sauces; bean dips; frozen guacamole; canned chilies and nacho chips.

Holland's long association with Indonesia is reflected in the many Indonesian restaurants that feature the formal Indonesian *rijsttafel* or "rice table" consisting of numerous dishes with rice as the central course. It might include at least three different types of rice, several fish, meat, poultry and vegetable dishes and side dishes or condiments. The *Nasi rames* is a simpler version. These restaurants should not be confused with the ubiquitous Indonesian/Chinese restaurants. They are also different from the Chinese restaurants where the Chinese population eats in the larger cities.

Almost as prolific are the *toko* or mom and pop Asian stores which are purveyors of nearly everything necessary to prepare Indonesian and other Asian meals. The shop keepers in the *toko* carry a large selection of imported foods and spices, as well as some produced locally. Some have their own in-house specialties of prepared Indonesian dishes. There are also several Chinese supermarkets in the larger cities. Look for *oosterse producten* in the Yellow pages. Besides Chinese ingredients, vegetables and frozen Dim Sum snacks, they also sell products from all over Asia. See the listing of International Food Shops in the Appendices. Most supermarkets also have a special section devoted mainly to locally-made Indonesian and other Asian food products. These products appear with the native or generally-accepted spelling and, when applicable, with the Dutch phonetic spelling in brackets indicated by D. The 'c' in *Bahasa* Indonesian is pronounced like a 'ch'.

POPULAR INDONESIAN RIJSTTAFEL DISHES:

Indonesian cooking encompasses the cooking of over 300 ethnic groups which live on about 6,000 of Indonesia's 18,000 islands. But what we generally see is basically Javanese, Sumatran and Balinese. There are also very strong Chinese and some Dutch influences. Many of the vegetables used in Indonesian cooking were introduced by the Dutch during their long relationship with Indonesia and the word *rijsttafel* is a purely Dutch invention. Somehow, the Indonesian restaurant owners have managed to condense this rich cuisine into a *rijsttafel* menu of up to 21 dishes.

Acar - atjar (D) The term applies to one or a mixture of pickled vegetables that are served as side dishes in most Indonesian meals. The most popular dish is *acar campur - atjar tjampoer (D)* which is pickled mixed vegetables.

Ayam goreng - ajam goreng (D) Fried - *goreng* chicken - *ayam*. The chicken is usually boiled first and then fried. The stock is used in other dishes. Each island or region has its own method.

Babi kecap - babi ketjap (D) This Javanese dish consists of small strips of pork - *babi* simmered in a sweet soy - *kecap* sauce.

Bahmie goreng - bami (D) Noodles - *bahmie* fried - *goreng* with chicken and/or shrimps, cabbage, carrots, red onions or shallots and garlic seasoned with soy sauce. Although it is Chinese in origin, it is one of Indonesia's national dishes. Bahmie goreng is a main dish and not usually a part of the *rijsttafel* but some restaurants serve it because their customers like it.

Bawang goreng Indonesian onion - *bawang* flakes fried until crispy. Indonesian cooks use the small Indonesian red shallots - *bawang merah* but the European shallots are often used here. These crispy onions flakes are generously sprinkled over fried rice and noodles, soups and vegetables and give the dishes a boost in terms of flavor.

Gado-gado Another national favorite, *gado gado* is a salad made of a selection of parboiled cabbage, bean sprouts, carrots, beans or potatoes topped with a peanut sauce dressing.

Ikan Bali Deep-fried fish covered with a sauce of onions, *sambal ulek, laos,* lemon grass, tamarind juice, ginger, brown sugar and soy sauce.

Ikan kari Fish in a curry sauce.

Krupuk udang or krupuk emping - kroepoek oedang or emping (D) Prawn - *udang* and melinjo - *emping* crackers or wafers - *krupuk* deep fried until light and crispy. They are served with most Indonesian meals.

Lumpia - loempia (D) A large Indonesian version of the Chinese spring roll, *lumpia* is an Indonesian favorite. It is stuffed with meats, bean sprouts and cabbage leaves and flavored with soy sauce, garlic and green onions.

Nasi goreng Rice - *nasi* fried - *goreng* with chicken, shrimps, onions, red chilies, garlic and soy sauce. *Nasi goreng* is another Chinese-inspired dish and is usually a main course wuth several accompaniments such as fried chicken, fried shrimp, serundeng, sliced cucumbers and tomato wedges.

Nasi kuning - nasi koening (D) A savory yellow - *kuning* rice - *nasi* cooked with turmeric, coriander seed, *salam* leaf, garlic and onion, it is always served on special occasions in Indonesia.

Nasi putih Plain white - *putih*, steamed rice - *nasi*.

Pisang goreng Peeled banana - *pisang* fried - *goreng* which is usually dipped in a rice flour batter then deep-fried.

Rendang Daging A delicious dry, beef dish which is long-cooked in coconut milk and spices until the gravy has all but disappeared and the meat begins to fry in the coconut oil.

Rujak - roedjak (D) A hot, spicy fruit salad.

Sambal The name *sambal* applies to a family of hot chili relishes or condiments tremendously popular in Indonesia and Holland. Here you can buy it prepared; but in Indonesia, cooks often grind their own *sambal* with a stone mortar and pestle. The salty *sambal olek - ulek* (D) is the most common in Holland. *Sambal bajak - badjak* (D) is a sweet paste flavored with garlic and shrimp paste (good for frying spicy chicken), *sambal manis* is relatively mild and sweet, *sambal kemeri* is made with candle nuts and *sambal udang* is made with shrimps or prawns.

Sambal goreng telur is made with hardboiled eggs - *telur*, fried with *sambal*, *laos*, onions, garlic, brown sugar and coconut milk.

Saté or satey One of the most well-known Indonesian dishes, saté consists of barbecued skewered pieces of chicken - *ayam*, pork - *babi*, beef - *daging*, duck - *bebek*, lamb/goat - *kambing* or fish - *ikan*. They are often served with a spicy peanut dipping sauce, but there are numerous methods for preparing them.

Saus kacang pedis A spicy hot - *pedis*, peanut - *kacang*, sauce - *saus* usually used as a dipping sauce for saté or satey.

Sayur lodeh A rich, spicy mixed vegetable - *sayur* stew.

Serundeng - seroendeng (D) A side dish made with roasted, grated coconut and fried peanuts.

Smor - Smoor (D) Chicken, beef or duck braised in a sweet soy sauce with onions and nutmeg. It is obviously Dutch influenced.

Tempe goreng *Tempe* is a solid slab of treated whole soy beans. *Tempe goreng* is *tempe* fried with shallots, garlic and tamarind water.

POPULAR CHINESE DIM SUM DISHES

蝦 餃	Ha Kau	Steamed shrimp moon dumplings
燒 賣	Siu Mai	Steamed minced pork dumplings
冬菇燒賣	Tong Ku Siu Mai	Steamed minced pork dumplings with mushrooms
牛肉燒賣	Ngau Yuk Siu Mai	Minced beef baskets
糯米雞	Lau Mei Kai	Steamed lotus leaf stuffed with rice and duck
蝦腸粉	Hai Tsjong Fan	Rice noodle rolls with shrimp
牛肉腸粉	Ngau Yuk Tsong Fan	Rice noodle rolls with beef
叉燒腸粉	Tsa Siu Tsong Fan	Rice noodle rolls with barbecued pork
咸水角	Haam Soi Kok	Sweet rice dumplings with barbecued pork
荔芋角	Loi Wook Kok	Deep-fried taro dumplings with pork
春 卷	Tsijn Kuun	Spring rolls
鍋 貼	Woh Teep	Pot stickers
叉燒飽	Tsa Siu Pau	Steamed barbecued pork buns
釀青椒	Jang Tsjen Tien	Steamed bell peppers with minced pork
鼓椒排骨	Si Tsjiu Pai Kwat	Steamed spare ribs in black beans sauce
梅子排骨	Mui Gee Pai Kwat	Steamed spare ribs in plum sauce
煎堆仔	Thsin To Chai	Sweet sesame seed balls with lotus seed stuffing
楊洲炒飯	Yeung Chau Chow Fan	Chinese fried rice
雞絲炒麵	Kai She Chow Mein	Crisp noodles with chicken filet and mushroom sauce
炒 麵	Chow Mein	Chinese fried noodles
鼓椒牛河	Si Tsjin Ngau Hoe	Rice noodles with beef, sweet bell pepper and black bean sauce
炸水餃	Tja Soy Kau	Deep fried dumpling in sauce
炸蝦球	Tja Ha Yun	Deep-fried shrimp balls
生煎肉飽	San Tjin Yu Pau	Pan-fried buns stuffed with vegetables and meat
燒 腩	Siu Nam	Roast pork with crispy skin
蒜蓉芥菜胆	Kai Choy Sum	Stir-fried mustard cabbage with garlic sauce

ESSENTIAL INDONESIAN AND OTHER ASIAN INGREDIENTS:

Agar agar The Indonesian name for a gelling agent extracted from various species of seaweed, *agar agar* gels without refrigeration and has no taste of its own. It is available in powdered form and in strands. Gelatin can sometimes be substituted but the texture is quite different.

Basil. Although other Asian countries use some forms of basil, it is central to many Thai dishes either as an ingredient or a garnish. Three types are used in Thai cooking: horaph basil - *bai horapah;* holy, hot or opal basil - *bai grapao*, and hairy basil - *bai mengluk*. European sweet basil can be used as a substitute however, the green-leafed **horaph basil** is probably the closest to its European cousin. It has a pronounced anise flavor. **Holy basil** has pretty purple leaves and its aroma has a hint of cloves. It should be used in cooked dishes. **Hairy basil** has tiny leaves and a lemony scent and a peppery flavor. It is sprinkled it over Thai salads and soups. See also Basil in the Herbs and Spices Chapter.

Bawang merah The diminutive Indonesian red shallots are related to the shallots sold in Holland. They are most often used to make the crispy fried onions flakes.

Bean curd Better known as Indonesian *tahu* or Japanese *tofu*, bean curd is a soft but firm, cream-colored custard or cheese made from curdled soya milk extracted from cooked soya beans. Rich in nutrients, it is sold in packets in Asian stores, health food stores and supermarkets. The local tahu is more sour than the Asian tofu. It can be blanched for seconds to remove some of the sour taste. The other Asian bean curd also differs from Chinese *doufu* in that it is denser in consistency and the natural flavor of soy beans is removed.

Bean sauce and paste - Chinese There are several types of Chinese bean sauces. **Yellow bean sauce** is thick, salty and aromatic and is made with yellow beans, flour and salt which are fermented together. It adds a distinctive flavor to **Peking Duck** and other meat dishes. It comes in two forms: the beans are either whole or crushed (paste). The difference is basically in the texture but the paste is somewhat saltier. The yellow bean paste comes in tins here under the names Yellow Bean Sauce or Paste, *Bohnesosse* or *Bonensaus* (whole beans), or *gemahlene Sojabohnensosse* or *gemalen Bonensaus* (paste). **Red bean paste** is made from red beans and sugar and is mostly used in desserts. **Chili bean sauce** (Toban Djan) is a salty chili sauce of chilies, water, salt and monosodium glutamate thickened with broad beans. It is used in the cooking of western China and is available in jars. It must be kept refrigerated after opening.

Black beans (fermented and salted) These small salted black soya beans are preserved by fermentation with salt and spices. Some of the salt is rinsed off in cold water before cooking, but some of the salt still remains. Do not add salt automatically but adjust the seasoning at the end of the cooking process. They are intensely flavorful so should be used sparingly. **Crab** or **Chicken in Black Bean Sauce** are mouthwatering Chinese dishes.

Candlenuts - *kemiri* (Indonesia) Candlenuts are similar to but not quite the same as macadamia nuts. They are crushed or ground and used as a thickening agent in many Indonesian recipes. Raw *kemiri* are slightly toxic, so must be cooked or roasted before eating.

Chilies The most common chilies sold here are the Indonesian *cabé*: *cabé hijau* - green, *cabé merah* - red and *cabé rawit/cabé Lombok* which are four-alarm hot chilies. See chilies under **Herbs and Spices**.

Chili sauce, Chinese The Chinese chili sauce is medium to hot. It is very red and is made from chili peppers, vinegar and salt. It is used mainly as a dipping sauce. There are many brands so you should experiment with them until you find one you like. Don't confuse them with the chili bean sauce described under **Bean Sauce and Paste**.

Chili sauce, Thai The Thais make some excellent chili sauces for export. They are dipping sauces for meats, fish and poultry that are much appreciated by Asians of other countries. The **Sriracha Hot Chili Sauce** is renowned for its very hot, lightly-sweetened flavor and the simply-stated **Sweet Chili Sauce** is more sweet than hot. The Sweet Chili Sauce is also a good dipping sauce for **Spring Rolls**, crispy **Won Tons** and other **Dim Sum** snacks.

Coconut - *kokosnoot* Central to many South and Southeast Asian dishes, **coconuts - *kokosnoten*** are basically used in the form of a **coconut milk - *kokosmelk* (D)** or ***santen* (Indon)** which is a mixture of the water and oils pressed from fresh, desiccated or powdered coconut meat, not the coconut juice of a fresh coconut. Coconut milk is used to thicken and flavor vegetable and curry dishes. It comes in frozen, canned and solid forms. **Coconut cream - *kokosroom*** is the thick white liquid which separates from the milk when it sets in the refrigerator. It can be stirred back into the milk or can be used in some recipes which call for coconut cream. Less common is the sweetened "cream of coconut" which is used mainly in desserts.

Coriander, Chinese parsley or cilantro - *ketumbar* (Indon) or *ketoembar* (D) - see **Herbs and Spices**.

Dashi is a Japanese soup stock which is basically made of hot water, dried bonito flakes and kelp - *kombu*. It is central to Japanese cooking. Liquid and granular *dashi* is available in shops here that cater to the Japanese.

Fish Sauce Central to some Asian cooking, fish sauce is made from fermented fish or seafood packed in wooden barrels with salt. Only the liquid that runs off from the fish is used. There are different grades; the Vietnamese *nuoc mam* is darker and stronger than the Thai *nam pla*. You can dilute it but there is no real substitute. It is used in dipping sauces and as a seasoning in cooking. It smells much worse than it tastes.

Galangal, galingale The greater galingal (*Alpinia galanga*) is known in Indonesia as *laos* (**lengkuas** in Malaysia and *khaa* in Thailand); the lesser (*Languas officinarum/ Alpinia officinarum*) as *kencur* - see **Herbs and Spices**. A third type (*Kemferia galangal*) known as *temu kunci* or as Chinese keys, is mostly used in Indonesian cooking as an aromatic and in their traditional folk medicine *jamu*.

Ginger - *gember (D, jahe Indon)* See **Herbs and Spices** and **Exotic Asian Vegetables**.

Hoisin sauce A thick, dark brownish-red sauce which is basically made from soy beans, garlic, vinegar and sugar. Hoisin is sweet and spicy and is widely used in Chinese cookery as a flavoring for meat, poultry and shellfish dishes. Many people in the West know it as the sauce which accompanies **Peking Duck**.

Kaffir lime - *jeruk purut* (Indon) - see **Herbs and Spices**.

Kecap manis - see **Soya sauce**

Kemiri - see **Candlenuts**

Lemon Grass - *sereh (Indon)* - see **Herbs and Spices**.

Monosodium Glutamate (MSG) - *mononatrium glutamaat, Ve Tsin or Ajinomoto* A crystalline salt widely used to enhance the flavors of Asian cooking, monosodium glutamate is a natural amino acid which comes from seaweed gluten and some vegetables. It is a controversial seasoning for some people claim they have experienced headaches and other maladies from MSG. The noted Chinese Chef Ken Hom in his book ***A Taste of China*** advises that "best chefs, cooks and restaurants should rely instead on the freshest and finest ingredients that need no enhancing". Yet, tons of MSG are sold to homemakers every year.

Miso is a fermented bean paste popular in Japanese cooking. It can be used as a soup base, a salad dressing, and as a condiment.

Mushrooms, Asian There are two main types of Chinese mushrooms; those which grow on the sides of trees and those which are grown on straw. The tree mushrooms are known as **Black or Fragrant Mushrooms** and are usually sold dried in packets. They are used in many dishes as a complimentary vegetable because of their special flavor and aroma. They must be soaked in warm water before using. They can be used in most Asian recipes calling for dried mushrooms. The **straw mushrooms** are sold in tins. The Chinese black or fragrant mushroom is the same as the large, flat chestnut-colored Japanese (and Korean) ***shiitake***. It has a steak-like flavor and is sold fresh in supermarkets and greengrocers and dried in Asian stores. The dried mushrooms come in three grades: the best have floral patterns on the cap surface, the second best have thick caps that slightly curl inwards and the ordinary have thin flat caps. While the taste is not the same, the European fresh mushrooms such as *cèpes* can be substituted. **Enokitaki or enoki mushrooms** are small mushrooms with long, spaghetti-like, yellowish-white stems and tiny round caps. Enoki mushrooms have a mild aroma and crispy texture. They are mostly used in soups and one-pot dishes. Look for fresh enoki mushrooms in stores which cater to Japanese and Koreans and canned ones in Chinese/Indonesian shops.

Muu (Korean) - see *daikon*

Noodles Most noodles sold in the Indonesian/Chinese *toko* are basically Chinese in origin, but are used extensively in Indonesian and other Asian cooking. In addition, other Asian countries have their own types of noodles. **Wheat and egg noodles - *bahmie or bamie*** are made from hard or soft wheat flour. When eggs are added to wheat noodle paste, they are simply known as egg noodles. They generally look like tangled masses of thin yellow spaghetti. The imported Indonesian *mie telur Asli* makes superior *Bahmie Goreng*. In Holland, the round or flat egg noodles called *mie* are popularly used in this dish. **Rice noodles or vermicelli - *miehun, sen mee*** are made from rice flour and are usually eaten with seafood. They look like a skein of whitish wire. A thicker type known as "rice sticks" are about the length of a normal Chinese chopstick and look like white ribbon. Soak them in warm water for 15 minutes or until they are soft. **Cellophane or bean thread noodles - *biehun, woon sen*** are almost transparent noodles made from mung bean starch. They are very thin and are added to soups or braised dishes or are deep-fried and used as a garnish. Soak them for about five minutes in warm water before using. Two of the most common types of Japanese noodles are ***Soba***, a buckwheat noodle which is used in soups; and ***udon***, a thick white noodle made from wheat flour. Others are ***harusame***, a very fine translucent noodle made from cornstarch and potato flour for use in cold noodle soups; ***ramen***, an egg noodle usually sold as a dry soup packet with flavoring spices; and ***somen***, a fine white wheat noodle.

Oyster sauce This is a thick dark-brown sauce which is made from oysters cooked in soy sauce and brine. In spite of its name, it does not taste fishy but has a wonderful flavor. It is used not only as a condiment but as a flavoring for vegetable, meat and poultry dishes.

Panko are Japanese bread crumbs normally used in deep-fried, batter-dipped dishes such as *tempura*. They are also good in Western-style dishes such as meat loaf and Wiener Schnitzel. These bread crumbs give a lighter taste to your dishes and many Western cooks prefer them to fresh bread crumbs.

Radish - see *daikon*

Rice In Asian countries where rice is eaten as a staple, different cuisines usually require a special type and variety of rice. It can depend on the eating utensils people use; for instance, the Chinese, Japanese and Koreans eat with chopsticks and a sticky rice is preferred. On the other hand, the Indonesians and Thais eat with spoon and fork and they prefer either a rice that is slightly sticky or a rice that is light and fluffy and each grain has separated after cooking. An American-grown **Japanese rice** suitable for these cuisines is available here in some *toko* or shops catering to the Japanese while the **Thai "perfumed" or jasmine rice** is an excellent choice for the Indonesian *rijsttafel*. It is not perfumed as such but gives off a lovely aroma as it cooks. It can be cooked sticky or fluffy depending on the amount of water used. Many supermarkets now carry it. The Indians, Pakistanis, and Sri Lankans prefer hard, fluffy rice and ***Basmati***, literally meaning "queen of fragrance", is one of their favorites. It is grown in the foothills of the Himalayas and has a fragrant, nut-like aroma. It is a long-grain rice with a fine texture. It is also sold in many supermarkets and most Asian stores or *toko*. **American and Surinam long grain rice** is available in most supermarkets. There is also a peculiar type of **glutinous** or **sticky rice** - ***kleefrijst*** which some Asians use for desserts. It is also available in most Asian shops. The make-up of the rice determines the percentage of amylose which is the starch component. The more amylose, the harder and fluffier the rice will be. Asian rice usually needs about 1¼ cups water to one cup rice while American rice is drier and thus needs at least 1½ cups of water to one cup rice. If the rice is mushy and the kernels shapeless, you have added too much water or cooked it too long.

Rice wine The Japanese ***saké*** and Chinese ***Shaozing*** are used extensively for cooking and drinking but they are quite different from each other. Both can be kept at room temperature after opening. A dry pale sherry can be substituted but again the flavor is quite different. ***Mirin*** is a sweetened *saké* used exclusively in cooking.

Salam leaf - *daun salam* (Indon) is confused with bay leaf. If you cannot get it, leave it out.

Seaweed - *zeewier* and kelp There are several types of seaweed used mostly in Japanese and Korean cooking. **Laver** is a type of paper-thin, dried seaweed sheet (Japanese *nori* and Korean *kim*) which is used as a ***Sushi*** or ***Kimpap*** wrap and as a garnish for many dishes. Dried laver can be made crispy by passing sheets over a gas burner two or three times or by oiling one side with sesame oil and frying it in a dry frying pan. It is also crushed into flakes and used as a flavor enhancer on rice and in soups. ***Kombu*** is a greenish-brown kelp. There are two main varieties: *dashikombu* is widely used in the Japanese soup stock - *dashi* and *nikombu* is often used in stew. ***Wakame*** or **lobe-leaf seaweed** is dusty-brown when dry but turns bright green when soaked. It is extremely nutritious and is used in soups such as the Japanese ***Miso*** and Korean ***Miyok Kuk***.

Sesame seed and oil - see **Herbs and Spices and Oil, other.**

Shichimi tõgarashi A "seven taste pepper" from Japan which consists of ground seaweed - *nori*, red pepper, *sansho* or ground prickly ash seed pods, and sesame, hemp and poppy seeds. The container is usually placed on the table so it can be sprinkled on soups and noodles just before eating.

Shrimp paste - ***terasi***, also *trassie*, *balachan* and *blachen* is a savory, pungent, salty, hard, shrimp paste used in Indonesian, Malaysian and Thai cooking. There is a lot of controversy over *terasi*; for some it is an acquired taste, while other cooks won't prepare an Indonesian meal without it.

Soy Sauce The word catsup or ketchup is derived from the Asian *ketsiap* or Indonesian *kecap*. It is made from a mixture of soy beans, wheat flour, water and salt. There are no tomatoes in it. It is fermented and aged, then distilled. As the sauce ages, it gets darker. In Indonesia, it comes in two varieties: ***kecap asin*** is salty and light and ***kecap manis*** is sweet, dark and syrupy. Use them for Indonesian cooking; but for other Asian cooking, you can't go wrong with a good Japanese ***shoyu*** like Kikkoman. The Japanese also make "thick" (*koikuchi)* and "thin" (*usukuchi*) varieties. The "thick" soy merely means it is darker in color and richer in flavor than the "thin" soy sauce. The thin sauce is saltier, the thick sauce is the standard sauce which is called *shoyu*. The Chinese also have light and dark soy sauces: ***Superior Soy*** is salty and light and is the best one to use in most Chinese recipes. The darker ***Soy Superior Sauce*** is best when used in Chinese stews.

Spring roll wrappers - ***loempiavellen*** are paper-thin, frozen rice paper wrappers which are sold in three different sizes. They can be used for other deep-fried items.

Tamarind - *asam or assem* (Indon) - see **Herbs and Spices**.

Tempe This solid slab of treated whole soy beans which looks like Brie and has a nutty flavor, comes from Indonesia.

Tahu (tofu) - see **Bean curd**

Tamari This sauce resembles the Japanese soy sauce, but is made without wheat and it is thicker. It is usually sold in the health food stores or health food counters in supermarkets. Use it for dipping sauces and as a base for basting sauces.

Turmeric - see **Herbs and Spices**.

Vinegar Rice vinegar is widely used in Chinese, Southeast Asian and Japanese cooking. It is less acidic than Western vinegars. White rice vinegar is clear and mild and is used in sweet and sour dishes. Black rice vinegar is dark and mild and is used in braised dishes. Red rice vinegar is sweet and spicy and is used in seafood dipping sauces. The Japanese ***su*** or white rice vinegar has the slightly sweet flavor of the glutinous rice from which it is made. Cider vinegar can be used as a substitute but a little sugar may have to be added.

Wasabi - see **Herbs and Spices**.

Won Ton wrappers - *wontonvellen* are squares of very thin pastry used to make won tons. There are two basic kinds, one made from the same dough as noodles that can be cooked in soup or deep-fried and the other that can only be deep-fried. They are sold frozen and dry out fairly quickly, so keep them covered with a damp cloth when working with them.

Wood ear fungus are often labelled 'dried black fungus'. They look unappetizing, but the appearance improves after they have been soaked in warm water for 30 minutes. They are used in spring rolls, *Mu Shu (pork)* and other Asian dishes.

Yakult This is a Japanese fermented milk drink made with water, sugar, low fat dried milk and active *Lactobacillus casei Shirota. Yakult* is marketed all over Japan, Korea and other Asian countries where *Yakult* ladies make daily deliveries to homes and offices where it is consumed regularly. The bacteria in *yakult* is not neutralized by the stomach acids and it thus travels to the intestines where it is turned into energy. The taste is not unpleasant and can become habit forming. It is available here in Asian stores and many supermarkets.

EXOTIC ASIAN VEGETABLES

It is sometimes difficult to identify some of the Asian vegetables for they differ in appearance and taste from country to country. For instance, the radishes of Korea are much larger than the white radishes sold here; however, the tastes are similar enough that they can be used interchangeably. See sketches of these vegetables toward the end of this chapter.

Since most of the Asian vegetables mentioned here are sold in local Chinese supermarkets that are quite often owned by Cantonese-speaking Chinese, names are given both in Cantonese (C) and Mandarin (M). When cooking with these vegetables, it is interesting to note that in Chinese cooking the nature of the ingredients are essential to their effects on the body. Or they may be cooked with specific combinations to balance the properties.

When pronouncing Mandarin names, use the following guideline: the "c" is like the *ts* in rats; the "h" is more guttural than the "h" in English and more like the German *ach*; the "q" is like *ch* as in cheap; the "r" is like a cross between a "j"and 'r', it has no English equivalent but it is rolled something like the "z" in azure; the "x" is like the *sh* in sheen; the "z"is like the *ds* in kids and the "zh" is like a hard "j" in jack. The rest are pronounced the same.

Leafy Greens

Chinese white cabbage - *baak choi, bok choy, pak choy* (C), *bai cai* (M) One of China´s earliest vegetables, the highly nutritious *bok choy* has been cultivated there since the 5th century AD. It has many varieties and relatives. In Holland you can usually find the following three: ***bok choy*** with succulent white spoon-shaped 8-to12-inch stems and dark green leaves; the smaller green-stemmed ***Shanghai bok choy***; and the squat or Cantonese **baby *bok choy***. The leaves retain their dark green color when cooked. *Bok choy* is stir-fried or used in soups and casseroles. The Shanghai and baby *bok choy* can be stir-fried but they are best when simply braised and served whole or cooked with olive oil and sliced garlic and/or oyster sauce. Some compare *bok choy* to Swiss chard (silver beet) but *bok choy* is much sweeter and juicier. The leaves taste a little like spinach. Cut the *bok choy* according to the recipe then wash thoroughly to get rid of the sand deposits between the stems and leaf bases.

Chinese celery, Peking, Tiensin or napa cabbage - *siu choy, wong nga bak, huang yao bai* (C), *pe-tsai shao cai* (M). It also sometimes called *bok choy*. There are basically three kinds sold in Holland: the stout barrel kind or napa cabbage); a green-leafed type that looks much like romaine lettuce; and the long cylindrical type or Peking cabbage. All can be used interchangeably. It has a mild sweet taste and is widely used in Chinese cooking in all provinces. It is braised in hotpots and casseroles, stir-fried with other vegetables and/or meats and noodles, or sliced into dumplings. Blanched leaves can be rolled and filled with shrimps or meats. In America, it is eaten raw in salads or baked au gratin. Koreans use it in soups and to make the famous pickled *kimchee*. Ignore the tiny black spots that appear on some leaves for they are a natural occurrence.

Chinese flowering cabbage - *choi sum or choy sum* (C), *cai xin* (M) Some people argue that this is the best of the Chinese cabbage family. It is closely related to *bok choy* and the flavor is pleasantly mild taste with only a hint of the cabbage flavor. You might serve it cooked, or raw on top of a bowl of noodles or as a garnish on other dishes. It is also served as a stir-fried vegetable dish but it usually benefits from the use of garlic or a slice of ginger or a little oyster sauce. The flowering stems are the best part but the leaves are used as well. It should be cooked very briefly to maintain its crunchy texture.

Flat cabbage - *tai goo choy* (C), *tai gu cai* (M) Another relative of the *bok choy*, this cabbage is round and flat or plate-like with white stalks and dark green leaves. You will most likely see it under the name *Tatsoi*, which is Japanese. Because it grows very close to the ground, it can be easily protected from frost and survives when other vegetables cannot. It tastes like *bok choy* except when it ages, then the flavor gets stronger. It can be cooked in any dish that calls for it cousin, *bok choy*. It benefits from the addition of garlic when used. In Western cooking, the baby flat cabbage is used as a salad green.

Oil seed rape - *yau choy* (C), *you cai* (M) Although best known for its seed, which is used to make canola oil, the Chinese like to eat the green leaves, stalks and flowers in a very simple manner. They can be blanched and stir-fried or simply stir-fried with garlic and olive oil and served when still crisp. Oil seed rape is sweeter than the Italian broccoli rape that the Italians fry, steam or braise and use in soups or salads

Chinese broccoli or Chinese kale - *gai lan* (C), *jie lan* (M) The only thing about this vegetable that resembles the broccoli used in Western cooking, is its delicate broccoli taste. Use it in place of broccoli in stir- fry dishes such as beef and broccoli. You can eat everything about the vegetable - stalk, leaves and flowers. However, when cooking, you may want to separate the leaves from the stalks for the stalks need to be cooked a little longer. Like broccoli, you should peel the lower stem if it is old and fibrous. There should be more buds on the plant than flowers when you buy it.

Mizuna - *siu cai, xiu cai* (M) This green is sold when still young and in Western cuisines the leaves are used in salads made of baby greens and mesclun. However, the Chinese steam or stir-fry it with a little garlic. It is similar to arugula but is milder and sweeter.

Mustard cabbage - *gai choy* There are several kinds of mustard cabbage and the names often get confused with each other. The three most common are: **Swatow mustard cabbage - *bao sum gai choy* (C), *kun sum jie cai*; wrapped heart or headed mustard cabbage - *dai gai choy (C), da jie cai* (M); and bamboo mustard cabbage - *fook gai choi, juk gai choy* (C); *zhu jie cai* (M).** They all have a mustard flavor. The **Swatow mustard cabbage** is a rather pretty vegetable that looks very much like a large, loose-leafed iceberg lettuce, although the stalks are more stout. It is often pickled and canned. **Wrapped or headed mustard cabbage** looks very much like a large loose-headed cabbage. It also should be used in long-cooking soups or cooked until soft then stir-fried in a little oil and garlic. The **bamboo mustard cabbage** looks quite different from the other two. Its appearance is like loose-leafed Romaine lettuce but with thin stalks. All of the mustard cabbages can be blanched then stir-fried with garlic or served with a dab of oyster sauce or used in long-cooking soups.

Amaranth or Chinese spinach - *een choy* (C); *xian cai* (M) This is another pretty vegetable of which there two types. One is the common green variety and the other the red leaf where the leaves are colored red at the base and then turn green at the other edges. It has a more pleasant taste and the leaves have more texture than the spinach used in Western cooking. Both stems and leaves are edible. The young leaves can be used in salads or cooked like spinach but it is also delicious in soups. The Chinese also stir-fry, sauté or steam it.

Garland chrysanthemum - *tung ho* (C); *tong hao* (M) While the leaves of this vegetable look much like the garden variety flowering chrysanthemum, it is another species. The leaves have a slightly perfumed flavor and they can either be used in soups or cooked then stir-fried and flavored with a little oyster sauce. The Japanese use it in their batter-dipped, deep-fried tempura. It must be cooked quickly or the leaves turn bitter.

Water *spinach* - *ong choi (C); weng cai* (M) There are two varieties of this vegetable, *soi ong choi* and *hon ong choi.* There is a slight difference in their color, leaf shape and form. Botanically, it is not related to spinach but like spinach it has a high water content and wilts fairly quickly so you need lots of it to make a side dish. The taste is quite mild. Eat both leaves and stems. In Western cooking it is sautéed with butter and garlic but in Asian cooking, it is used in various ways: in soups, stir-fried, batter-fried or raw. The Indonesians call it *kangkong* or *kungkong.*

Slippery vegetable, Ceylon spinach - *saan choy* (C); *chan cai* (M) The word *saan* in Chinese has two meanings. One is mucilaginous and the other is slippery. The former refers to the texture and the latter to the fact that it is considered to be a mild laxative. Both leaves and stems are basically eaten in soups but it is sometimes used as a substitute for okra. It is also stir-fried, blanched and used in stews that require thickening agents. If stir-frying, cook the stalks separate from the leaves as the stalks take longer to cook.

Chinese boxthorn - *gau gei choy* (C); *gou qi cai* (M) This is one of the most nutritious of the Chinese vegetables for it is high in protein and is loaded with iron and calcium. This plant, also know as the matrimony vine, sometime bears hidden thorns. Pick the thorns off first then run your hand down the length of the stem to remove the leaves. The Chinese believe that boxthorn and pork liver soup is good for the eyes. They add scallions, ginger, soy sauce and sherry to disguise its slightly bitter flavor.

Bok choy

Shanghai bok choy

Chinese cabbage

Chinese flowering cabbage

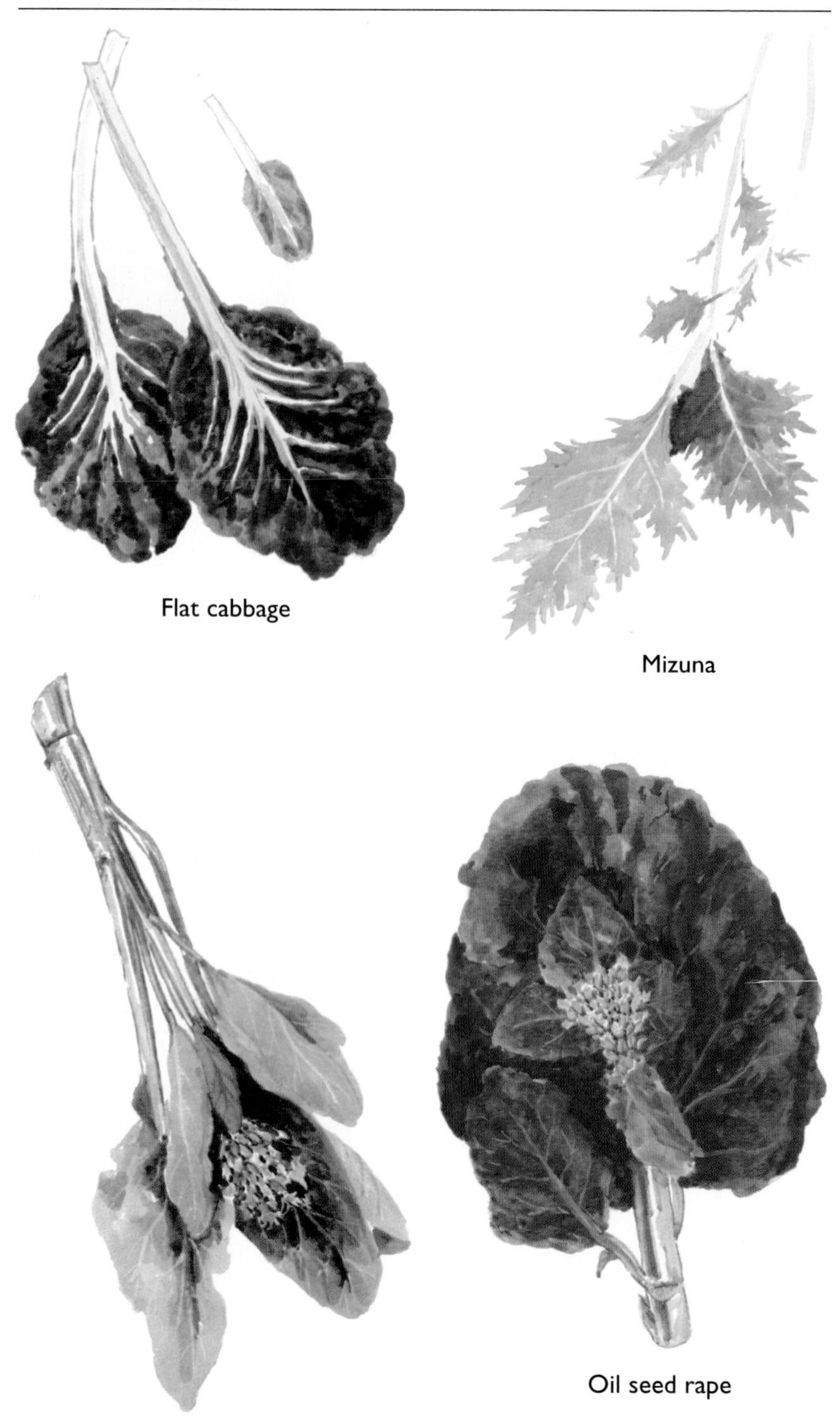

Flat cabbage

Mizuna

Oil seed rape

Chinese broccoli

Swatow mustard cabbage

Wrapped heart mustard cabbage

Bamboo mustard cabbage

Amaranth - red leaf

Slippery vegetable

Garland chrysanthemum

Water spinach

Chinese boxthorn

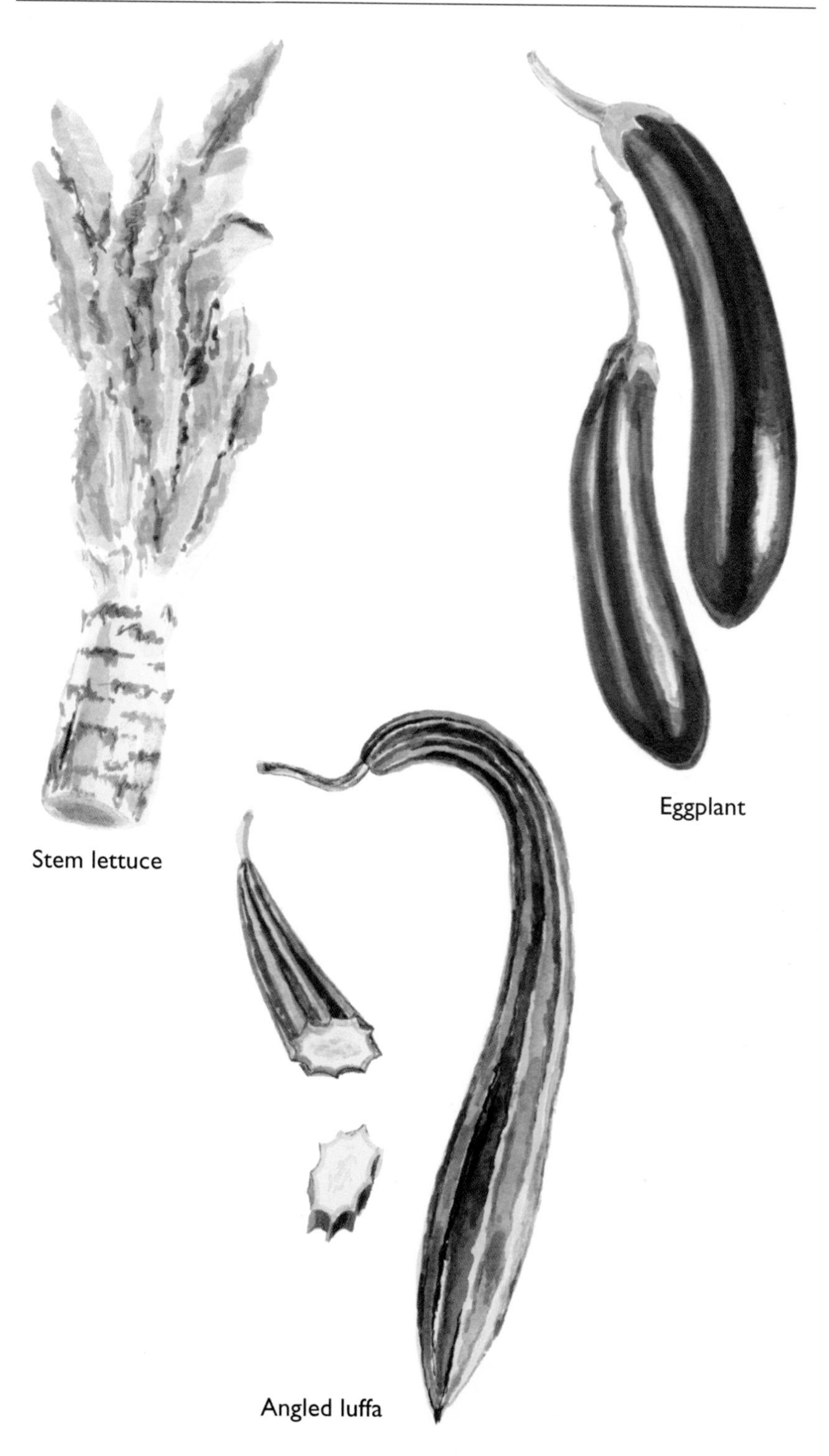
Stem lettuce
Eggplant
Angled luffa

Bottle gourd

Chayote

Winter squash

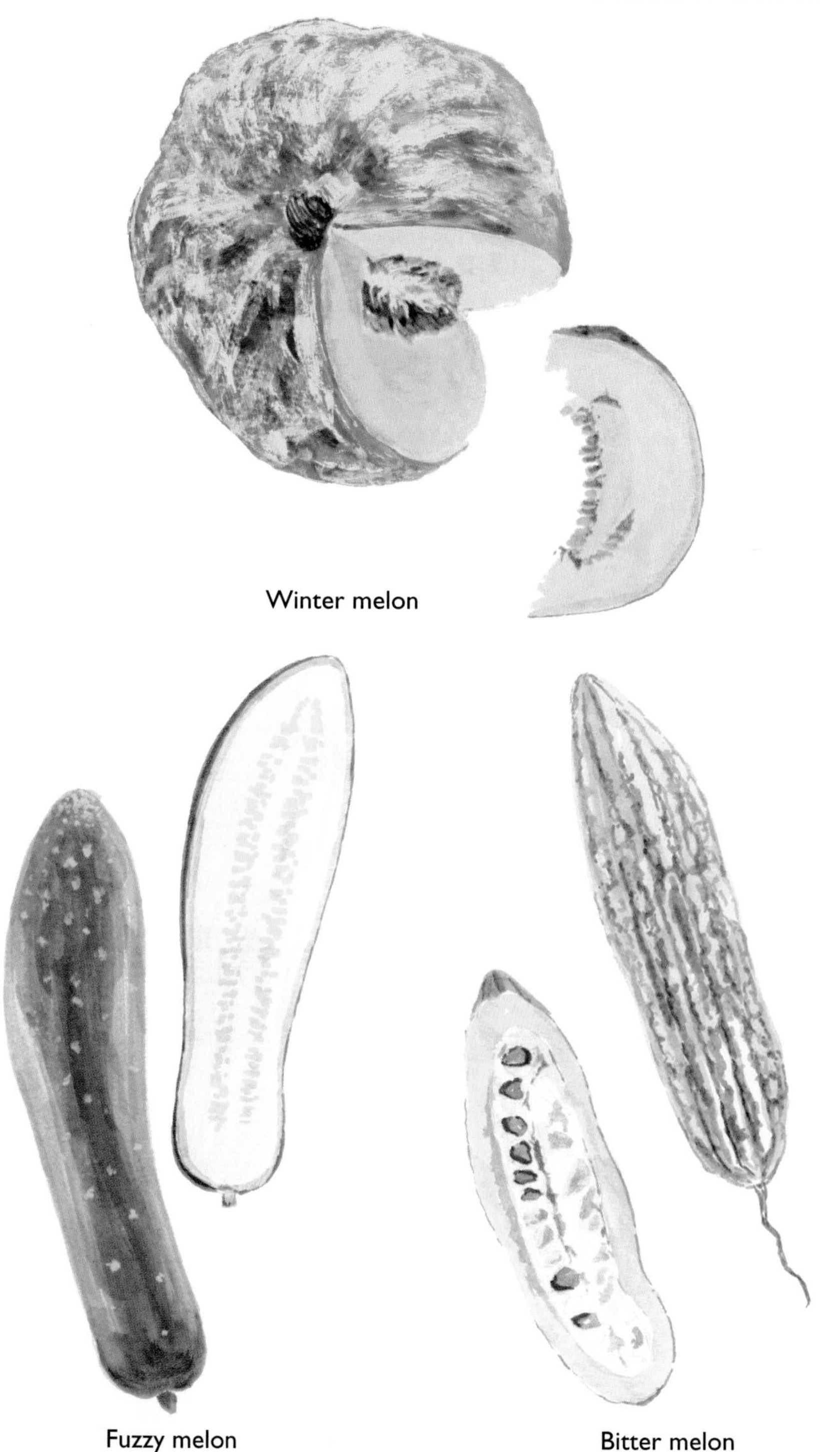
Winter melon
Fuzzy melon
Bitter melon

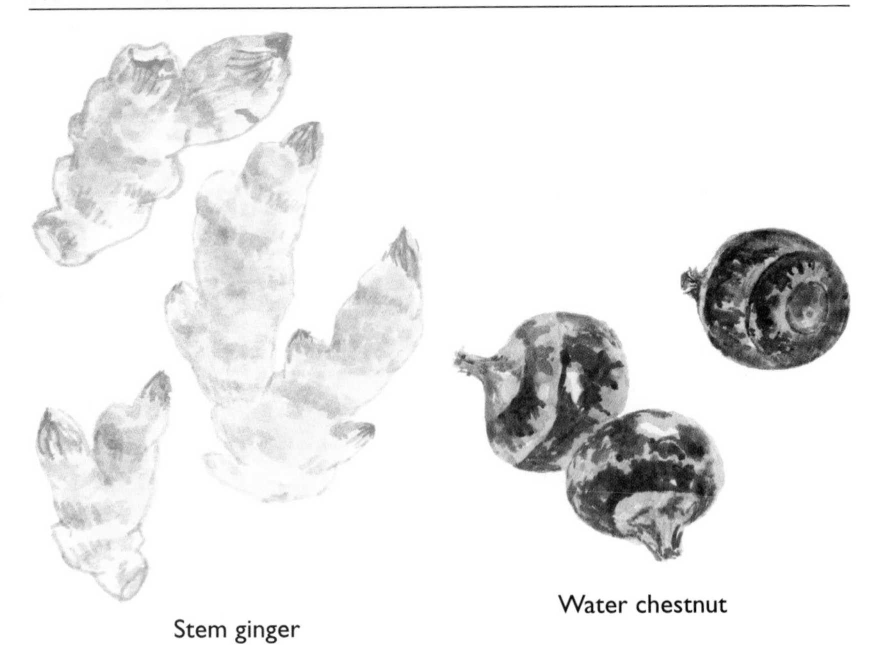

Stem ginger

Water chestnut

Green and white radish (daikon)

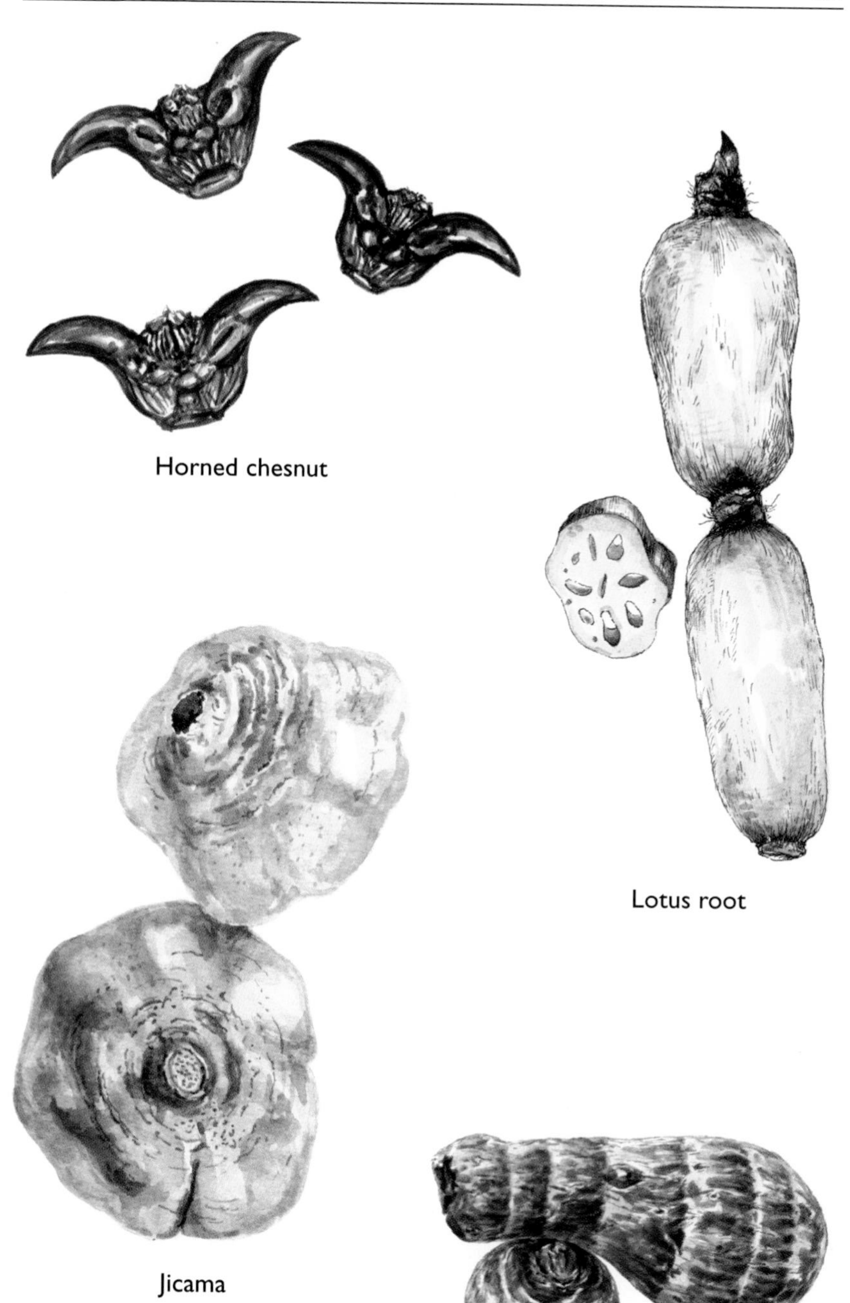

Horned chesnut

Lotus root

Jicama

Taro

Kudzu

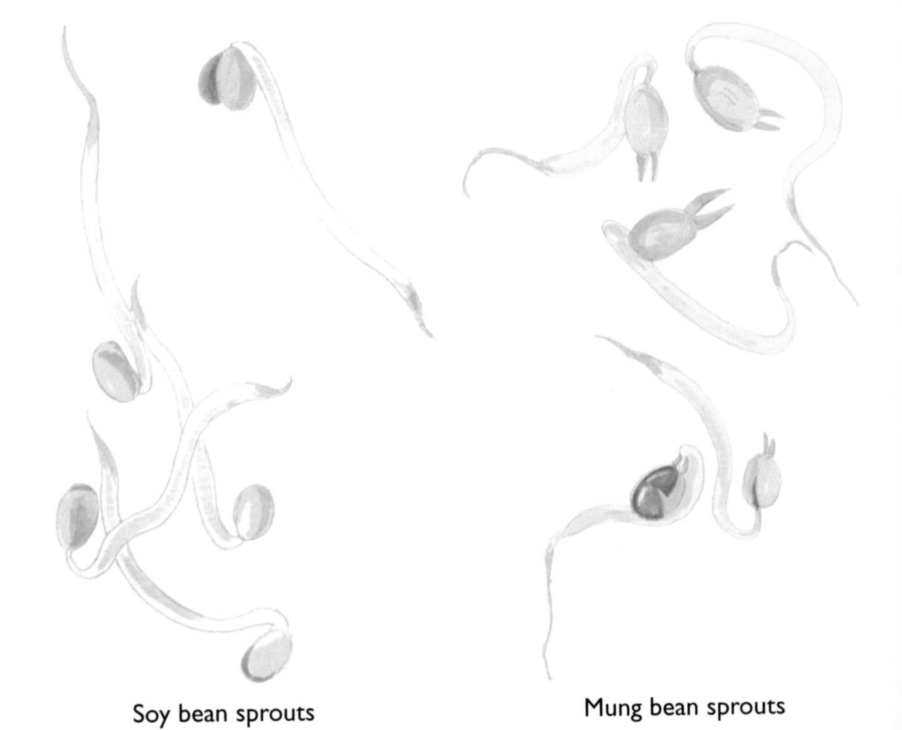

Soy bean sprouts

Mung bean sprouts

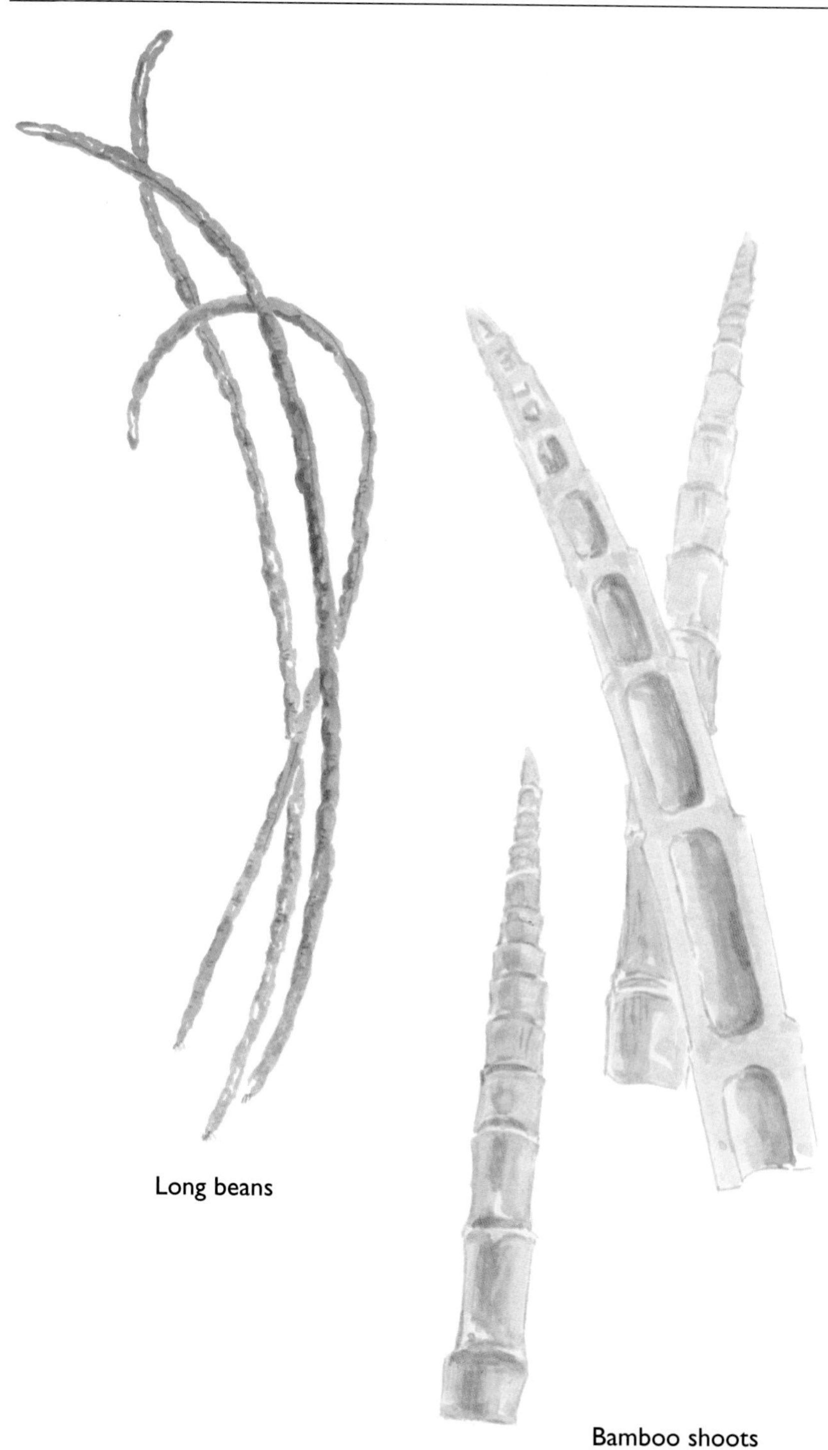

Long beans

Bamboo shoots

Chinese garlic chives

Chinese flowering chives

Chinese yellow chives

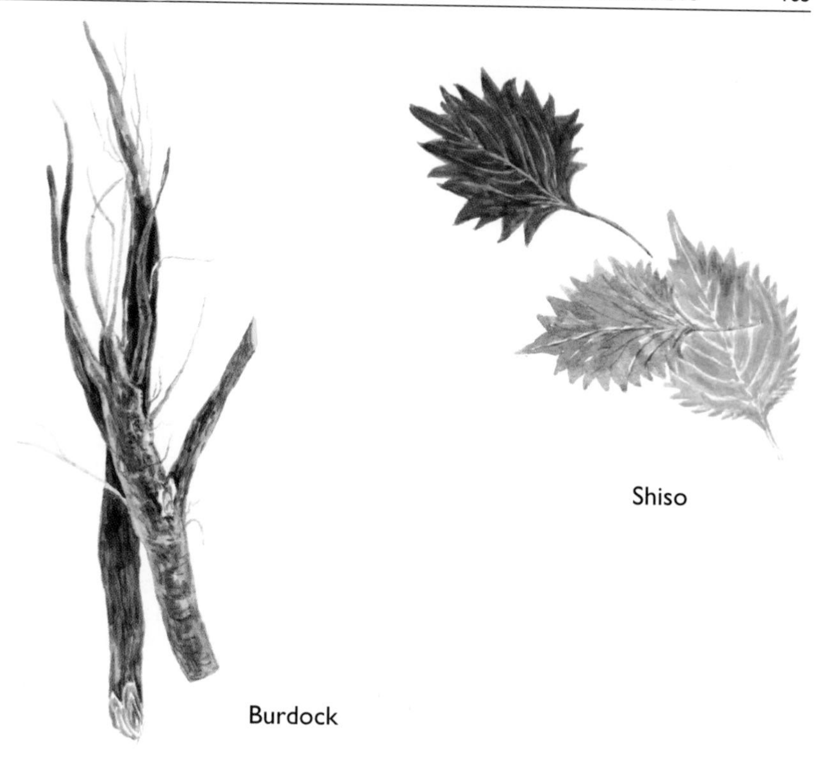

Shiso

Burdock

Stem lettuce - *wo sun (C); wo sun* (M). Stem lettuce, as the name implies, grows around the long thick stem. It tastes much like Western lettuce but since the Chinese rarely eat vegetables raw, the leaves are usually cooked. However, to the Chinese, the choicest part of this vegetable is the stem which when peeled has a pleasant celery taste. You can cut the stem into match stick strips and stir-fry with peas, spring onions and chicken or stir-fry it as a vegetable on its own.

Watercress - *sai yeung choi* (C); *xi yang cai* (M). (See Cress in the Fruits and Vegetables Chapter.)

Gourds, Melon and Squashes

Eggplant - *ai qwa* (C); *ai gua* (M) Also known as Chinese and Japanese eggplants, this vegetable is thought to have originated in India and has been cultivated in Asia since 600 BC., only reaching Europe in the 12th century. The most common is the long slim vegetable ranging in color from mauve to deep purple. There are also egg-shaped eggplants in various colors: white, yellow, green, or green with white stripes at the top, and the tiny Thai pea-sized egg plant which because it is sour is usually used in curries or chutneys. Although it does not get as bitter as the larger European eggplant, you still might want to cut and salt Asian eggplants to drain out any bitterness and extra water. The Chinese usually cook eggplant stuffed and deep-fried, braised with pork or batter-fried. Young eggplant need not be peeled.

Angled luffa or silk squash and smooth or sponge luffa - *sze qwa, seui qwa, soi gwa, si gua* (C); *shui gua* (M) There are two kinds of luffa: angled and smooth. Both taste very similar to zucchini flowers and are firm on the outside and slightly spongy on the inside when cooked. Select the younger luffa as older ones can be bitter. Scrape with a potato peeler to remove the ridges. Slice it across in 1/2-inch slices and use it in soups, or stir-fries. It can also be sautéed and braised by itself.

Bottle gourd - *po qwa, woo lo qwa* (C); *hu lu gua* (M) There are two main types of bottle gourd: one is bat-shaped (*po gwa*), and the other is more like a bottle or ewer (*woo lo qwa*). Both are mild tasting, much like summer squash, and have a smooth texture. They are mainly used in soups and stir-fries but can also be cut lengthwise, the seeds scooped out and stuffed with meats and vegetables and then baked.

Chayote - *hop jeung qwa, faat sau* gwa (C); *he zhang* (M) A South American vegetable, chayote is now quite popular in Asia because of its mild flavor and smooth texture. It can be cooked in its skin if the skin is tender. Peeling is rather difficult because of its ridges. It can be used in soups or braised or stuffed. Cook it much like you would cook a summer squash. In Western cooking, it is eaten raw with a dip or in salads.

Winter squash - *naam qwa* (C); *nan gua* (M) A member of the pumpkin family, and indeed it tastes like pumpkin, this squash is firm, sweet, and flavorful and is less watery than the pumpkin. It can be used in soups, stir-fried or braised. It can also be deep-fried in tempura batter.

Winter melon - *doenggwa, tung qwa* (C); *dong gua* (M) The winter melon looks very much like its cousin, the water melon, but its flesh is white. It is at its best when used in strongly seasoned meat-based soups. The taste is not unlike zucchini and it can be stuffed and baked with meat-based stuffing.

Fuzzy melon - *tseet gwa, mo qwa* (C), *mao qwa, jie gwa* (M) Because this vegetable has a rather bland taste, it can be stir-fried or braised with a wide variety meats and other vegetables. Wash and peel before using.

Bitter melon - *fu gwa* (C); *ku gua* (M) While an acquired taste to Western palates, the Asians love it because of its bitter taste. This bitterness is caused by the presence of quinine. It absorbs other flavors well and can be used with a black bean sauce with chicken, beef and pork. It can be stir-fried, braised, curried and stewed or steamed.

Roots, Rhizomes and Tubers

Stem ginger - *chee geung, tsee gueng, geung* (C); *zi jiang, jiang* (M) Although this rhizome flavors many Asian dishes, it is also prized for its medicinal properties. See also Ginger in the Herbs and Spices Chapter.

Water chestnut - *ma tai* (C); *ma ti* (M) Unlike its namesake, the true chestnut that grows on trees, the water chestnut is a bulb that grows in the swamps. Its soft skin makes it easy to peel. It is one of the few Chinese vegetables that are eaten out-of-hand as snacks. The Chinese also eat them minced and mixed with meats in stir-fries and dim sum snacks. You can also eat them raw in salads. While the fresh ones are far superior to the canned, the canned chestnuts are more readily available.

Horned water chestnuts or caltrops - *ling kok* (C); *ling jiao* (M) Although they are called water chestnuts, the horned water chestnuts look entirely different—their horns make them look like the heads of water buffaloes. Their taste is bland like the potato. To eat them as a snack or in salads, simply boil them in water for 5 to 10 minutes. You can also braise them with pork or chicken or boil them in soup.

Green and white radish (daikon) - *tseng loh bak, loh* bak (C); *quing lua bo, lua bo* (M) The Japanese name for a large, crispy, juicy Asian radish, *daikon* can grow up to 15 inches in length. There are two types of fresh *daikon* found here: the white *rettich* sold at most green grocers and supermarkets, and the green, sold in Chinese supermarkets. White radish can be eaten raw in salads but the green must be cooked. Both have a sweet, radish-like flavor with a hint of turnip. They can also be pickled - a typical Japanese preparation - or braised, stir-fried or deep-fried. The Chinese and other Far East Asians love to use it in soups. In Cantonese cooking, it is a part of the dim sum tradition. The radish is grated and made into turnip pudding, then cooled sliced and sautéed. The Korean radish or *muu* grows to an enormous size and it is a very important ingredient in the Korean **Kkaktugi** and **Nabak Kimchee**, and the summer salad, **Muuch'ae Namul**. See also Radish in the Fruits and Vegetables Chapter.

Lotus root - *leen ngau* (C); *lian ou* (M) The lotus root might look like a string of fat sausages but when it is sliced across, the air passages form an attractive lovely lacy pattern. Thus, Western cooks use it for garnish. It has a sweet flavor and a crunchy texture much like a raw potato; however, the texture remains crunchy even after being boiled for hours. Peel it first and then use it in sweet or savory dishes. It can be candied, pickled, boiled in soups, deep-fried (like in the Japanese tempura) or braised. Lotus stems and flowers are also edible and the dried leaves are used to wrap lotus parcels of sticky rice stuffed with chicken, pork or duck.

Taro - *woo tau, woo chai* (C); *yu tou, yu zi* (M) There are two basic types of taro: one is the large betel nut taro and the other the eddoe. Asians, Africans and Polynesians have been cultivating it for over 2,000 years. Most people know it as the Hawaiian starchy staple, *poi,* which is actually cooked taro that has been mashed into a paste. The Cantonese eat it as a part of the dim sum meal. They mash the taro and then wrap it around a filling of meat, mushrooms and bamboo shoots. As it is deep-fried, the taro develops a crisp lacy outer layer. Raw taro can cause allergenic reactions so it must be cooked - both varieties can be boiled, braised, steamed and fried.

Jicama, yam bean - *sa got, sa kot* (C); *sha ge* (M) Jicama is a native tropical American plant that was introduced by the Spanish to the Philippines. The Asians like it in many ways. It has a fresh and sweet taste and can be eaten raw in salads, creamed, steamed and braised and used in soups and stir- and deep-fried dishes.

Kudzu - *fun got, fun kot* (C); *fen ge* (M) A relative of the Jicama, it is used almost exclusively in soups. The flavor is sweet so it has mostly been replaced by the sweet potato.

Sprouts, Shoots and Beans

Soy bean sprouts - *daai dau nga choy; da dou ya cai* (M) Soy bean sprouts may look like mung bean sprouts but they are much larger and have bright yellow heads about 1/4 inch long, the sprout itself is about 4 to 5 inches long. They are among the most nutritious foods available. However, the Chinese believe that they disrupt the stomach functions and since ginger is the antidote, dishes with soy beans or sprouts must be accompanied by a chunk of ginger. Unlike the mung bean sprouts, they cannot be eaten raw. They are usually used in soups, stir-fried or chopped and mixed in with minced meats for texture.

Mung bean sprouts - *nga choi, nga choy* (C); *ya cai* (M) Mung bean sprouts have been cultivated in China for 5,000 years. Like the soy bean sprouts, they are highly nutritious. Unlike the soy bean sprouts, these highly rated sprouts can be eaten raw or blanched very briefly then used in soups, used in stuffing for egg or spring rolls, or used with other vegetables in stir-fries.

Long beans, yard long beans - *dau gok , bak dau gok; tseung dau gok* (C); *dou jiao* (M) See beans in the Fruits and Vegetables Chapter.

Snow peas - *hoh laan dau* (C); *he lan dou* (M). See Peas in the Fruits and Vegetables Chapter.

Bamboo shoots - *sun, chuk sun* (C); *zhu sun* (M) There are three major kinds of bamboo shoots: spring (*mo sun*), summer (*jook sun*) and winter (*doeng sun*), the difference in taste is subtle but winter shoots are considered to be the best. You will rarely find summer bamboo shoots outside parts of Asia. If you find fresh bamboo shoots in Holland, they most likely will already be cooked. They are always available canned. However, use fresh bamboo if you can get it because the shoots are crunchier and sweeter. Only the pith of the shoot is edible and what you buy is usually stripped of the coarse outer leaves. They are toxic so bamboo shoots must always be cooked. Parboil before using them in a variety of stir-fry dishes. They can also be braised or stewed and cut-up shoots are also added to rice, soups, ground meat, and noodle and vegetable dishes.

Herbs

Scallions, spring onions, welsh onions - *tsung, choeng* (C); *cong* (M) See Scallion, green onion and spring onion in the Fruits and Vegetables Chapter.

Chinese parsley, coriander, cilantro - *yuen sai* (C); *yuan qian* (M) See the Herbs and Spices Chapter.

Chinese garlic chives - *gau choi (C), jiu cai (M)*; blanched or **yellow chives - *gau wong (C), jiu huang (M),*** and **flowering garlic chives - *gau choi fa* or *gau choy sum*) (C), *jiu cai hua* (M)** There are three types of garlic chives (also known as *knoflook bieslook* in Dutch supermarkets) : the green-leafed plant, the same plant which is grown under cover (blanched), and the flower or bud. At first glance, garlic chives are distinguished from regular chives by their flat leaves and their robust garlic flavor – regular chives are round and hollow. The green chives are used in stir-fries, soups, omelets and dips. The blanched or yellow chives are softer and pricier than green chives and are used a similar manner. The bud or flower stalk is usually cut in 1-inch strips and stir-fried as a vegetable. However, it is also served with seafood or braised with bean curd.

Chinese celery - *kun choy* (C); *qin cai* (M) Chinese celery is similar to the Dutch *selderij* and is more an herb than a vegetable. See Celery in Fruits and Vegetables Chapter.

Leek - *dai suen.* While the leeks grown in Asia are smaller than the leeks you find in Holland, you can use them interchangeably. See Leeks in the Fruits and Vegetables Chapter.

Shiso - *shiso (Japanese), zi si* (C); *zi su* (M) This is an ancient Chinese leaf but today it is used almost exclusively by the Japanese and Koreans. The flavor can have a hint of mint, licorice or cinnamon. Also called perilla or Japanese basil, the Japanese deep-fry shiso in tempura dishes or use it in meat, fish or rice dishes, and to flavor soups and barbecues. It also makes a pretty garnish. The Koreans call it *kkaenip namul* or wild sesame leaf and it is popularly prepared with hot sauce eaten with steamed rice. They also can it in this manner. Red and green shiso sprouts are sold here for use in salads. See also Sprouts in the Fruits and Vegetable Chapter.

Burdock - *gobo* (Japanese); *uong* (Korean), *ngao pong* (C); *niu bang* (M) Burdock has been used in China since ancient times but as a medicine and not food. It is eaten in Japan and Korea as a delicacy. Its taste is sweet and mild. It must be peeled and then should be soaked in acidulated water for about an hour, to remove the bitterness. It can be parboiled until tender then can be stir-fried, roasted or stewed. In Korea, it is either cooked and flavored with sesame seed and oil or cut into shoestring strips and deep-fried then sprinkled with sesame seed and oil and a little sugar.

Many guest workers from the Mediterranean and North African countries now make Holland their home. For food from these areas, look for the *Turkse Winkel* (Turkish shop) in your neighborhood.

V. APPENDICES

A. HOUSEWARES AND KITCHEN SUPPLIES

There is a very big selection of housewares, kitchen supplies and gadgets that are either made locally or are imported primarily from France, Belgium, Italy, Germany, Luxembourg and the United States. They are sold in department stores and household shops. Look for ***Warenhuizen*** and ***Huishoudelijke apparaten en artikelen*** in the *Gouden Gids* or **Yellow Pages** of the telephone book. Shops specializing in **porcelain** and **crystal** are listed under ***Glas, porselein en aardewerk***. Look for a greater variety of equipment and utensils for gourmet cooking in the larger cities, but for more commonly used housewares, the chain store Blokker is convenient. Ethnic stores carry more exotic cooking wares.

Dutch craftsmen have long been famous for their superb earthenware or pottery, silverware and glassware. To supplement the selection, all the other well-known names in European **porcelain, earthenware, silverware, crystal** and **kitchen equipment** manufacturers are represented here. Many expatriate housewives take advantage of their location and visit factories and factory outlets to pick up porcelain, earthenware and crystal at lower prices. The American Women's Clubs in Holland even arrange special buying tours to Luxembourg, Great Britain and The Czech Republic for this purpose.

Some **Corning ware** and **Pyrex glass** baking forms are sold here and dimensions are expressed in inches, cups and quarts. However, the dimensions for traditional European **baking pans** and **tins** are based on the metric system. When substituting, the pans or tins should have the same volume and a similar depth. As long as the volume remains the same, the depth can vary up to ½ inch. Volume is measured by the amount of liquid a pan holds when filled to the rim. If the pan is deeper than specified, pies, cakes and breads may need to be baked longer.

Local stoves have standard European gas or electric heating elements. The electric elements are mostly flat with a small, round, indented center. There are no electric stoves with elements made of coils. The European heating plates take longer to heat and longer to cool and require flat, heavy-bottomed **pots and pans** which are ¼ inch to ¾ inch larger than the heating unit. The standard elements are 6, 7, and 9 inches. Stainless steel pots and pans are the most popular here and most are of exceptional quality. Teflon- and Silverstone-coated frying pans are also available. The stoves and kitchen equipment are all 220 volt.

It is convenient to have an **oven thermometer** with temperatures expressed in Fahrenheit and Celsius and **measuring cups and spoons** with American and metric measures. It is best to bring them from home but they can also be purchased locally in some housewares shops. If you are using Dutch recipes, you will need to have one or two **kitchen scales** for many ingredients are expressed in weight.

Everything you need in terms of **kitchen supplies** for food storage in the refrigerator or freezer is available here; however, some items like heavy duty aluminum foil and zip-loc bags are not generally sold commercially.

Paclan is now marketing a deep-freeze bag that can be dropped from the deep freezer into boiling water or the micro-wave oven and heated to 100°C/212°F.

When stocking the kitchen, it is important to remember that what may not be available one day, may be the next. While the home made deep-dish fruit pies have not yet become fashionable in Holland, muffins have; and muffin tins which were not sold a year ago are now in major housewares shops.

General Terms:

Materials:

aluminum	*aluminium*
cast iron	*gietijzer*
copper	*koper*
crystal	*kristal*
earthenware	*aardewerk*
enamel	*email*
plastic	*plastic*
stainless steel	*roestvrij staal*
wood	*hout*

Shapes:

oval	*ovaal*
rectangular	*rechthoekig*
round	*rond*
square	*vierkant*

Kitchen Equipment and utensils:

Small Kitchen Equipment:	***keukenapparatuur:***
blender	*mengbeker*
coffee grinder, electric	*koffiemolen*
coffee maker	*koffiezetapparaat*
deep fryer, electric	*electrische frituurpan*
food processor	*keukenmachine*
hand mixer	*handmixer*
iron	*strijkijzer*
juicer, electric	*citruspers*
kitchen scale	*keukenweegschaal*
knife sharpener	*messeslijper*
meat grinder	*vleesmolen*
microwave oven	*magnetron*
pressure cooker	*hogedrukpan*
toaster	*broodrooster*
waffle iron	*wafelijzer*

Pots and pans:	***pannen:***
casserole	*schotel*

Corning ware ovenproof dish	*glas-keramische pan*
deep fryer	*frituurpan*
double boiler	*au bain marie pan*
Dutch oven	*braadpan*
frying pan	*koekenpan*
microwave-safe casserole	*magnetronveilige schotel*
ovenproof glass baking dish	*vlamvaste glazen pan*
roasting pan	*braadslee*
saucepan	*kookpan*
wok	*wok*
Baking pans and tins:	***bakvormen en dergelijke:***
baking sheet	*bakplaat*
baking pan	*bakvorm*
bread pan/loaf	*broodvorm*
cake pan (like bread pan)	*cakevorm*
springform	*springvorm*
Utensils:	**keukenbestek:**
bottle opener	*flessenopener*
bowl	*kom*
mixing bowl	*beslagkom*
cake rack	*taartrooster*
canning jars	*wekpotten*
can opener	*blikopener*
cheese cleaver	*kaasmes*
cheese shaver	*kaasschaaf*
citrus press	*citruspers*
colander, strainer	*vergiet*
cork screw	*kurktrekker*
cutting board	*vleesplank*
egg beater, rotary	*slagroomklopper*
egg cutter	*eiersnijder*
egg timer	*eierwekker*
flour sifter	*meelzeef*
funnel	*trechter*
garlic press	*knoflookpersje*
garnishing utensils	*garneer-apparaatjes*
apple corer	*appelboor*
butter curler	*boterkruller*
citrus fruit zester	*citroentrekker*
citrus and vegetable knife	*citrus en groente mesje*
melon ball spoon	*meloenbolletjes lepel*
radish cutter (flowerlets)	*radijssnijder*
spiral cutter	*spiraaltrekker*
grater	*universeelrasp*
grill, grill spit	*braadroaster, braadspit*
grilling tongs	*grilleertang*
kettle	*ketel*

kitchen mitt or glove	*lange ovenwant*
kitchen shears	*keukenschaar*
knives, kitchen	*messen*
bread knife	*broodzaagmes*
cleaver	*hakmes*
electric knife	*elektrisch mes*
grapefruit knife	*grapefruitmesje*
meat or French knife	*vleesmes*
palette knife (for icing)	*paletmes*
paring knife	*schilmesje*
measuring cup - large	*litermaat*
measuring spoons - individual	*maatlepeljes*
mushroom brush	*paddestoelen borstel*
nutmeg grater	*nootmuskaatrasp*
pastry brush	*boterkwastje*
pepper mill	*pepermolen*
potato masher	*aardappelstamper*
potato peeler	*dunschiller*
rolling pin	*deegroller*
sieve	*zeef*
slotted spoon	*schuimspaan*
spatula	*spatel*
string	*touw*
thermometer, meat	*vleesbraadthermometer*
thermometer, oven	*oventhermometer*
timer	*keukenwekker*
wire whisk	*eiklopper or garde*
wooden spoon	*pollepel*
Dinnerware:	***serviesgoed:***
beaker, milk beaker	*beker, melkbeker*
cup	*kop*
egg cup	*eierdopje*
glasses	*glazen*
beer glass	*bierglas*
brandy snifter	*cognac glas*
champagne glass	*champagne glas*
liqueur glass	*likeur glas*
sherry glass	*sherry glas*
standard cocktail glass	*cocktail glas*
tumbler	*bekerglas*
wine glass	*wijnglas*
plates	*borden*
dinner plate	*groot bord*
salad plate	*ontbijt bord*
bread plate	*broodmanje*
dessert plate	*dessert bord*
soup plate	*soep bord*
bowls	*kommen*

salad bowl	*slakom*
soup bowl	*soepkom*
saucer	*schotel*
serving pieces	*serviesgoed*
bowl	*schaal*
bowl with lid	*dekschaal*
bread basket	*broodmandje*
butter dish	*botervlootje*
candy dish	*bonbondoos*
coffee pot	*koffiekan*
food warmer	*Réchaud*
fruit dish	*fruitschaal*
meat platter	*vleesschotel*
milk pitcher	*melkkan*
pepper shaker	*peperstrooier*
salt shaker	*zoutstrooier*
soup terrine	*soepterrine*
sugar bowl	*suikerpot*
tart or pie dish	*taartschotel*
Flatware/Silverware:	***bestek/tafelzilver:***
forks	*vorken*
cocktail fork	*cocktail vork*
dinner fork	*grote vork/tafelvork*
fish fork	*visvork*
salad/dessert fork	*ontbijt vork*
dessert fork	*taartvorkje*
knives	*messen*
butter/cheese knife	*boter/kaasmesje*
dessert knife	*dessertmes*
dinner knife	*groot mes/tafelmes*
steak knife	*vleesmes*
fish knife	*vismes*
fruit knife	*fruitmesje*
spoons	*lepels*
demitasse spoon	*theelepeltje*
dessert spoon	*dessertlepel*
egg spoon	*eierlepeltje*
ice cream spoon	*ijslepeltje*
soup spoon	*soeplepel*
tablespoon	*eetlepel* or *tafellepel*
teaspoon	*theelepel* or *koffielepel*
serving pieces	*serveer gerei*
cheese knife	*kaasmes*
fish server	*visschep*
gravy or sauce ladle	*juslepel* or *sauslepel*
large ladle (punch/soup)	*soeplepel*
pie or cake server	*taartschep*
salad fork and spoon	*sla vork en lepel*

serving spoon	*serveer lepel*
sugar spoon	*suiker lepeltje*

Kitchen supplies:

aluminum foil	*aluminiumfolie*
cocktail pick/toothpick	*cocktail prikker, tandestoker*
deep-freeze bags	*diepvrieszakjes*
food wrap	*huishoudfolie*
garbage can	*pedaalemmer*
microwave safe food wrap	*magnetronfolie*
paper napkins	*papieren servetten*
parchment paper	*bakpapier*
tablecloth	*tafel laken*

B. CLEANING SUPPLIES

"All the streets are pav'd with broad stones, and before the meanest artificer's doors, seats of various colour'd marbles, and so neatly kept that I'll assure you I walk'd allmost all over Town Yesterday, incognito, in my slippers without receiving one spot of Dirt, and you may see Dutch maids washing the Pavement of the street with more application than ours do our bed chambers". Lady Mary Wortley Montagu, Letter to Lady Mar, From Rotterdam, 3 August 1716.

Holland still lives up to its reputation in terms of cleanliness with one exception. Because of the large dog population, one might step into the "culture", so to speak. However, all of the necessary cleaning supplies are available in supermarkets to take care of these problems and more; some special cleaners such as spot removers or rug cleaning compounds are usually found in the drugstores and department stores. Since the international companies such as Unilever and Johnson have factories here, many name brands will be familiar to you. Some supermarkets, such as Albert Heijn, have their own in-house brands; theirs are identified with the "ah" symbol or the name Albi. New products continue to be introduced into the market. Pictures on the containers make the use of the product clear.

Warning or information labels are in the form of round-cornered squares. A square with an "**i**" in it alerts the consumer to special environmental information - *milieu informatie*; an "**x**" means the product is an irritant - *irriterend* or is detrimental to one's health - *schadelijk*; a round lid means it has a child-proof lid - *kinderveiligde dop*; a flame means it is lightly flammable - *licht ontvlambaar* or flammable - *ontvlambaar*; and a triangle in the square with two bottles means do not mix - *niet mengen.*

Antiseptic - disinfectant A diluted solution of Dettol disinfects cuts and abrasions and is useful for soaking clothes that are dirty from children's "accidents". It can also be used to disinfect kitchen tiles and bathroom tubs and sinks.

Bathroom cleaner - *badkamer reiniger* Dutch water in many areas tends to have a high amount of calcium. Thus, many bathroom cleaners, usually liquid, are designed to remove calcium and soap residue from bathroom wall tiles, floors, tubs and sinks. Many local housekeepers use a cleaning vinegar - *schoonmaakazijn*. Others use **Badkamer Crofty**, **Ajax Badkamer**, **Toilet Bruispoeder**, **HG hagesan blauw**, and **'t Groene Hart**. For other persistent calcium deposits they may need a **calcium remover - *ontkalker*** such as **Viakal** or **Citin**. **Kalkeend**, literally meaning "calcium duck" is a special toilet bowl calcium remover. **Glorix WC Fris** and **WC-Eend plus** and **mild** are specifically for cleaning toilet bowls.

Bleach - *bleekwater and bleekmiddel* The **liquid bleach - *bleekwater*** sold here under the name **Loda** is primarily used for getting rid of mildew spots and for cleaning sinks and toilets.

Brooms, brushes, sponges and mops Most supermarkets carry some form of household **brush - *borstel*** and **sponge - *spons***. However, department stores and household shops such as Blokker carry a larger selection; plus they market (hard bristle) **push brushes - *boender(s)***, (soft bristle) **push brooms - *veger(s)*** and **mops - *zwabber(s)***. For the long-handled, long-bristled garden broom, check with the local garden center.

Carpet and upholstery cleaner - *tapijt reiniger* **Citin, Haggarty Shampoo** and **HG vlekkenspray for tapijt en bekleding** are all carpet and upholstery cleaners that are sold in most drug stores. Some dry cleaners sell a dry cleaning powder and rent a **cleaning machine - *tapijtreiniger***.

Cleaning and dusting supplies Most supermarkets, household shops and department stores market cleaning and dusting supplies such as **chamois - *zeem***, **mopping rag - *dweil***, **dust cloth - *stofdoek***, **dish towel - *theedoek***, **hand towel - *hand doek***, **dish brush - *afwasborstel***, **bar soap - *stuk zeep***, and **soft soap - *cremesoap***. The *dweil* is a handy traditional Dutch mopping cloth. **Unicura** makes a **disinfectant-*disinfecterend*** bar soap and soft hand soap.

Cleansers and scouring pads **Vim** is a reliable brand of **cleansing powder - *schuurmiddel*** and **Jiff**, ***Brillo***, and **'t Groene Hart** are **liquid cleansers - *vloeibaar schuurmiddelen***. They are suitable for use on tiles, sinks, toilets, showers, ovens, microwaves, refrigerators and counter tops. **Brillo soap pads - *schuursponsjes*** by Johnson are steel wool scouring pads with soap added and are great for cleaning stove tops, grills, tools and pots and pan.

Decalcifier - *ontkalker* **Melitta snelontkalker** can be used for coffee machines and irons; however, before using a decalcifier in your coffee and tea pots and irons, consult the manufacturer's instructions. The drugstore or department store salespersons may also be of some assistance.

Dish detergent - ***afwasmiddel*** There are several good **dish washing detergents - *afwasmiddelen*** in liquid form at supermarkets. Some are brand names, others are in-house brands.

Dishwasher detergent Department stores, supermarkets and drug stores sell **Machine Sun**, **Ultra**, **Dreft**, and **Calgonit Reiniger** which are powdered **dishwasher detergent(s) - *machine afwasmiddel(en)***. In addition, you may also need a **liquid rinse - *glansspoelmiddel***, and **water softener - *Broxo Matic***, which is a coarse salt water softener that prevents hard-water stains.

Fabric softener **Robijn** makes sheets of **anti-static clothes softeners - *zachtdoekjes*** for dryers but they are some times hard to find. Other **fabric softeners - *wasverzachter*** are sold in liquid form and are added to the wash. Some laundry detergents also have fabric softening elements in them. Fabric softeners are sold in supermarkets and department stores.

Floor wax and oil **Citin, Johnson's Plavuis** and **Kiwi Plavuis** are types of **floor wax** - ***vloerwas*** and/or **self-polishing floor wax** - ***zelf-glanzende vloerwas*** which can be used to clean and shine tile and flagstone floors. **Bruynzeel Parketwas, Brenolin *Parketwas*** and **Parketreiniger** are especially designed for cleaning and polishing parquet floors.

Furniture wax and oil - ***meubelwas*** and ***meubelolie*** are mediums with which to clean, protect and polish all types of wooden furniture. Some are especially designed for **antiques** - ***antiek was*** **(Ca-va Seul)** or woods like **teak** - **teakolie** **(*Peli Teakolie*)**. Most waxes are liquid; but Johnson's Pledge is an easy to use **furniture spray** - ***meubelspray***. ***Casa vloeibare zeep*** and ***Alles Reiniger*** are recommended wood cleaners.

Garden furniture cleaners **HG International** makes a variety of products which are helpful for cleaning garden furniture which is made of **PVC** - ***kunststof*** and PVC window and door frames.

Household liquids **Wood alcohol** - ***brandspiritus***, **drain opener** - ***afvoer ontstopper*** and **cleaning fluid** - ***wasbenzine*** are available in supermarkets and drugstores.

Ironing - ***strijken*** **Crackfree** makes a **powder or spray starch** - ***stijfsel***. The powder is the stiffest. Both are labelled *textiel-appret*. **Johnson Jubilee** and **Vlot & Glad** are **sizing sprays** - ***strijkspray***. They are available at supermarkets and drug stores as is **distilled water** - ***gedistilleerd water***.

Laundry detergents - ***wasmiddel(en)*** are available in liquid or powdered form. The liquid detergents are often heavily concentrated. **BioTex** (blue box) is a pre-wash powder for hard to clean clothes; **Dash 3** is a detergent with fabric softener; **Dixan**, **Ariel**, **Perzil Liquid** and **All** are tougher detergents suitable for all temperatures; **Fleuril** is suitable for colored clothes; and **Dreft** and **Robijn** are designed for gentle wash. Liquid hand wash soaps such as **Woolite** and **Robijn wol en fijn** are designed for wool, silk, linen, lingerie, lycra and other fine fibers. **BioTex** (green box) is a powdered hand wash soap.

Metal polish **Silvo** and **Wrights** make **silver polish** - **zilverpoetsmiddel**; ***Delu Kupferfix*** makes a **copper polish** - ***koperpoetsmiddel*** and ***Brasso***, a **brass polish** - ***koperglans*** which works on copper, pewter and chrome. **Andy Alles Reiniger**, **Jif**, **Forza** and **Staalfix** can be used for cleaning **stainless steel** - ***roestvrij staal*** sinks and counters. ***Staalfix*** is designed for polishing stainless steel pots and pans and for other items made of enamel, porcelain, copper, chrome and tin. **Quick** makes a cleanser for **gas burners** - ***reinigingsmiddel voor gasbranders***; it can also be used on other metals.

Multi-purpose cleaner - ***alles reiniger*** There are several all-purpose cleaners in liquid form. Look for **Andy**, **Ajax**, **Spidi snel reiniger**, **Glorix**

reiniger and **'t Groene Hart**. **Zachte zeep** such as that made by **Driehoek** is nature friendly soap made from natural ingredients that can be used as an all-purpose cleaner. It can also be diluted and sprayed on plant leaves to rid them of aphids and plant lice. This soap comes in gel, liquid or bar forms. **Driehoek Fijne Soda** neutralizes household odors.

Oven cleaner - *ovenreiniger* ***Johnson*** makes two foam oven cleaners - *ovenreinigers*: **Brillo** and **Forza** which can be used against persistent fat stains and burned fat deposits on ovens, grills, barbecues and electric stove burners. **K2r** is another brand.

Stain remover, fabrics For years the only type of effective fabric spot or stain remover on the market was **Ossegal zeep** which came in bars or tubes. However, **Citin** now has several new types of stain removing powders on the market called *vlekkentovenaar* that are aimed at specific difficult spots like blood, ink, fat and oil, etc. They also make a stain removing stick - *vlekkenstift* and a stain removing salt - *vlekkenzout* aimed at all stains. They are available in drug stores and department stores. Other popular stain removers are **Biotex vlekkenspray** and **Shout vuil en-vlekkenspray** by ***Johnson***. **Dylon** makes a color remover for whites that have been stained by other colored fabrics.

Vacuum cleaner bags - *stofzuigerzakken* are available at household stores such as Blokker and at department stores and some open market stalls.

Window cleaner - *ruiten reiniger* The local housekeepers have traditionally washed their windows with ammonia dissolved in water and wiped dry with chamois and a newspaper. It works. However, the standard window cleaning sprays, **Glassex** and **Ajax**, and **Lustra** which must be diluted with water do very well if you want to break with Dutch tradition. For those who hate to do windows, the "local window cleaner" will come on an arranged schedule for a reasonable fee and clean both inside and outside the house as you wish.

C. WEIGHTS AND MEASURES

The Dutch use the metric system affecting weight, volume and temperature. Milliliters (ml) and cubic centimeters (cc) are identical in this system and there are 1000 of each in a liter. Another metric unit sometimes used in recipes is the deciliter (dl): there are 10 deciliters to a liter. Weights are straightforward: there are 1000 grams to the kilogram. The Dutch also have a folksy way of expressing weights when ordering meats, cheeses and vegetables (see Dutch Equivalents below).

Cooking with recipes expressed in weight measurements is often more efficient than with cup measurements. If you are going to be working with both, buy a simple measuring cup which has the majority of dry ingredients printed on it. Also buy one or two kitchen scales of different weights. The weight equivalents in metric and the Dutch *ons* and *pond* and British/American ounces and pounds are listed below along with length measures, liquid measures and equivalents for common ingredients. Symbols commonly used are as follows: oz = ounce, lb = pound, g = gram, kg = kilogram, fl oz = fluid ounces, ml = milliliter and dl = deciliter.

WEIGHTS

Metric	Dutch Equivalent
100 grams	*een ons*
150 grams	*anderhalf ons*
250 grams	*half pond*
500 grams	*een pond*
750 grams	*anderhalf pond*
1,000 grams	*een kilo*

Ounces	Actual Grams to Nearest Two Decimals	Conversion to most Convenient Unit
1 oz	28.35 gr	30 gr
2 oz	56.70 gr	60 gr
3 oz	84.05 gr	90 gr
4 oz	112.40 gr	120 gr
5 oz	141.75 gr	150 gr
6 oz	170.10 gr	180 gr
7 oz	198.45 gr	210 gr
8 oz	226.80 gr	240 gr
9 oz	255.15 gr	270 gr
10 oz	283.50 gr	300 gr
11 oz	311.85 gr	330 gr
12 oz	340.20 gr	360 gr
13 oz	368.55 gr	390 gr
14 oz	396.90 gr	420 gr
15 oz	425.25 gr	450 gr
1 lb	453.60 gr	480 gr
2 lbs	907.20 gr	900 gr

Metric Liquid to Ounces (liquid) Imperial and American

American	Imperial	Metric
1 teaspoon (5 ml)	1 teaspoon (5 ml)	
1 tablespoon (15 ml)	1 tablespoon (20 ml)	
2 tablespoons (30 ml)	2 tablespoons (40 ml)	
3 tablespoons (45 ml)	3 tablespoons (60 ml)	
4 tablespoons (60 ml)	4 tablespoons (80 ml)	
¼ cup	2 fl oz	60 ml
½ cup	4 fl oz	120 ml
¾ cup	6 fl oz	180 ml
1 cup	8 fl oz	240 ml
1¼ cups	10 fl oz	300 ml
1½ cups	12 fl oz	360 ml
1¾ cups	14 fl oz	420 ml
2 cups	16 fl oz	480 ml
3 cups	24 fl oz	720 ml
4¼ cups	34 fl oz	1 liter

The Dutch teaspoons - *theelepels* (3 cc) are smaller than the American and British (5 cc). Dutch and American tablespoons - *eetlepels* are nearly the same 15 cc) while the British are a bit larger (20 cc).

Inches to Metric (Centimeters)

Inches	Centimeters
1	2.5
2	5
3	7.5
4	10
5	12.5
6	15.0
7	17.5
8	20
9	22.5
10	25
11	27.5
12	30.5
13	33
14	35.5
15	38
16	40.5
17	43
18	45.5
19	48
20	61

EQUIVALENTS FOR COMMON INGREDIENTS

8 ounces butter = 7.3 ounces hydrogenated fats
8 tablespoons butter = 4 ounces (1 stick) = 125 grams
1 cup granulated sugar = about 8 ounces = about 224 grams
1 cup all-purpose or white flour = about 4 ounces = about 112 grams
2 large number 3 eggs = 3 fl oz = about 100 grams
2 cups uncooked rice = 6 cups cooked
¼ teaspoon finely-powdered dried herbs = ¾ to 1 teaspoon crumbled dried herbs = 1½ to 2 teaspoons chopped fresh herbs
2 lb/1 kg fresh spinach = 1 lb/½ kg cooked spinach
2 lb/1 kg frozen leaf spinach = 3 lb/1 ½ kg fresh = 1½ lb/¾ kg cooked

D. OVEN TEMPERATURES

The 8-Mark figures are applicable to Dutch stoves, the 10-Mark to American stoves. Marks 2 to 9 on American stoves correspond to the same numbers on the British stoves. The mark settings are only approximates but sufficient for most cooking purposes.

Fahrenheit Degrees F.*	Centigrade Degrees C.*	8-Mark Stove	10-Mark Stove
225	107	1	¼
250	121	1	½
275	135	1-2	1
300	149	1-2	2
325	163	2-3	3
350	177	3-4	4
375	191	4-5	5
400	204	4-5	6
425	218	5-6	7
450	232	6-7	8
475	246	6-7	9
500	260	7-8	10
525	274	8	

*(Rounded)

COMMON TEMPERATURES

Centigrade to Fahrenheit Common Temperatures

	Fahrenheit (F.)	Centigrade (C.)
Boiling Point	212	100
Freezing Point	32	0
Freezer	0	-18
Refrigerator	40	4
Room Temperature	65-70	17-21

E. VOCABULARY

BASIC BAKING AND COOKING INGREDIENTS

General terms:	
box	*doos, pak(je)*
can	*blik*
instant	*kant en klaar*
jar	*pot*
quick or fast cooking	*vlug or vlugkokend*
salted	*gezouten*
salted, light	*licht gezouten*

Staple foodstuffs:	***levensmiddelen:***
almond paste	*amandelspijs*
baking powder	*bakpoeder*
baking soda	*maagzout*
bread crumbs	*paneermeel*
cake and pie garnish	*garnituur*
chocolate glaze	*chocoladeglazuur*
fruit glaze	*vruchteglazuur*
clear	*helder*
red	*rood*
candied fruit	
cherries	*glacé* or *bigarreau*
mixed	*pudding vruchten*
citron peel	*sukade*
cereal grains	*granen*
amaranth	same
barley	*gerst*
hulled barley	*gort*
pearl barley	*parelgort*
quick-cooking	*vluggort*
buckwheat	*boekweit*
buckwheat groats	*boekweitgrutten*
bulgur	*bulgur*
corn	*mais*
cornmeal, coarse	*maismeel, maisgriesmeel*
couscous	*couscous*
kamut	kamut
millet	*gierst*
oats	*haver*
oat bran	*haverzemelen*
oatmeal	*havermout, havervlokken*
quinoa (Incan rice)	*quinoa*
rice	*rijst*
broken	*gebroken*
dry	*droog*

long grain	*langgraanrijst*
parboiled	*parboiled*
quick cooking/instant	*snelrijst*
unpolished	*zilvervliesrijst*
white or polished	*witte* or *geslepen*
wild	*wilde rijst*
rye	*rogge*
spelt	same
wheat	*tarwe*
wheat germ	*tarwekiemen*
bran	*tarwezemelen*
cream of wheat	*tarwe griesmeel*
chocolate, baking	*puur chocolade*
extra bitter	*extra bittere*
milk chocolate	*melkchocolade*
semi-sweet	*semi-sweet*
white	*witte*
chocolate chips	same
chocolate cups	*chocolade bakjes*
chocolate for dipping or coating	*couverture*
chocolate sprinkles or jimmies	*hagelslag*
chocolate flakes	*chocolade vlokken*
cocoa powder	*cacaopoeder*
coconut, grated	*kokosnoot, gemalen*
young coconut	*jong kokosnootvlees*
cream of tartar	same
crumb crust	*kruimel bodem*
extracts and essences	*extract* or *aroma*
almond	*amandel*
cherry water	*kirsch*
lemon	*citroen*
maraschino	*marasquin*
mocha	*mokka*
rum	*rhum*
vanilla	*vanille*
vanilla sugar	*vanille suiker*
bean	*stokje*
fats, solid	*vetten*
animal fat	*dierlijkvet*
beef suet	*rundniervet, rundvet*
butter	*boter* or *roomboter*
butter for frying	*boter voor bakken en braden*
deep-frying fat	*frituurvet*
lard	*reuzel*
margarine	*margarine*
margarine for frying	*margarine voor bakken en braden*
vegetable fat	*plantaardig*
flour, wheat	*tarwe bloem, meel*

all-purpose flour	*patentbloem*
bread flour	*brood bloem*
brown wheat flour	*tarwemeel*
instant	*alles binder or vlug bloem*
pastry flour	*bloem voor patrisserie*
self-rising flour	*zelf-rijzend meel*
white bread flour	*witbrood bloem*
white wheat flour	*tarwebloem*
whole wheat flour	*volkoren meel*
flour, non-wheat	*andere bloem*
arrowroot	*pijlwortel meel*
buckwheat	*boekweit*
cornstarch	*maizena*
potato flour	*aardappelmeel*
rice flour	*rijstbloem*
rye	*rogge*
tapioca	*tepung tapioca*
gelatin	*gelatine*
leaf gelatin	*gelatine blaadjes*
powdered or packets	*poeder gelatine zakjes*
honey	*honing*
marshmallow	*marshmallow, spekkie/spekken*
noodles	*pasta*
nuts	*noten*
almonds	*amandelen*
Brazil nuts	*paranoten*
cashew	*cashewnoten*
chestnuts	*kastenjes*
coconuts	*kokosnoten*
hazel nuts	*hazelnoten*
macadamia nuts	*macadamia noten*
mixed nuts	*gemengde noten*
peanuts	*pindas*
pecan nuts	*pecan noten*
pine nuts	*pijnboomnoten*
pistachio	*pistachenoten*
walnuts	*walnoten*
oil, cooking	*olie*
corn oil	*maisolie*
deep frying oil	*frituurolie*
olive oil	*olijfolie*
mild	*mild*
extra virgin	*extra vergine*
virgin	*vergine*
peanut oil	*arachideoile*
safflower oil	*saffloer olie*
sesame oil	*sesamolie*
soya oil	*sojaolie*
sunflower oil	*zonnebloemolie*

vegetable oil	*slaolie*
oil, other	*andereolie*
almond oil	*huile d'amande*
grape-seed	*huile de pepin de raisin*
hazelnut	*huile de noisette*
walnut	*huile de noix*
pastry dough	*deeg*
croissant	*croissant deeg*
dough for savory tarts	*deeg voor hartige taart*
filo (phyllo)	*fillo*
pizza	*pizzadeeg*
puff pastry	*bladerdeeg*
spring roll or lumpia wrappers	*loempiavellen*
won ton wrappers	*wontonvellen*
peanut butter	*pindakaas*
chunky	*met stukjes noot*
pectin	*pectine*
sugar with pectin	*geleisuiker*
salt	*zout*
iodized salt	*Jozo met jodium*
mineral salt	*Jozozout*
salt substitute	*dieet zout*
sea salt	*zeezout*
sodium reduced salt	*Jozo Vitaal*
stock, broth, bouillon	*fond, bouillon*
bouillon	*bouillon*
beef, chicken, herb, fish	*rundvlees, kip, kruiden, vis*
stock or broth	*fond*
brown stock	*bruine fond, fond brun*
fish stock	*visfond, fond de poisson (fumet)*
game stock	*wild fond, fond de gibier*
lobster stock	*kreeftenfond, fonds d'homards*
vegetable stock	*groentefond*
white stock	*blanke fond, fond blanc*
sugar, cane, beet	*suiker, riet, biet*
candy	*kandij*
crystal, or coarse (granulated)	*kristalsuiker*
moist sugars	*basterd*
white	*witte basterdsuiker*
light brown	*lichtbruine basterdsuiker*
dark brown	*donkerbruin basterdsuiker*
powdered or confectioner's	*poedersuiker*
raw	*ruwe rietsuiker*
sugar cubes	*suikerklontjes*
super fine or castor	*zeer fijne tafelsuiker*
sugar, other	
grape or corn (dextrose)	*druivensuiker*
fruit sugar (fructose)	*fructose*
Javanese palm	*gula Jawa*

syrup	*stroop/siroop*
corn	substitute Golden syrup
heavy	*stroop*
heavy but liquid	*schenk stroop*
light and liquid	*siroop*
maple	*ahoornstroop*
molasses (cane)	*melasse (van rietsuiker)*
tomato sauce, paste	*tomaten puree*
condensed	*gecondenseerde*
concentrated	*geconcentreert*
vinegar	*azijn*
apple cider vinegar	*ciderazijn*
balsamic	*balsamic azijn*
herb vinegar	*kruidenazijn*
natural	*natuurazijn*
pickling	*inmaakazijn*
raspberry	*frambozenazijn*
red wine	*rode wijnazijn*
tarragon	*dragonazijn*
white wine	*witte wijnazijn*
whipped cream stabilizer	*slagroom versteviger*
yeast	*gist*
dry	*gist poeder or korrels*
instant	*instant or gist levure*
moist	*verse gist or bakkersgist*

HERBS AND SPICES

General Terms:

broken	*gebroken*
dried	*gedroogde*
ground	*gemalen*
kernels	*korrels*
leaves	*blaadjes*
mild	*mild*
powder	*poeder*
root (like ginger)	*wortel*
salt	*zout*
seed	*zaad*
snipped, finely chopped	*gesnipperd*
sprig	*takje*
strong or sharp	*scherp*
sweet or sweet/sour	*zoet/zoetzuur*
whole	*heel*

Herbs and spices:	***kruiden en specerijen:***
allspice	*piment, Jamaica peper*
anise	*anijs*
basil	*basilicum*

bay leaf	*laurierblad*
capers	*kappertjes*
caraway seed	*karwijzaad*
cardamom	kardemom
cayenne pepper	*cayennepeper*
celery leaf	*selderij*
celery seed	*selderij zaad*
chervil	*kervel*
chili pepper	*Spaanse peper*
chives	*bieslook*
cinnamon, stick	*kaneel, stokje*
clove	*kruidnagel*
coriander/ Chinese parsley/ cilantro	*koriander*
coriander seed	*koriander zaad*
cumin	*komijn*
dill	*dille*
fennel seed	*venkelzaad*
fenugreek	*fenegriek*
galangal	*laos/kencur*
ginger, root	*gember, wortel*
horseradish, grated	*mierikswortel, geraspte*
juniper berry	*jeneverbes*
kaffir lime leaf	*daun jeruk purut (Indon.)*
lemon balm	*citroenmelisse*
lemon grass	*sereh (Indon.)*
lovage	*lavas*
mace	*foelie*
marjoram	*marjolein, marjoraan*
mint	*munt*
peppermint	*pepermunt*
spearmint	*kruizemunt*
mustard seed	*mosterdzaad*
nutmeg	*nootmuskaat*
oregano	*oregano*
paprika (Hungarian style)	*paprikapoeder*
parsley	*peterselie*
pepper, black/white/green	*peper, zwart/wit/groen*
peppercorn	*peperkorrel*
peppercorn, pink	*baies frais*
poppy seed	*maanzaad*
rosemary	*rozemarijn*
rue	*wijnruit*
saffron	*saffraan*
sage	*salie*
salam leaf	salamblad, *daun salam (Indon.)*
savory	*bonekruid*
sesame seed	*sesamzaad*
Sichuan pepper/Szechwan pepper	*fagara*

star anise	*steranijs*
tamarind	*asam* or *assem*
tarragon	*dragon*
thyme	*tijm*
turmeric	*koenjit* or *kunyit, kurkuma*
wasabi	*wasabi*

Herb Blends:

bouquet garni	*bouquet garni*
fines herbes	*fines herbes*
herbes de Provence	*herbes de Provence*
Italian seasoning	*italiaanse keukenkruiden*
Indonesian herb and spice mix	*bumbu (Indon.), boemboe (D)*

Spice Blends:

chili powder	*chilipoeder*
curry powder	*kerriepoeder*
garam masala	*garam masala*
chicken spices	*kipkruiden*
pickling spices	*inmaakkruiden*
sambal	*sambal*
sambal olek	*sambal ulek*
sambal bajak	*sambal badjak*
shoarma spices	*shoarma kruiden*
four spices	*quatre épices*

DAIRY PRODUCTS

General terms:

box	*doos*
bottle	*fles*
carton	*karton*
glass	*glas*
packet	*pakje*
plastic bag	*plastik zakje*
tube	*tube*

Cheese:

Cheese cuts and forms:

flat chunk	*plat stuk*
grated	*geraspte*
ground	*gemalen*
slice	*plakken*
wedge	*punt stuk*

Cheese types:

blue-veined cheese	*schimmel kaas*

diet cheese	*dieet kaas*
goat cheese	*geitekaas*
factory cheese	*fabriekskaas*
farmer's cheese	*boerenkaas*
fresh cheese	*verse kaas/fromage frais*
curd cheese	*verse kaas*
cream cheese	*roomkaas*
cottage cheese	*hütenkäse*
kwark or quark	*kwark*
garlic cheese	*knoflook kaas*
herb cheese	*kruiden kaas*
May cheese	*Meikaas*
sheep's cheese	*schapekaas*
spreading cheese	*smeerkaas*
smoked cheese	*rookkaas*

Terms found on cheese packages:

aromatic	*aromatisch*
creamy	*romig*
firm	*stevig*
fresh/sour	*friszuur*
less fat	*minder vet*
less salt	*minder zout*
melting cheese	*smeltkaas*
mild	*mild*
nutty	*nootachtig*
piquant	*pikant*
tasty	*pittig*
soft	*smeuig*
spreadable	*smeerbaar*
taste	*smaak*

Dairy products:	***zuivelproducten:***
biogarde, garde	same
butter, unsalted	*boter* or *roomboter*
lightly salted	*licht gezouten*
salted	*gezouten*
herbed	*kruiden*
frying butter	*voor bakken en braden*
buttermilk	*karnemelk*
cheese	*kaas*
coffee milk, condensed/evaporated	*koffiemelk*
condensed	*gecondenseerde melk*
evaporated	*geevaporeerde melk*
full cream	*volle melk*
half full	*half volle*
sweetened condensed milk	*gecondenseerde volle melk met suiker* or *gesuikerde gestilliseerd gecondenseerde melk*

cream	*room* or *slagroom*
cooking cream	*kookroom* or *room culinaire*
creme fraiche	*crème fraîche*
non-dairy whipping cream	*klop klop* or *slag slag*
sterilized cream, whipping	*lang houdbare slagroom*
whipping cream	*slagroom*
eggs - see Poultry	
ice cream	*ijs, roomijs, schepijs*
margarine	*margarine*
low fat	*halvarine*
diet	*dieet margarine*
frying margarine	*voor bakken en braden*
milk	*melk*
full fat	*volle melk*
half full	*halfvolle melk*
low fat or skim	*magere melk*
farmer's milk	*boerenmelk*
powdered milk	*melkpoeder*
sterilized	*lang houdbaar* or *gesteriliseerd*
sour cream	*zure room* or sour cream
toetje	a small custard-like dessert
vla	custard or pudding
yoghurt	*yoghurt*
full cream	*volle yoghurt*
low fat	*magere yoghurt*
yoghurt drink	*yoghurt drank*

DELICATESSEN AND GOURMET FOODS

Main Course:	***hoofdgerecht:***
hodgepodge	*hutspot*
sauerkraut with sausage	*zuurkool met worst*
curly kale with sausage	*boerenkool met worst*
pea soup	*erwtensoep*
brown bean soup	*bruinebonensoep*
Indonesian fried rice	*nasi goreng*
Indonesian fried noodles	*bahmi goreng*
Indonesian skewered beef, pork, chicken	*saté*

Nuts - see Basic Baking and Cooking Ingredients

Salads:	***salade:***
celeriac root	*knolselderij*
cucumber	*komkommer*
egg	*ei*

ham and leek	*ham en prei*
hussar's (potato and meat)	*huzaren*
mixed vegetable or fruit without dressing	*rauwkost*
salmon	*zalm*
shrimp	*garnalen*

Sauces:	***sausen**:*
curry	*kerrie*
dill	*dille*
fish sauce or tartar	*vis*
garlic	*knoflook* or *aioli*
whiskey	*whiskey cocktail*

Snacks:	***hapjes:***
sausage in puff pastry	*saucijzen broodjes*
Dutch meatballs	*bitterballen*
minced meat morsels	*frikadel* and *croquette*
Flemish liver paste	*vlaamse likkepot*

BREADS AND PASTRIES

General terms:	
almond paste	*amandelspijs*
coarse grind	*grof*
filled	*gevuld*
fine grind	*fijn*
half loaf	*half brood*
sliced	*gesneden*
whole loaf	*heel brood*

Bread:	***brood:***
brown	*bruin brood*
currant	*krentenbrood*
four or five grain	*vier or vijf granen brood*
French bread	*Frans stokbrood*
French bread, Dutch-style	*Hollands stokbrood*
raisin	*rozijnenbrood*
rye, Scandanavian	*roggebrood*
rye, German style	*pumpernickel*
sandwich	*casino brood*
white	*wit*
brown	*bruin*
white, regular	*wittebrood*
white milk	*melkbrood*
white, with spotted crust	*tijgerbrood*
white, with cut crust	*knipbrood*
white round loaf	*lampionnebrood*

whole grain	*vier of vijf granen*
whole wheat	*volkoren brood*
Rolls:	*broodjes:*
currant rolls	*krentenbollen*
rolls, soft	*zachte broodjes*
round (hamburger buns)	*bolletjes*
oval	*puntjes*
rolls, hard crusts	*harde broodjes*
round	*bolletjes*
oval	*puntjes*
rusks, Dutch	*beschuit*
Cookies and pastries:	***koekjes en banket:***
butter or pound cake	*boter cake*
cake	*cake*
cookies	*koekjes*
sweet	*zoete koekjes*
salt	*zoutjes*
butter	*roomboter koekjes*
cream puffs, regular	*soezen*
small	*soesjes*
Danish pastries	*koffie broodjes*
puff pastry shells	*pasteitjes*
tart	*taart*

Dutch specialties, including holiday breads and pastries:

appelbeignets	apple fritters
appelbollen	apple balls
appelflap	apple turnovers
appelgebak	apple cake
boterkoek	shortbread
botercake	butter cake
gevulde boterkoek	shortbread, filled
Kerstkransjes	Christmas wreaths
Kersttol	Christmas bread
Kerst Tulband/Paas Tulband	Christmas or Easter turbans
Limbursge vlaai	custard pie with fruit or rice
oliebollen	oil balls
ontbijtkoek	spiced breakfast cake
speculaas	spiced cookie
speculaas, gevulde	spiced cookie, filled

FISH AND SHELLFISH

General terms:	
bones	*graten*
cleaned (head and skin off)	*kop en vel eraf*

deep fried	*gebakken*
fillet (to cut into)	*gefileerd*
fresh	*verse*
new (as in raw herring)	*nieuwe*
salted and smoked	*kippered*
scaled (to scale)	*geschrapt (schrappen)*
smoked	*gerookte*
stewed	*gestoofd*

Fish:	***vis:***
anchovy	*anjovis*
Angler (monkfish, goosefish, lotte)	*zeeduivel*
brill	*griet*
carp	*karper*
catfish, European	*meerval*
cod, deep-fried pieces	*kabeljauw, kibbling*
dab	*schar or limande*
eel, freshwater/sea	*paling/zeepaling*
flounder	*bot*
garfish	*geep*
haddock (deep-fried)	*schelvis (lekkerbekje)*
hake	*heek*
halibut	*heilbot*
herring	*haring*
herring, smoked	*bokking*
ling	*leng*
mackerel	*makreel*
monkfish (see angler)	
mullet, gilthead, thicklip grey	*diklipharder*
red/goatfish	*mul/rode mullet or rouget*
perch (bass)	*baars*
pike (pike/perch)	*snoek, snoekbaars*
plaice	*schol*
pollack	*pollak*
ray	*rog*
redfish, Norwegian haddock	*roodbaars*
red snapper	*rode zeebaars*
roe, deep fried	*kuit, gebakken kuit*
salmon	*zalm*
salmon trout	*zalmforel*
sardine	*sardine*
sea bass	*zeebaars*
sea bream, gilthead	*goudbrasem (dorade)*
sea robin, gurnard	*rode poon, knorhaan, zeehaan*
smelt	*spiering*
sole	*tong, zeetong*
sprat	*sprot*
trout	*forel*
tuna	*tonijn*

turbot	*tarbot*
whiting	*wijting*
white bait	*witvis*
wolf fish	*zeewolf*

Shellfish:

abalone	*zeeoor*
clam	*clam*
cockle	*kokkel*
crab	*krab*
crayfish or crawfish	*rivierkreeft* or *ecrevisse*
cuttlefish	*inktvis, zeekat*
lobster	*kreeft*
mussel	*mossel*
oyster	*oester*
octopus	*octopus*
prawn	*kreeft garnalen*
scallop	*Sint-Jacobsschelp*
sea cucumber, sea slug	*zeekomkommer*
shrimp	*garnaal*
squid, calamari	*pijlinktvis*

POULTRY, GAME BIRDS AND GAME

General terms:

corn	*mais*
legs	*poten*
saddle of hare	*hazerug*
tame	*tam*
wild	*wild*

Eggs:	***eieren:***
chicken eggs	*kippen* eieren
battery eggs	*batterij*
free range	*scharrel*
corn fed free range	*maischarreleiereen*
4-grain free range eggs	*viergranen scharrel* eieren
semi-free range	*voliereeiren*
organic eggs	eko-eieren
duck eggs	*eende eieren*
lapwing	*kievit eieren*
quail	*kwarteleieren*

Poultry and game birds	***gevogelte:***
chicken	*kip* or *kuiken*
Bresse chicken	*Bresse poularde*
broiler	*jong haantje*
corn-fed	*mais kip*

Cornish game hen (or very young chicken)	*poussin*
roasting/stewing	*poularde*
roasting/pullet	*braadkip* or *braadkuiken*
soup	*soepkip*
spring	*piepkuiken*
chicken parts	
breast, with bone	*kipborst*
breast, deboned	*kipfilet*
cutlets, breaded	*kipschnitzel*
drumsticks	*kippepootjes*
drumstick & thigh	*kuikenbouten*
liver/heart/gizzard	*lever/hart/maag*
rolled roast	*rollade*
chicken thigh rolled roast	*kipdij rollade*
chicken filet rolled roast	*kipfilet rollade*
whole chicken rolled roast with skin	*kiprollade met vel*
wings	*vleugels*
wing drumsticks	*t.v. sticks*
duck (domestic)	*eend*
duck, wild	*wilde eend*
goose	*gans*
grouse	*korhoen*
guinea fowl	*parelhoen*
partridge	*patrijs*
pheasant	*fazant*
pigeon (domestic)	*duif*
pigeon, wild	*houtduif*
quail	*kwartel*
turkey	*kalkoen*
turkey breast	*kalkoen filet* or *fricandeau*
turkey thighs	*kalkoen dij*
rolled roast	*kalkoen rollade*

Game:	***wild:***
boar, wild	*wild zwijn*
deer	*ree* or *hert*
frog's legs	*kikkerbilletjes*
hare	*haas*
saddle of hare	*hazerug*
two front legs	*hazenvoorbout(en)*
two back legs	*hazenachterbout(en)*
rabbit	*konijn*
tame	*tam*
legs	*konijnbout(en)*
wild, dune rabbit	*wild duinkonijn*
venison	*wildbraad*

FRUITS AND VEGETABLES

General terms:	
box (berries)	*doosje*
bunch (grapes & bananas)	*tros*
bunch (onions, carrots)	*bos*
hand (as in out-of-hand eating)	*hand*
head (lettuce)	*krop*
stewing	*stoof*
tips	*punten*
Fruits:	***verse vruchten:***
apple	*appel*
apple sauce	*appelmoes*
apricot	*abrikoos*
banana	*banaan*
cooking, plantain	*bakbanaan*
berries	*bessen en krenten*
blackberry	*braam*
blueberry	*blauwebes*
cranberry	*cranberry* or *veenbes*
gooseberry	*kruisbes*
raspberry	*framboos*
strawberry	*aardbei*
wild strawberry	*bosaardbei*
carambola	*carambola*
cherimoya, custard apple	*cherimoya* or *annona*
cherry	*kers*
currant	*krent*
black currant	*zwarte bes* or *cassis*
red currant	*rode bes* or *aalbes*
white currant	*witte bes*
fig	*vijg*
grape, grape leaves	*druif, druiven bladeren*
grapefruit	*grapefruit* or *pompelmoes*
pink/red grapefruit	*rode/dubbele rode grapefruit*
pomelo or pamplemousse	*pompelmoes*
tangelo	same
ugli	same
kiwi	*kiwi fruit* or *Chinese kruisbes*
kumquat	same
lemon	*citroen*
litchi, lichee, lichi, lychee	*lychee* or *litchi*
lime	*limoen*
mango *mango* or *manga*	
mangosteen	*mangosteen*
melon(s)	*meloen(en)*
cantaloupe	*cantaloup*

galia melon	*galiameloen*
honeydew	*honingmeloen*
net melon	*netmeloen*
Ogen	*ogenmeloen*
sugar melon	*suikermeloen*
watermelon	*watermeloen*
nectarine	*nectarine*
olive	*olijf*
orange, mandarin	*sinaasappel(en), mandarijn*
blood	*bloed*
juicer	*pers sinaasappel*
navel	*navel*
mandarin/tangerine	*mandarijn/tangerine*
clementine	*clementine*
papaya	*papaya*
passion fruit	*passievrucht*
peach	*perzik*
pear	*peer*
Asian pear	Chinese, Japanese, Korean or apple pear
persimmon	*kaki* or *Sharon fruit*
pineapple	*ananas*
plum	*pruim*
pomegranate	*granaatappel*
pomelo - see grapefruit	
prickly pear	*cactus* or *woestijnvijg*
rambutan	*rambutan*
ugli - see grapefruit	
Dried or candied fruits:	
apple	*gedroogde appel*
apricot	*gedroogde aprikoos*
candied cherry	*bigarreaux*
candied citron	*sukade*
currant	*krent*
date	*dadel*
fig	*vijg*
prune	*gedroogte pruim*
mixed dried fruits	*tutti frutti*
raisin	*rozijn*
Fresh vegetables:	***verse groenten:***
artichoke	*artisjok*
asparagus	*asperge*
avocado	*avocado*
beans	*bonen*
azuki, adzuki bean	*azuki boon*
black-eyed peas	*zwarte ogenboon*
black or turtle	*zwarte boon*
broad or fava bean	*tuinboon*

brown bean	*bruine boon*
dwarf French green bean	*haricots vert*
flageolet bean	*flageolet*
French string, snap bean	*sperziebonen (aka princessenbonen or sla bonen)*
kidney bean	*kidneyboon or niuerboon*
lima bean or butter bean	*boterboon/lima boon*
mung bean	*katjang idjo*
pinto bean	*kievitboon*
runner bean	*snijboon*
scarlet runner	*pronkboon*
soybean	*soyaboon*
yard long bean	*kouseband*
yellow snap, wax or butter bean	*boterboon*
white bean	*witteboon*
bean sprouts	*bonenkiem*
alfalfa sprouts	*alfalfa groente*
bean sprout mix	*kiemmix*
mung bean sprouts	*taugé*
radish sprouts	*radijssla*
red beet	*rode bieten kiemen*
shiso green/red	*shiso groen/rood*
beets, red	*rode biet*
cooked	*gare*
Belgian or French endive	*witlof* or *Brusselslof*
broccoli	*broccoli*
Brussels sprouts	*spruitjes*
cabbage	*kool*
cabbage, pointed head	*spitskool*
Chinese or napa cabbage	*Chinese kool*
Chinese white cabbage	*bok choy, bok choi* or *paksoi*
curly kale	*boerenkool*
green	*groene kool*
Savoy cabbage	*savooie kool*
red cabbage	*rode kool*
sauerkraut	*zuurkool*
white cabbage	*witte kool*
carrot	*wortel* or *peen*
carrot bunch with greens	*bospeen*
winter carrot	*winterpeen*
small round carrots	*mini worteljes* or *parisienne*
cauliflower	*bloemkool*
celery	*selderij*
celery root or celeriac	*knolselderij*
soup green	*selderij*
stalk celery	*bleekselderij*
chicory (endive)	
Belgian or French endive or chicory (UK)	*witlof* or *Brusselslof*

escarole	*andijvie*
curly endive (UK), chicory (US)	*krul andijvie, frisé*
red-leafed Italian chicory:	
radicchio di Verona	*radicchio or roodlof*
radicchio de Treviso	*radicchio de trevisio (trevisla)*
corn	*mais*
baby corn	*babymais*
corn on the cob	*maiskolven*
sweet corn	*zoete mais*
corn salad, field lettuce, lamb's lettuce, or mâche	*veldsla*
courgette - see zucchini	
cress	*kers*
garden cress	*tuinkers or sterrekers*
watercress	*waterkers*
cucumber (European)	*komkommer*
gherkin	*augurk*
eggplant	*aubergine*
endive, Belgian or French	see chicory
endive, curly	see chicory
escarole	see chicory
fennel	*venkelknol*
garden cress - see cress	
garlic	*knoflook*
garlic clove	*knoflook teentje*
garlic salt	*knoflook zout*
garlic paste or minced garlic	*knoflook pasta*
kale, curly - see cabbage	
kohlrabi	*koolrabi*
leek	*prei*
lentil	*linze*
lettuce	*sla*
Batavia red	*Batavia rood*
butterhead	*kropsla*
cooking lettuce	*stoof sla*
Cos or Romaine	*cos sla or sla romaine*
iceberg, head lettuce	*ijsbergsla*
red leaf	*rode kropsla*
oak leaf	*eikenblaadsla*
lollo red, green	*lollo rosso, biondo*
mushroom(s)	*paddestoel(en)*
button	*champignon*
cépes, bolete, porcini	*cepe or eekhiirntjesbrood*
chanterelle, girole	*cantharel*
chestnut	*kastanje*
crimini	same
hedgehog (sweet tooth, wood urchin, pig's trotter	*pied du mouton*
large common mushroom	*reuzenchampignon*

lion's mane, monkey's head, yamabushi-take	*pom pom blanc*
morel	*morielje*
oyster	*oesterzwammen*
portobello	same
shiitake or golden oak	*shiitake*
truffle	*truffel*
trumpets of death or horn of plenty	*trompette de la mort or hoorn van overvloed*
okra	*okra*
onion(s)	*ui(en)*
fresh onion	*stengelui*
red onion	*rode ui*
silver or pearl	*zilveruitje*
shallot	*sjalot*
small Indonesian red	*bawang merah*
spring or green	*sla or lente uitje*
parsnip	*pastinaak* or *witte peen*
pea	*erwt*
chick pea, garbanzo	*kikkererwt*
green pea, small	*doperwt*
green pea, large	*groene erwt*
marrow fat pea	*kapucijner*
snow, Chinese	*peultje*
split pea	*spliterwt*
sugar snap	same
pepper, sweet	*paprika*
green bell pepper	*groene paprika*
red bell pepper	*rode paprika*
yellow bell pepper	*gele paprika*
pimiento, pimento	*zoete rode paprika*
peppers, hot	*Spaanse peper*
small Asian chili	*lombok* or *cabe rawit*
potato	*aardappel*
baking	*om te poffen*
mashing	*om te pureren*
small new	*nieuwe* or *krieltje*
clay grown potatoes	*klei aardappel*
pumpkin - see squash	
purslane	*postelein*
radish, regular red	*radijs*
large white	*rettich*
brown/black	*ramenas*
rhubarb	*rabarber*
rutabaga or Swedish turnip	*koolraap*
samphire, salicornia	*zeekraal*
salsify or oyster plant	*schorseneer*
sorrel	*zuring*
spinach	*spinazie*

squash	*pompoen*
acorn squash	same
butternut squash	same
hubbard squash	same
pattypan	*pattison*
pumpkin	*pompoen*
rouge vif d'etamps	same
spaghetti squash	same
winter luxury pie pumpkin	*gele centenaar*
zucchini	*courgette*
sweet potato	*zoete aardappel, bataat*
Swiss chard	*snijbiet*
tomato	*tomaat*
beef steak	*vleestomaat*
cherry	*kriel-cocktail-kers-tomaat*
Italian plum or pomodori	*pomodori*
sun dried tomato	*gedroogde tomaten*
turnip	*knolraap* or *koolraap*
turnip leaves	*raapstelen*
watercress - see cress	
zucchini	*courgette*

MEATS

General terms:

and, or, with, without	*en, of, met, zonder*
bone	*been*
broth	*bouillon*
breast, back, belly	*borst, rug, buik*
cartilage	*kraakbeen*
foot(feet)	*poot(jes)*
fresh	*verse*
front, rear, shoulder	*voor, achter, schouder*
gristle	*bindweefsel*
lard	*reuzel*
lean	*mager*
marrow	*merg*
muscle	*spier*
soup meat	*poelet*
stock	*fond*
slice	*schijf*
streaky (like bacon)	*doorregen*
tender	*mals(e)*
terms of doneness	*gaarheid*
rare	*rood/saignant*
medium	*roze*
well done	*doorbakken*

General Meat cuts:

Beef:

biefstuk - steak
biefstuk van de haas - filet mignon
biefstuk van de boven bil of ronde bil - rump or round steak
borststuk or *klapstuk* - brisket
braadstuk - large roasting piece
chateaubriand - chateaubriand (a steak for two)
doorregen borstlappen met been or *klaprib met been* - short ribs
entrêcote or *lendebiefstuk* - similar to New York steak
half om half - half ground beef, half ground pork
haaskarbonade - loin chop (with tenderloin)
hacheevlees - stew meat
klapstuk - similar to brisket
kogelbiefstuk - eye of the round
lap(pen), lapjes - cut(s) or slices, small
- *baklap* - a frying piece
- *braadlappen* - frying slices
- *borstlappen* - breast slices
- *borstlappen met been* - short ribs
- *doorregen runderlappen* - streaky slices
- *lendelappen* - loin slices
- *magere runderlappen* - lean beef slices
- *middenrif, lap van de klaprib,* and *vlees van middenrif* - cuts from the short loin and flank
- *riblap met been* - bone-in rib roasts
- *riblappen* - rib slices or steaks
- *schouderlappen* - shoulder slices of lamb
- *sucadelappen* - slices from the shoulder

losgesneden ribben - individual beef ribs
mergpijp - marrow bone
karbonade, kotelet - chop, cutlet
ossehaas or *haas* - fillet or tenderloin
Porterhouse - Porterhouse
rib eye steak - rib eye steak
ribstuk - rib piece
rollade - rolled roast
- *lenderollade* - top loin rolled roasts
- *doorregen rollade* - streaky rolled roasts

rosbief - roast beef
- *lende rosbief* - roast beef from the loin

rundergehakt - hamburger or ground meat
runderquicksteak - beef minute steak
schenkel met been - shank cross cut with marrow bone
staart, ossestaart - tail, oxtail
staartstuk - rump roast
stoofvlees, stooflappen - stewing meat
tartaar - minced beef

T-bone steak - T-bone steak
tournedos - medallions

Veal:
braadstuk - roasting piece
fricandeau - veal roasts from the leg (round)
kalfsgehakt - ground veal
kalfsbiefstuk(je) - veal steak or small veal steak
kalfshaas - tenderloin
kalfsborst, heel - whole veal breast
kalfsnierstuk - veal kidney piece
kalfspoten - calves feet
kalfsoesters or *médaillon de veau* - small , round, trimmed slices
kalfsschnitzel - scallops or cutlet
kalfsquicksteak - veal minute steak
koteletten - chops or cutlets
    vangkotelet - boneless flank veal cutlet
    koteletten van de dunne lende - loin cutlets
lappen - slices
    lendelappen - loin slices
    vanglap - veal flank slice
ossobuco - cross cut veal shanks
ribben - veal rib piece
ribkarbonade - veal riblets
rollade
    lenderollade - loin rolled roast

Pork:
Casselerrib - salted, smoked pork loin
ham - ham
    achterham - smoked, cooked ham from the leg
    rauwe ham - uncooked, salt-cured, air-dried ham
    schouderham - smoked, cooked ham from the shoulder
lappen or *varkenslappen* - pork slices
    hamlappen - fresh ham slices
    hamschijf - cross cut fresh ham slices
    verse lappen - streaky fresh pork cuts
krabbetjes - pork spare ribs
ribkarbonade - rib pork chop
rollade - rolled roast
    doorregen varkensrollade - streaky rolled pork roast
    schouderfiletrollade - blade rolled pork roast
schouderfilet - boneless blade pork chop or blade steak
schouderkarbonade - blade pork chop
spek - fat
    bacon - salted and lightly smoked bacon
    bardeerspek - barding fat
    borst, buik, or *doorregen spek* - pork belly
    doorregen lappen or *speklapjes* - fresh slices

katenspek - smoked and cooked bacon
lardeerspek - larding fat
ontbijtspek - salted and smoked breakfast bacon
pekelspek or *zuurkoolspek* - pork cured in a salt brine
rookspek - smoked and salted pork belly
rugspek - fat back
vers mager spek - fresh lean pork belly
vet spek - salt pork

varkensbiefstuk - pork steak
varkensfricandeau - pork fricandeau
varkensgehakt - ground pork
varkenshaas - pork fillet or tenderloin
varkensoester - medallions

Lamb:

halskotletten - lamb cutlets
lamsbout - leg of lamb
lamspootjes - lamb's feet
lamsrugribstuk or *zadel* - rack of lamb
rollade

lamsrib rollade - rib roast of lamb
schijf lamsrib rollade - slices of lamb's rolled rib roast
schouderrollade - rolled lamb roast from the shoulder

schouder - shoulder or lamb's shoulder meat
spinnekop - crown roast of lamb

Variety meats or offal:

hersen - brains
hart - heart
nieren - kidney
lever - liver
zwezerik - sweetbreads
tong - tongue

SAUSAGES AND COLD CUTS

General terms:

coarse	*grof*
cooked	*gekookt*
fine	*fijne*
fresh	*verse*
lightly smoked	*lichtgerookt*
roasted	*gebraden*
smoked dried (chipped) beef	*rookvlees*
salted	*gezouten*
sliced	*gesneden*
smoked	*gerookt*

Sausages and cold cuts:	***worst en vleeswaren:***
bacon	*bacon*
smoked, cooked	*katenspek*
breakfast bacon (cold)	*ontbijtspek*
beef	*rundvlees*
roast beef, rare	*rosbief*
salted and boiled	*pekelvlees*
smoked (chipped) beef	*runder rookvlees*
blood sausage	*bakbloedworst*
bologna/with fat	*gekookte worst/boterhamworst*
cervelat	*cervelaat*
chicken, roasted	*gebraden kip*
chorizo	*chorizo*
corned beef	*corned beef*
Frankfurters	*knackworstjes*
ham	*ham*
ham from hind leg	*achterham*
ham from shoulder	*schouderham*
raw ham	*rauwe ham*
smoked pork chop	*casselerrib*
head cheese	*zure zult*
horse meat, smoked	*paarderookvlees*
hot dogs	*Frankfurter knakworstjes*
liverwurst	*leverworst*
spreadable	*smeer leverworst*
liverwurst, coarse	*Hausmacher leverworst*
liverwurst spread	*Vlaamse leverworst*
meat loaf	*gebraden gehakt*
pâté and terrine	*pâté*
mushroom	*champignon*
green peppercorn	*groene peper*
garlic	*knoflook*
pork, roasted	*gebraden fricandeau*
ox tongue	*ossetong*
Rotterdammers (a type of salami)	*Rotterdammers*
salami	*salami*
sausage	*worst*
fresh	*verse worst*
smoked	*rookworst*
Bavarian bratwurst	*beierse braadworst*

CHILDREN'S FOOD

General terms:

acid	*zuur*
with acid added	*aangezuurd*
amino acid	*aminozuur*
ages	*leeftijd*
baby	same

infant	*zuiggeling*
toddlet (about 18 mos. to 4 yrs.)	*peuter*
child (4 to 5 yrs. old)	*kleuter*
dairy products with fruit	*zuivelhapjes met fruit*
follow-up milk	*opvolgmelk*
6 mos. to 1 year	*6 maanden - 1 jaar*
food	*voeding*
gluten free	*gluten vrij*
lactose reduced	*lactosebeperkt, laag lactose*
meals	*maaltijd*
mixed	*gemengd*
no chicken eggs	*kippen-eiwit vrij*
rich in fiber	*rijk aan vezels*

Children's food:	***kindervoeding:***
baby food	*baby voeding*
baby juice	*puur sap*
biscuits, children's	*kindervoeding*
Liga from 6 months	*Liga van 6 maanden*
Liga Junior from 18 mos.	*Liga van 18 maanden*
bread toppings	*brood beleg*
chocolate paste	*chocolade pasta*
chocolate lumps	*hagel*
fruity bits	*muisjes*
flakes	*vlokken*
hazelnut paste	*hazelnotenpasta*
peanut butter	*pindakaas*
breakfast cereal	*groei ontbijt*
oatmeal	*havermout*
porridge	*pap*
baby cereals or pablums	*Molenaar's Kindermeel*
rice flour	*rijstmeel*
grain flakes	*graanvlokken*
wheat flour	*tarwebloem*
infant formulas	*volledige zuigelingen voeding*
vitamins	*vitaminen*

BEVERAGES

Drinks:	***dranken:***
apple juice	*appel sap*
apple wine	*cidre*
apple jack, brandy	*Calvados*
beer	*bier*
coffee	*koffie*
caffeine-free	*caffeinevrij*
fine or filter grind	*snelfiltermaling*
instant freeze-dried	*vriesdroog*

regular grind	*normaal gemalen*
whole beans	*bonen*
coffee milk	*koffie melk*
creamer	*koffiecreamer*
full fat	*volle*
half full	*half volle*
liquor and liqueurs	*dranken*
soft drinks	*fris dranken*
tea	*thee*
water	*water*
carbonated	*koolzuurhoudend*
spring water	*bronwater*
wine	*wijn*
red	*rood*
white	*wit*
rosé	*rose*
dry	*droog*
very dry	*brut*
sweet	*zoet*
light	*licht*
full-bodied	*vol*
sparkling	*mousserend*
ice cubes, with	*ijsblokjes, met*

INDONESIAN RIJSTTAFEL TERMS

(Note: The Dutch spelling is indicated by a (D) when it differs from the Indonesian.)

acar - atjar (D)	assorted pickled vegetables
ayam - ajam (D)	chicken
babi	pork
bahmi, bami	noodles
mie	wheat flour egg noodles
miehoen	rice vermicelli
bawang	onion
bawang goreng	fried onions
bebek	duck
beras	rice
bumbu - boemboe (D)	mixed spices
bumbu sate	mixed sate spices
cabé	chilies
cabé hijau	green
cabé merah	red
cabé rawit/Lombok rawit	small very hot chilies
cengkeh	cloves
dadar	omelet
daging	meat

daun salam - daon salam (D)	Indonesian bay
gado gado	Indonesian salad
goreng	fried
gula Jawa - goela Djawa (D)	Javanese palm sugar
ikan	fish
jahe - djahe (D)	ginger
jinten - djinten (D)	cumin
kambing	goat/lamb
kari - kerrie (D)	curry
kacang - katjang (D)	peanuts
kayu manis	cinnamon
kemiri	candle nut
kencur - kentjoer (D)	ginger-like root
ketumin - ketimoen (D)	cucumber
kecap - ketjap (D)	Indonesian soy sauce
asin	salty
manis	sweet
kelapa - kokos (D)	coconut
kunyit - koenjit (D)	turmeric
krupuk - kroepoek (D)	crispy wafers
udang - oedang (D)	shrimp/prawn
emping - melindjo (D)	melingo nut wafers
laos	a spice root
lumpia - loempia (D)	Indonesian style spring roll
nasi putih	rice, cooked white
nasi goreng	rice, fried
nasi kuning - koening (D)	yellow rice
nasi rames	a miniature *rijsttafel*
panggang	roasted
pedis	hot, spicy
pisang	bananas
pisang goreng	fried banana
rujak - roedjak (D)	hot, spicy fruit salad
saté, satey	skewered barbecued meats
sambal	hot chili pastes
olek - ulek (D)	salty
bajak - badjak (D)	sweet
santen - kokosmelk (D)	coconut milk
sapi	beef
saus kacang, pedis	peanut sauce, hot
sayur - sajoer (D)	vegetable dishes
sereh	lemon grass
soto ayam - soto ajam (D)	chicken soup
tahu - tahoe (D)	soy bean cake
telur - telor (D)	eggs
tempe soy	bean cake
tepung	flour
tepung beras	rice flour

EXOTIC ASIAN VEGETABLES

Leafy Greens:

Chinese white cabbage - *baak choi, bok choy, pak choy* (C), *bai cai* (M)
Chinese celery, Peking, Tiensin or napa cabbage - *siu choy, wong nga bak, huang yao bai* (C), *pe-tsai shao cai* (M).
Chinese flowering cabbage - *choi sum* or *choy sum* (C), *cai xin* (M)
flat cabbage - *tai goo choy* (C), *tai gu cai* (M)
oil seed rape - *yau choy* (C), *you cai* (M)
Chinese broccoli or Chinese kale - *gai lan* (C), *jie lan* (M)
mizuna - *siu cai, xiu cai* (M)
mustard cabbage - *gai choy*
Swatow mustard cabbage - *bao sum gai choy* (C), *kun sum jie cai*;
wrapped heart or headed mustard cabbage - *dai gai choy (C), da jie cai* (M);
bamboo mustard cabbage - *fook gai choi, juk gai choy* (C); *zhu jie cai* (M).
amaranth or Chinese spinach - *een choy* (C); *xian cai* (M)
garland chrysanthemum - *tung ho* (C); *tong hao* (M).
Water *spinach - ong choi (C); weng cai* (M
slippery vegetable, Ceylon spinach - *saan choy* (C); *chan cai* (M)
Chinese boxthorn - *gau gei choy* (C); *gou qi cai* (M)
stem lettuce - *wo sun (C)*; *wo sun* (M). Watercress - *sai yeung choi* (C)*; xi yang cai* (M).

Gourds, Melon and Squashes:

eggplant - *ai qwa* (C); *ai gua* (M)
angled luffa or silk squash and smooth or sponge luffa - *sze qwa, seui qwa, soi gwa, si gua* (C); *shui gua* (M)
bottle gourd - *po qwa, woo lo qwa* (C); *hu lu gua* (M)
bat-shaped (*po gwa)*
bottle or ewer (*woo lo qwa*)
chayote - *hop jeung qwa, faat sau* gwa (C); *he zhang* (M*)*
winter squash - *naam qwa* (C); *nan gua* (M)
winter melon - *doenggwa, tung qwa* (C)*; dong gua* (M)
fuzzy melon - *tseet gwa, mo qwa (C), mao qwa, jie gwa* (M)
bitter melon - *fu gwa* (C)*; ku gua* (M)

Roots, Rhizomes and Tubers:

stem ginger - *chee geung, tsee gueng, geung* (C)*; zi jiang, jiang* (M)
water chestnut - *ma tai* (C); *ma ti* (M)
horned water chestnuts or caltrops - *ling kok* (C); *ling jiao* (M)
green and white radish (daikon) - *tseng loh bak, loh* bak (C); *quing lua bo, lua bo* (M)
lotus root - *leen ngau* (C); *lian ou* (M)
taro - *woo tau, woo chai* (C); *yu tou, yu zi* (M)
jicama, yam bean - *sa got, sa kot* (C); *sha* ge (M)
kudzu - *fun got, fun kot* (C); *fen* ge (M)

Sprouts, Shoots and Beans:

soy bean sprouts - *daai dau nga choy; da dou ya cai* (M)

mung bean sprouts - *nga choi, nga choy* (C); *ya cai* (M)
long beans, yard long beans - *dau gok , bak dau gok; tseung dau gok* (C); *dou jiao* (M)
snow peas - *hoh laan dau* (C); *he lan dou* (M).
bamboo shoots - *sun, chuk sun* (C); *zhu sun* (M)
  spring (*mo sun*)
  summer (*jook sun*)
  winter (*doeng sun*)

Herbs:
Scallions, spring onions, welsh onions - *tsung, choeng* (C); *cong* (M)
Chinese parsley, coriander, cilantro - *yuen sai* (C); *yuan qian* (M)
Chinese garlic chives - *gau choi (C), jiu cai (M)*
blanched or yellow chives - *gau wong (C), jiu huang (M)*
flowering garlic chives - *gau choi fa* or *gau choy sum*) (C), *jiu cai hua* (M)
Chinese celery - *kun choy* (C); *qin cai* (M)
leek - *dai suen*
shiso - *shiso (Japanese), zi si* (C); *zi su* (M)
burdock - *gobo* (Japanese); *uong* (Korean), *ngao pong* (C); *niu bang* (M)

CLEANING SUPPLIES

General terms:

bar of soap	*stuk zeep*
cloth	*doek*
tube	*tube*

Cleaning Supplies:	**schoonmaakmiddelen:**
antiseptic - disinfectant	*antisepticum - desinfectans*
bathroom cleaner	*badkamer reiniger*
bleach *bleekmiddel or chloor*	
broom/American type	*bezem/veger*
bucket *emmer*	
brush *borstel*	
calcium remover/decalcifier	*schoonmaakazijn/ontkalker*
carpet cleaner	*tapijt reiniger*
chamois skin	*zeem*
cleaning fluid	*wasbenzine*
cleansing pads - metal	*schuursponsjes*
cleansing powder	*schuurpoeder*
liquid cleansing powder	*vloeibaar schuurmiddle*
dish detergent	*afwasmiddel*
dishwasher detergent	*machine afwasmiddel*
rinse	*glansspoelmiddel*
water softener	*Broxo Matic*
dish towel	*theedoek*
distilled water	*gedistilleerd water*
drain opener	*afvoer ontstopper*

dust cloth	*stofdoek*
dustpan	*vuilnisblik*
fabric softener	*wasverzachter*
furniture polish	*meubelolie*
furniture wax	*meubelwas*
floor wax	*vloerwas*
floor wax, self-polishing	*zelf-glanzende vloerwas*
laundry detergent	*wasmiddel*
metal polisher	*poetsmiddel*
mop	*zwabber*
mopping rag	*dweil*
multi-purpose cleaner	*allesreiniger*
oven cleaner	*ovenreiniger*
soap	*zeep*
sponge	*spons*
stain remover	*Ossegal zeep (bar or tube)*
starch	*stijfsel*
starch, sizing	*strijkspray*
toilet bowl cleaner	*WC reiniger*
vacuum cleaner bags	*stofzuigerzakken*
water softener	*waterontharder*
window cleaner	*ruiten reiniger*
wood alcohol	*brandspiritus*

Terms Found on Food Labels:

additives	*toevoegingen*
no additives	*geen toeviegingen*
care/caution in use	*voorzichtig bij gebruik*
cooking instructions	*kookinstrukties*
ingredients	*ingredienten*
artifical color	*kunstmatige kleur*
artifical flavoring	*kunstmatige smaak*
artifical preservative	*kunstmatig conserveringsmiddel*
artifical sweetener	*kunstmatige zoetstof*
use before	*ten minste houdbaar tot*
salt	*zout*
sugar	*suiker*
synthetic (artificial)	*kunstmatig*
instant	*klaar voor gebruik*
method of handling	*wijze van behandeling*
method of preparation	*wijze van bereiding*

F. INTERNATIONAL FOOD SHOPS

American, Irish and British:

A Taste of Ireland
Herengracht 228hs
Amsterdam ☎ (020) 638 16 42
(150 m behind the Dam)
Fax (020) 625 68 27
E-mail tasteirl@euronet.nl
Importers of fine foods from Ireland, England, Scotland, and Wales.

Bitter's Delicatessen
Naarderstraat 34-36
Laren ☎ (035) 538 34 65
Has a good selection of American and some British and Japanese imports. Also has Indonesian food stuffs and Thai and Chinese spice packets and gourmet vegetables. (Now operated by the Vreeken people of Wassenaar.)

Supermarket van Dijk
Ursulalaan 80
The Hague ☎ (070) 385 64 65
Handles American imports plus French, Italian, German and Spanish wines. Also carries fresh milk, fruit and vegetables.

Eichholtz Delicatessen
A. J. Ernststraat 191
Amsterdam ☎ (020) 744 47 64
and
Leidsestraat 48
Amsterdam ☎ (020) 622 03 05
Has a very large selection of imported American food stuffs from General Mills, Old El Paso, S&W, Campbell's. Great selection of cereals.

Kingsalmarkt Delicatessen
Rembrandtweg 617-635
Amstelveen ☎ (020) 643 37 51
A full service supermarket that also carries American, British and some Japanese imports.

Albert Heijn *#5 supermarkets whose branches in larger cities also carry imported items from the U.S. and Asia.*

The English Shop
Wijnegem Shopping Center
near Antwerp, Belgium ☎ 00-32-3- 3537834 (from Holland)
Imports English and American food stuffs plus English language greeting cards, paperback, and weekly and monthly magazines.

Grare
Prins Boudewijnlaan 175
Wilrijk, Belgium
(near Antwerp) ☎ 00-32-3-4494118 (from Holland). *Second store open in Antwerp with kosher products.*
Has arguably the largest stock of American foods in Europe. Also features Mexican foods.

Marks and Spencer
Kalverstraat 66-72,
Amsterdam ☎ (020) 531 24 68
and Grote Marktstraat 44
The Hague ☎ (070) 361 21 68
This well-known U.K. department store has an interesting food department which carries English foods, some Indian breads and chutneys, and U.S. style apple and berry pies and cheese cakes.

Den Toom Koopcentrum
Oudedijk 149
Rotterdam (Kralingen) ☎ (010) 240 02 49
Large supermarket with a small American foods section: Duncan Hines cake mixes, Philadelphia Cream Cheese, Tang, Kool Aid, Skippy peanut butter, Marshmallows, etc.

Vreeken
Windlustweg 12
Wassenaar ☎ (070) 511 07 00
Importer of fine American and other International food products.
(See Bitter's Delicatessen)

Asian, Middle Eastern and Caribbean shops:

In addition to the shops and markets listed below, you will also find many Asian, Middle Eastern and Caribbean shops in the De Pijp around Albert Cuyp Market and around the Oudezijds Voorburgwal in Amsterdam and the Westkruiskade in Rotterdam.

Chinese Supermarkets:

The following supemarkets stock all types of mostly Chinese food stuffs including Chinese spices, noodles, oils, various types of rice, tea and vegetables and Chinese, Indonesian, Thai and Vietnamese sauces. In the deep freeze they stock prawns, dim sum snacks for steaming or deep frying and won ton and spring roll wrappers. They also have some cooking implements, Chinese language cards and arts and crafts. Most also carry some Indian and Pakistani lentils, breads and curry and marsala spice mixes.

Wah Nam Hong Supermarket
Gelkdersekade 90-92
Amsterdam ☎ (020) 627 0303
and West Kruiskade 4-6
Rotterdam ☎ (010) 241 7355
and Gedempte Burgwal 8
Den Haag ☎ (070) 360 1977
and de Flinesstraat 18 (by Macro)
Amsterdam ☎ (020) 463 8883
Fax: (020) 463 5000

Shopping Center Oriental
Upstairs, Ocean Paradise Restaurant. Next to Euromast.
Rotterdam ☎ (010) 436 25 22

Cheung Kong
Wagenstraat 94A
The Hague
☎ 070 360 9052
Fax: 070 345 9127

Chinese / Indonesian:

The following *toko* carry Indonesian, Chinese, Thai and other Asian food stuffs including rice, sauces, noodles, herbs and spices, cosmetics, herbal teas and some exotic fresh ingredients such as banana leaves. If they don't have what you need, they will often order it for you.

Toko Tjin
1e vd Helstraat 64
Amsterdam ☎ (020) 671 77 08
Also has many American products.

Toko Asia Baru
Oude Zijds Voorburwal 37-39
Amsterdam ☎ (020) 625 82 33

Toko Dun Yong
Stormsteeg 9
(Corner Geldersekade 84)
Amsterdam ☎ (020) 622 17 63 / 626 75 13

Roeraade
Naarderstraat 13
Hilversum ☎ (035) 624 65 50

Toko Centraal
1e Hogeweg 16,
Zeist ☎ (030) 692 06 75
and
Toko Centraal
Achter Clarenburg 55
Utrecht ☎ (030) 231 22 90

Toko Lezat
Laarderweg 12
Bussum ☎ (035) 693 71 29

Toko Mee Sin
Groest 86 Wc Hilvertshof 1 et.
Hilversum ☎ (035) 623 35 05

Toko Mie Wah
Langestraat 69
Amersfoort ☎ (033) 461 83 81

Japanese/Korean:

Meidi-ya
Beethovenstraat 18
Amsterdam ☎ (020) 673 74 10
Carries a full range of Japanese food stuffs including dried noodles, tofu, some Japanese-preferred fresh vegetables, fish cake, pickled vegetables, snacks, canned fish, U. S. Extra Fancy Japanese rice and sweet rice, seaweed for sushi and imported Korean kimchee.

Oriental Delicatessen Shilla
Gelderlandplein 34
1082 LB Amsterdam ☎(020) 642 84 23
Similar to Meidi-ya but the accent is on Korean food.

Indian/Pakistani:

India Pakistan's Tropisch Center en Saree House
Albert Cuyp Straat 360-38
Amsterdam ☎ (020) 679 11 86

Indian Market
Wagnerstraat 63
Den Haag ☎ (070) 364 53 40
Carry Indian and Pakistani foods such as dal, rice, spices, ghee, plus cooking utensils and Indian and Pakistani traditional clothes.

Italian:

The following Italian delicatessens have fresh homemade Italian pastas, sauces, salads, breads, cheeses and sausages and Italian coffee, coffee makers.

Tira Mi Su
9A Groest
(outside Koemarkt in Silver Parking complex)
Hilversum ☎ (035) 624 5421

Spiga D'Oro
P.C. Hooft straat 140
Amsterdam ☎ (020) 6713268

Italy
Piet Heinstraat 40a
The Hague ☎ (070) 363 9652

Kosher Foods:

Mouwes Koschere Delicatessen
Kastelenstraat 261
Amsterdam ☎ (020) 661 0180
Carries kosher foods such as gefilte fish; turkey pastrami from Israel.

Albert Heijn on **Gelderlandplein** in **Amsterdam**, for one, has a kosher food section.

Butcher Shops:

Chateau Briand
Vasteland 42
Rotterdam ☎ (010) 433 11 45
or Ninneweg 163
Heemstede ☎ (023) 528 26 55
or Grote Krocht 7
Zandvoort ☎ (023) 571 90 67
Beautiful butcher shop with Scottish beef several branches.

Groeneveld Slagerij
Luifelbaan 26
Wassenaar ☎ (070) 511 24 81
Specialize in sausage making and has a large selection of homemade gourmet foods in the deep freeze.

B. Thornhill, Your English Butcher
Pluvierstraat 273
Scheveningen ☎ (070) 354 50 44

De Leeuw Slagerij
Utrechtsestraat 92
Amsterdam ☎ (020) 623 02 35
Not only do Fred and Yolanda de Leeuw have beautiful meats, they are proud of their truffles as well.

Erciyes Imp/Exp
Zuidsingel 65
Amersfoort ☎ (033) 472 11 17
Muslim butcher specializing in lamb. Also carries Turkish food stuffs.

Tek Yol
1e vd Helstraat 47
Amsterdam ☎ (020)676 78 95
Muslim butchers.

Coffee and Tea:

Geels & Co.
Warmoesstraat 67
Amsterdam
Located in a beautiful 17th century house, this shops has 140 different types of coffee and tea from all over the world. Also has a coffee and tea museum.

Improc.
Denneweg 126
Den Haag ☎ (070) 346 15 41

Cheese shops:

De Franse Kaasmakers
Marnixstraat 192
Amsterdam ☎ (020) 626 22 10
Huge selection of French cheeses.

De Kaasspecialist
Shops in various locations.

Fish shops:

Schmidt Vis
Vasteland 60
Rotterdam ☎ (020) 412 27 69
The largest selection of seafood in Holland.

Vishandel Simonis
Visafslagweg
Scheveningen ☎ (070) 350 99 42
and
Markthof
Scheveningen ☎ (070) 360 53 54
Has a large selection of fish and seafood, some of which you may not find in the smaller neighborhood fish shops.

Frozen Food Home Delivery Services:

Bofrost
Locations at ***Beringe, Woudenberg, and Pijnacker.*** Call ☎ (015) 369 8964 for information.

Health Food Stores:

Most health food stores carry fresh and packaged tofu; rice waffles; pulses, beans grains; whole wheat bread flour; teas; coffee substitutes, and vitamins.

Bitter Reform Huis
Naarderstraat 34
Laren ☎ (035) 538 3465

De Graanschuur
Bloemendalstr. 19,
Amersfoort ☎ (033) 470 19 61

Erica
has shops in ***Amersfoort, Amsterdam Central Station, Gouda, Maastricht, 's-Hertogenbosch, Nijmegen, Tilburg Utrecht, Zeist, Zutphen.*** For information ☎ (020) 626 18 42

Wassenaar Reformhuis
Johan de Witt straat 6/A
Wassenaar ☎ 070 511 18 20

Gala Natuurvoeding
Aert van der Goesstraat 35/37
The Hague ☎ 070 35428 27

Herbs and Spices:

Jacob Hooy & Co.
Klovenier Burgwaal 10-12
Amsterdam ☎ (020) 624 30 41

Bread Flour:

Roerade - see *toko*

Open Markets:

The Albert Cuyp Market
Albert Cuypstraat between Ferdinand Bolstraat
Amsterdam
Has many specialty stalls including Indian, Greek, Moroccan, and Italian stalls which sell fresh herbs, live crabs and langoustines, squid, tuna, trout, salmon, cockles, winkles, oysters, pots and pans, among others.

The Oosterse Markt
Beverwijk
A large indoor market open on Satudays and Sundays. Stalls carry mostly food stuffs for Middle Eastern cooking including vegetables, spices, rice, and sweets. Next door there is an oriental bazaar and across the road is a weekend flea market.

Grotemarkt on Herman Costerstraat & Hobbemastraat, ***The Hague*** is open on Mon., Wed. and Fri. 9 a.m. – 6 p.m. & Sat. 9 a.m. – 5 p.m. and the ***Markhof*** market on Gedempte Gracht, downtown behind the Bijenkorf is open Mon. 11 a.m. - 6 p.m. and Tues. – Sat. 9a.m. – 6 p.m. & Thurs. until 9.p.m.

The Fish Market in the ***Scheveningen*** Inner Harbor on Visafslagweg is open on Fridays 7 a.m. until 10 a.m. or until sold out.

Kitchen wares:

See also large department stores: Bijenkorf BV; Metz & Co; Habitat; V&D; and Hema plus Blokker, a general housewares store.

Mulders Kookwinkel
Gedempte Nieuwsloot 56
Alkmaar ☎ (072) 515 49 56

Oldenhof Kookkado
Langestraat 77
Amersfoort ☎ (035) 475 95 82

La Cucina
Keisersgracht 709
Amsterdam ☎ (020) 622 28 58

Duikelman
Ferdninand Bolstraat 68
Amsterdam☎(020) 671 22 30

Studio Bazaar
Reguliers warsstraat 60
Amsterdam ☎ (020) 622 08 30

Het Pauwtje
Voldersgracht 5
Delft ☎ (015) 212 26 36

En Garde
Prinsestraat 63
Den Haag ☎ (070) 364 73 52

De Heksenketel
Dennenweg 67
Den Haag ☎ (070) 365 01 97

De Kookwinkel van Heemskerk
Brinkmanpassage 33-35
Haarlem ☎ (023) 532 33 70

De Huismuis
Warmoesstraat 15-19
Haarlem ☎ (023) 532 20 66

De Kookwinkel van Heemskerk
Hilvertshof Shopping Center
Hilversum ☎ (035) 623 47 54

Kitchen Art
Botermarkt 13
Leiden ☎ (071) 513 46 21

Het Kookpunt
Noordplein 81
Rotterdam ☎ (010) 466 32 66

Betsies Kookwinkel
Vismarkt 6
Utrecht ☎ (030) 232 19 33

Au Bain Marie
Kerkweg 9-11
Zeist ☎ (030) 691 94 00

Oldenhof Tafelkado
Nieuwe Markt 23
Zwolle ☎ (038) 423 0981

Oldenhof Kookkado
Gasthuisplein 1-5
Zwolle ☎ (038) 421 1222

ENGLISH INDEX

A
abalone **63**
acorn squash **96, 98**
adzuki bean **82**
acar **140**
agar agar **143**
alcoholic beverages **133, 134**
alfalfa sprouts **83**
all-purpose flour **18**
allspice **28, 91**
almonds **20, 48**
almond extract **17**
almond oil **22**
almond paste **13, 21**
Althena cheese **42**
aluminum foil **176**
amaranth **14, 152, 155**
anchovy **60**
angled luffa **157, 166**
angler **55,57**
anise **28**
Appenzeller cheese **43**
apple **71**; dried **74**
apple ball **53, 137**
apple brandy **132**
apple cake **53, 137**
apple cider **132**
apple cider vinegar **25**
apple corer **173**
apple fritter **53,137**
apple juice **72, 132**
apple sauce **72**; canned **125**
apple turnover **53, 137**
apple wine **132**
apricot **72**
  dried **72,74**
Arab bread **50, 100**
arborio rice **15**
aroma **17**
arrowroot **19**
artichoke **22, 80**
  canned **125**
Asian foods **139**
Asian noodles **20, 83, 125, 142,146**
asparagus **3, 22, 80**
  canned **125**
  with ham and boiled eggs **136**
asparagus bean **82, 163**
avocado **81**
ayam goreng **140**

B
babi kecap **140**
bahmie goreng **37, 48, 140, 146**
bawang goreng **140**
baby corn **86**
baby food **9,127, 128**
  in jars **128**
  infant formula **127**
  beverages **128**
  biscuits **129**
  bread topping **129**
  cereal **129**
  vitamins **129**
bacon **112, 114, 116, 121**
bake, to **100, 101**
bakeries **50**
bakery goods **9**
baking ingredients **13**
baking pans **171**
baking powder **13**
baking soda **14**
balsamic vinegar **26**
bamboo shoots **163, 168, 169**
banana **72**
barbecue sauce **126**
bard, to **100**
barley **14**
  hulled **14**
  pearl **14**
  quick cooking **14**
basil **27, 28, 143**
bathroom cleaner **177**
bawang merah **94, 140, 143**
bay leaf **24, 28**
beans **81, 82**
  canned **125**
  frozen **125**
bean curd **130, 143**
bean dip **139**
bean sauce & paste, Asian **143**
bean sprouts **83, 162, 168**
bean sprout mix **83**
Beaufort cheese **43**
beef **100, 102**
  wholesale & retail cuts **103, 104**
  preparation of **105**
  roasted **123**
beef, chipped **122**
beefsteak tomato **99**
beef stock **23**
beef suet **17**
beer **132**
beet, red **83**
  canned **125**
beet leaves **83**
beet sprouts **83**
beet sugar **24**
Belgian endive **86**
  with ham & cheese **137**
Belle de Champs cheese **43**
bell pepper **34, 92**
Bel Paese cheese **43**
berries **72, 124**
  frozen **125**
  canned **125**
berry pie filling **125**
beverages **128, 132**
  Dutch **134**
bicarbonate of soda **14**
biogarde **43, 45**
Bishop's wine **134**
biscuits **129**
bitter melon **159, 166**
black beans **82**
black beans, fermented & salted **143**
black berry **72, 73**
black currant **74**
black-eyed pea **82**
black strap molasses **25**
bleach **177**
blender **172**
blood orange **77**
blood sausage **121**
blue berry **72, 73**
blue cheese **44**
boar, wild **69**
boil, to **100**
bok choy **85, 150, 153**
Bologna **121**
bonbons **50**
bottle gourd **158, 166**
bottle opener **173**
bouillon **23**
bouquet garni **37**
bourbon **133**
bowl **173, 174, 175**
brains **105**
braise, to **100**
brandy **133**
Brazil nuts **20, 48**
bread **11, 50, 51**
bread, flour for **18, 19**
bread basket **175**

bread crumbs **14**
bread mixes **9**
bread pan **173**
bread toppings **129**
breakfast cereals **9, 129**
Bressot cheese **43**
Brie cheese **43**
brill **55, 57**
Brillat-Savarin **43**
broad beans **82**
broccoli **83**
brooms **178**
broth **23**
brown beans **82**
  canned **125**
brown stock **23**
brown wheat flour **19**
brush **178**
Brussels sprouts **84**
buckwheat **14, 15**
buckwheat flour **15, 19**
buckwheat groats **15**
buckwheat noodles **146**
bulghur **14**
bumbu **37**
burdock **169, 165**
butcher shop **10, 100, 102**
butter **17, 18, 45**
butter cake **52, 53, 137**
butter curler **173**
butter dish **175**
butterhead lettuce **89**
butternut squash **96, 98**
buttermilk **45**

C
cabbage **84, 85**
cake **52**
cake decorations **14**
cake flour **19**
cake garnishes **14**
cake glazes **14**
cake mixes **9, 19**
cake pan **173**
cake rack **173**
cake server **175**
calcium remover **177**
Camembert cheese **43**
candied fruit **14**
candy **9, 15, 50, 135**
candy dish **175**
candy sugar **24**
candlenuts **144**
cane sugar **24**
canned foods **124**
canning jars **173**
can opener **173**
Cantal cheese **43**
cantaloupe **77**
Cape gooseberry **73**
capers **28**
carambola **73**
caraway seed **29**
cardamom **29**
carp **62**
carpet cleaner **178**
carrot **85**
cashew nuts **20, 21, 48**
Casselerrib **121**
casserole **172**
cassis **74**
castor sugar **24**
catfish **62**
catsup **126**
cauliflower **85**
cayenne pepper **29**
celeriac **29, 85**
celery **29, 85**
celery leaf **29, 85**
  Chinese **169**
celery root **29, 85**
celery seed **29**
Centenaar cheese **42**
cepes or porcini
  mushroom **89**
cereal, breakfast **9, 129**
cereal grains **14, 15**
cervelat **121**
chamois skin **178**
chanterelle **90**
chayote **158, 166**
cheddar cheese **43**
cheese 9, kinds of **40**
  Dutch **40-42**
  soft to semi-soft **43**
  semi soft **43**
  semi-firm to firm **43**
  firm to hard **44**
  goat/sheep **44**
  blue-veined **44**
  whey cheese **44**
  processed cheese **44**
  string/spun cheese **44**
cheese cleaver **173**
cheese farmers **11, 41**
cheese knife **175**
cheese shaver **173**
cheese shops **1, 40**
cheese soufflé,
  frozen **126**
cherimoya **73**
cherry **73**
  canned **125**
cherry, candied **14, 73**
cherry tomato **99**
cherry water **17**
chervil 27, **29**
chestnut **20, 21, 49**
chestnut mushroom **89**
chevre cheese **44**
chicken **11, 67**
  frozen **125**
  roasted **123**
chicken eggs **67**
chicken spices **38**
chicken stock **23**
chick peas **91**
chicory **85**
chicory root **85**
children's food **127**
chili **29, 92, 144**
chili pepper **30**
chili powder **30**
chili powder blend **37**
chili sauce **126**
  Thai **144**
  Chinese **144**
Chinese boxthorn **152,**
  156
Chinese broccoli **151, 154**
Chinese cabbage **84, 85,**
  150, 153
Chinese flowering cabbage
  151, 153
Chinese gooseberry **75**
Chinese kale **151, 154**
Chinese leaves **84, 85,**
Chinese long bean **82, 163,**
  168
Chinese parsley **27, 31, 169**
Chinese snow pea **91, 168**
Chinese white cabbage **84,**
  150, 153
Chinese spinach (Amaranth)
  152, 155
chipped beef **122**
chive **27, 30,**
  Chinese garlic chives **164,**
    169
  Chinese flowering chives
    164, 169
  Chinese yellow chives
    164, 169
chocolate **15**
chocolate chips **15**
chorizo **122**
cider vinegar **25, 149**
cilantro **31**
cinnamon **30**
citroen, candied **14**
citrus fruit zester **173**

citrus and vegetable knife **173**
citrus press **173**
clam **63**
cleaning fluid **179**
cleaning supplies **9, 178**
cleansing pads **178**
cleansing powder **178**
clementine **78**
clotted cream **43, 46**
clove **4, 27, 30**
cockle **64**
Coca cola **133**
cocktail pick **176**
cocktail sausages **126**
cocoa powder **16**
coconut **16, 20, 144**
coconut cream **16, 144**
coconut milk **16, 144**
coconut powder **144**
cod **54, 55, 57**
  frozen **122**
coffee **9, 132**
coffee creamer **45, 132**
coffee grinder **172**
coffee maker **172**
coffee milk **45, 132**
coffee pot **175**
colander **173**
cold cuts **9, 121**
condensed milk **45, 132**
confectioner's sugar **24**
confectionary shops **50**
cookies **52, 138**
cooking lettuce **89**
cooking oil **22**
coriander **27, 31**
coriander seed **31**
cork screw **173**
corn **14, 15, 86**
  frozen **125**
corned beef **122**
corn meal **15**
corn oil **22**
corn salad **86**
corn starch **19**
corn syrup **25**
Corning ware **173**
cos lettuce **89**
cottage cheese **43**
courgette **95**
couscous **14**
cow pea **82**
crab **64**
  frozen **124**
  imitation **64**
cranberry **73**
crayfish **64**
cream, whipping **46**
  sterilized **46**
cream cheese **42, 43**
cream of tartar **16**
cream of wheat **15**
cream puff **52**
créme fraîche **46**
crepes **137**
cress **87**
crimini mushroom **89**
croissant **50, 124**
croquettes **49**;
  frozen **126**
crumb crust 16, **17**
cucumber **87**
cucumber salad **49**
cumin **31**
cup **174**
curd cheese **42, 43**
curly kale **84**
  frozen **125**
  with sausage **48, 136**
curly endive **85**
currant **72, 74**
  dried **74**
curry powder **37**
curry sauce **49**
custard apple **73**
custard/pudding **47, 136**
cuttle fish **64**
cutting board **173**

D

dab **55, 57**
daikon radish **146, 160, 167**
dairy products **40**
Danish pastry **52**
dashi **144**
date **74**
decalcifier **178**
deep freeze bags **176**
deep fryer, electric **172**
deep frying fat **17**
deer **70**
delicatessen **48**
delicatessen foods **9, 48**
Demerara sugar **24**
deposits on bottles **7**
diet T.V. dinners **126**
diet cheese **41**
dill **31**
dill sauce **49**
dill pickles **87**
dinner ware **174**
dish brush **178**
dish detergent **178**
dish towel **178**
dishwasher
  detergent **178**
dishwasher rinse **178**
dishwasher water softener **179**
distilled water **173**
double boiler **173**
dough for savory pies **22, 122**
drain opener **179**
dried fruit **74**
duck **68**
  frozen **125**
duck eggs **67**
dust cloth **178**
Dutch gin **135**
Dutch food & drink **134**
Dutch oven **173**
Dutch pea soup **49, 135**
Dutch phrases **5**
Dutch vegetable soup **136**
dwarf green beans **82**

E

Eastern market **139**
Edam cheese **41, 43**
eel **54, 55, 60**
egg **44, 67**
egg beater **173**
egg cup **173**
egg cutter **173**
eggplant **87**
  Asian **157, 165**
egg timer **173**
electric knife **174**
Emmenthaler cheese **43**
endive, curly **85**
English breads **50**
English pea **91**
enokitaki mushroom **146**
escarole **85**
essence **17**
evaporated milk **45, 132**
exotic Asian vegetables, **150**
  see also individual names
extract **17**

F

fabric softener **178**
fagara **36**
farms **11**
fats, solid **17**
fava bean **82**
fennel root **87**
fennel seed **31**
fenugreek **31**

field lettuce **86**
fig **74**
  dried **74**
filo pastry **22, 124**
fines herbes **37**
fish **11, 54**
  frozen, canned **124**
fish fork **175**
fish knife **175**
fish sauce **49**
  Asian **144**
fish server **175**
fish shop **10, 24**
fish stock **23, 24**
five spice powder **38**
flat cabbage **151, 154**
flatware/silverware **175**
floor wax and oil **179**
flounder **54, 55, 58**
flour, non-wheat **19**
flour, wheat **18, 19**
flour sifter **173**
foil, aluminum **176**
fondue au fromage **43**
food processor **172**
food warmer **175**
food wrap **176**
forks **175**
fragrant mushrooms **145, 146**
fragrant rice **147**
frankfurters **122**
French breads **50, 51**
French fried potatoes, **93**
  frozen **125**
French knife **174**
frisée **86**
Frisian clove cheese **42**
frog's legs **70**
fromage blanc **42**
fromage frais **42**
fructose **24**
fruit **9, 11, 71** - see also individual fruits;
  frozen, canned **125**
fruit cocktail **125**
fruit dish **175**
fruit knife **175**
fry, to **101**
frying pan **173**
funnel **173**
furniture wax **179**
fuzzy melon **159, 166**

G

gado gado **140**
galangal **32, 145**
galia melon **77**
game and game birds **67**
  frozen **125**
garam masala **38**
garbage can **176**
garbonzo **91**
garden cress **87**
garden furniture cleaner **179**
garfish **55, 61**
garland chrysanthemum **152, 156**
garlic **88**
garlic paste **88**
garlic powder **88**
garlic press **173**
garlic salt **88**
garlic sauce **49**
garnishing utensils **173**
gelatin **20**
geranium water **17**
gherkin **87, 126**
giblets **68, 69**
gilthead **59**
gin **133, 135**
ginger **32, 145**
  stem **160, 166**
glasses, drinking **174**
glucose **24**
goat cheese **41, 44**
goatfish **59**
golden oak mushroom **89**
Golden syrup **25**
goose **68**
gooseberry **72, 73**
goosefish **57**
Gorgonzola cheese **44**
Gouda cheese **4, 40, 41, 43**
Goudse stroopwafels **137**
gourmet foods **48**
Graham crackers **16**
grains **14, 15**
grape **74**
grapefruit **75**
grapefruit knife **174**
grape leaves **74**
grapeseed oil **22**
grape sugar **24**
grater **173**
gravy/sauce ladle **175**
green beans **81**;
  frozen **125**
green cabbage **84**
green lollo **89**
green onion **94**
green pepper **91**
greengrocer **7, 71**
grill, to **101**
grill spit **173**
grilling tongs **173**
grouse **68**
Gruyere cheese **43**
Guacamole, frozen **139**
guinea fowl **68**
gula Jawa **24**
gunnard **59**

H

haddock **54, 55, 58**
hake **55, 58**
halibut **55,58**
ham **112, 114, 116, 122**
hamburger patties **125**
hand mixer **172**
hand towel **178**
hare **70**
hash brown potatoes **93, 125**
haricots vert (dwarf French beans) **82**
harissa **38**
harusami **146**
hazelnuts **20, 21, 49**
hazelnut butter **129**
hazel nut oil **22**
head cheese **122**
head lettuce **89**
health food **130**
heart **105**
hearts of palm **125**
hedge hog mushroom **90**
herbs **27,** see also individual herbs
herbes de Provence **38**
herring **54, 55, 61**
hodgepodge **48, 136**
hoisin sauce **145**
honey **20**
honeydew melon **77**
horned water chestnut **161, 167**
horn of plenty mushroom **90**
horse meat **122**
horseradish **32**
hot dogs **122**
household liquids **179**
housewares **171**
hubbard squash **96, 97**

I

iceberg lettuce **89**
ice cream **46, 125**
icing sugar **24**
ikan Bali **140**

ikan kari **140**
Indonesian food **139, 140, 141**
infant formulas **127**
infant vitamins **129**
instant flour **19**
International food products **11, 139**
iron, clothes **172**
ironing supplies **179**
Italian pastas **125**
Italian seasoning **38**

J
jalepeño pepper **92**
Jamaica pepper **28**
jams and jellies **23**
jelling powder **23, 128**
jelling sugar **23**
jicama **161, 168**
juice **133**
  frozen **125**
  baby **128**
juicer, electric **172**
Julia Child **102**
juniper berry **32**

K
kaffir lime **33, 145**
kaffir lime leaves **33**
kale, curly **48, 84, 136**
  frozen **125**
kamut **14**
kangkong **152, 156**
kasha **14**
kecap manis **145**
kelp **147**
kettle **173**
kidney **105**
kidney bean **82**
kippered herring **61**
kitchen equipment and utensils **172**
kitchen mitt or glove **172**
kitchen scale **172**
kitchen shears **174**
kitchen supplies **171**
kiwi **75**
knife sharpener **172**
knives, kitchen **174**
knives, flatware **175**
kohlrabi **88**
kombu **144**
krupuk udang **140**
kudzu **162, 168**
kumquat **75**
kwark or quark **42, 43**

L
ladle **175**
lamb **100, 117**
  wholesale/retail cuts **117**
  preparation of **118**
lamb's lettuce **86**
lapwing eggs **67**
lard **17**
lard, to **101**
lasagne, frozen **125**
laundry detergent **179**
leek **88, 169**
Leerdammer cheese **42**
Leiden cheese **42**
lemon **75**
lemon balm **33**
lemon extract **17**
lemon grass **33, 145**
lentil **89**
  dal **89**
  Egyptian **89**
lettuce **89**
  stem **157, 165**
lima bean **82**
Limburger cheese **43**
lime **76**
ling **55, 58**
lion's mane mushroom **90**
liqueur **132, 133**
liquor **132, 133**
liquor stores **132**
litchi **76**
  dried **76**
liver, beef **105**
liver, chicken **68**
liver sausage **122, 123**
loaf pan **173**
lobster **64**
lollo red, green **89**
lotte **55, 57**
lotus root **161, 167**
lovage **33**
lumpia **140**
lumpia wrapper **148**

M
Maasdammer cheese **42**
macadamia nut **20, 21, 49**
macaroni, frozen **125**
mace **4, 27, 33**
mâche **86**
mackerel **54, 55, 61**
main courses **48**
malsouqua **23**
mandarin orange **77**
mango **76**
mangosteen **76**
maple syrup **25**
maraschino cherry **73**
maraschino extract **17**
margarine **17, 46**
marjoram **33**
marrowfat pea **91**
mascarpone cheese **43**
marshmallows **20**
marzipan **13**
mayonnaise **126**
measurements **7, 181**
measuring cup **174**
measuring spoons **174**
meat balls **135**
meat grinder **172**
meat knife **172**
meat loaf **123**
meat platter **175**
meats **9, 100,125** - see also individual meats
meat thermometer **174**
Melba toast **126**
melon **76**
melon ball spoon **175**
metal polish **179**
microwave oven **172**
microwave casserole **173**
microwave food wrap **176**
milk **40, 45, 47**
  powdered **47**
milk, coffee **45, 132**
milk pitcher **175**
milk products **9, 40**
millet **14,15**
Milner cheese **42**
mineral water **133**
mint **33**
miso **145**
mixed fruit **14**
mixed nuts **49**
mizuna **154**
mocha essence **17**
molasses **24**
monkfish **57**
monosodium glutamate **145**
mop **178**
mopping rag **178**
Morbier cheese **43**
morel mushroom **89**
mortadella sausage **121**
mozzarella cheese **44**
muesli **129**
muffin tin **172**
mullet **55, 58, 59**
multi-purpose cleaner **179**
mung bean **83**

mung bean sprouts **83, 162, 168**
mushroom **89, 90**
mushroom, Asian **145**
mushroom brush **174**
musk melon **76, 77**
mussels **54, 65**
mustard **34**
mustard cabbage **151, 155**
mustard seed **34**

N
nacho chips **139**
Napa cabbage **84**
nasi goreng **48, 140**
nasi kuning **141**
nasi putih **141**
natural vinegar **25**
navel orange **77**
nectarine **77**
net melon **77**
noodles and pasta **9, 20, 125**
noodles, Asian **146**
nori **147**
nougatine **14**
nutmeg 4, **27, 34**
nutmeg grater **174**
nuts **20, 48**

O
oakleaf lettuce **89**
oat bran **15**
oatmeal **14, 15**
oats **14**
octopus **64**
Ogen melon **77**
oil, cooking **22**
oil, other **22**
oil seed rape **151, 154**
okra **90**
Old Amsterdam cheese **42**
olive **77**
olive oil **22**
onion(s) **90**
onion powder **91**
onion flakes **91**
open markets **11**
orange **77**
orange flower water **17**
oregano **34**
oven cleaner **180**
ovenproof dish **173**
oven thermometer **174**
oyster **65**
oyster mushroom **89**
oyster plant **94**
canned **125**
oyster sauce **146**

P
pablum **127**
paella **48**
palette knife **174**
pan-fry, to **101**
panko **14, 146**
pancakes **137**
papaya **78**
paper napkins **176**
paprika powder **34**
parchment paper **176**
Pardano cheese **42**
paring knife **174**
Parisian carrots **85**
Parma ham **122**
Parmesan cheese **40, 44**
parsley **27, 34**
parsnip **91**
partridge **69**
Passendale cheese **43**
passion fruit **78**
pasta **9, 20, 125**
pastries **11, 50, 124, 134, 137**
pastry brush **174**
pastry dough **22, 124**
pastry flour **19**
pastry for savory pies **22, 124**
paté **123**
frozen **124**
pattypan squash **95, 97**
pea **91**
frozen **125**
peach **78**; canned **125**
peanut butter **23**
peanut oil **22**
peanuts **20, 21**
pear **78**
canned **125**
pear nectar **78**
pea soup, Dutch **48, 135**
pecan nut **20, 21, 49**
pectin **23, 130**
Pecorino Romano **44**
Peking cabbage **84, 150, 153**
pepper **34**
pepper, bell or sweet **91**
pepper, chili, hot **92, 144**
peppercorns **34**
peppermill **174**
peppermint **33**
pepperoni sausage **123**
pepper shaker **175**
Pepsi cola **133**
perch (bass) **63**
persimmon **79**
pet food **9, 11**
pheasant **69**
pickles, gherkins **87**
pickling spices **38**
pie **52**
pie filling **52, 74**
pie server **175**
pigeon **69**
pike (pike/perch) **63**
pimento **92**
pineapple **79**;
canned **125**
pine nuts **20, 21, 49**
pinto bean **82**
pisang goreng **141**
pistachio nuts **20, 21, 49**
pita bread **50**
pizza **124, 125**
plaice **54, 55, 58**
plates **174**
plum **79**
plum tomato **99**
poach, to **101**
pollack **55, 59**
pomegranate **79**
pomelo **75**
pomodoro tomato **99**
pop corn **86**
poppy seed **35**
porcini mushroom **89**
pork **100, 112**
wholesale & retail cuts **112**
preparation of **114**
frozen **125**
roasted **123**
portobello mushroom **89**
Port Salut cheese **43**
porridge **129**
potato **92**
potato chips **49**
potato flour **19**
potato masher **174**
potato peeler **174**
pots and pans **172, 175**
poultry **67, 68**
frozen **125**
poultry seasoning **38**
poultry shops **10, 67**
prawns 54, **65**
pressure cooker **172**
prickly pear **80**
processed cheese **41, 44**
prosciutto ham, see Parma ham

provolone cheese 44
prune **74, 79**
pudding **47**, **136**
puff pastry dough **22**, **124**
puff pastry shells **53**
pumpkin **93, 95, 96, 97**
pumpkin pie sauce **95**
pumpkin pie spice **38**
purslane **93**

Q
quail **69**
quail eggs **67**
quatre epices **38**
quiche **22**, **124**
quinoa **15**

R
rabbit **70**
raclette cheese **43**
radicchio **85, 86**
radish **93**, **160, 167**
radish cutter **173**
radish sprouts **83**
raisin **74**
raisin bread **51**
rambutan **80**
ramen **126**, **146**
raspberry **73**
raspberry vinegar **26**
ray **53, 59**
recycling **7**
red beet **83**
  canned **125**
red cabbage **84**
red currant **74**
redfish **55, 59**
red leaf lettuce **89**
red lollo **89**
red mullet **58**
red onion **90**
red snapper **55,59**
rendang daging **141**
rémoulade sauce **54**
rhubarb **72, 93**
rice **15**
  Asian **147**
rice flour **19**
rice vinegar **26**, **148**
rice wine **147**
ricotta cheese **42**, **44**
rijsttafel **134, 139, 140**
Reijpenaer cheese **42**
roast, to **101**
roasted meats **123**
roasting pan **173**
roe **54, 63**
rolling pin **174**
rolls **51**
rolmops **61**
Romaine (cos) lettuce **89**
Roquefort cheese **44**
rosehip syrup **128**
rosemary **35**
rosewater **17**
Rotterdammers **123**
rouge vif d'etamps squash
  96, 97
rue **35**
rujak **141**
rum **133**
rum aroma **17**
rusk, Dutch **52**
rutabaga **94**
rye bread **51**, **126**
rye flour **19**
rye grain **15**

S
safflower oil **22**
saffron **35**
sage **35**
saimin **126**
salad, Dutch **49**
salad dressing **126**
salad fork **175**
salad fork & spoon **175**
salami **123**
salam leaf **35**, **147**
salicornia **94**
salmon **61**
  frozen **124**
salmon trout **62**
salsa **139**
salsify **94**
  canned **125**
salt **23**
salt shaker **175**
sambal **39**, **141**
sambal goreng telur **141**
samphire **94**
sandwiches **133**
sardine **55, 62**, **124**
saté **48**, **141**
  frozen **126**
saucepan **173**
sauces **9, 49**, **126**
sauerkraut **84**
  with sausage **84, 137**
saus kacang pedis **141**
sausages & cold cuts **121**,
  129
savings stamps **10**
savory **36**
Savoy cabbage **84**
sayur lodeh **141**
scales **172**
scallion **94, 169**
scallop **66**
scampi **65**
scarlett runner **81**
scotch whiskey **133**
scouring pads **178**
sea bass **59**
sea bream **55, 59**
sea cucumber **66**
sea robin **55, 59**
sea salt **23**
sea weed **147**
seed sprouts **83**
self-rising flour **19**
serundeng **141**
sesame oil, Asian **22, 36,**
  148
sesame oil, white **22**
sesame seed **36**
Seven-up **133**
shaddock **75**
shallot **94**
sheep's milk cheese **43, 44**
shellfish **54, 63**
shichimi togarashi **148**
shiitaki mushroom **89, 145**
shiso green, red **83, 165,**
  169
shopping hours **5**
shopping procedures **6**
short bread **52**
shortening, vegetable **17, 18**
shrimp **54**, **55, 65**
  canned **125**
shrimp paste (*terasi*) **148**
schwerma sandwiches **100**
shwerma spices **39**, **100**
sieve **174**
silver onion **90**
  canned **126**
simmer, to **101**
sizing starch **179**
skate **59**
slippery vegetable **152**
slotted spoon **174**
smelt **55, 62**
smoke, to **101**
smoked beef **122**
smoor **141**
snacks **49**, **126**
snap beans **81**
snow pea **91**
soap **155, 178, 180**
soap pads **178**

soba **146**
soda crackers **126**
soft drinks **9, 133**
sole **54, 55, 60**
  frozen **124**
sorrel **94**
sour cream **47**
sour sop **73**
soups **49, 126, 135**
soup tureen **175**
soya milk **128, 130**
soya oil **22**
soy bean **83**
soy bean sprouts **162, 168**
soy sauce **148**
spaghetti **125**
spaghetti squash **96, 98**
spatula **174**
spearmint **33**
specialty shops **10**
spelt **15**
spinach **95**
  frozen **125**
spices **9, 27** - see also individual spices
spiral cutter **173**
split pea **91, 125**
sponges **178**
spoons **175**
sprat **55, 62**
spray starch **179**
spring form **173**
spring roll wrappers **148**
spring onion **94**
sprouts **83**
squash **93, 95**
squid **64**
stain remover, fabrics **180**
star anise **36**
star fruit **73**
starch, laundry **179**
steam, to **101**
stew, to **101**
Stilton cheese **44**
stir-fry, to **101**
stock **23**
strawberry **72**
straw mushrooms **145**
string **174**
string bean **81**
Subenhara cheese **42**
sucrose **24**
sugar **24**
sugar bowl **175**
sugar melon **77**
sugar snap pea **91**
sugar spoon **176**
sun-dried tomatoes **99**
sunflower oil **22**
supermarkets **9**
Swede **94**
Swedish turnip **94**
sweet onion **90**
sweet potato **96**
sweetbreads **105**
sweetened condensed milk **45, 132**
Swiss chard **96**
Swiss cheese **43**
syrup **24**
  fruit **128**
Szechwan pepper **36**

T
tabasco pepper **92**
tabasco sauce **30**
table cloth **176**
taco **139**
taco seasoning **139**
tahini **36**
tamari **148**
tamarind **36**
tangarine **78**
tangelo **75**
tapioca flour **19**
taro **161, 167**
tarragon **27, 36**
tarragon vinegar **26**
tart **52**
tart fillings **52**
tartar sauce **49, 54**
tart dish **175**
tart glazes **14**
tatsoi **151, 154**
tea **9, 133**
tempe **130, 148**
tempe goreng **141**
terrine **123**
thermometer, meat/oven **174**
thyme **27, 36**
timer **174**
tival **131**
toaster **172**
tofu **130, 143**
toilet bowl cleaner **155**
tomato **99**
  canned **125**
  dried **99**
tomato paste **25**
tomato puree **25**
tomato sauce **25**
tongue **105**
tongs, grilling **173**
toothpick **176**
tortilla **139**
Trenta cheese **42, 130**
trout **63**
truffle **89**
trumpets of death **90**
tuinbonen **82**
tuna **62**
  canned **124**
turban squash **95**
turbot **55, 60**
turkey **69**
turmeric **37**
turnip **99**
turnip leaves **99**
TV dinner **124, 126**

U
ugli **75**
upholstery cleaner **178**

V
vacuum cleaner bags **180**
Valencia orange **77**
vanilla **17**
vanilla bean **17**
vanilla sugar **17**
variety meat **100, 105**
veal **100, 108**
  wholesale and retail cuts **108**
  preparation of **110**
vegetable oil **17, 22**
vegetables **9, 11, 71, 80**
  - see also individual vegetables
  frozen **122, 125**
vegetarian foods **130**
venison **70**
Vienna sausage **126**
vinegar **25**
  Asian **148**
vitamins (infant) **128, 129**
vodka **133**

W
waffle iron **172**
waffles **137**
walnut **20, 21, 49**
walnut oil **22**
wasabi **37**
water chestnut **160, 167**
watercress **87**
water melon **76**
water, mineral **133**
water softener **178**
water spinach **152, 156**

wax bean **82**
weights **181**
wheat **15**
wheat bran **15**
wheat germ **15**
whipping cream **46**
whipping cream
  stabilizer **26**
white beans **82**
  canned **125**
white bait **62**
white bread **51**
white cabbage **84**
white currant **74**
white wheat flour **19**
whiting **55, 60**
whole wheat bread **51**
whole wheat crackers
  biscuits **17, 126**
whole wheat flour **19**
wild boar **69**
wild rice **15**
window cleaner **180**
wine **9, 133**
wine vinegar **25**
winter luxury pie pumpkin
  96, 97
winter melon **159, 166**
winter squash **158, 166**
wire whisk **152**
wok **173**
wolf fish **55, 60**
won ton wrappers **149**
wood alcohol **179**
wood ear fungus **149**
Worcestershire sauce
  126

Y
yakult **47, 149**
yam **96**
yard long bean **82, 163, 168**
yeast **26**
yellow snap bean **82**
yoghurt **47**
yoghurt drink **47**
yoghurt ice cream **46**

Z
zucchini **95**

DUTCH INDEX

A

aardappel **92**
aardappelmeel **19**
aardappelstamper **174**
aardbei **72**
abrikoos **72**
gedroogd **72, 74**
acar **140**
advocaat **133**
adzuki **82**
afvoer onstopper **179**
afwasborstel **178**
afwasmachine poeder **178**
afwasmiddel **178**
agar agar **143**
ahornstroop **25**
alcoholische dranken **132**
alfalfa groente **83**
allesreiniger **179**
Althena kaas **42**
aluminiumfolie **176**
amandelen, **20, 48**
amandel aroma **17**
amandel olie **22**
amandelspijs **13, 21**
Amerikaanse whisky **133**
amaranth **14, 152**
Amsterdams vet **86**
ananas **79**
in blik **125**
andijvie **86**
anijs **28**
ansjovis **60**
annona **73**
appel **71**
gedroogd **74**
appel azijn **25, 147**
appelbeignets **53, 137**
appelbollen **53, 137**
appelboor **173**
appelcidre **132**
appelflappen **53, 137**
appelgebak **53, 137**
appelmoes **72**
in blik **125**
appelsap **72, 132**
Arabisch brood **50, 100**
arachideolie **22**
arborio rijst **15**
aroma **17**
artisjok **22, 80**
in blik **125**
asam **36**
asperges **83, 22, 80**
in blik **125**
asperges met ham & eieren **136**
au-bain-marie pan **173**
aubergine **87, 157, 165**
augurk **87, 124**
avocado **81**
ayam goreng **140**
Aziatische pasta **146**
Aziatische voeding **139**
Aziasche paddestoel **146**
Aziatische pasta **123, 144**
azijn **25, 148**

B

baars **63**
babi kecap **140**
baby mais **86**
baby voeding **9, 127**
in potten **128**
baby maaltijd **128**
kleuter formule **127**
dranken **128**
biscuits **129**
brood beleg **129**
ontbijt granen **129**
vitaminen **129**
bacon **112, 114, 116, 121**
badkamer reiniger **177**
bahmie goreng **48, 140**
bak benodigdheden **13**
bakken **100, 101**
bakkerij artikelen **9**
bakkerijen **50**
bakpapier **176**
bakpoeder **13**
bakvorm **171**
balsam azijn **26**
bamboe scheuten **141**
banaan **72**
banket bakkerijen **50**
barbecue saus **124**
barderen **100**
basilicum **27, 28, 143**
bawang goreng **140**
bawang merah **94, 140, 143**
Beaufort kaas **43**
bekleding reiniger **178**
belegde broodjes **135**
Bel Paese kaas **43**
beschuit **52**
bessen **72, 124**
bevroren, in blik **124**
bessen jenever **135**
bestek **174**
bier **132**
bieslook **27, 30**
Chinese **164, 169**
bigarreau **14**
biogarde **43,45**
biscuits, kinder **129**
Bisschop's wijn **134**
bitterballen **135**
bladerdeeg **22, 124**
bladerdeeg voor hartige taarten **22, 124**
blauwe bessen **72, 73**
blauwe kaas **44**
bleekmiddel (bleekwater) **177**
bleekselderij **29, 85**
blikopener **173**
blinde vinken **136**
bloed sinaasappel **77**
bloedworst (bak) **121**
bloem **19**
bloemkool **85**
bloem voor patisserie **19**
boekweit **14, 15**
boekweit meel **15, 19**
boekweit grutten **15**
boekweit pasta (soba) **146**
boerderijen **11**
boerenjongens **134**
boerenkool **84**
bevroren **125**
boerenkool met worst **48, 136**
boerenmeisjes **134**
bok choy **85, 150, 153**
bokking **61**
bonbon doos **175**
bonbons **50**
bonekruid **36**
bonensaus & pasta, Aziatisch **143**
bonenspruit **83, 162, 168**
boon **81**
in blik **125**
borden **174**
borstel **178**
bosui **94**
boter **17, 45**
boterboon **82**
botercake **52, 137**
boterhamworst **119**
boterkoek **52, 53, 137**
boter kruller **173**

boterkwastje **174**
botervloot **173**
bouillon **23**
bouquet garni **37**
braadpan **173**
braadslee **173**
braadspit **173**
braden **101**
bramen **72, 73**
brandewijn **132**
brandspiritus **179**
brie **43**
broccoli **83**
broeivet **86**
brood **11, 50, 51**
brood beleg **129**
broodbloem **19**
broodjes **51**
broodkruimels **14**
broodmandje **175**
broodmengsel **9**
broodrooster **172**
broodvorm **173**
Broxo Matic **178**
bruine bonen **82**
  in blik **125**
bruine bonensoep **136**
bruine fond **23**
bulghur **14**
bumbu **37**
butternut squash **94, 98**

C
cacaopoeder **16**
cactus vijg **79**
cake **52**
cake meel **19**
cake mengsels **9, 19**
cakevorm **173**
cake versiering **14**
Calvados **132**
Camembert kaas **43**
cantaloup **77**
canterelle **90**
carambola **73**
cashew noten **20, 21, 48**
Casseler rib **121**
cassis **74**
catsup **126**
cayenne peper **29**
cervelaat **121**
champignons **89, 90**
cheddar kaas **43**
chèvre kaas **44**
cherimoya **73**
chili poeder **30**
chili poeder mengsel **37**
chili saus **126**
  Thai **144**
  Chinese **144**
Chinese kool **84, 150, 153**
chips **49**
chocolade **15**
chocolate chips **15**
chocolade glazuur **14**
chorizo **121**
cider azijn **25**
citroen **75**
citroen aroma **17**
citroen gras **33, 145**
citroenmelisse **33**
citroen aroma **17**
citroen trekker **173**
citrus en groenten mesje **173**
citruspers **173**
clotted cream **46**
Coca cola **133**
cocktail prikker **176**
cocosroom **16, 144**
coriander blad **27, 31**
coriander zaad **31**
corned beef **122**
cos sla **89**
courgette **95**
cranberry **73**
crème fraîche **46**
crimini mushroom **89**
croissant **50, 124**

D
dadel **74**
daon djeruk perut **33, 145**
daon salam **35, 147**
dashi **144**
deegroller **174**
deeg voor hartige taart **22, 122**
delicatessen artikelen **48**
delicatessen **9, 48, 139**
dieet kaas **41**
dieet TV maaltijden **126**
diepvries zakjes **176**
dieren voeding **9, 11**
diklip harder **58**
dille **31**
dille saus **49**
djeruk perut **32, 145**
dragon **27, 36**
dragonazijn **26**
dranken **128, 132, 134**
drankwinkel **132**
druif **74**
druiven bladeren **74**
druiven zaad olie **22**
dry gin **133, 135**
duif **69**
dunschiller **174**
dweil **178**

E
ecrevisse **64**
eekhoorntjesbrood **89**
Edammer kaas **41**
eend **68**
  bevroren **125**
eendeneieren **67**
ei **44, 67**
eierdopje **173**
eierklopper **173**
eiersnijder **173**
eierwekker **173**
eikenbladsla **89**
elektrische frituurpan **172**
elektrische fruitpers **172**
elektrisch mes **174**
Emmenthaler kaas **43**
enokitaki paddestoel **146**
erwt **91**
  bevroren **125**
erwtensoep **49, 135**
exotische Aziatische groenten **150**
  see also individual English names

F
fabriekskaas **44**
fagara **36**
fazant **69**
fenegriek **31**
fijne kruiden **37**
filo deeg **22, 124**
fines herbes **38**
flensjes **137**
flageolet **81**
fles opener **173**
foelie **4, 27, 33**
fond blanc **23**
fond brun **23**
fond de gibier **24**
fond de volaille **23**
forel **63**
framboos **72**
framboosazijn **26**
frankfurters **122**
Friese nagelkaas **42**
fritessaus **126**
frituurvet **17**
fromage blanc **42**
fromage frais **42**

fructose **24**
fruit **9, 11, 71**
  bevroren **125**
fruit bordje **175**
fruit cocktail **125**
fruit mesje **175**

G
gado gado **140**
galangal **32, 145**
galiameloen **77**
gans **68**
garam masala **38**
garde **173**
garnalen **54, 65**
garnalen pasta (terasi) **148**
garneer-apparaatjes **173**
gebak **11, 50, 122**
gebraden fricandeau **123**
gebraden gehakt **123**
gebraden kip **123**
gebraden vlees **123**
gecondenseerde melk **45, 132**
gedistilleerd water **179**
gedroogde pruim **74, 79**
gedroogde tomaten **99**
geep **55, 61**
geiten kaas **41, 44**
gelatine **20**
gelatine poeder **23, 130**
gelei suiker **23**
gember **32, 160, 167**
gemengde noten **49**
geranium water **17**
gerst **14**
gesteriliseerde
  geëvaporeerde melk **45, 132**
gesuikerde
  gecondenseerde melk **45**
gewichten **181**
gevogelte **67, 68**
  bevroren **125**
gevogelte fond **23**
gierst **15**
gist **26**
glans spoelmiddel **178**
glas-keramische pan **173**
glazen **174**
glucose **24**
Golden syrup **25**
Gorgonzola kaas **44**
gort **14**
  parelgort **14**
goudbrasem **59**
Goudse kaas **4, 40, 43**
Goudse stroopwafels **137**
gourmet maaltijden **48**
granaatappel **79**
grapefruit **75**
grapefruitmesje **174**
granen **14, 15**
griet **57**
grilleren **101**
grilleer tang **173**
groene kool **84**
groentefond **23**
groenteman **10, 71**
groentensoep **136**
groenten **9, 11, 71, 80,**
  bevroren **124, 125**
  Zie ook afzonderlijke namen
Gruyere kaas **43**
guacamole **136**
gula Jawa **24**

H
haas **70**
hachee **136**
ham **112, 114, 116, 122**
hamburger **125**
handdoek **178**
handmixer **172**
haricot vert **82**
haring **54, 61**
harissa **38**
hart **105**
harusami **146**
haver **14**
havermout **14**
haverzemelen 15
hazelnoot **21, 20, 49**
hazelnoot pasta **129**
hazelnoot olie **22**
heek **58**
heilbot **58**
herbes de Provence **38**
hersens **105**
hert **70**
hogedruk pan **172**
hoisin saus **145**
hom **54, 63**
honing **20**
honingmeloen **77**
hoofdschotels **48**
hoorn van overvloed **90**
hotdogs **122**
huile de noisette **22**
huile de pepin de raisin **22**
huishoud folie **176**
huishoudelijke apparaten **171**
huishoudelijke artikelen **171**
hutspot **48, 136**
hüttenkäse **43**

I
iceberg sla **89**
ijs **46, 125**
ikan Bali **140**
ikan kari **140**
inktvis **64**
Indonesische gerechten **139, 140, 141**
inmaakkruiden **38**
internationale
  voedingsstoffen **11, 139**
Italiaanse kruiden **38**
Italiaanse pasta **125**

J
jalepeño pepper **92**
jam **23**
Jamaica peper **28**
jenever **130, 133, 135**
jenever bessen **32**
jeroek nipis **76**
juslepel **175**

K
kaasboerderij **11, 41**
kaasmes **175**
kaasmesje **174**
kaasschaaf **173**
kaassoesjes **135**
kaassoorten **40**
  Nederlands **40-42**
  zacht to semi-zacht **43**
  semi-zacht - semi soft **43**
  semi-stevig tot stevig **43**
  stevig tot hard **44**
  geit/schaap **44**
  blauwe kaas **44**
  weikaas **44**
  fabriekskaas **44**
kaasschaaf **173**
kaassoorten **40**
kaaswinkel **1, 40**
kaassoufflé, bevroren **126**
kabeljauw **54, 57**
  bevroren **124**
kaki **79**
kalfsvlees **108, 108**
  groothandel en
  kleinhandel **108**
  bereiden van **110**
kalkoen **69**
kamut **15**
kandijsuiker **24**

kaneel **30**
kappertjes **28**
kapucijner **91**
in blik **125**
kardemom **29**
karnemelk **45**
karper **62**
karweizaad **29**
kasha **14**
kastanje **20**, **21**, **49**
kastanje paddestoel **89**
katenspek **114**
katjang idjo **82**
kecap manis **145**
kemiri **144**
kerrie poeder **37**
kerry saus **49**
kers **73**
in blik **125**
kerst tulband **53**,**137**
kerstkranjes **53**, **137**
kerststol **53**, **137**
kervel **27**, **29**
ketel **173**
ketoembar **31**
keukenmachine **172**
keukenmes **174**
keukenschaar **174**
keuken weegschaal **172**
keuken wekker **174**
kibbeling **54**
kiemgroenten **83**
kiemmix **83**
kievietboon **82**
kievietseieren **67**
kindervoeding **127**
kikkerbilletjes **70**
kikkererwten **91**
kip **11**, **67**
bevroren **125**
gebraden **123**
kipkruiden **38**
kippeneieren **67**
kippered haring **61**
kirsch **17**
kiwi **75**
knakworstjes **122**
knoflook **88**
knoflook poeder **88**
knoflook pasta **88**
knoflookpers **173**
knoflook zout **88**
knoflook saus **49**
knolselderij **29**, **85**
knolselderij salade **49**
koekepan **173**
koekjes **52**
koenjit **37**
koffie **9**, **132**
koffie broodjes **52**
koffiecreamer **45**, **132**
koffiemelk **45**, **132**
koffiemolen **172**
koffiezet apparaat **172**
koffiekan **175**
koken **100**
kokkel **64**
kokosnoot **16**, **20**, **144**
kokosroom **16**, **144**
kokosmelk **16**, **144**
kom **172**, **173**, **175**
kombu **144**
komkommer **87**
komkommer salade **49**
komijn **31**
konijn **70**
kool **84**, **85**
koolraap **93**
koolrabi **88**
kookpan **173**
kopje **174**
kouseband boon **82**, **163**
korhoen **68**
koriander **27**, **31**
koriander zaad **31**
krab **63**
imitation **64**
in blik **124**
kreeft **64**
kreeften-fond **24**
kreeft garnaal **34**
krent, bes **72**, **74**
gedroogd **74**
kriel- en kers-tomaten **99**
kroketten **49**
bevroren **126**
kropsla **89**
kruiden, **27** zie ook individuele kruiden
kruiden voor pompoen taart **38**
kruidnagel **4**, **27**, **30**
kruimelbodem **16**, **17**
kruisbes **72**, **73**
kruizemunt **33**
krul andijvie **86**
krupuk **140**
kuit **54**, **63**
kumquat **75**
kurketrekker **173**
kurkuma **37**
kwark **42**, **43**
kwartel **69**
kwartel eieren **67**

L

lange ovenwant **174**
lam **100**, **117**
groothandel/kleinhandel **117**
bereiding van **118**
laos **32**, **145**
larderen **101**
lasagne, bevroren **125**
laurierblad **28**
lavas **33**
Leerdammer kaas **42**
lekkerbekje **54**
leng **58**
lepel **175**
lever, rund **105**
lever, kip **68**
leverworst **122**, **123**
likeur **132**
Limburgse kaas **43**
limoen **76**
linzen **89**
litermaat **175**
loempia **140**
loempia vellen **148**
lollo biondo **89**
lollo rosso **89**
lychee **76**
gedroogd **76**

M

maagzout **14**
maanzaad **35**
Maasdammer kaas **41**
maatjes haring **61**
maatlepeltjes **174**
macadamia noot **20**, **21**, **49**
macaroni, bevroren **125**
magnetron **172**
magnetron-veilige schotel **173**
magnetron vershoud folie **176**
mais **14**, **15**, **86**
bevroren **125**
maismeel **15**
maisolie **22**
maizena **19**
makreel **55**, **61**
malsouqua **23**
mandarijn **78**
mango **76**
mangosteen **76**
maraschino kers **73**
maraschino aroma **17**
margarine **17**, **46**
marjolein **33**

markten **11**
mascarpone kaas **43**
marsepein **13**
mayonnaise **126**
meelzeef **173**
meerval **62**
meiknol **97**
melasse **24**
Melba toast **126**
melk **40, 45, 47**
melkkan **175**
melk poeder **47**
meloen **76**
messenslijper **172**
meloenbolletjes lepel **175**
metaal poetsmiddel **179**
meubelwas **179**
mierikswortel **32**
mineraalwater **133**
miso **145**
mokka aroma **17**
Mon Chou **42**
mononatrium
glutamaat **145**
morieltje **89**
mortadella **121**
mosselen **54, 65**
mosterd **34**
mosterd zaad **34**
mozzarella kaas **44**
meusli **128**
muffin vorm **172**
mul **58, 59**
munt **33**

N
nacho chips **139**
nasi goreng **48, 141**
nasi koening **141**
nasi putih **141**
natrium bicarbonaat **14**
natuurazijn **25**
navel sinaasappel **77**
nectarine **77**
netmeloen **77**
nier **105**
nierbonen **82**
niervet **17**
nootmuskaat **4, 27, 34**
nootmuskaat rasp **174**
nori **147**
noten **20, 48**
nougatine **14**

O
octopus **64**
oester **65**
oester zwammen **89**
ogen meloen **77**
okra **90**
olie **22**
oliebollen **11, 53, 137**
olijf **77**
olijfolie **22**
ontbijt granen **9, 129**
ontbijtkoek **138**
ontbijtspek **121**
ontkalker **178**
ontstopper **179**
Oosterse markt **139**
openings tijden **5**
opsnit **121**
oregano **34**
Oud Amsterdam kaas **41**
ovenreiniger **180**
oventermometer **174**
ovenwant **172**
oyster sauce **146**

P
paardenvlees **122**
paas tulband **53, 137**
paddestoel **89**
paddestoelen borstel **174**
paella **48**
paletmes **174**
paling **54,55, 60**
palmhart **125**
paneermeel **14**
panko **14, 146**
pannenkoek **137**
pap **129**
papaja **78**
papieren servetten **176**
paprika **92, 144**
paprika poeder **34**
parelgort **14**
parelhoen **68**
paranoot **20, 48**
Parisienne worteltjes **85**
Parma ham **122**
Parmesaanse kaas **44**
Passendale kaas **43**
passie vrucht **78**
pasta **9, 20, 125**
pasteitje **53**
pastenaak **91**
patat friet **93,**
bevroren **125**
pâté **123**
bevroren **124**
patentbloem **18**
patisserie bloem **19**
patrijs **68**
pattison **95**
pecan noten **20, 49**
Pecorino Romano
kaas **44**
pectine **23, 130**
pedaalemmer **176**
peen **85**
peer **78**
in blik **125**
peterselie **27, 34**
peper **34**
peperkorrels **34**
pepermolen **174**
pepermunt **33**
pepperoni worst **123**
peperstrooier **175**
Pepsi Cola **133**
perzik **78**
in blik **125**
peultjes **91**
physallis **73**
pijlinktvis **64**
pijlwortel **19**
pijnboomnoten **20, 21, 49**
piment **28**
pindakaas **23**
pinda's **20, 21**
pisang goreng **141**
pistachonoten **20, 21, 49**
pizza **124, 125**
plantaardige olie **17, 22**
pocheren **101**
poedersuiker **24**
poelier **10, 67**
poffertjes **11, 138**
pollak **55,59**
pomelo **75**
pomodoro **99**
pompoen **96, 97**
pop corn **86**
portobello **89**
prosciutto, zie Parma ham
122
postelein **93**
potten en pannen **172, 173**
prei **88**
princesseboon **81**
bevroren **125**
pronkboon **81**
provolone kaas **44**
pruim **79**
pudding vruchten **14**
purée voor pompoen taart
95

Q
quatre epices **38**

quiche **22**, **124**
quinoa **15**

R
raapstelen **99**
rabarber **72**, **93**
radicchio **85**, **86**
radijs **93**, **160**, **167**
radijssla **83**
radijssnijder **173**
rambutan **80**
ramen **126**, **146**
rechaud **175**
ree **70**
reform artikelen **130**
rémoulade saus **54**
rendang daging **141**
rettich **93**, **160**, **167**
reuzel **17**
ricotta kaas **42**, **44**
rijst **15**
  Aziatisch **147**
rijst azijn **26**, **148**
rijstmeel **19**
rijsttafel **134**, **139**,**140**
rijst wijn **147**
rivierkreeft **64**
rode bessen **74**
rode biet **83**
  in blik **125**
rode bietbladeren **83**
rode kool **84**
rode mullet **58**, **59**
rode poon **59**
rode ui **90**
rode zeebaars **59**
roesti **92**, **125**
rog **53**, **59**
roggebrood **51**, **126**
rogge graan **15**
rogge meel **19**
roken **101**
rolmops **61**
roodbaars **59**
rookvlees **122**
rookworst **123**
roomijs **46**, **125**
rosbief **123**
rozijn **74**
rozijnen brood **51**
Roquefort kaas **44**
rooswater **17**
Rotterdammers **123**
rozebottel siroop **128**
rozemarijn **35**
ruitenreiniger **180**
rujak **141**
rum **133**
rum aroma **17**
runder bouillon **23**
rund niervet **17**
rundvlees **100**, **102**
  groot- en kleinhandel stukken **103**
  bereiden van **105**
ruwe rietsuiker **24**

S
saffloerolie **22**
saffraan **35**
saimin **126**
salade **49**
salade serveer vork en lepel **175**
salam blad **35**, **147**
salami **123**
salie **35**
salsa **139**
sambal **39**, **141**
sambal goreng telur **141**
San Francisco
  volkoren biscuits **17**, **126**
santen **144**
sap **132**;
  bevroren **125**, **128**
sardines **62**, **124**
saté **48**, **141**
  bevroren **126**
saucijzen broodje **49**, **135**
saus kacang pedis **141**
sauslepel **175**
sauzen **9**, **49**, **126**
Savooie kool **84**
sayur lodeh **141**
schaaf **173**
schaal **173**, **174**, **175**
schapen kaas **43**, **44**
schar **57**
schelvis **54**, **58**
schepijs **46**, **125**
schelpdieren **54**, **55**, **63**
schilmesje **174**
schol **54**, **58**
schoonmaak
  artikelen **9**, **178**
schorseneer **94**
  in blik **125**
schotel **172**
schuimspaan **174**
scotch whiskey **133**
schuursponsje **178**
schuurmiddel **178**
selderij **29** Chinese selderij
selderij knol **29**, **85**
selderij zaad **29**
sereh **33**
serundeng **141**
serviesgoed **174**
sesam olie, wit **22**
  Aziatische sesam olie **22**, **36**
sesamzaad **36**
Seven-up **133**
Sharon frucht **79**
shichimi togarashi **148**
shiitake paddestoel **89**, **145**
shoarmabroodjes **100**
shoarma kruiden **39**, **100**
sinaasappel **77**
sinaasappel bloem water **17**
siroop **24**
sjalot **94**
sla **89**
sla bonen **81**
slagerijen **100**, **102**
slagroom **46**
slagroom klopper **173**
slagroom versteviger **26**
sla olie **22**
sla Romein **89**
sla saus **126**
slijterijen **132**
smoor **142**
smoren **101**
snacks **126**
snijboon **81**
snoek **63**
snoepje **135**
soba **146**
soep **49**, **126**, **135**
soeplepel **175**
soepterrine **175**
soesje **52**
sojaboon **83**
sojamelk **128**, **130**
sojaolie **22**
soja saus **148**
spaar zegels **10**
spaghetti **125**
Spaanse peper **19**, **92**
spatel **174**
speculaas **53**, **138**
spekkies **20**
spelt **15**
spercieboon **81**
spiering **62**
spinazie **95**
  bevroren **125**
spiraal trekker **173**
spliterwt **91**, **125**
spons **178**

springvorm **173**
sprot **62**
spruitjes **84**
statiegeld **7**
steranijs **36**
sterke drank **132, 133**
St. Jacobs schelp **65**
stijfsel **179**
Stilton kaas **44**
stir-fry, to **101**
stofzuiger zakken **180**
stofdoek **178**
stokbrood **50, 51**
stomen **101**
stoofsla **89**
stoven **101**
straw mushrooms **145**
strijkijzer **172**
strijk spray **172**
stroop **24**
Subenhara kaas **42**
sucade **14**
sudderen **101**
sugar snap pea **91**
suiker **24**
suikerpot **175**
suikerlepeltje **176**
suikermeloen **77**
supermarkten **9**
surimi **63**
Szechwan pepper **36**

T
taai taai **138**
taart **52**
taart rooster **175**
taartschep **175**
taartschotel **175**
taartvulling **52, 74, 125**
Tabasco peper **92**
Tabasco saus **30**
taco **139**
taco seasoning **139**
tafellaken **176**
tafelmessen **175**
tafelzilver **175**
tahini **36**
tahoe **130, 143**
tamari **14**
tamarind **36**
tangelo **75**
tangerine **78**
tapijtreiniger **175**
tapioca meel **19**
tarbot **55, 60**
tartaar saus **49, 54**
tarwe **15**
tarwebloem **19**
tarwegriesmeel **15**
tarwe kiemen **15**
tarwemeel **19**
tarwe zemelen **15**
taugé **83**
tempe **130, 148**
tempe goreng **141**
terasi **148**
terrine **123**
thee **9, 133**
theedoek **178**
thermometer,
 vlees/oven **174**
tijm **27, 36**
toetje **47**
tofu **130, 143**
tomaat **99**
 in blik **124**
tomaat gepeld **25**
tomaat gedroogt **99**
tomaten puree **25**
tong **105**
tong (zee) **54, 55, 60, 124**
tonijn **62**
 in blik **124**
tortilla **139**
touw **174**
traiteur artikelen **48**
trechter **173**
Trente kaas **42, 130**
truffel **89**
tuinbonen **82**
tuinerwtjes **91**
tuinkers **86**
turban squash **95**
tutti-frutti **74**
TV maaltijden **124, 126**

U
ugli **75**
ui(en) **90**
uienpoeder **91**
uienvlokken **91**
uitsmijter **135**
universeel rasp **173**

V
vanille **17**
 stokje **17**
 suiker **17**
varkensvlees **100, 101**
 groot- en kleinhandel **112**
 klaarmaken van **114**
veenbessen **72**
veger **178**
vegetarisch **130**
veldsla, grof **86**
venkelknol **87**
venkel zaad **31**
vergiet **173**
verse worst **123**
vet, niet vloeibaar **17**
vieux (brandy) **133**
vijg **74**
 gedroogd **74**
vis **11, 54**
 bevroren, in blik **124**
visfond **24**
vismes **1177**
vissaus **49**
 Aziatische **144**
visschep **177**
visvork **177**
viswinkel **10**
vitaminen, baby **129**
vla **47, 136**
vlaai **74, 138**
vlamvaste glazen
 pan **173**
vlees **9, 100, 125** - zie ook
 individuele namen
vlekkenverwijderaar **180**
vleesmes **172**
vleesmolen **172**
vleesplank **173**
vleesschotel **175**
vlees termometer **174**
vleestomaat **99**
vloerwas, vloerolie **179**
vlugbloem **19**
vodka **133**
voedsel in blik **125**
volkoren biscuits **16**
volkorenmeel **19**
vorken **175**
vruchten glazuur **14**
vulling voor
 bessentaart **52, 74**

W
wafelijzer **172**
walnoot **20, 21, 49**
walnoot olie **22**
wasabi **37**
wasbenzine **179**
waspoeder **179**
wasverzachter **175**
water kastanje **160, 167**
waterkers **87**
watermeloen **76**
water verzachter **178**
weegschaal **172**
wekpotten **173**

wildbraad **70**
wilde rijst **15**
wildfond **24**
wild en gevogelte **67, 125**
wild zwijn **69**
witlof **85**
witlof met ham en kaassaus **137**
witte bessen **74**
witte bonen **82**
  in blik **125**
wittebrood **51**
witte kool **84**
witte peen **90**
witvis **62**
wijn **9, 133**
wijn azijn **25**
wijnruit **35**
wijting **55, 60**
wok **173**
won ton vellen **149**
wood ear fungus **149**
Worcestershire sauce **126**
worteltje **84**
worst en vleeswaren **9, 121**
winkel proceduren **6**

Y
yakult **47, 149**
yoghurt **47**
yoghurt drink **47**
yoghurt ijs **46**

Z
zalm **61**
  bevroren **124**
zalm forel **62**
zeebaars **59**
zeeduivel **57**
zeef **174**
zeekomkommer **66**
zeekraal **93, 94**
zeem **178**
zeeoor **63**
zeep **178**
zeer fijne tafel suiker **24**
zeetong **54, 60, 124**
zeewier **147**
zeewolf **60**
zeezout **23**
zelfrijznd bakmeel **19**
zilveruitjes **90**
  in blik **125**
zoete aardappel **96**
zoete rode paprika **91**
zoete uien **90**
zonnebloem olie **22**
zout **23**
zoutstrooier **175**
zuivel produkten **40**
zure zult **122**
zuring **94**
zure room **47**
zuurkool **84**
zuurkool met
  worst **48, 137**
zuurzak **73**
zwabber **178**
zwarte bessen (cassis) **74**
zwarte bonen **82**
  gefermenteerd en
    gezouten (oosters) **143**
zwarte ogen bonen **82**
zwarte melasse **25**
zwezerik **105**
Zwitserse kaas **43**